Lecture Notes in Computer Science 16177

Founding Editors

Gerhard Goos

Juris Hartmanis

Editorial Board Members

Elisa Bertino, *Purdue University, West Lafayette, IN, USA*
Wen Gao, *Peking University, Beijing, China*
Bernhard Steffen, *TU Dortmund University, Dortmund, Germany*
Moti Yung, *Columbia University, New York, NY, USA*

The series Lecture Notes in Computer Science (LNCS), including its subseries Lecture Notes in Artificial Intelligence (LNAI) and Lecture Notes in Bioinformatics (LNBI), has established itself as a medium for the publication of new developments in computer science and information technology research, teaching, and education.

LNCS enjoys close cooperation with the computer science R & D community, the series counts many renowned academics among its volume editors and paper authors, and collaborates with prestigious societies. Its mission is to serve this international community by providing an invaluable service, mainly focused on the publication of conference and workshop proceedings and postproceedings. LNCS commenced publication in 1973.

Xiaofeng Chen · Haibo Hu · Ding Wang
Editors

Data Security and Privacy Protection

Third International Conference, DSPP 2025
Xi'an, China, October 16–18, 2025
Proceedings, Part II

 Springer

Editors
Xiaofeng Chen
Xidian University
Xi'an, China

Haibo Hu
The Hong Kong Polytechnic University
Hong Kong, China

Ding Wang
Nankai University
Tianjin, China

ISSN 0302-9743　　　　　　　ISSN 1611-3349　(electronic)
Lecture Notes in Computer Science
ISBN 978-981-95-3184-4　　　ISBN 978-981-95-3185-1　(eBook)
https://doi.org/10.1007/978-981-95-3185-1

This Springer imprint is published by the registered company Springer Nature Singapore Pte Ltd.
The registered company address is: 152 Beach Road, #21-01/04 Gateway East, Singapore 189721, Singapore

If disposing of this product, please recycle the paper.

Preface

The 3rd International Conference on Data Security and Privacy Protection (DSPP 2025) was held during October 16–18, 2025, in Xi'an, China.

This year the conference received 105 submissions. These papers were double-blindly peer reviewed and subsequently discussed based on their novelty, quality, and contribution by at least three members of the Program Committee. The submission of the papers and the review process were carried out using the EasyChair platform. Based on the reviews and the discussion, 36 full papers were selected for presentation at the conference (resulting in an acceptance rate of 34.3 %). While revisions were expected to take the reviewers' comments into account, this was not enforced and the authors bear full responsibility for the content of their papers. On the other hand, though many high-quality submissions were not included in the proceeding because of the high technical level of the overall submissions, we are certain that many of these submissions will, nevertheless, be published in other competitive forums in the future.

The DSPP 2025 conference promoted and stimulated discussion on the latest theories, algorithms, applications, and emerging topics in data security and privacy protection. It encouraged the cross-fertilization of ideas and provided a platform for researchers, professionals, and students worldwide to discuss and present their research results. In addition, we were honored to have eight distinguished keynote speakers for the main conference: Elisa Bertino from Purdue University (USA), Robert H. Deng from Singapore Management University (Singapore), Mianxiong Dong from Muroran Institute of Technology (Japan), Fuchun Guo from University of Wollongong (Australia), Qian Wang from Wuhan University (China), Qingqing Ye from Hong Kong Polytechnic University (China), Moti Yung from Columbia University (USA), and Tianqing Zhu from City University of Macau (China). We were also pleased to feature four invited talks by Chao Lin from Nanjing University of Aeronautics and Astronautics (China), Yi Wang from National University of Defense Technology (China), Zhedong Wang from Shanghai Jiao Tong University (China), and Cong Peng from Wuhan University (China). Their erudition and expertise were on full display as they delivered a series of illuminating talks that provided profound insights into the latest trends, challenges, and opportunities within the domain of data security and privacy protection. These thought-provoking presentations served as a cornerstone of the conference, inspiring attendees to explore new dimensions of research and fostering a collaborative environment that encouraged the sharing of innovative ideas and constructive dialogue.

DSPP 2025 received the support of many volunteers and organizations. A multitude of individuals selflessly contributed their valuable time and energy to ensure the smooth organization and operation of this conference, and their efforts are truly commendable and warrant our deepest appreciation. First, we extend our heartfelt thanks to all the authors who submitted their scholarly papers to DSPP 2025. Their willingness to share their research and insights was a key factor in the conference's success. Thanks to all the members of the Program Committee and the external reviewers for their hard work in evaluating the papers; their expertise and commitment to the peer-review process ensured that only the most valuable and impactful research was presented at the conference. We thank all of the co-chairs for helping with the organization and taking care of local arrangements. Finally, we thank many institutes for their strong support: State Key Laboratory of Integrated Service Networks (ISN), NSCLab, the 111 center (B16037), and Xi'an ISTC Base for Data Security and Privacy Preservation. We also appreciate the great support from Springer.

August 2025

Xiaofeng Chen
Haibo Hu
Ding Wang

Organization

Honorary Chairs

Elisa Bertino	Purdue University, USA
Willy Susilo	University of Wollongong, Australia
Yang Xiang	Swinburne University of Technology, Australia
Moti Yung	Columbia University, USA

Technical Program Committee Chairs

Xiaofeng Chen	Xidian University, China
Haibo Hu	Hong Kong Polytechnic University, China
Ding Wang	Nankai University, China

General Chairs

Jin Li	Guangzhou University, China
Zheng Yan	Xidian University, China
Xiaokang Zhou	Kansai University, Japan

Steering Committee

Xiaofeng Chen	Xidian University, China
Xinyi Huang	Jinan University, China
Kuan-Ching Li	Providence University, Taiwan, China
Kui Ren	Zhejiang University, China
Yang Xiang	Swinburne University of Technology, Australia

Organizing Chairs

Debiao He	Wuhan University, China
Zheli Liu	Nankai University, China
Meixia Miao	Xi'an University of Posts and Telecommunications, China

Jian Shen	Zhejiang Sci-Tech University, China

Publication Chair

Xiaoyu Zhang	Xidian University, China

Publicity Chairs

Weizhi Meng	Lancaster University, UK
Chunhua Su	University of Aizu, Japan
Guohua Tian	Xidian University, China
Wei Zong	University of Wollongong, Australia

Program Committee

Joonsang Baek	University of Wollongong, Australia
Arcangelo Castiglione	University of Salerno, Italy
Chao Chen	RMIT University, Australia
Rongmao Chen	National University of Defense Technology, China
Xiaofeng Chen	Xidian University, China
Chi Cheng	China University of Geoscience, China
Yang-Wai Chow	University of Wollongong, Australia
Jie Cui	Anhui University, China
Ashok Kumar Das	International Institute of Information Technology Hyderabad, India
Steven Furnell	University of Nottingham, UK
Dieter Gollmann	Hamburg University of Technology, Germany
Prosanta Gope	University of Sheffield, UK
Fuchun Guo	University of Wollongong, Australia
Marko Hölbl	University of Maribor, Slovenia
Yuan Hong	Hong Kong Polytechnic University, China
Haibo Hu	Hong Kong Polytechnic University, China
Qiong Huang	South China Agricultural University, China
Xinyi Huang	Jinan University, China
Jonas Juffinger	Graz University of Technology, Austria
Imtiaz Karim	Purdue University, USA
Masoud Kaveh	Aalto University, Finland
Kuan-Ching Li	Providence University, Taiwan

Zengpeng Li	Lancaster University, UK
Jay Ligatti	University of South Florida, USA
Joseph Liu	Nokia Bell Labs, Finland
Shushu Liu	Monash University, Australia
Xin Liu	Lanzhou University, China
Feng Lin	Zhejiang University, China
Mehrnoosh Monshizadeh	Nokia Bell Labs, Finland
Siqi Ma	University of New South Wales, Australia
Weizhi Meng	Lancaster University, UK
Gerardo Pelosi	Politecnico di Milano, Italy
Jun Shao	Zhejiang Gongshang University, China
Chunhua Su	University of Aizu, Japan
Willy Susilo	University of Wollongong, Australia
Zhiyuan Tan	Edinburgh Napier University, UK
Norbert Tihanyi	Eötvös Loránd University, Hungary
Ding Wang	Nankai University, China
Zhibo Wang	Zhejiang University, China
Yu Wei	Georgia Institute of Technology, USA
Qianhong Wu	Beihang University, China
Yang Xiang	Swinburne University of Technology, Australia
Bin Xiao	Hong Kong Polytechnic University, China
Guomin Yang	Singapore Management University, Singapore
Wun-She Yap	University Tunku Abdul Rahman, Malaysia
Ilsun You	Kookmin University, South Korea
Moti Yung	Columbia University, USA
Fangguo Zhang	Sun Yat-sen University, China
Lei Zhang	East China Normal University, China
Mingwu Zhang	Hubei University of Technology, China
Tianwei Zhang	Nanyang Technological University, Singapore
Xuyun Zhang	Macquarie University, Australia
Yang Zhang	CISPA Helmholtz Center for Information Security, Germany
Yifan Zhang	Aalto University, Finland
Yudi Zhang	University of Wollongong, Australia
Xiaokang Zhou	Kansai University, Japan
Tianqing Zhu	University of Technology Sydney, Australia
Yunkai Zou	Nankai University, China

Additional Reviewers

An, Zhiyuan
Jiang, Hanrui
Wang, Fuyi
Chang, Yijia
Jiang, Yan
Wang, Wenli
Chen, Yu
Lang, Yongkang
Wang, Yujue
Chen, Yumin
Li, Chen
Wei, Jiaheng
Chu, Junjie
Li, Hongbo
Wu, Changdi
Deng, Fuyang
Li, Jiawei
Wu, Wenbo
Ding, Zhengyang
Li, Minghang

Xiao, Meiyan
Hao, Xiaohan
Li, Yanting
Yang, Xu
He, Hongzhi
Liang, Zi
Yu, Peng
Huang, Jianye
Liao, Ziwen
Zhang, Bonan
Huang, Lifeng
Lin, Yuliang
Zhang, Xiaoyu
Huang, Mengdie
Tang, Li
Zhang, Yingmiao
Huang, Yixuan
Tian, Guohua
Zhu, Liufu

Contents – Part II

AI-based Security Applications and Technologies

Cryptographic Protocols Design and Analysis

Model Security and Copyright Protection

Contents – Part I

AI and System Security

Blockchain and Related Technologies

Privacy Preserving/Enhancing Technologies

Cryptographic Primitives

Privacy-Aware Federated Learning

AI-based Security Applications and Technologies

AI-based Security Applications and Technologies

Dual-FER: A Dual-Network Approach to Facial Expression Recognition with Enhanced Generalization

Junwei Liu[1], Qingwu Fu[2], Hongyang Yan[1,3,4,5]([envelope]), and Shaowei Wang[1]

[1] School of Artificial Intelligence, Guangzhou University, Guangzhou 510006, China
hyang_yan@gzhu.edu.cn
[2] School of Computer Science and Cyber Engineering, Guangzhou University, Guangzhou 510006, China
[3] Huangpu Research School of Guangzhou University, Guangzhou University, Guangzhou 510006, China
[4] Guangdong Key Laboratory of Blockchain Security, Guangzhou University, Guangzhou 510006, China
[5] Pazhou Lab, Guangzhou 510330, China

Abstract. Facial Expression Recognition (FER) has garnered significant attention in recent years due to its wide applications in human-computer interaction, psychological analysis, and affective computing. With the advancements in deep learning, FER models have achieved remarkable accuracy on benchmark datasets. However, most existing methods perform well on in-distribution datasets but struggle with out-of-distribution data, revealing weak generalization ability. This limitation hampers their effectiveness in real-world scenarios, where the distribution of test data often differs from that of the training data. To address this challenge, we propose a dual-network framework that integrates a global network and a local network to extract complementary features from images. The extracted features are subsequently fused to enhance the model's generalization capability. Furthermore, we propose a novel loss function that integrates cross-entropy loss with contrastive loss to optimize model training. The contrastive loss is designed to measure the discrepancy between global and local features, encouraging the model to learn more complementary representations. Ablation experiments validate the effectiveness of the proposed loss function. Experimental results demonstrate that our method outperforms existing approaches on multiple FER datasets, achieving superior generalization to out-of-distribution datasets.

Keywords: Facial expression recognition · Out-of-distribution generalization · Deep learning · Neural networks

1 Introduction

Facial Expression Recognition (FER) refers to the automated identification and interpretation of human facial expressions using computer algorithms [3,8,10].

X. Chen et al. (Eds.): DSPP 2025, LNCS 16177, pp. 3–13, 2026.
https://doi.org/10.1007/978-981-95-3185-1_1

This process involves analyzing facial features and their dynamic variations to infer an individual's emotional state or intent. In recent years, FER has emerged as a crucial task in the fields of computer vision and human-computer interaction (HCI). It demonstrates significant application potential across various domains, including sentiment analysis, mental health assessment, and multimedia content management. By analyzing facial expressions, FER facilitates the inference of human emotions and intentions, thereby fostering more natural, effective, and intuitive interactions between humans and machines.

Despite significant progress in FER research, existing methods achieve high accuracy on their respective training datasets. However, when evaluated on out-of-distribution (OOD) [11] datasets, these models often exhibit inadequate generalization capabilities. For example, a model trained on the RAF-DB [5] dataset may perform well on its corresponding test set but experience a substantial performance drop when evaluated on other FER datasets, such as FERPlus [1] and MMA. This highlights a significant limitation of current FER methods: their insufficient generalization capability. In real-world applications, FER models frequently encounter scenarios that differ significantly from the training data, thereby imposing stringent requirements on the model's generalization capacity.

To address the challenge of generalization in FER, we propose an innovative framework that integrates a global network and a local network to extract complementary features from images. Given the strong semantic representation capabilities of CLIP [6], we first employ it to extract semantic features from facial images. Inspired by multi-scale feature fusion, we design both the global and local networks based on ResNet-18 [2] to capture hierarchical features at different levels. The extracted hierarchical features undergo global average pooling (GAP) and are subsequently fused through element-wise addition. To enhance generalization, the fused features are further processed through ReLU and Sigmoid activation functions. These refined features are then element-wise multiplied with the semantic features to obtain the final feature representation. Notably, the global network captures holistic facial representations, providing a comprehensive understanding of the overall context and emotional tone. In contrast, the local network focuses on critical facial regions, such as the eyes, eyebrows, and mouth, which are essential for capturing subtle emotional variations. By integrating these two perspectives, our framework effectively learns the complexity and nuanced nature of facial expressions, thereby improving its generalization capability across diverse datasets. Furthermore, we introduce a contrastive loss term to measure the distance between global and local features. By maintaining a balance between these two representations, the model leverages both perspectives to achieve more accurate and robust expression recognition. This contrastive loss is combined with cross-entropy loss to form the final loss function, which guides the training process and enhances model performance.

Experimental results demonstrate that our proposed method outperforms existing methods in terms of performance and generalization capability, thereby validating its adaptability to various real-world scenarios. In summary, our contributions are as follows:

- We propose a novel FER framework that effectively integrates both global and local networks to capture facial features at various scales. This dual-network architecture enhances the model's generalization capabilities, particularly for out-of-distribution FER datasets.
- We introduce a contrastive loss function that balances the relationship between global and local features. This loss function is integrated with cross-entropy loss to optimize training and enhance overall generalization capability.
- Experimental results demonstrate that our method outperforms existing approaches on multiple FER datasets, achieving superior generalization to out-of-distribution datasets.

2   Related Work

Facial Expression Recognition. With the increasing application of facial expression recognition (FER) in human-computer interaction, extensive research has been conducted to improve the performance of FER models. POSTER [15] enhances feature integration by employing a dual-stream pyramidal cross-fusion design, which effectively combines facial landmark and image features. EAC [13] mitigates the impact of noisy samples in the FER task by leveraging random erasure and flip consistency. However, while these methods perform well on in-distribution test data, their effectiveness significantly degrades on OOD test samples. In this study, our objective is to enhance the generalization capability of FER models, ensuring their robustness in real-world deployment. Specifically, we train FER models on a single FER dataset and evaluate their performance across various unseen FER test sets.

Out-of-Distribution Generalization. Let $P_{tr}(X, Y)$ and $P_{te}(X, Y)$ denote the probability distributions of the training and test data, respectively. The objective is to develop a model that achieves optimal performance under the test distribution. When $P_{tr}(X, Y) \neq P_{te}(X, Y)$, distribution shift occurs, transforming the problem into an out-of-distribution (OOD) generalization challenge. In such cases, discrepancies between distributions can lead to significant performance degradation on the test data. To address this issue, StableNet [11] enhances the generalization capability of deep models under distribution shifts by eliminating statistical correlations between features through sample reweighting. Fishr [7] improves OOD generalization by aligning the gradient variance across different training domains.

3   Method

3.1   Overall Framework and Goals

Our goal is to enhance the generalization capability of FER models, thereby improving classification accuracy on OOD test samples. To achieve this, we propose an innovative framework that integrates global and local networks to extract

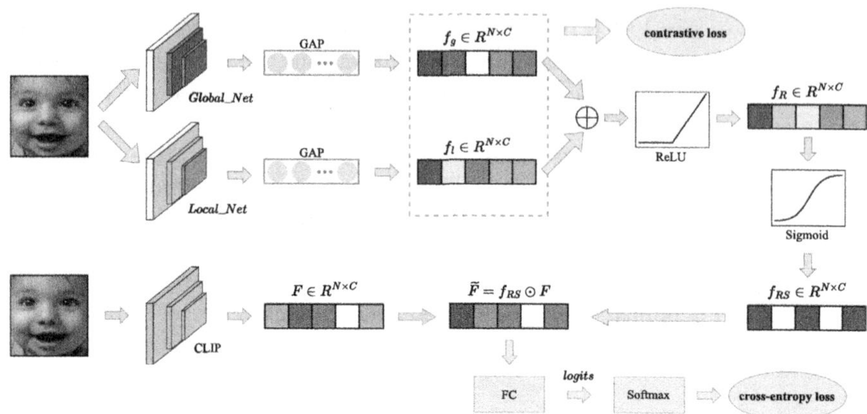

Fig. 1. The framework of the proposed dual-network method for enhancing the generalization capacity of facial expression recognition.

complementary features from facial images. First, we employ a pre-trained CLIP model to extract semantic features. Next, we utilize a global network and a local network to capture global and local facial features, respectively. The extracted global and local features undergo global average pooling (GAP) and are subsequently fused through element-wise addition. To enhance generalization, the fused features are further processed through ReLU and Sigmoid activation functions. Finally, these processed features are element-wise multiplied with the semantic features to obtain the final feature representation, which serves as the basis for classification decisions. The framework of our proposed method is shown in Fig. 1.

3.2   Dual Network for Enhanced Generalization

Given an image x from the training set D_{train}, we employ the CLIP model [6] to extract its semantic features $F \in R^{N \times C}$, where N denotes the number of images and C represents the dimensionality of the feature space.

Inspired by multi-scale feature fusion, we design two hierarchical feature extraction networks based on ResNet-18 [2]: a global network ($Global\_Net$) and a local network ($Local\_Net$). The $Global\_Net$ utilizes the high-level residual layers of ResNet-18 to extract global features. These features have a larger receptive field, capturing holistic facial expression information. In contrast, the $Local\_Net$ employs the low-level residual layers of ResNet-18 to extract fine-grained local features. This network focuses on subtle variations in facial expressions to enhance generalization. Specifically, after processing through a global average pooling (GAP) layer, the extracted global and local features are represented as $f_g \in R^{N \times C \times 1 \times 1}$, and $f_l \in R^{N \times C \times 1 \times 1}$, respectively. We then resize them to $N \times C$ and fuse the features f_g and f_l through element-wise addition, followed by ReLU activation to obtain f_R, formulated as follows:

$$f_R = ReLU(f_g + f_l) \tag{1}$$

To improve the model's generalization capability on unseen test samples, we apply the Sigmoid function to f_R, obtaining f_{RS}:

$$f_{RS} = Sigmoid(f_R) \tag{2}$$

Next, the semantic feature F is element-wise multiplied with f_{RS} to generate the fused feature $\widetilde{F}$:

$$\widetilde{F} = f_{RS} \odot F \tag{3}$$

3.3 Loss Function

To optimize the training of the entire network, we propose a novel loss function that combines cross-entropy loss with contrastive loss. The fully connected (FC) layer maps $\widetilde{F}$ to the class space, generating logits. To quantify the discrepancy between the model's predictions and the ground truth labels, the logits are processed through the Softmax function. The cross-entropy loss is computed as follows:

$$L_{ce} = -\frac{1}{N} \sum_{i=1}^{N} \left(\log \frac{e^{W_{y_i} \widetilde{F}_i}}{\sum_{j}^{L} e^{W_j \widetilde{F}_i}} \right) \tag{4}$$

where N is the number of samples, L is the number of facial expression categories, $\widetilde{F}_i$ is the fused feature of the image x_i, W_{y_i} corresponds to the y_i-th weight of the fully connected (FC) layer, and y_i is the ground truth label of x_i.

We introduce a contrastive loss term to measure the distance between global and local features, defined as follows:

$$L_{gl} = \frac{1}{N} \sum_{i=1}^{N} \left(f_l^i - f_g^i \right)^2 \tag{5}$$

where f_l^i and f_g^i represent the local and global features of the i-th sample, respectively.

The proposed network is trained using a composite loss function that combines cross-entropy loss and contrastive loss. The final objective function is formulated as follows:

$$L_{total} = \lambda_1 L_{ce} + \lambda_2 L_{gl} \tag{6}$$

where λ_1 and λ_2 are hyperparameters that balance the contributions of the two loss functions.

4 Experiments

In this section, we outline the experimental dataset and implementation details, followed by a presentation of the experimental results and a comparison with existing methods. Finally, we conduct ablation experiments and analyze the network architecture.

4.1   Datasets

RAF-DB [5] comprises 12,271 images for training and 3,068 images for testing. The annotation process was conducted by a group of 40 certified experts, who classified the facial expressions into seven primary categories.

FERPlus [1] consists of 28,709 training images and 3,589 test images, which were collected through the Google search engine. This dataset enhances FER2013 with improved label quality, and we adopt the same seven basic facial expression categories as RAF-DB.

MMA is a comprehensive FER resource, primarily featuring individuals of European and American descent. It includes 92,968 training images, 17,356 validation images, and 17,356 test images. Each image is labeled with one of seven basic emotional expressions, providing a robust foundation for the development of FER models.

4.2   Implementation Details

The FER model is trained on the training set $D_{train} = \{(x_i, y_i)\}_{i=1}^{N}$, where x_i denotes the i-th training image, $y_i \in Y = \{1, ..., L\}$ represents the corresponding expression label, N is the total number of training samples, and L denotes the number of facial expression categories. In this study, we utilize a FER dataset comprising seven expression categories, i.e., $L = 7$. The model is subsequently evaluated on the test set $D_{test} = \{(x_i, y_i)\}_{i=1}^{M}$, where M represents the number of test samples.

In our experiments, we set the learning rate lr to 0.0002 and apply the Adam optimizer with a weight decay of 0.0001. An ExponentialLR scheduler with a gamma of 0.9 is used. The model is trained for 60 epochs with a batch size of 32.

4.3   Results

We sequentially use the RAF-DB, FERPlus, and MMA datasets as training sets, while all three datasets serve as test sets for evaluation. Our primary focus is on the model's generalization capability on out-of-distribution test samples. For instance, when the model is trained on the RAF-DB dataset, we place greater emphasis on its classification accuracy on the FERPlus and MMA test sets rather than on RAF-DB.

We conduct experiments using three FER datasets and compare with FER methods published in top conferences in recent years, such as SCN [9], RUL [12], OFER [4], and CAFE [14]. The experimental results, presented in Table 1, demonstrate that our method consistently outperforms existing approaches across all test sets. Notably, our method exhibits strong generalization capability on out-of-distribution test sets. For example, when trained on the MMA dataset, our model achieves a classification accuracy of 77.81% on the FERPlus test set, outperforming CAFE by 4.24%. While previous methods perform well on in-distribution test samples, they struggle with out-of-distribution test

Table 1. The comparative experimental results of our method compared with other existing approaches. The highest-performing results among all methods are highlighted in bold.

Train Dataset	Method	Test Dataset		
		RAF-DB	FERPlus	MMA
RAF-DB	SCN(CVPR2020)	87.32	58.37	36.52
	RUL(NeurIPS2021)	88.86	57.89	37.11
	OFER(ICCV2023)	89.07	53.90	36.43
	CAFE(ECCV2024)	88.72	73.16	56.80
	Dual-FER	**89.50**	**76.09**	**58.23**
FERPlus	SCN(CVPR2020)	68.71	86.80	59.12
	RUL(NeurIPS2021)	51.89	88.40	58.00
	OFER(ICCV2023)	55.67	89.26	59.37
	CAFE(ECCV2024)	72.91	89.51	60.14
	Dual-FER	**74.15**	**89.61**	**61.78**
MMA	SCN(CVPR2020)	74.09	73.99	63.00
	RUL(NeurIPS2021)	71.94	69.05	61.70
	OFER(ICCV2023)	72.85	69.69	64.74
	CAFE(ECCV2024)	78.36	73.57	65.97
	Dual-FER	**79.74**	**77.81**	**66.08**

samples, indicating limited generalization capabilities. In contrast, our method significantly enhances generalization, making it more applicable to real-world scenarios.

4.4 Ablation Study

Analysis of the Loss Function. The proposed method employs a loss function comprising two components: cross-entropy loss and contrastive loss. The contrastive loss is introduced to enhance the training process of the dual-network architecture. To evaluate its effectiveness, we compared model performance when using only cross-entropy loss, as presented in Table 2. The results clearly demonstrate that the model trained with the combined loss function, incorporating both cross-entropy and contrastive losses, achieves superior performance compared to the model trained solely with cross-entropy loss. Notably, when RAF-DB and MMA are used as training datasets, the combined loss function leads to a significant performance improvement over the use of cross-entropy loss alone.

Analysis of Hyperparameter. As previously discussed, we introduce the hyperparameters λ_1 and λ_2 to balance the contributions of cross-entropy loss and contrastive loss. In this ablation study, we assess the impact of different values of these hyperparameters on classification accuracy. Specifically, when using

Table 2. The classification accuracy of the model across different loss components.

Method	Train Dataset	Test Dataset		
		RAF-DB	FERPlus	MMA
$L_{total} = L_{ce}$	RAF-DB	88.17	75.20	57.40
	FERPlus	74.90	89.10	61.07
	MMA	78.13	77.72	64.94
$L_{total} = L_{ce} + L_{gl}$	RAF-DB	89.50	76.09	58.23
	FERPlus	74.15	89.61	61.78
	MMA	79.74	77.81	66.08

the RAF-DB dataset for training, λ_1 is set to 0.1, 0.25, 0.5, 0.75, and 1.0, while λ_2 takes the same set of values. We evaluate the classification accuracy for each combination of λ_1 and λ_2 across three test datasets and visualize the results using heatmaps. To provide a comprehensive analysis, we compute the average classification accuracy across the three test sets and generate an aggregated heatmap, as shown in Fig. 2. As observed in Fig. 2(a), the highest classification accuracy is achieved when $\lambda_1 = 1.0$ and $\lambda_2 = 0.75$. Similarly, when training on FERPlus, the optimal classification accuracy is obtained with $\lambda_1 = 0.25$ and $\lambda_2 = 0.75$. Additionally, when using MMA as the training set, the best performance is observed at $\lambda_1 = 1.0$ and $\lambda_2 = 0.1$.

4.5   Different Backbones

In our experimental design, we employed distinct backbone architectures to validate the efficacy of our proposed method. Specifically, we utilized MobileNet, ResNet-18, and ResNet-50 as the backbone networks for our experiments. The results obtained from our method Dual-FER were compared with those from the CAFE method, as shown in Table 3. The outcomes demonstrated that our approach achieved superior performance compared to CAFE. This not only corroborates the effectiveness of our method but also highlights its adaptability across different backbone networks, indicating a stronger generalization capability.

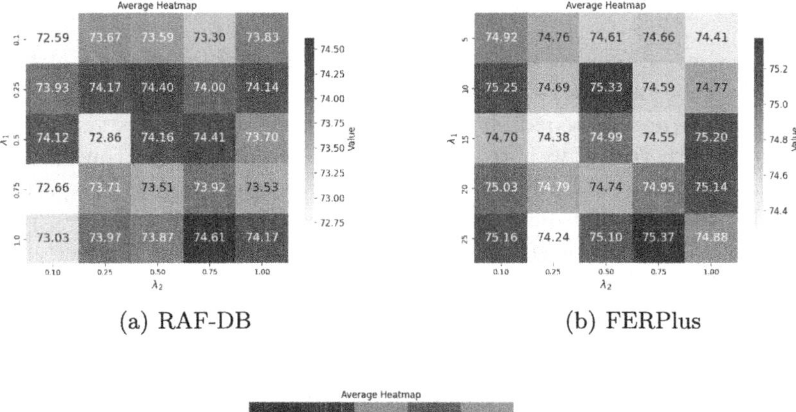

(a) RAF-DB   (b) FERPlus

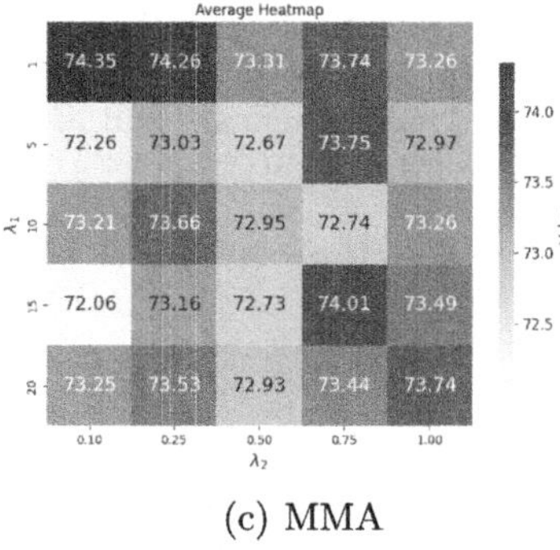

(c) MMA

Fig. 2. Classification accuracy for different combinations of hyperparameters λ_1 and λ_2. Darker shades represent higher accuracy values.

Table 3. The accuracy of our proposed method, when compared to the CAFE method trained on the RAF-DB dataset with different backbones, demonstrates that our method achieves superior generalization capability.

Backbones	Test Dataset		
	RAF-DB	FERPlus	MMA
MobileNet	84.65	61.33	40.67
MobileNet + CAFE	85.07	64.97	43.11
MobileNet + Dual-FER	**87.39**	**75.74**	**60.53**
ResNet-18	88.40	58.05	42.61
ResNet-18 + CAFE	88.72	73.16	56.80
ResNet-18 + Dual-FER	**89.50**	**76.09**	**58.23**
ResNet-50	88.49	70.13	48.90
ResNet-50 + CAFE	89.05	75.26	57.46
ResNet-50 + Dual-FER	**89.89**	**76.63**	**60.41**

5   Conclusion

In summary, we propose a dual-network framework that integrates a global network and a local network to extract complementary features from facial images. These features are subsequently fused to enhance the model's generalization capability. Furthermore, we introduce a novel loss function that combines cross-entropy loss with contrastive loss to optimize model training. Experimental results demonstrate that our method outperforms existing approaches, particularly in out-of-distribution scenarios. These findings highlight the effectiveness of our approach in improving FER model generalization, making it more applicable to real-world scenarios with diverse data distributions.

Acknowledgments. This work is funded by the Guangzhou basic and applied basic research Project (2024A03J0397, 2023A04J1725), the National Natural Science Foundation of China (No. 62372130), the Research Project of Pazhou Lab for Young Scholars (No. PZL2021KF0002), and the Open Research Fund of Guangdong Key Laboratory of Blockchain Security, Guangzhou University.

References

1. Barsoum, E., Zhang, C., Ferrer, C.C., Zhang, Z.: Training deep networks for facial expression recognition with crowd-sourced label distribution. In: Proceedings of the 18th ACM International Conference on Multimodal Interaction, pp. 279–283 (2016)
2. He, K., Zhang, X., Ren, S., Sun, J.: Deep residual learning for image recognition. In: Proceedings of the IEEE Conference on Computer Vision and Pattern Recognition, pp. 770–778 (2016)
3. Kim, D., Song, B.C.: Emotion-aware multi-view contrastive learning for facial emotion recognition. In: European Conference on Computer Vision, pp. 178–195. Springer (2022). https://doi.org/10.1007/978-3-031-19778-9_11
4. Lee, I., Lee, E., Yoo, S.B.: Latent-OFER: detect, mask, and reconstruct with latent vectors for occluded facial expression recognition. In: Proceedings of the IEEE/CVF International Conference on Computer Vision, pp. 1536–1546 (2023)
5. Li, S., Deng, W., Du, J.: Reliable crowdsourcing and deep locality-preserving learning for expression recognition in the wild. In: Proceedings of the IEEE Conference on Computer Vision and Pattern Recognition, pp. 2852–2861 (2017)
6. Radford, A., et al.: Learning transferable visual models from natural language supervision. In: International Conference on Machine Learning, pp. 8748–8763. PmLR (2021)
7. Rame, A., Dancette, C., Cord, M.: FISHR: invariant gradient variances for out-of-distribution generalization. In: International Conference on Machine Learning, pp. 18347–18377. PMLR (2022)
8. She, J., Hu, Y., Shi, H., Wang, J., Shen, Q., Mei, T.: Dive into ambiguity: latent distribution mining and pairwise uncertainty estimation for facial expression recognition. In: Proceedings of the IEEE/CVF Conference on Computer Vision and Pattern Recognition, pp. 6248–6257 (2021)

9. Wang, K., Peng, X., Yang, J., Lu, S., Qiao, Y.: Suppressing uncertainties for large-scale facial expression recognition. In: Proceedings of the IEEE/CVF Conference on Computer Vision and Pattern Recognition, pp. 6897–6906 (2020)
10. Zeng, D., Lin, Z., Yan, X., Liu, Y., Wang, F., Tang, B.: Face2Exp: combating data biases for facial expression recognition. In: Proceedings of the IEEE/CVF Conference on Computer Vision and Pattern Recognition, pp. 20291–20300 (2022)
11. Zhang, X., Cui, P., Xu, R., Zhou, L., He, Y., Shen, Z.: Deep stable learning for out-of-distribution generalization. In: Proceedings of the IEEE/CVF Conference on Computer Vision and Pattern Recognition, pp. 5372–5382 (2021)
12. Zhang, Y., Wang, C., Deng, W.: Relative uncertainty learning for facial expression recognition. Adv. Neural. Inf. Process. Syst. **34**, 17616–17627 (2021)
13. Zhang, Y., Wang, C., Ling, X., Deng, W.: Learn from all: erasing attention consistency for noisy label facial expression recognition. In: European Conference on Computer Vision, pp. 418–434. Springer (2022). https://doi.org/10.1007/978-3-031-19809-0_24
14. Zhang, Y., Zheng, X., Liang, C., Hu, J., Deng, W.: Generalizable facial expression recognition. In: Leonardis, A., Ricci, E., Roth, S., Russakovsky, O., Sattler, T., Varol, G. (eds.) European Conference on Computer Vision, pp. 231–248. Springer (2024). https://doi.org/10.1007/978-3-031-72630-9_14
15. Zheng, C., Mendieta, M., Chen, C.: Poster: a pyramid cross-fusion transformer network for facial expression recognition. In: Proceedings of the IEEE/CVF International Conference on Computer Vision, pp. 3146–3155 (2023)

Digital Forensics in Ransomware Analysis for Windows-Based Computer Systems

Hoang Anh Nguyen[(✉)], John Le[(✉)], Joonsang Baek, and Willy Susilo

Institute of Cybersecurity and Cryptology (IC2), University of Wollongong,
Wollongong, NSW 2522, Australia
{hoanganhng,john_le,joonsang_baek,willy_susilo}@uow.edu.au

Abstract. The increasing sophistication of ransomware attacks on computer systems presents a significant cybersecurity challenge. This paper evaluates the application of digital forensics methodology in ransomware analysis for Windows-based desktops. We propose a forensically sound dynamic analysis framework integrating key digital forensics principles, including evidence integrity and chain of custody, and processes for ransomware investigation. The methodology involves executing ransomware samples in a sandbox environment, collecting system artefacts, and analysing behavioural patterns. To assess the practicality of the proposed approach, machine learning models are trained on forensic-based features extracted from ransomware activity. Experimental results on seven types of models demonstrate that Decision Tree and XGBoost ones achieve the highest accuracy (93%), validating the effectiveness of our forensic-driven approach. These findings suggest digital forensics can enhance ransomware detection, investigation, and mitigation.

Keywords: Digital forensics · Malware · Ransomware analysis · Windows · Machine learning

1 Introduction

The Operating Systems Market Report 2025 estimates a two per cent annual growth in market share, from \$47.53 billion in 2024 to \$52.6 billion by 2029 [18]. Windows remains dominant in desktop systems with around 70% market share despite minor fluctuations [23]. Consequently, Windows-based cybersecurity threats, particularly ransomware, continue to rise as Windows systems are widely employed for financial and operational activities. On the other hand, global ransomware damages are projected to reach \$265 billion annually by 2031 [7], and Australia reports losses of \$7.6 million per incident without law enforcement involvement [2]. In 2023 alone, the Internet Crime Complaint Centre recorded 2,800 ransomware complaints, an 18% increase from 2022, resulting in \$59.6 million in losses, with critical sectors such as healthcare and energy being prime targets [11]. Furthermore, in 2024, the Ransomware Task Force reported an increasing focus on critical infrastructure, including military facilities, pipelines, and hospitals, which raises national security and public safety risks [17].

While the increasing prevalence of ransomware highlights the urgent need for effective countermeasures, digital forensics could be crucial in understanding and mitigating these threats from legal and criminal investigations perspectives. However, current research on applying digital forensics to ransomware remains limited. Several studies focus on analysing a specific type of malware or ransomware, such as Android malware [20,21], or conducting case studies on particular incidents [8,14] employed digital forensics in the analysis of network traffic, while [22] examined the limitations of dynamic analysis in digital forensics, focusing on memory forensics.

Despite ongoing efforts, key research gaps remain. No comprehensive studies assess whether fundamental digital forensics principles entirely apply to ransomware and malware analysis. Moreover, research beyond memory and network forensics, such as API calls, registries, and system behaviours, is also limited. Additionally, few case studies address diverse ransomware families. Bridging these gaps is essential for advancing forensic techniques to identify and counter ransomware threats.

This study addresses these challenges by examining whether dynamic malware analysis in sandbox environments aligns with the principles of digital forensics. Subsequently, it proposes a forensically sound framework for ransomware analysis, which, to our knowledge, is the first to integrate digital forensics methodology into dynamic ransomware analysis. We then apply the proposed framework to a ransomware collection, generating a dataset of forensic-based features. Finally, the proposal's performance and practicality are evaluated by analysing and training the dataset with seven machine learning models for the classification task.

The main contributions of the paper are as follows:

- We prove that the results of dynamic ransomware analysis suit the fundamentals of digital forensics methodology.
- We propose a novel framework integrating the digital forensics principles and standards with the dynamic ransomware analysis methodology.
- We apply the proposed framework in several ransomware detection Machine Learning (ML) models to assess the practicality of the methodology.

The paper is organised as follows: Sect. 2 reviews related work. The methodology for applying digital forensics in ransomware analysis is outlined in Sect. 3. Section 4 describes the experimental setup and evaluate the results. The conclusion and future work are discussed in Sects. 5.

2   Related Works

Several works have tried integrating digital forensics with static malware analysis for classification tasks. In 2021, Sharma et al. [21] performed forensic analysis on Android-based ransomware by extracting seven static features: permissions, intents, strings, images, encrypt, lock, and encode methods from the ransomware's Android Package Kits (APKs). Besides, Zola et al. [27] considered the concept drift issue in malware structures, which dampened the performance of machine learning (ML) models. In particular, the work extracted the control flow graphs (CFGs) from the malware before extracting the representative nine graph properties. Despite being unable to pinpoint the root cause of concept drift, the work suggested sufficient data for training and a need for regular re-training.

There has been an attempt to apply digital forensics to analyse malware in the network. In particular, Ganachari et al. [8] selected five among twenty-three Internet of Things (IoT) network traffic scenarios and performed feature selection by removing timestamps, identifications, and historical data, which were considered redundant. The processed data was then trained with six widely used models for malware classification tasks.

Furthermore, analysing the memory of malware-infected systems was an aspect of applying digital forensics. Shosha et al. [22] utilised the dynamic malware analysis (DMA) scheme to profile Windows kernel memory for a signature-based malware detection mechanism. However, a more significant contribution of the work was the discussion of the current imperfections of DMA in digital forensics. Specifically, state-of-the-art DMA failed to acquire complete knowledge of malware's behaviours, as it did not support multiple execution paths and could not analyse the relationship between suspected objects. Similarly, Norman et al. [15] utilised digital forensic tools to investigate the WannaCry ransomware in a live system, dissecting its processes, Dynamic Link Libraries (DLLs), binaries, and network connections. Nonetheless, the work failed to consider the memory dump files, a fundamental component in performing memory forensics.

On the other hand, Schmutz et al. [20] analysed 64 samples of the Hook malware using a combination of static and dynamic analysis. The authors investigated their packers and code obfuscation methods, installation sequences, permissions acquisition, hard-coded configuration, interfaces, attack behaviours, and the Command and Control (C&C) server address based on the reverse-engineered source code and from the end user's perspective. This hybrid method was also implemented for forensic analysis in the work of Kara et al. [13], where a general framework approaching a ransomware attack scenario was proposed. Using free-licensed tools and software, the authors performed a case study on the "Onion" ransomware, which operates on Windows - the most targeted operating system for ransomware.

Additionally, Suk-On et al. [25] provided a case study on the Lockbit ransomware, attempting to categorise their attack patterns using ransomware attack frameworks. Specifically, the authors employed dynamic analysis to reveal 50 steps of the system behaviours during the attack involving processes run, files created, and system IP acquired. Likewise, Nakhonthai et al. [14] also analysed four industrial case studies on REvil, Lockbit 2.0, Conti, and CryptoLocker ransomware for malicious action categorisation. However, the work performed digital forensic analysis of these attacks from the end users' perspective.

Finally, Kao et al. [12] proposed a protocol following the digital triage forensics (DTF) framework. In detail, the work provided a toolkit to collect volatile and non-volatile data from compromised, live Windows systems, along with an action plan. However, the procedure required manual efforts in forensic data collection, which might fail to preserve data integrity and fullness promptly.

Overall, there are several research gaps in the body of knowledge. Firstly, there is a lack of association between the work and digital forensics methodologies. Specifically, this isolation from digital forensics theories was observed in [15,25], which could be seen as independent malware analysis works from digital forensics. Moreover, although the authors proposed different techniques and analysis schemes for various malware and ransomware, they focused mainly on the machine learning perspective, distinct from key digital forensics concepts [8,21,27]. Thus, it poses a demand to evaluate integrating digital forensic principles with malware analysis and its ML application. Secondly, there is a lack of comprehensive investigation into ransomware attributes from the system's perspective. While some works dived into network traffic [8] and memory data [15,22], others attempted to analyse the attack from the end users' or victims' perspective [12–14], missing crucial background or hidden behaviours. Thirdly, state-of-the-art digital forensic analysis targets specific families or instances of ransomware [13–15,20,25]. The ever-evolving ransomware landscape requires a more comprehensive analysis methodology applicable to a broader range of families and instances.

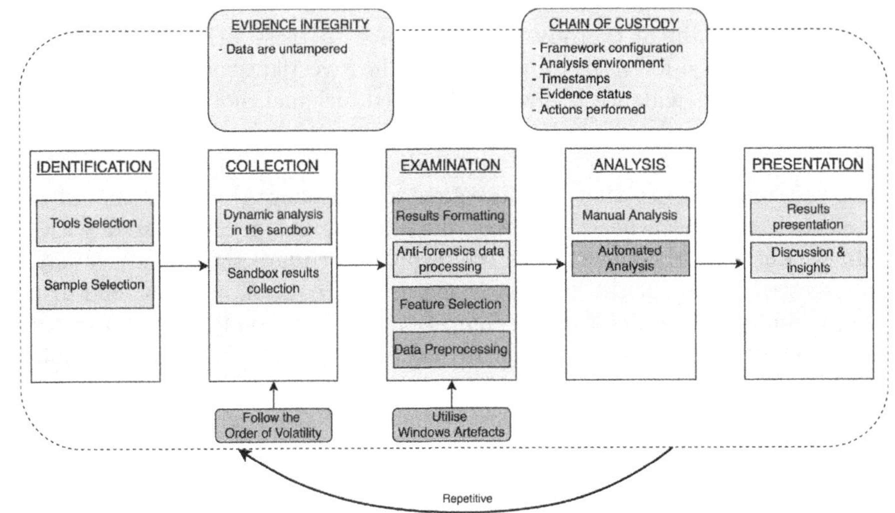

Fig. 1. Proposed Digital Forensics Framework for Ransomware Analysis.

3   Methodology

Digital Forensics is a branch of forensic science that aims to apply scientific methods to derive facts answering legal problems [1], which is based on Locard's Exchange Principle: "Whenever two objects come into contact with one another, there is an exchange of materials between them [1]." Regarding ransomware attacks on computing devices, we interpret the principle as that ransomware must leave digital traces on the victim's machine at every step of its attack. Moreover, dynamic ransomware analysis (and malware analysis in general) shares similar interests with digital forensics, as it also strives to anticipate unauthorised, illegal, or vandalistic actions. However, ransomware analysis must follow digital forensics principles, standards, and processes for its results to be forensically valid.

In this section, we discuss the two essential rules of digital forensics and their interpretation in dynamic ransomware analysis. We then examine the investigation process in digital forensics as a framework for the dynamic ransomware analysis procedure. In addition, the study details Windows system artefacts. However, while the principles and process hold, the paper does not cover memory, network, Internet, and mobile device forensics, as they are dedicated subbranches of digital forensics and would require extensive work.

3.1   Evidence Integrity and Chain of Custody

The two fundamental principles of digital forensics are the integrity of the evidence and the chain of custody [1]. Adherence to these principles during all phases of the digital forensics process proves the investigation's trustworthiness. It guarantees that evidence is always protected, original, not missing, nor contaminated, therefore legally valid.

In dynamic ransomware analysis, evidence integrity means the analysis framework must ensure that the investigated ransomware and its digital evidence, such as the cache or memory dump files, are not tampered with or modified. Likewise, the chain of custody principle requires the dynamic analysis framework to document the evidence's acquisition, control, analysis, and disposition, including the framework configuration, analysis conditions, timestamps, evidence status, and actions conducted. Besides supporting legal admissibility, complying with the two principles validates the investigation process and results and keeps track of all artefacts, making the analysis transparent, verifiable, and reproducible.

3.2 Five Phases of Digital Forensics

The digital forensics process incorporates five consecutive but iterative stages: identification, collection, examination, analysis, and presentation [1] (as shown in Fig. 1).

Firstly, the identification step aims to identify the incidence to initiate the investigation. In dynamic analysis, since the ransomware is predetermined, one needs to specify the sandbox environment executing the ransomware, which is termed a live system.

Secondly, in the collection step, one must make a forensically sound copy of the evidence. In the sandbox environment, all evidence only comes from the analysed machine. However, live systems contain a high risk of compromising the evidence and should be collected following the order of date and time, running applications, running processes, and volatile data [19]. Furthermore, based on the persistence and transfer characteristics of the evidence [9], volatile data collection must adhere to the order of volatility [1]. Specifically, one should prioritise collecting data with short lifespans or easy to eradicate. While the sandbox environment conceals its underlying data-collecting order, one can assess its alignment with these principles by verifying if it gathers all required data.

Thirdly, the examination phase seeks to extract potential evidence from the data collection and prepare it. In digital forensics, this step involves parsing, carving, and recovering broken, deleted, or scattered data. While state-of-the-art sandbox systems retain records of interacted files and data during the ransomware infiltration and attack, one might need to employ external tools for data carving and recovery. However, in the abundance of ransomware samples and their evidence, carving and recovering all possible contents over-stretches the investigation time and creates data overload, distracting the analysis where several crucial data points could be sufficient. On the other hand, the examination step also requires formatting the forensic results into an informative and readable structure, in which the JSON format provided from dynamic analysis results is suitable. Similarly, digital forensics encourages investigators to remove non-relevant and known-good files, which is similar to feature selection and data preprocessing in dynamic analysis. Nonetheless, timestamps are non-crucial in ransomware analysis since time in the sandbox environment can be manipulated to match the analysis's requirements. Additionally, anti-forensics techniques, including compression, encryption, and obfuscation, should be considered and may be collected manually if not supported by automated tools.

Table 1. Windows System Artefacts in Digital Forensics from the Dynamic Ransomware analysis perspective

Windows System Artefacts	Dynamic Ransomware Analysis Artefacts
Deleted data	Deleted files
Hibernation files (Sleep/Hibernation/Hybrid Sleep)	Not collected
Registry	Opened/Read/Modified/Removed registries
External drives	Not collected
Print Spooling	Connection attempts to printers via IPP
Recycle Bin	Deleted files
Metadata	Metadata
Thumbnail cache	Not collected
Most Recently Used (MRU)	Opened/Closed/Read/Modified/Deleted files
Restore Points and Shadow Copy	Not collected
Prefetch	Not collected
Link files	Created files
Install program	Run executables Imported PEs Originated DLLs

Fourthly, the analysis step involves processing the information given the investigation objectives to provide facts, evidence assessment, and the responsible person or people. In ransomware analysis, the step involves both manual and automated analysis. While AI/ML and other tools can work continuously, consistently, and with large-scale data, they usually extrapolate evidence to the results mechanically, without fully understanding the underlying contexts or intentions of the ransomware makers. Thus, they are prone to errors when obfuscation techniques are involved, which then requires manual examination.

Finally, the presentation phase in digital forensics has a similar objective to ransomware analysis: to share the results with the parties involved.

3.3   Windows System Artefacts

Digital forensics identifies a list of artefacts or footprints scattered in a Windows-based machine upon interaction and everyday use [19], as shown in Table 1. From the ransomware (and malware) analysis perspective, although not all artefacts are equally crucial, some resemblances can be deduced.

The two disciplines share the concern of registries. While digital forensics focuses on registries and their status in general, dynamic analysis with the sandbox environment records all interactions involving these registries, including opening, reading, modifying, or deleting. Likewise, since digital forensics works in a post-mortem environment, it can only analyse the artefacts in their final states. The dynamic ransomware analysis also agrees with examining deleted or recently used files. However, it extends the scope to all files interacted with by the investigating sample with their actions and outcomes since legitimate software will not attempt to act suspiciously (e.g., inject a process or open an unauthorised system registry/file). Moreover, Windows-based ransomware analysis extends the spectrum of installed programs inspected to executables run and imported Portable Executables (PEs).

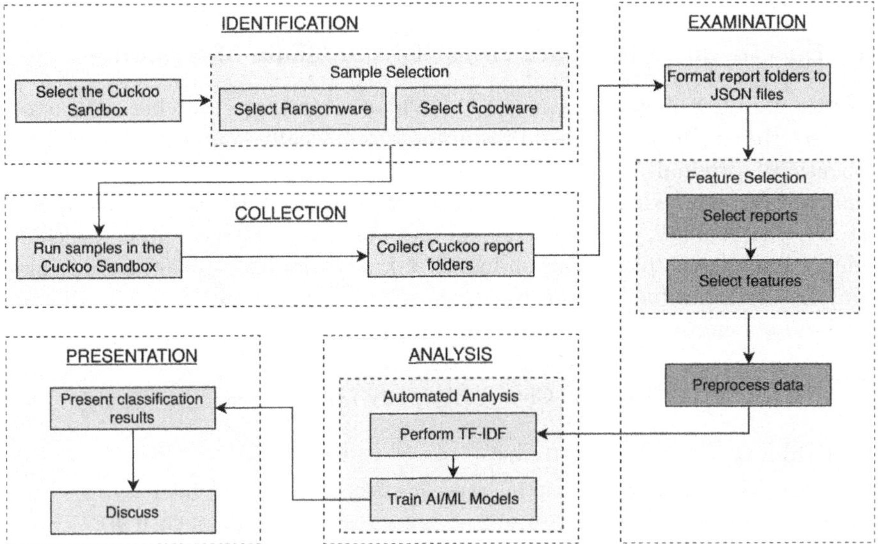

Fig. 2. The process diagram of the experiment based on the proposed framework.

On the other hand, because the dynamic analysis with the sandbox environment records the crime from start to finish, thumbnail cache, prefetch, restore points, and shadow copies are duplicative. Similarly, since the analysis environment manages all connected drives and data storage and does not sleep, analysing external drives and hibernated data is unnecessary.

Print spooling is a special case of implementing Windows artefacts from digital forensics into dynamic ransomware analysis. Conventionally, a legitimate program does not attempt to use the printer without the user's consent. Furthermore, the automated dynamic analysis does not involve human interaction for consent affirmation. Thus, queries to the printer are already questionable and could serve as an fully legitimate evidence.

4   Experiments and Results

The experiment applies the proposed framework to analyse ransomware and everyday-used software from a digital forensics perspective. As shown in Fig. 2, it comprises five steps: Identification, Collection, Examination, Analysis, and Presentation. The process also adheres to the two principles of digital forensics: Data Integrity and Chain of Custody. In general, while the Identification phase introduces the tools and data used, the following three phases (Collection, Examination, and Analysis) describe the acquisition and processing of the data while applying digital forensics methodology. Finally, the Presentation discusses the results of the experiment.

The GitHub project containing all related scripts, programs, and data is available at: https://github.com/hoanganhnguyen1198/gongrsw24.

4.1   Enactment of Evidence Integrity and Chain of Custody

The process must obey the principles of evidence integrity and chain of custody to ensure the experiment and its results are forensically sound. Regarding data authenticity, original and processed data at every stage of the experiment are untampered, archived, and documented. Furthermore, we secure the chain of custody with Table 2, documenting the actions and environment in which the evidence is acquired, processed, and analysed. Additionally, since the experiment is universally reproducible, the timestamps are independent of the results and, therefore, not needed.

Table 2. Chain of Custody List of items

Criteria	Items	Contents
Framework Configuration	Sandbox host machine specification	Ubuntu 22.04, Intel: - 32GB RAM, 1TB HDD
	AI/ML host machine specification	Google Colab - 51GB RAM, 225.18GB Disk
	Sandbox system configuration	Virtual machines: 02 Sandbox subnet: 192.168.30.1/24
	Virtual machine configuration	Windows 10 64-bit, 2 CPUs: - 4GB RAM, 128GB HDD - Recommended installation [5] - Network connected
Analysis environment	AI/ML models architecture	Model 1: K-Nearest Neighbours Model 2: Support Vector Machine Model 3: Gaussian Naive Bayes Model 4: Decision Tree Model 5: Random Forest Model 6: Multi-layer Perceptron Model 7: XGBoost
Evidence status	Ransomware	Ransomware collection
	Goodware	Goodware collection
	Processed file and data	GitHub gongrsw24
Timestamps	Timestamps	Not collected
Actions performed	Data processing & models training scripts	GitHub gongrsw24

4.2   Identification

We use the Cuckoo3 Sandbox System to perform dynamic ransomware analysis [6]. The work utilises two Windows 10 virtual machines to process samples simultaneously. We select this Windows version since it still accounts for over 53% of all Windows operating machines [24] and may remain in use for years to come. The system only uses the shared subnet to control and manage the machines, and the machines do not communicate with one another.

The samples contain 1,500 ransomware samples from [26] and 250 Windows-based legitimate software samples from [4].

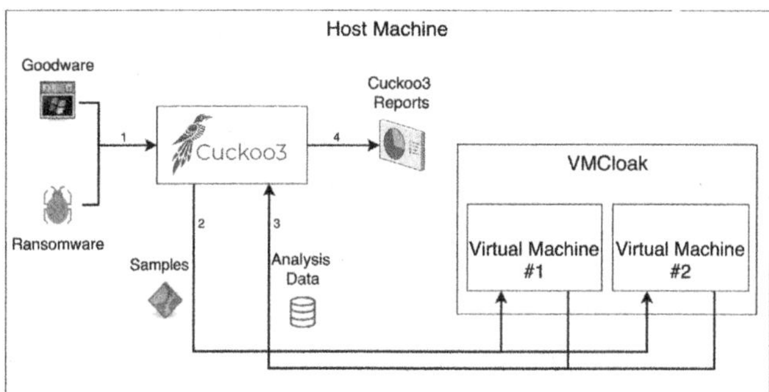

Fig. 3. The configuration of the Cuckoo3 Sandbox system.

4.3   Collection

The collection (1,750 samples) is fed into the Cuckoo Sandbox system in batches of 250. The system executes and records their behaviours and interactions separately in the two virtual machines. The host system is isolated from the running samples and maintains its integrity against samples attempting to modify system settings. After each run, the virtual sandbox machine is reset to its original state so that every run is independent, clean, and reproducible. Consequently, we collect 1,750 folders, each containing the dynamic analysis results of one sample. The configuration of the system is shown in Fig. 3.

4.4   Examination

The Cuckoo3 Dynamic Analysis runs all samples in the sandbox environment, returning 1,750 result folders. The details of the folder's contents are listed in Table 3. Most files are in JSON format, besides a log file in txt format and a set of memory dump files in dmp format. Although not listed, the report folder also contains several screenshots taken randomly during the analysis.

Table 3. Analysis Report Files and Selected Features

File Name	Description	Selected Features
`analysis.json`	Overall analysis results	None
`analysis.log`	Analysis log	None
`identification.json`	Sample identification	None
`pre.json`	PEs imported list	- DLL - APIs imported
`file.json`	File interaction list	- Source path - Destination path - Action performed - Effect
`mutant.json`	Mutants interaction list	None
`process.json`	Processes running list	None
`registry.json`	Registry interactions list	- Registry path - Action performed - Value type - Effect
`machine.json`	Target VM configuration	None
`*.dmp`	Memory dump files	None
`report.json`	Detailed analysis report	Process: - Process name & command line - PID & PPID - Is it injected? Network: - Hosts resolved - UDP Src/Dst IP & Port - UDP Packet size - DNS query Src/Dst IP & Port - Domain name

Select Reports. We select the `report.json` file from the folder since it contains comprehensive details of the analysis. The `pre.json`, `file.json`, and `registry.json` files are also collected because they include details about all affected Portable Executables (PEs), files, and registries when a sample runs. Notably, while uncollected files are valuable for other analysis tasks, they are not relevant to the experiment's scope.

Select Features. We select information that aligns with the digital forensics methodology. Details regarding the selected features in each file are listed in Table 3. Specifically, the experiment concerns Windows System artefacts. Based on 3.3, we categorise them into Behaviours and Static data. Behaviour data includes all registries and files with actions performed on them, processes, and hosts resolved. Especially for processes, we consider whether they are injected, a more suspicious action compared to start, stop, or terminate, assuming that a legitimate program does not need to inject its processes. Regarding Static data, the paper selects the list of PE imports, including the Dynamic Link Libraries (DLLs) and their corresponding API imported.

Preprocess Data. This step reformulates the nominated static and behaviour data into features and parameters for analysis and model training. Static data processing examines explicitly dynamically linked libraries (DLLs). We consider each DLL name a unique word and record its number of appearances, which is always one. Similarly, APIs imported by the program are treated as distinct words, and their appearance count remains one.

Algorithm 1. Data preprocessing

```
      for each feature_file do
2:       Read the content of feature_file
         txt_dict = {}                                   ▷ Create a dictionary to store preprocessed data
4:       for each pe_import do                           ▷ Handle selected features from PE imports
            Convert dll name to all lowercase
6:          txt_dict[dll] = count(dll)                    ▷ Count the appearances of dll
            for each import do
8:             Convert import name to all lowercase
               txt_dict[import] = count(import)           ▷ Count the appearances of import
10:         end for
         end for
12:      for each process do                              ▷ Handle selected features from Process list
            Convert commandline to all lowercase
14:         Split commandline to parts by spaces
            for each part do
16:            txt_dict[part] = count(part)               ▷ Count the appearances of part
            end for
18:         if injected == True then
               txt_dict[is_injected] += 1                 ▷ Count if process injection happened
20:         end if
         end for
22:      for each host_resolved do                        ▷ Handle selected features from Network
            txt_dict[host_resolved] = count(host_resolved) ▷ Count the appearances of hr
24:      end for
         for each file do                                 ▷ Handle selected features from File interaction
26:         Convert all keys' values to all lowercase
            Create the entry sda = srcpath_dstpath_action
28:         txt_dict[sda] = count(sda)                     ▷ Count the appearances of sda
            Create the entry ae = action_effect
30:         txt_dict[ae] = count(ae)                       ▷ Count the appearances of ae
         end for
32:      for each registry do                             ▷ Handle selected features from Registry interaction
            Convert all keys' values to all lowercase
34:         Create the entry pva = path_valuetype_action
            txt_dict[pva] = count(pva)                     ▷ Count the appearances of pva
36:         Create the entry ae = action_effect
            txt_dict[ae] = count(ae)                       ▷ Count the appearances of ae
38:      end for
         Save the recorded dictionary txt_dict
40: end for
```

Regarding Behaviour data, the processing focuses on how a program interacts with the system. The process list is an essential component, with particular attention paid to the process command line. The analysis considers the process and its arguments, recording the number of times each unique combination appears. In addition, the work investigates process injection, recording the number of instances where process injection occurs. However, process identifiers (PIDs) and parent process identifiers (PPIDs) vary between analyses and are therefore not tracked.

Network activity is another critical aspect of Behaviour data processing. In particular, the study considers hosts resolved, treating each hostname as a separate word along with the number of appearances.

On the other hand, we scrutinise source paths, destination paths, and actions performed for file operations. Different actions may serve different purposes even with the same path, so the combination of source, destination, and action is documented with its frequency. Furthermore, the effect of an action is assessed to determine whether it aligns with the intended outcome under the assumption that legitimate programs do not misrepresent their activities.

Similarly, registry modifications are examined by analysing the registry path, the action performed, and the value type. Different actions serve distinct purposes even with the same registry, so a combination of these factors is recorded along with its frequency. Additionally, the experiment evaluates the effect of registry actions, ensuring that the reported effect matches the performed action. Again, it is assumed that legitimate programs do not misrepresent their operations.

The algorithm used for the process is shown in Algorithm 1.

4.5   Analysis

Step 4.4 results in a collection of files where each file represents the analysis of one sample, describing characteristics as parameters (e.g., DLL name, hosts resolved, process command line) with their corresponding frequency. The experiment deploys automated analysis, utilising AI/ML models. However, while pre-processed data in 4.4 are presentable for manual analysis, they are further processed for AI/ML model training.

Perform TF-IDF. We consider each parameter equivalent to a word or a term. Thus, each file can be regarded as a text file in the text analysis task. A corpus of all parameters (terms) that appeared is also created.

For the Term Frequency calculation, according to Zipf's Law [3], we argue that the relevance of a sample's characteristic is also non-linearly proportional to its raw appearance count. Therefore, the term frequency is calculated with the log formula:

$$TF = \log(1 + tf_{f,d}) \tag{1}$$

where $tf_{f,d}$ is the raw term frequency term (the number of times that term t occurs in the document d).

Regarding the Inverse Document Frequency, we employ the formula:

$$IDF = \log(\frac{N}{df_t}) \tag{2}$$

where N is the number of documents in the collection and df_t is the number of documents in the given collection that contain the term t.

The Algorithm 2 describes the process of applying the two formulas to compile the dataset.

Algorithm 2. Dataset compilation using TF-IDF

    Read the *corpus*
2: $idf\_dict = \{\}$ ▷ Create a dictionary to store IDF data
    $N = count(txt\_dict)$
4: **for each** *term* **in** *corpus* **do**
      $term\_idf = \log(\frac{N}{corpus_{[term]}})$ ▷ Calculate a term's IDF
6:     Record $idf\_dict_{[term]} = term\_idf$
    end for
8: $tf\_idf\_dict = \{\}$ ▷ Create a dictionary to store TF-IDF data
    for each *txt_dict* **do**
10:     Read the content of *txt_dict*
      $tf\_dict = \{\}$ ▷ Create a dictionary for a document's TF data
12:     **for each** *term* **in** *corpus* **do**
        Initiate $tf\_dict_{[term]} = 0$
14:       **if** $term \in txt\_dict$ **then**
          $tf\_dict_{[term]} = \log(1 + txt\_dict_{[term]})$ ▷ Calculate a term's TF
16:       **end if**
      end for
18:     $tf\_idf\_t\_dict = \{\}$ ▷ Create a dictionary for a document's TF-IDF data
      for each *term* **in** *txt_dict* **do**
20:       $tf\_idf\_t\_dict_{[term]} = tf\_dict_{[term]} \times idf\_dict_{[term]}$ ▷ Calculate a term's TF-IDF
      end for
22:     Record $tf\_idf\_dict_{[term]} = tf\_idf\_t\_dict$
    end for
24: Create an empty data frame *df*
    for each *key, value* **in** tf_idf_dict **do**   ▷ Create the dataset
26:     Append as a new line to *df*
    end for

AI/ML Model Training. We employ seven types of AI/ML models to train the dataset as a binary classification task between ransomware and goodware. The seven models are: K-Nearest Neighbours (KNN), Support Vector Machine (SVM), Gaussian Naive Bayes (GNB), Decision Tree (DT), Random Forest (RF), Multi-Layer Perceptron (MLP), and XGBoost (XGB).

Table 4. Comparison between datasets utilising TF-IDF from Sandbox Report

Comparison Criteria	This work	[10]	[16]
Sample size (Goodware/Malware)	1690 (249/1441)	22,200 (11,735/10,465)	1076 (72/1004)
No. of Parameters	548,820	25,066,934 (15,542 samples)	332,481 (164 samples)
Parameter types	Digital Forensics-based	Full report	APIs, network, text
Availability	Yes	No	Yes

4.6 Presentation

Table 4 compares the final datasets to two other works that employ TF-IDF to process data from reports from Sandbox Systems. While each work represents different feature selection methods, to the best of our knowledge, this study introduces the first dataset integrating with digital forensics disciplines. Moreover, it shows a more efficient size of parameters over the number of samples used (548,820 parameters derived from 1690 samples). In contrast to the private dataset used in the work of [10], it is public and comprises more samples than the one in [16].

Table 5. The experiment results on the test dataset

Model	Goodware		Ransomware		Accuracy
	Precision	Recall	Precision	Recall	
KNN	73%	71%	73%	76%	73%
SVM	91%	86%	88%	92%	89%
GNB	85%	79%	82%	87%	83%
DT	**96%**	90%	91%	**97%**	**93%**
RF	91%	88%	89%	92%	90%
MLP	92%	78%	82%	94%	86%
XGB	93%	**93%**	**94%**	94%	**93%**

Table 5 illustrates the performance of the test dataset of 120 samples with 58 goodware and 62 ransomware, measuring three criteria: accuracy, precision, and recall. Specifically, the accuracy measures the ratio of correct predictions over the total number of predictions with the formula:

$$Accuracy = \frac{TP + TN}{TP + TN + FP + FN} \tag{3}$$

where TP, TN, FP, FN are true positives, true negatives, false positives, and false negatives, respectively. The paper also considers precision, which counts the number of correctly predicted positive cases, and recall, which measures the proportion of accurately identified true positive instances. The formula for precision is:

$$Precision = \frac{TP}{TP + FP} \tag{4}$$

and one for recall is:

$$Recall = \frac{TP}{TP + FN} \tag{5}$$

Among seven models, the DT and XGB models achieved the highest overall accuracy of 93%. Specifically, the XGB model had a more balanced precision and accuracy, with the highest ransomware precision of 94%. On the other hand, the DT model had the highest ransomware recall rate of 97%. It was also more precise in classifying goodware than XGB, 96% compared to 93%. The reasons for these high performances lie in the characteristics of the data and the two models' fundamentals. In particular, each feature contains a large number of data points as parameters, creating a highly dimensional dataset. Moreover, different ransomware deploying multiple attack strategies results in complex decision boundaries, non-linear parameter relationships, and some indications are more consequential than others. Fortunately, the DT model could address these challenges as it utilises the tree structure and the feature-selection algorithm, which opts for the most information gained, solving the discrete and categorical data nature and its varied feature importance. Similarly, since XGB trains decision trees sequentially (with gradient descent optimisation), it performs well with complicated, biased, and highly dimensional data.

In opposition, the KNN and GNB models failed to handle such issues, achieving worse results (77% and 83% in accuracy, respectively). The KNN model, which classifies instances based on their distances to others, suffers in high-dimensional spaces where distance is less meaningful. Nonetheless, the GNB model assumes features are independent and normally distributed, which seems unrealistic in this case.

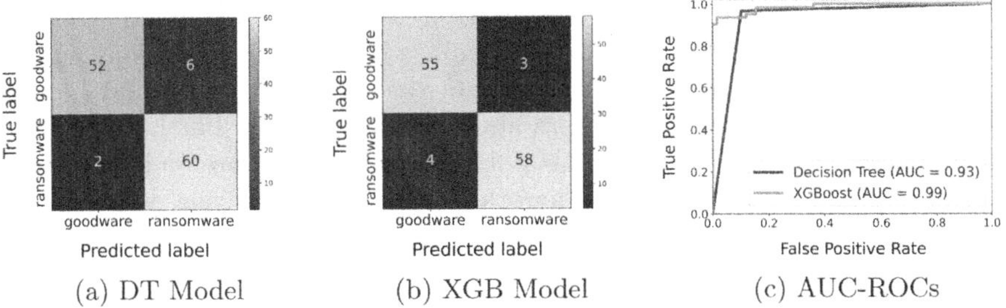

(a) DT Model   (b) XGB Model   (c) AUC-ROCs

Fig. 4. The confusion matrices and AUC-ROCs of DT and XGB models.

The confusion matrices of the two best-performed models (DT and XGB) are shown in Fig. 4(a) and 4(b). Notably, the DT model only misclassified two ransomware, while the XGB model misclassified twice as many. However, the DT model mistakenly sorted six legitimate software instances as ransomware, three more than its counterpart.

Since these two models had equal accuracy and comparable precision and recall, we employed the Area Under the Curve for the Receiver Operating Characteristic (AUC-ROC), which plots the recall against the false positive rate at different thresholds, as a distinguished metric. The false positive rate is calculated as follows:

$$FPR = \frac{FP}{FP + TN} \tag{6}$$

Despite sharing the tree architecture, the XGB model combines multiple trees, utilises the probability scores rather than hard if-else decisions, and improves misclassified samples with gradient descent optimisation. Figure 4(c) illustrates this, as the XGB model outperforms the DT model with an under-the-curve area of 0.99 compared to 0.93.

In conclusion, the XGBoost model achieves high accuracy, high precision, comparable recall, and a nearly-perfect AUC-ROC. However, the Decision Tree model is useful for interpretable forensic analysis, revealing insights into ransomware's distinctive behaviours.

5   Conclusion and Future Work

This paper presents a novel framework that integrates digital forensics into dynamic ransomware analysis, thereby bridging the gap between the two. The proposed approach enhances interpretability and reliability by aligning forensic principles with machine learning-based ransomware classification. Experimental results demonstrate that Decision Tree and XGBoost achieve the highest accuracy (93%), validating the framework's effectiveness. These findings suggest that digital forensics methodologies can improve ransomware detection and classification, ensuring forensic soundness in cyber investigations.

However, some challenges remain. The current implementation primarily focuses on binary classification (ransomware vs. goodware), which limits its ability to differentiate between ransomware families or malware types. The methodology also introduces numerous parameters that may add noise and increase computational cost, affecting interpretability and scalability. Furthermore, real-world adversarial techniques, such as polymorphic ransomware and obfuscation strategies, could challenge the framework's robustness, requiring adaptation to evasive threats.

Future research will expand beyond binary classification to multi-class models, which will distinguish ransomware families and malware types, offering deeper forensic insight. To further enhance accuracy, advanced machine learning techniques, especially deep learning architectures, transformer-based models, and Graph Neural Networks (GNNs), will be investigated to improve pattern recognition, feature extraction capabilities, interpretability, and performance.

Additionally, incorporating memory and network forensics could broaden the framework's forensic capabilities and improve reliability. Moreover, future work could extend the framework to analyse other malware categories, such as spyware, rootkits, banking trojans, and Advanced Persistent Threats (APTs). Finally, anomaly detection methods, including unsupervised learning and autoencoders, will be explored to detect unknown ransomware behaviours.

By incorporating these enhancements, we aim to develop an intelligent, adaptive, and forensic-driven malware detection framework capable of addressing modern ransomware threats and evolving cyberattack tactics.

Acknowledgement. This study was funded by UOW AEGiS (Advancement and Equity Grants Scheme for Research - University of Wollongong) fund.

References

1. Arnes, A.: Digital Forensics. Wiley (2017)
2. Australian federal police: Don't hack it alone: calls for australians to report ransomware attacks. Tech. rep., Australian Federal Police (2024). https://shorturl.at/ficcU
3. B., M., Zipf, G.K.: Human behavior and the principle of least effort; an introduction to human ecology. Am. J. Psychol. **64**(1), 149–150 (1951)
4. CNET download: free software download (2023). https://download.cnet.com. Accessed 10 May 2023
5. Cuckoo3: Creating an image (2024). https://cuckoo-hatch.cert.ee/static/docs/creating/vms/#creating-an-image. Accessed 20 Dec 2024
6. Cuckoo3: What is cuckoo3? (2024). https://cuckoo-hatch.cert.ee/static/docs/about/cuckoo/. Accessed 20 Dec 2024
7. Cybersecurity ventures: global ransomware damage costs predicted to reach \$265 billion by 2031 (2023). https://shorturl.at/ji2MY, accessed: Feb. 20, 2025
8. Ganachari, S., Nandigam, P., Daga, A., Mohanty, S.N., Sudha, S.V.: Machine learning based malware analysis in digital forensic with IoT devices. In: Nandan Mohanty, S., Garcia Diaz, V., Satish Kumar, G.A.E. (eds.) Intelligent Systems and Machine Learning, pp. 169–183. Springer Nature Switzerland, Cham (2023)
9. Houck, M.M., Siegel, J.A.: Fundamentals of Forensic Science. Elsevier, Amsterdam (2015)
10. Ilić, S., Gnjatović, M., Tot, I., Jovanović, B., Maček, N., Gavrilović Božović, M.: Going beyond API calls in dynamic malware analysis: a novel dataset. Electronics (Basel) **13**(17), 3553 (2024)
11. Internet crime complaint center: 2023 internet crime report. Tech. rep., FBI Internet Crime Complaint Center (IC3) (2023). https://www.ic3.gov/AnnualReport/Reports/2023_IC3Report.pdf
12. Kao, D.Y., Wu, G.J.: A digital triage forensics framework of window malware forensic toolkit: based on ISO/IEC 27037:2012. In: 2015 International Carnahan Conference on Security Technology (ICCST), pp. 217–222 (2015). https://doi.org/10.1109/CCST.2015.7389685
13. Kara, I., Aydos, M.: The rise of ransomware: forensic analysis for windows based ransomware attacks. Expert Syst. Appl. **190**, 116198 (2022)

14. Nakhonthai, P., Chimmanee, K.: Digital forensic analysis of ransomware attacks on industrial control systems: a case study in factories. In: 2022 6th International Conference on Information Technology (InCIT), pp. 416–421 (2022). https://doi.org/10.1109/InCIT56086.2022.10067356

15. Norman, J., Joseph, P.: Systematic memory forensic analysis of ransomware using digital forensic tools. Int. J. Nat. Comput. Res. **9**(2), 61–81 (2020)

16. Parisot, A., Bento, L.M.S., Machado, R.C.S.: Ransomware detection: leveraging sandbox, text mining techiques and machine learning. In: 2024 IEEE International Workshop on Metrology for Industry 4.0 & IoT (MetroInd4.0 & IoT), pp. 446–451 (2024). https://doi.org/10.1109/MetroInd4.0IoT61288.2024.10584155

17. Ransomware task force: April 2024 progress report. Tech. rep., Institute for Security and Technology (2024). https://securityandtechnology.org/wp-content/uploads/2024/04/April-2024-RTF-Progress-Report-Doubling-Down.pdf

18. Research and markets: operating systems market report 2025. Tech. rep., Research and Markets (2025). https://www.researchandmarkets.com/report/operating-systems

19. Sammons, J.: The Basics of Digital Forensics: The Primer for Getting Started in Digital Forensics. Syngress, 225 Wyman Street, Waltham, MA 02451, USA (2012)

20. Schmutz, D., Rapp, R., Fehrensen, B.: Forensic analysis of hook android malware. Forensic Sci. Int. Digit. Invest. **49**, 301769 (2024)

21. Sharma, S., Krishna, C.R., Kumar, R.: RansomDroid: forensic analysis and detection of android ransomware using unsupervised machine learning technique. Forensic Sci. Int. Digit. Invest. **37**, 301168 (2021)

22. Shosha, A.F., James, J.I., Hannaway, A., Liu, C.C., Gladyshev, P.: Towards automated malware behavioral analysis and profiling for digital forensic investigation purposes. In: Rogers, M., Seigfried-Spellar, K.C. (eds.) Digital Forensics and Cyber Crime, pp. 66–80. Springer, Heidelberg (2013). https://doi.org/10.1007/978-3-642-39891-9_5

23. Statcounter: desktop operating system market share worldwide (2025). https://gs.statcounter.com/os-market-share/desktop/worldwide/#monthly-202204-202504. Accessed 1 Apr 2025

24. statcounter: Windows version market share worldwide (2025). https://gs.statcounter.com/windows-version-market-share/desktop/worldwide/#monthly-202204-202504. Accessed 1 Apr 2025

25. Suk-On, N., Thiratitsakun, N., Chimmanee, K.: Digital forensic analysis of lockbit ransomware attack on operational technology. In: 2024 8th International Conference on Information Technology (InCIT), pp. 624–629 (2024). https://doi.org/10.1109/InCIT63192.2024.10810564

26. VirusShare.com: Virusshare.com - because sharing is caring (2023). https://virusshare.com. Accessed 10 May 2023

27. Zola, F., Bruse, J.L., Galar, M.: Temporal analysis of distribution shifts in malware classification for digital forensics. In: 2023 IEEE European Symposium on Security and Privacy Workshops (EuroS&PW), pp. 439–450 (2023). https://doi.org/10.1109/EuroSPW59978.2023.00054

Evaluating Deep Learning in Gait Recognition

Haotian Liu[1], Zheng Zhu[1], Weizhi Meng[1,2(✉)], and Xiaojiang Du[3]

[1] SPTAGE Lab, Technical University of Denmark, Kgs. Lyngby 2800, Denmark
[2] School of Computing and Communications, Lancaster University, Lancaster, UK
weizhi.meng@ieee.org
[3] Department of Electrical and Computer Engineering, Stevens Institute
of Technology, Hoboken, USA

Abstract. User recognition is an important technology to identify and distinguish individuals based on certain characteristics or biometric data in various contexts such as in a system and application. It is a basis for building a secure user authentication or identification scheme. For example, gait recognition aims to verify and identify an individual based on the walking style with features such as stride length, speed, and joint angles. With continuous technological advancements, gait recognition is expected to be employed in more practical scenarios, bringing convenience and enhanced security. For better processing the data, deep learning has been widely applied in gait recognition. However, high variability in gait is still an open challenge to build a practical gait recognition system. In this work, we aim to investigate the usage of deep learning in gait recognition. In particular, we explore different neural network models including C3D, CNN-LSTM, CNN-Res-LSTM, ViViT and CNN-Transformer, and study the effect of different gait video directions on model accuracy. In the end, we discuss the potential security threats and open challenges of deep learning-based gait recognition.

Keywords: Gait recognition · User authentication · Deep learning · Biometric security · Neural network

1 Introduction

Biometric recognition [22,34] is an identity verification technology that identifies or verifies individuals by analyzing their biological or behavioral features. Humans have various biometric characteristics for identification and authentication such as iris [43], fingerprints [33], face [16,41], handwriting [30], keystroke [47], touch dynamics [37], gait [23], etc. These features can be used in areas such as identity verification, criminal investigations, and biometric recognition. It is worth noting that facial features, fingerprints, and iris patterns have been widely adopted in the commercial sector and have become part of our daily lives.

Over the past few decades, the field of gait recognition has undergone significant changes, incorporating advancements from related disciplines such as

X. Chen et al. (Eds.): DSPP 2025, LNCS 16177, pp. 33–50, 2026.
https://doi.org/10.1007/978-981-95-3185-1_3

computer vision, machine learning, and biometrics. *Gait recognition* can be considered as a technology that identifies individuals based on their unique walking patterns [44]. Many early studies were conducted using film cameras, but the widespread application of gait analysis in individuals with pathological conditions such as cerebral palsy, Parkinson's disease, and neuromuscular disorders began in the 1970s when camera systems became available for detailed studies of individual patients within realistic costs and time constraints [35]. Treatment plans based on gait analysis results, often involving orthopedic surgery, made significant progress in the 1980s.

Compared to fingerprint recognition and facial recognition, gait recognition is non-intrusive in nature. It does not require active user participation and enables remote and continuous monitoring and identification. Thus, gait recognition presents an exciting opportunity to complement and even surpass traditional biometric identification techniques in certain applications.

Nowadays, gait recognition primarily relies on video analysis and sensor technology to capture individuals' gait information. By extracting features and utilizing efficient algorithms such as deep learning [39], gait patterns can be modeled and recognized. The application scope of gait recognition technology is extensive, including areas such as human identification, medical rehabilitation, and security systems. Nowadays, many leading orthopedic hospitals worldwide have gait laboratories, typically used for designing treatment plans and conducting follow-up monitoring. However, we found that gait recognition still encounters several main issues as below.

- **Diversity and complexity:** Gait patterns exhibit diversity and complexity, influenced by individual variations, environmental factors, and behavioral changes. Developing gait recognition systems that are widely adaptable and robust is a challenge.
- **Real-time processing and efficiency:** Many practical applications of gait recognition require real-time processing, such as in security surveillance and border control. Therefore, gait recognition systems need to be efficient with high processing speed and low latency.
- **Privacy and ethical concerns:** Gait recognition involves the collection and analysis of individuals' biometric features, raising concerns about privacy and ethics. Ensuring data security and privacy protection are significant issues in the development of gait recognition technology.
- **Limited datasets and annotations:** Gait recognition relies on large labeled datasets for training and evaluation. However, acquiring and annotating large-scale gait datasets is a complex and time-consuming task. Additionally, existing datasets may suffer from sample bias and diversity lacking.
- **Dependency on wearable devices:** Some gait recognition systems require individuals to wear sensor devices or use specific camera setups, limiting the practical application scope. Developing gait recognition techniques that do not rely on additional devices or conventional monitoring equipment remains a challenge.
- **Environmental interference and noise:** The accuracy of gait recognition can be affected by environmental interference and noise, such as changes in lighting conditions, camera angles, and occlusions.

Related Work. Deep learning has been widely explored in gait recognition. For instance, Liu et al. [10] introduced spatial-temporal gait features with deep learning. It can leverage a gait energy image (GEI) based Siamese neural network to automatically extract robust and discriminative spatial gait features. A deep convolutional neural network (DCNN) was also explored to help detect the early fall of persons with walking disabilities [38]. Battistone and Alfredo [3] introduced TGLSTM, a Time based Graph Long Short-Term Memory network with temporal information to dynamically learn graphs when there are chances during time for gait recognition systems. Gul et al. [11] introduced a 3D convolutional deep neural network (3D CNN) for gait recognition by capturing the spatio-temporal features of a gait sequence (e.g., the shape and motion characteristics of the human gait). Deng et al. [6] introduced a frontal-view gait recognition method using gait dynamics and deep learning. They particularly characterized the binary walking silhouettes with three different kinds of frontal-view gait features such as kinematic features, spatial ratio features and area features. Sepas-Moghaddam and Etemad [39] provided a review to introduce breakthroughs and recent developments in gait recognition with deep learning including datasets, protocols and a taxonomy with four dimensions (such as body representation, temporal representation, feature representation, and neural architecture). Some other related surveys can refer to [12, 19].

Contributions. Motivated by the current trend of using deep learning in gait recognition, our work aims to evaluate its performance. This is because gait features may pose high variability that can greatly affect the performance of learning models. Also, there is a lack of evaluation studies on deep learning in gait recognition. For instance, we notice there are many studies proposing a tuned classifier to achieve better recognition performance, but few studies aim to provide a performance evaluation among existing methods.

Hence, this work delves into the mechanisms of gait recognition and explores the utilization of deep learning with 5 different neural network models. Then we discuss potential security threats and investigate the open challenges in this field. We have two primary contributions:

- One is to compare the performance of different deep learning models in gait recognition, including C3D, CNN-LSTM, CNN-Res-LSTM, ViViT and CNN-Transformer;
- The second is to examine the impact of different gait video directions on the model accuracy, which can provide a reference for designing a suitable and practical gait recognition scheme.

The rest of this work is organized as follows. Section 2 describes the gait dataset preprocessing and the primary neural network models in gait recognition. Section 3 presents the performance evaluation regarding different models and the impact of different gait video directions. Section 4 further discusses the threshold settings, potential threats and open challenges in gait recognition. Section 5 concludes our work with future trends.

2   Deep Learning Models in Gait Recognition

In this section, we present how deep neural networks are applied in gait recognition tasks, including dataset preprocessing, different neural network modeling, and neural network training.

2.1   Dataset Preprocessing

In this work, we selected the CASIA gait database [1] as the training and testing datasets. This database has three sub-datasets: *Dataset A* (small-scale library), *Dataset B* (multi-view library), and *Dataset C* (infrared library).

- **Dataset A** (the former NLPR gait database) was created on December 10, 2001, which contains the data of 20 people, where each person has 12 image sequences, and 3 walking directions (parallel to the image plane at $0°$, $45°$, and $90°$, respectively), with 4 image sequences for each orientation. The length of each sequence varies with walking speed of the person, and the number of frames in each sequence ranges from 37 to 127. The entire database contains 13,139 images with around 2.2 GB in size.
- **Dataset B** is a large-scale, multi-view gait library collected in January 2005. It contains a total of 124 people, each with 11 viewing angles (0, 18, 36, ..., 180°), which were collected under three walking conditions (e.g., normal conditions, wearing a coat, and carrying a package).
- **Dataset C** is a large-scale database taken at night by an infrared (thermal) camera, collected from July to August 2005, including 153 people, each person walked under four conditions: normal walking, fast walking, slow walking, and walking with Pack away.

Figure 1 shows the gait image sequence used in this work.

Fig. 1. Gait Image Sequence.

Because of the limitation of GPU resources, we used *Dataset A* for our training and testing to validate the performance of deep learning networks. In particular, *Dataset A* includes three parts: background image sequences, RGB image sequences of people walking, and single-valued image sequences of people walking after image segmentation. To eliminate potential confounding factors from apparel characteristics such as clothing color variations across subjects, which remain constant for each individual throughout the dataset–we exclusively employed single-channel image sequences for gait analysis.

To process the data, the first step is to split the dataset into both training and testing sets. For each image sequence, we extract the last 20 frames of all sequences as the test set and the previous sequences as the training set. The length of each image sequence is usually 70–90 frames, and the number of frames of the image sequence fed by a single training session is set to 16 frames.

It is worth noting that *Dataset A* has only 240 image sequences in total, which is relatively small. To mitigate the limited frame number in the original dataset, we employ a 16-frame sliding window with single-frame stride for data augmentation. This approach generates non-overlapping training (1,918 sequences) and testing (240 sequences) subsets while preserving temporal continuity. The method of using a sliding window both expands the training dataset and maintains strict separation between training and testing data. Every image is normalized with 0.5 mean and 0.5 standard deviations.

2.2 Neural Network Modeling

In this work, several different neural networks are tested based on their popularity, such as C3D (3D convolutional neural network), CNN-LSTM, CNN-Res-LSTM, ViViT, and CNN-Transformer.

C3D Description. The architecture of the C3D neural network is shown in Fig. 2. The C3D model contains 6 '*3D convolutional neural network blocks*' and a fully connected layer to obtain the final classification. Each convolutional neural network block contains 3 layers: a 3D convolutional layer, a batch normalization layer, and a ReLU activation function layer, as shown in Fig. 3. The convolution kernel size of the convolution layer of each convolution block is 3×3, and the downsampling is realized by setting the stride to 2.

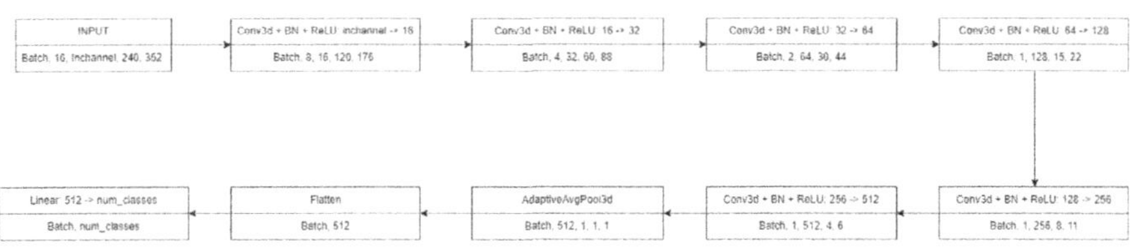

Fig. 2. The architecture of C3D neural network.

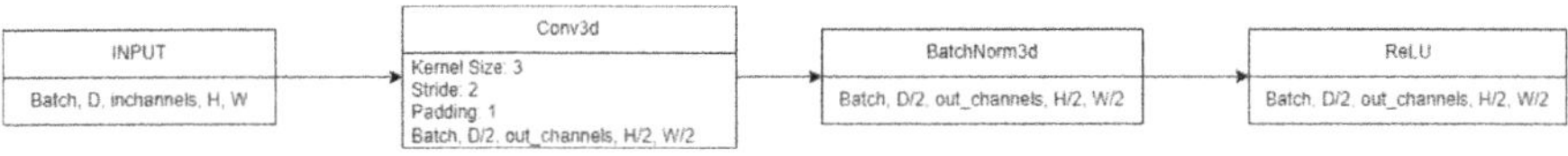

Fig. 3. C3D Block.

Following the convolutional layers, there is an Adaptive Average Pooling layer that reduces the feature map size of each channel to $1 \times 1 \times 1$. Then, a

Flatten operation is applied to the tensor so that it can be fed into the fully connected layer. The fully connected layer transforms the 512-dimensional input into an output of the dimension of the number of classes in the network.

CNN-LSTM Description. The long short-term memory (LSTM) [15] neural network is wildly used in Natural Language Processing (NLP) field because LSTM performs well in dealing with time series tasks. The gait recognition task needs to analyze the correlation of each frame of images in the gait video data in the time dimension, so as to classify the video information. However, the LSTM neural network cannot process image information well.

On the contrary, Convolutional Neural Network (CNN) [14] performs well in extracting image features. To accomplish the gait recognition task, each frame of the image is first fed into a convolutional neural network. The CNN performs frame-level feature extraction on each individual image in the sequence. These extracted spatial features are then sequentially fed into a LSTM network to model temporal dependencies across frames. Finally, the time sequence information output by the LSTM neural network is input into a fully connected neural network to obtain classification results, as shown in Fig. 4.

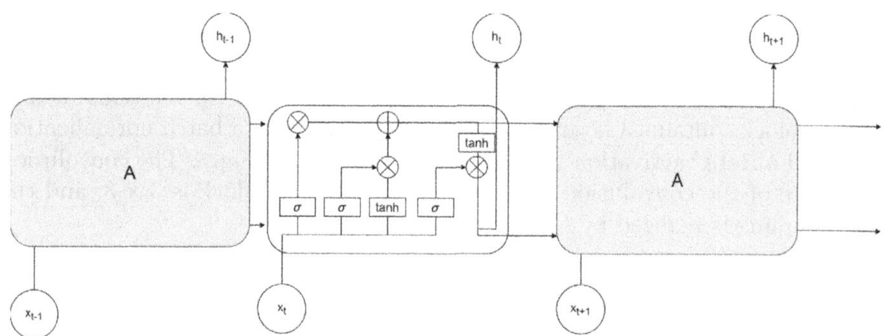

Fig. 4. LSTM Cell.

While in the process of model training, the LSTM training results are not ideal. Hence, we introduce the residual connection between LSTM layers called the *CNN-Res-LSTM model*. With the residual connection, the model accuracy can be greatly improved. This is because the introduction of residual connections may reduce the problem of multi-layer LSTM vanishing gradient, thereby improving the network performance. Figure 5 describes the CNN-LSTM model and Fig. 6 shows the CNN-Res-LSTM model.

Video Vision Transformer (ViViT). Transformer [48] is one of the most popular neural networks in the literature, which performs very well in various NLP tasks. The currently popular ChatGPT is an application of language model

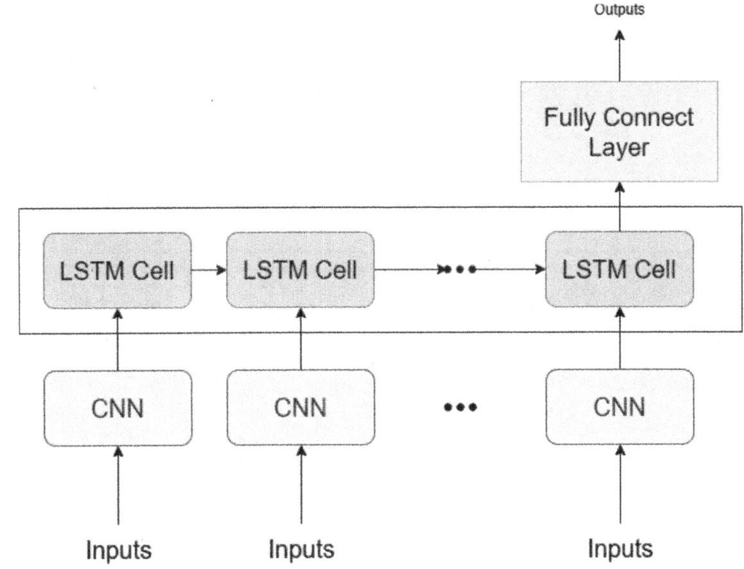

Fig. 5. CNN-LSTM Model.

Fig. 6. CNN-Res-LSTM.

based on Transformer design. The idea of the Transformer is to model the dependencies between different positions in the input sequence through a self-attention mechanism. Traditional recurrent neural networks, e.g., RNN and LSTM, face problems such as gradient disappearance or gradient explosion when processing long sequences, but Transformer can directly capture the dependencies between different positions in the sequence through the self-attention mechanism and handle the long-distance dependencies well.

In Transformer, input sequences are represented as queries, keys, and values, respectively. The attention weight is obtained by calculating the similarity between the query and the key, and then the weighted sum of the attention weight and the value can be obtained to present the context representation. This attention calculation is realized by calculating the dot product, and the attention weight is obtained after normalization.

In order to increase the expressiveness of the model and capture multiple different attention patterns, Transformer introduces a multi-head self-attention mechanism. In multi-head self-attention, the input is mapped multiple times, and different attention weights are computed separately. These attention weights are then weighted and summed to obtain the final context representation.

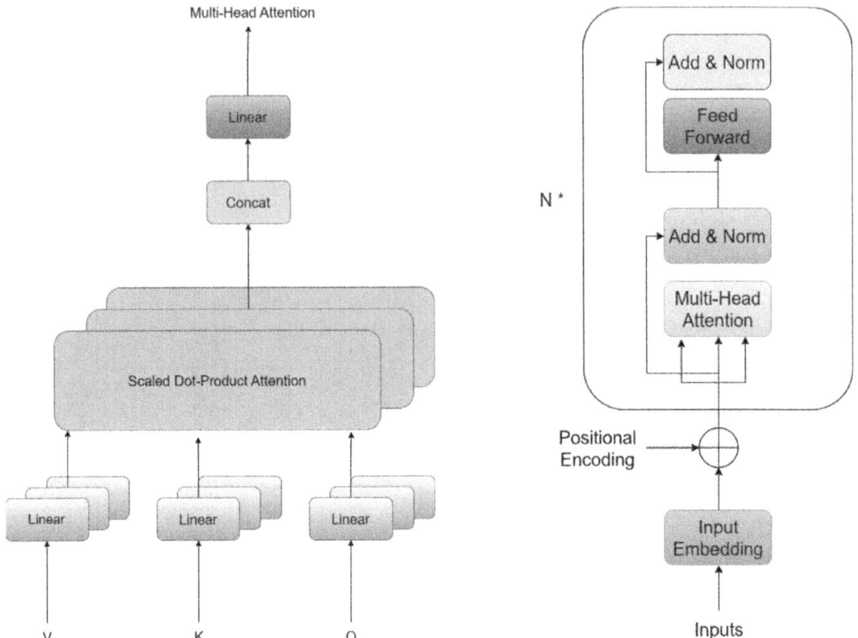

Fig. 7. Multi-head self-attention.　　　　**Fig. 8.** Transformer Encoder.

As shown in Fig. 7, multi-head self-attention allows the model to simultaneously focus on different positions in the input sequence, thus improving the model's ability to model the input. Through multiple attention heads, Transformer can learn different attention patterns, such as paying attention to semantic information or location information at different positions in the sequence. In addition, Transformer's performance in image processing is also competitive.

For processing images, the Vision Transformers (ViT) [49] neural network is designed for image-processing tasks. The idea of ViT is to segment the image into fixed-size tiles and feed these tiles into the Transformer model as a sequence.

It is noted that ViT first works by splitting the input image into a set of patches and then flattening each patch into a vector representation. These vector representations are treated as input sequences and passed to the Transformer encoder (as shown in Fig. 8). In the Transformer encoder, each patch vector is processed through a multi-layer self-attention mechanism and a feed-forward neural network. ViT can obtain the feature of the image through a method of dividing the image into many patches.

Then the ViViT neural network [2] is a video classification version of ViT, which contains two Transformer blocks. The first Transformer block is actually a ViT image processing layer that is able to extract features of each frame. The second Transformer block is a time sequence Transformer Layer, which extracts sequence information in the time dimension. Feeding the feature obtained by the

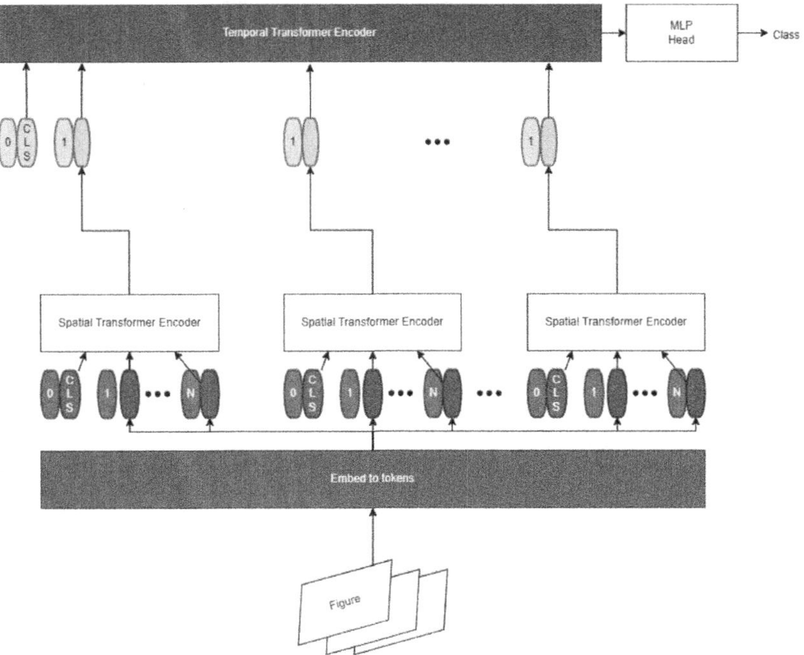

Fig. 9. Model of ViViT.

second Transformer block into a fully connected neural network can help obtain the video classification result. Figure 9 depicts the model of ViViT.

CNN-Transformer Description. Because CNN often performs better than other neural networks in image feature extraction tasks, the idea of a combined model–CNN-Transformer is to use a CNN to extract features of each frame of image, and then concatenate the extracted image features according to the time dimension. Feeding the concatenated tensor into a Transformer block can help obtain the features of the video in time series, and then feeding the obtained features into a fully connected neural network can obtain the result of video classification. Figure 10 shows the CNN-Transformer model.

2.3   Neural Network Training

In order to compare different models, it is important to ensure that the training hyperparameters are similar. However, the architecture of each model is different, there will still exist some differences in the hyperparameters used for training.

In this work, Adam optimizer with $\beta_1 = 0.5, \beta_2 = 0.999$ is used for C3D neural network and CNN-LSTM neural network training, while Adam optimizer with $\beta_1 = 0.9, \beta_2 = 0.98$ is used for ViViT neural network and CNN-Transformer neural network training. L2 regularization is used for training all neural networks to mitigate the overfitting problem. It is a technique by adding a penalty term

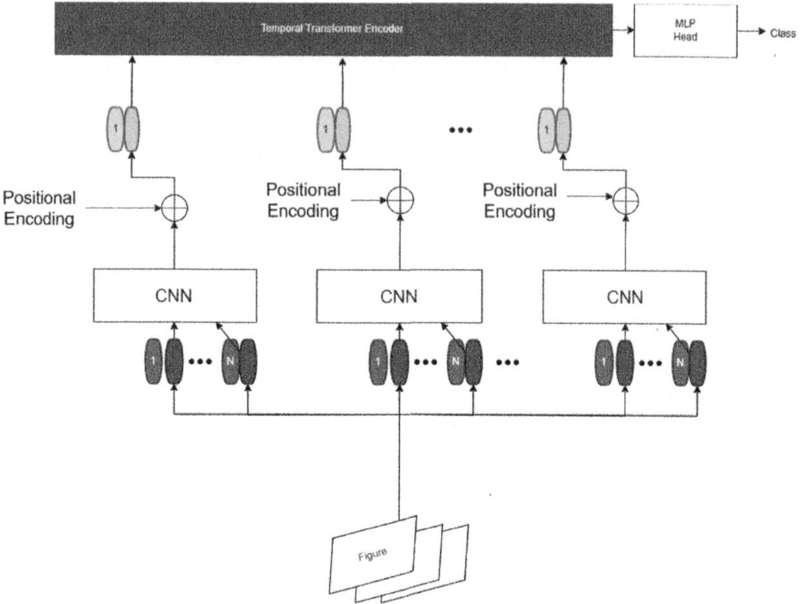

Fig. 10. CNN-Transformer Model.

to the loss function, in order to avoid assigning excessively large weights to features. Also, gradient clipping is used for all neural networks to mitigate the problem of exploding gradients during back-propagation, through thresholding the gradients to a maximum magnitude. Each model trains the entire training set for 50 times, that is, each model trains 50 epochs.

3 Evaluation of Gait Recognition Systems

In this work, the performance evaluation is mainly carried out in two aspects. One is to compare the testing results of different models (e.g., C3D, CNN-LSTM, CNN-Res-LSTM, ViViT, and CNN-Transformer) and the second is to explore the impact of different gait video directions on model accuracy.

3.1 Evaluation on Different Models

Table 1 shows the accuracy of all 5 models trained on 3 directions video combined dataset. It can be seen that the CNN-Transformer model could reach the highest prediction accuracy, followed by the CNN-Res-LSTM model, and the third highest accuracy was reached by the C3D model.

After adding the residual connection between LSTM layers, the accuracy of LSTM models increased by 7.92%. Trends in test accuracy for each model are depicted in Fig. 11 and trends in loss for each model are shown in Fig. 12. It is found that the convergence speed of the C3D model is the fastest, and

Table 1. Accuracy in 3 Directions Trained Together for Each Model

Model Name	Accuracy
C3D	86.25%
CNN-LSTM	79.58%
CNN-Res-LSTM	87.50%
ViViT	45.41%
CNN-Transformer	88.33%

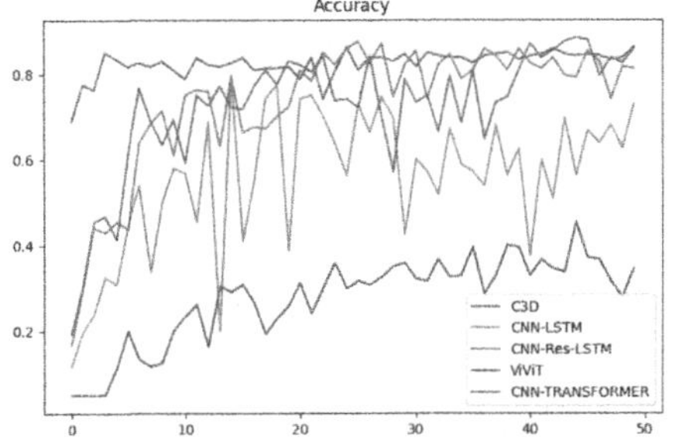

Fig. 11. Accuracy in 3 Directions Trained Together for Each Model.

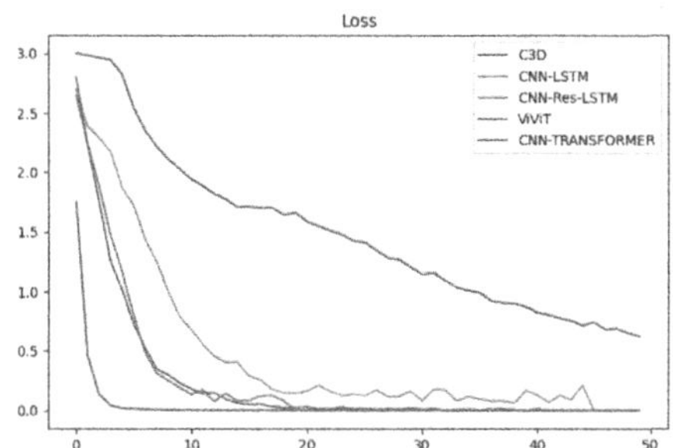

Fig. 12. Loss in 3 Directions Trained Together for Each Model.

it converges to the optimum in around the 5th epoch. On the contrary, the convergence speed of the ViViT model is the slowest, which even has not fully converged in the last epoch during the testing.

The accuracy results of different directions of 5 models (e.g., 0, 45 and 90°) are shown in Fig. 13, Fig. 14, and Fig. 15, respectively. It can be seen that different directions have the least influence on the C3D model. More specifically, the accuracy of the C3D model trained in a single direction is similar to the accuracy of the three directions trained together. The maximum accuracy of different models with different directions is summarized in Fig. 16.

3.2 Effect of Different Gait Video Directions

The accuracy of different directions is presented in Table 2. Note that the results in the table are intuitive. It is observed that the training accuracy based on video information in three directions could be better than those obtained by training with video information in any direction alone. Among the results obtained based on single-directional video training, the accuracy could be the highest trained by the 90-degree video information.

3.3 Result Analysis

According to the evaluation results, for the gait recognition, it is a promising idea to combine convolutional neural networks with other neural networks aiming at

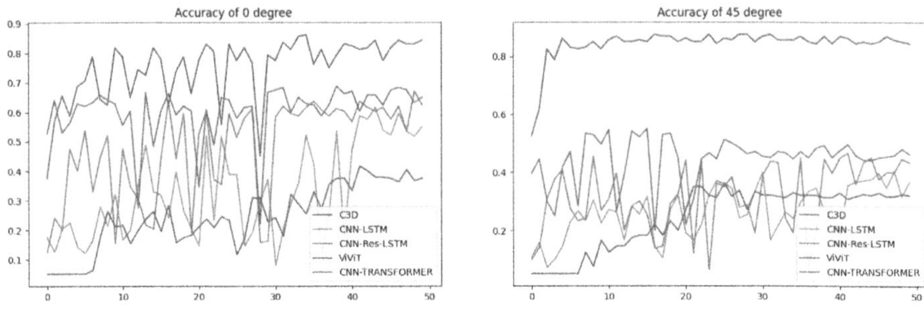

Fig. 13. Accuracy of 0°.   Fig. 14. Accuracy of 45°.

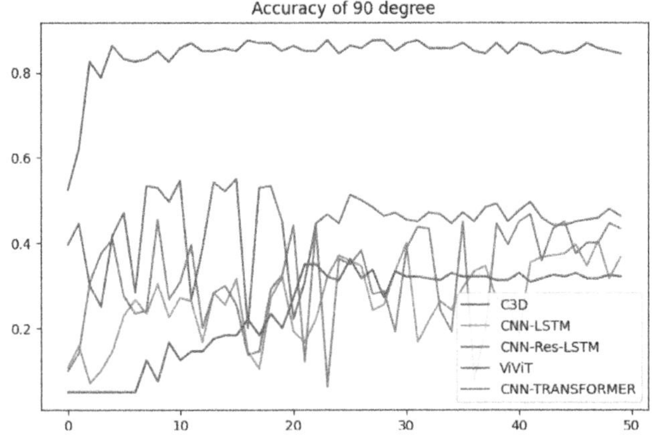

Fig. 15. Accuracy of 90°.

time sequence tasks such as recurrent neural networks, LSTM neural networks, and Transformer neural networks. Besides, when constructing several layers of LSTM neural networks, the residual connection is very helpful to reduce the issue of vanishing gradient. It occurs when gradients (used to update network weights during back propagation) become exponentially small as they propagate backward through the network, causing early layers to learn extremely slowly or stop learning altogether.

When we trained the ViViT model, the loss trained did not converge as quickly as other models. It is found that even after 50 epochs, the loss of the ViViT model is still relatively high, around 0.7. This may be caused by the fact that the ViT model divides each frame of the image according to a fixed-size patch for feature extraction. Because each patch of ViT segmentation does not overlap with each other, this may lead to the insufficient Field of View (FOV) of the neural network and insufficient extraction of the overall feature of the image. Therefore, the training results of ViViT are not ideal. FOV refers to the extent of the observable world or scene that is visible at any given moment through a visual system, e.g., a camera.

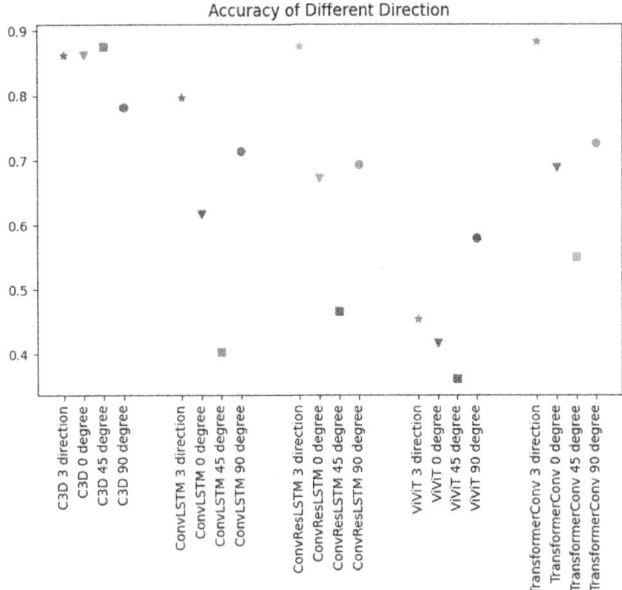

Fig. 16. Accuracy of Different Direction of 5 Models.

Table 2. Accuracy of Each Direction of All Models

Direction	Mean Accuracy
$0°$	65.08%
$45°$	53.17%
$90°$	69.79%
0, 45, 90° together	77.42%

In addition, simultaneously using video information from multiple directions for training can improve accuracy. These results might have important reference values for designing a suitable gait recognition scheme based on neural networks. However, based on Fig. 13, Fig. 14, Fig. 15 and Fig. 16, it is found that if only one direction is available, the C3D model might be the best option.

Also, we notice that the results of model training are easily affected by the datasets. For example, the gait video–*Dataset A*–in the experiment has fewer gait image sequences for each tester, which may lead to unstable model training and prone to overfitting problems. Future model tests should be performed with more larger datasets.

4   Further Discussion

4.1   Threshold Setting for Identification

While neural networks can provide a probabilistic output, decisions often need to be made in a binary manner, especially in the context of identification. This is where threshold setting comes into effect. By setting a threshold, we can decide the certainty level that we require from the model and make a proper decision.

For instance, we could set a probability threshold of 90%. When the classification probability output by the neural network reaches or exceeds 90% (in the gait recognition scenario, it refers to the recognition confidence of a specific individual), we determine that the recognition result is valid.

This approach can be used to reduce the chances of mis-identification. With a high threshold, we can only accept the decision where the model is highly confident. This is particularly useful in sensitive applications where the cost of a false positive is high.

4.2 Probability Threshold in Gait Recognition

The principle of threshold setting can be directly applied to the field of gait recognition. In our evaluation, we found that neural networks, particularly those combined convolutional layers with recurrent structures, have shown good performance in identifying individuals based on their gait patterns.

In practice, we could input a sequence of gait data into our trained neural network. The output could be a probability distribution over all individuals known to the system. If the highest probability is 90% or more (or any other pre-set threshold), we could conclude that the gait sequence belongs to the corresponding individual.

In conclusion, the use of a probability threshold for user identification (or user authentication) provides a useful method to control the trade-off between sensitivity and specificity in gait recognition systems. With all system parameters, we have to carefully fine-tune this threshold, which is crucial in ensuring that the system can perform optimally in its intended application.

4.3 Attacks and Potential Solutions

Gait recognition systems, similar to other biometric systems [34,40], are susceptible to various security threats. These include spoofing attacks [42] where an attacker imitates the gait of a target individual, and replay attacks where previously recorded gait data is used to fool the system. In addition, gait recognition systems can also be susceptible to machine learning-specific attacks such as adversarial attacks [29,31], where small perturbations are introduced to the input data in order to deceive the system.

To counter these threats, various anti-attack mechanisms have been proposed. Liveness detection methods [32], for example, can be used to differentiate between live subjects and recorded videos in an attempt to prevent replay attacks. For spoofing attacks, multi-factor authentication that combines gait recognition with other biometric modalities could potentially increase the cracking difficulty for attackers (e.g., two-factor authentication).

However, the effectiveness of these countermeasures varies, and there is a constant tug-of-war between the security of gait recognition systems and the usability of real-world applications. As such, it is still an open challenge to make a balance. There is also a need to consider combining with existing security solutions, such as intrusion detection [24,25,46], collaborative method [17,18,27], trust management [20,21,29], firewall [7,8,36], access control [9,13,26], privacy-preservation [4,28,45] and more. Large language models (LLMs) are also a promising add-on that can be considered [5].

4.4 Open Challenges

In this part, we discuss some open challenges for establishing a robust and practical gait recognition system.

1. *Data Collection:* Gait data needs to be collected from multiple angles and environments, which requires careful placement and adjustment of camera equipment, but it may not always be practical in many situations. Additionally, the accuracy of gait recognition often relies on high-quality video data, which may require expensive hardware equipment.
2. *Variability:* A person's gait features can gradually change due to factors such as fatigue, injury, aging, etc., or due to environmental factors such as the wearing shoes or the condition of the ground. These changes can impact the accuracy of gait recognition.
3. *Privacy Concerns:* Gait recognition requires the collection and analysis of personal gait data, which can raise privacy issues. For instance, though gait data will not disclose a user's identity as facial data, some people might still feel insecure or uncomfortable.
4. *Computational Costs:* The algorithms used for gait recognition typically require much computational resources, which can limit their application in low-power devices or the environments with limited resources.
5. *Regulatory Restrictions:* In some countries and regions, the use of gait recognition technology may be restricted by regulations, particularly when it comes to monitoring in public spaces, e.g., issues of personal privacy.

5   Conclusion

User identification and authentication is an important topic in securing modern network systems. This work focused on gait recognition and explored the application of deep learning in building gait recognition systems. Evaluation of different learning models demonstrated the effectiveness of certain architectures, particularly those combined convolutional neural networks with recurrent neural networks, LSTM neural networks, and Transformer neural networks. Further, it was observed that using multi-directional video data for training could significantly improve the model accuracy. We also discussed security issues in gait recognition systems, highlighting the need for designing robust anti-attack mechanisms in practice.

Our evaluation also suggested several promising trends. First, model architectures that effectively combine convolutional layers with components designed for sequence tasks can improve recognition accuracy. Future research might delve deeper into hybrid model architectures, examining ways to further leverage the strengths of various types of neural networks. Second, multi-directional data appears to enhance gait recognition results. This observation has implications for data collection methods, suggesting that the simultaneous capture of gait data from multiple angles could become standard practice.

References

1. CASIA Gait Database. Accessed on 1 July 2024. http://english.ia.cas.cn/db/201610/t20161026_169403.html
2. A. Arnab, M. Dehghani, G. Heigold, C. Sun, M. Lucic, and C. Schmid, ViViT: A Video Vision Transformer. In: 2021 IEEE/CVF International Conference on Computer Vision (ICCV), pp. 6836–6846 (2021)
3. Battistone, F., Alfredo, P.: Tglstm: a time based graph deep learning approach to gait recognition. Pattern Recognit. Lett. **126**, 132–138 (2019)
4. Chang, Y., Li, J., Li, W.: 2d2ps: a demand-driven privacy-preserving scheme for anonymous data sharing in smart grids. J. Information Security and Applications **74**, 103466 (2023)
5. Deng, L., Zhong, Q., Song, J., Lei, H., Li, W.: LLM-based unknown function automated modeling in sensor-driven system for multi-language software security verification. Sensors **25**(9), 2683 MDPI (2025)
6. Deng, M., Fan, Z., Lin, P., Feng, X.: Human gait recognition based on frontal-view sequences using gait dynamics and deep learning. IEEE Trans. Multimedia **26**, 117–126 (2024)
7. Coscia, A., Maci, A., Tamma, N.: Frog: a firewall rule order generator for faster packet filtering. Comput. Netw. **257**, 110962 (2025)
8. Chiu, W.Y., Meng, W.: BlockFW - towards blockchain-based rule-sharing firewall. In: The 16th International Conference on Emerging Security Information, Systems and Technologies (SECURWARE 2022), pp. 70–75 (2022)
9. Chiu, W.Y., Meng, W., Jensen, C.D.: My data, my control: a secure data sharing and access scheme over blockchain. J. Inf. Secur. Appl. **63**(103020), 1–11 (2021)
10. Liu, W., Zhang, C., Ma, H., Li, S.: Learning efficient spatial-temporal gait features with deep learning for human identification. Neuroinformatics, 457–471 (2018). https://doi.org/10.1007/s12021-018-9362-4
11. Gul, S., Malik, M.I., Khan, G.M., Shafait, F.: Multi-view gait recognition system using spatio-temporal features and deep learning. Expert Syst. Appl. **179**, 115057 (2021)
12. Filipi Gonçalves dos Santos, C., et al.: Gait recognition based on deep learning. ACM Comput. Surv. (CSUR) **55**, 1–34 (2022)
13. Meng, W., Li, W., Wang, Y., Au, M.H.: Detecting insider attacks in medical cyber-physical networks based on behavioral profiling. Futur. Gener. Comput. Syst. **108**, 1258–1266 (2020)
14. Girshick, R.: Fast R-CNN. In: 2015 IEEE International Conference on Computer Vision (ICCV), pp. 1440–1448 (2015)
15. Hochreiter, S., Schmidhuber, J.: Long short-term memory. Neural Comput. **9**(8), 1735–1780 (1997)

16. Li, Y., et al.: A closer look tells more: a facial distortion based liveness detection for face authentication. In: AsiaCCS 2019, pp. 241–246 (2019)
17. Li, W., Meng, W., Au, M.H.: Enhancing collaborative intrusion detection via disagreement-based semi-supervised learning in IoT environments. J. Netw. Comput. Appl. **161**(102631), 1–9 (2020)
18. Li, W., Tian, F., Li, J., Xiang, Y.: Evaluating intrusion sensitivity allocation with supervised learning in collaborative intrusion detection. Concurr. Comput. Pract. Exp. **34**(16), 1–15 (2022)
19. Alharthi, A.S., Yunas, S.U., Ozanyan, K.B.: Deep learning for monitoring of human gait: a review. IEEE Sens. J. **19**, 9575–9591 (2019)
20. Li, W., Meng, W., Kwok, L.F., Ip, H.H.S.: Enhancing collaborative intrusion detection networks against insider attacks using supervised intrusion sensitivity-based trust management model. J. Netw. Comput. Appl. **77**, 135–145 (2017)
21. Li, W., Meng. W.: BCTrustFrame: enhancing trust management via blockchain and IPFS in 6G era. IEEE Netw. **36**(4), 120–125 (2022)
22. Maiorana, E.: A survey on biometric recognition using wearable devices. Pattern Recognit. Lett. **156**, 29–37 (2022)
23. Marsico, M.D., Mecca, A.: A survey on gait recognition via wearable sensors. ACM Comput. Surv. **52**(4), 86:1–86:39 (2019)
24. Li, W., Wang, Y., Li, J.: A blockchain-enabled collaborative intrusion detection framework for SDN-assisted cyber-physical systems. Int. J. Inf. Secur. **22**, 1219–1230 (2023)
25. Li, W., Stidsen, C., Adam, T.: A blockchain-assisted security management framework for collaborative intrusion detection in smart cities. Comput. Electr. Eng. **111**, Part A, 108884, 1–13 (2023)
26. Li, W., Gleerup, T., Tan, J., Wang, Y.: A security enhanced android unlock scheme based on pinch-to-zoom for smart devices. IEEE Trans. Consum. Electron. **70**(1), 3985–3993 (2024)
27. Ma, Z., Liu, L., Meng, W., Luo, X., Wang, L., Li, W.: ADCL: towards an adaptive network intrusion detection system using collaborative learning in IoT networks. IEEE Internet Things J. **10**(14), 12521–12536 (2023)
28. Meng, Y., Li, W., Kwok, L.F., Xiang, Y.: Towards designing privacy preserving signature-based IDS As a service: a study and practice. In: The 5th IEEE International Conference on Intelligent Networking and Collaborative Systems (INCoS), IEEE, pp. 181–188 (2013)
29. Meng, W., Li, W., Zhu, L.: Enhancing medical smartphone networks via blockchain-based trust management against insider attacks. IEEE Trans. Eng. Manage. **67**(4), 1377–1386 (2020)
30. Fang, L., et al.: HandiText: handwriting recognition based on dynamic characteristics with incremental LSTM. ACM Trans. Data Sci. **4**(1), 25:1–25:18 (2020)
31. Li, Y., Zhang, J., Zhu, J., Li, W.: BlockFD: blockchain-based federated distillation against poisoning attacks. Neural Comput. Appl. **36**, 12901–12916 (2024)
32. Long, X., Zhang, J., Shan, S.: Generalized face liveness detection via de-fake face generator. IEEE Trans. Pattern Anal. Mach. Intell. **47**(3), 1818–1831 (2025)
33. Marasco, E., Ross, A.: A survey on antispoofing schemes for fingerprint recognition systems. ACM Comput. Surv. **47**(2), 28:1–28:36 (2014)
34. Meng, W., Wong, D.S., Furnell, S., Zhou, J.: Surveying the development of biometric user authentication on mobile phones. IEEE Commun. Surv. Tutorials **17**(3), 1268–1293 (2015)
35. Al-Zahrani, K.S., Bakheit, M.O.: A historical review of gait analysis. Neurosci. J. **13**(2), 105–108 (2008)

36. Pyke, M.S.C., Meng, W., Lampe, B.: Security on top of security: detecting malicious firewall policy changes via K-means clustering. In: The 5th International Conference on Machine Learning for Cyber Security (ML4CS 2023), pp. 145–162 (2023)
37. Meng, W., Li, W., Calugar, A.N.: BANN-TMGUARD: towards touch movement-based screen unlock patterns via blockchain-enabled artificial neural networks on IoT devices. IEEE Internet Things J. **12**(2), 1856–1866 (2025)
38. Sampath Dakshina Murthy, A., Karthikeyan, T., Vinoth Kanna, R.: Gait-based person fall prediction using deep learning approach. Soft Comput. **26**, 12933–12941 (2022)
39. Sepas-Moghaddam, A., Etemad, A.: Deep gait recognition: a survey. IEEE Trans. Pattern Anal. Mach. Intell. **45**(1), 264–284 (2022)
40. Sundararajan, A., Sarwat, A.I., Perez-Pons, A.: a survey on modality characteristics, performance evaluation metrics, and security for traditional and wearable biometric systems. ACM Comput. Surv. **52**(2), 39:1–39:36 (2019)
41. Tang, L., Ma, W., Grobler, M., Meng, W., Wang, Y., Wen, S.: Faces are protected as privacy: an automatic tagging framework against unpermitted photo sharing in social media. IEEE Access, IEEE **7**(1), 75556–75567 (2019)
42. Toprak, I., Toygar, O.: Detection of spoofing attacks for ear biometrics through image quality assessment and deep learning. Expert Syst. Appl. **172**, 114600 (2021)
43. Thanh, K.N., Proenca, H., Alonso-Fernandez, F.: Deep learning for iris recognition: a survey. ACM Comput. Surv. **56**(9), 223:1–223:35 (2024)
44. Wan, C., Wang, L., Phoha, V.V.: A survey on gait recognition. ACM Comput. Surv. **51**(5), 89:1–89:35 (2019)
45. Wang, Y., Meng, W., Li, W., Li, J., Liu, W.X., Xiang, Y.: A privacy-preserving approach for signature-based intrusion detection using fog computing in distributed networks. J. Parall. Distrib. Comput. **122**, 26–35 (2018)
46. Wu, C., Li, W.: Enhancing intrusion detection with feature selection and neural network. Int. J. Intell. Syst. **36**(7), 3087–3105 (2021)
47. Wu, J., Chiu, W.Y., Meng, W.: KEP: keystroke evoked potential for EEG-based user authentication. In: The International Conference on Artificial Intelligence Security and Privacy (AIS&P 2023), pp. 513–530 (2023)
48. Vaswani, A. et al.: Attention is all you need. In: the 31st International Conference on Neural Information Processing Systems (NIPS), pp. 6000–6010 (2017)
49. Zhang, T., Xu, W., Luo, B., Wang, G.: Depth-wise convolutions in vision transformers for efficient training on small datasets. Neurocomputing **617**, 128998 (2025)

Composite Weather Image Restoration Based on Two-Stage Feature Learning

Chenbo Ma, Zihan Chen, Maoyi Xiong, and Wentao Zhao[✉]

College of Computer Science and Technology, National University of Defense Technology, Changsha 410073, China
wtzhao@nudt.edu.cn

Abstract. Adverse weather conditions significantly degrade the visual quality of images and affect system performance. While existing research has achieved satisfactory results in single image restoration tasks under single adverse weather conditions, challenges remain in developing unified image restoration techniques for multiple adverse weather conditions, including low model efficiency, task conflicts, and insufficient generalization capabilities. To address these issues, this paper proposes an optimized composite weather image restoration technique based on two-stage training strategy. In the first stage, cross-weather universal features are extracted, and in the second stage, composite weather-specific parameters are adaptively expanded. By combining a dynamic weather combination identifier based on a marked vector, the technique achieves collaborative suppression of composite degradation. Experiments show that this method achieves a significant improvement in PSNR compared to traditional methods on a self-built composite weather dataset, especially in rain-haze composite scenes, where it significantly improves detail retention capabilities.

Keyword: Unified image restoration · Composite weather degradation · Two-stage feature learning

1 Introduction

With the rapid development of computer vision technology [1, 2], its applications have expanded to various practical scenarios, such as military reconnaissance, security surveillance [7], and autonomous driving [41]. In these practical applications, the quality of images is of critical importance, as it directly determines the success or failure of task execution. However, in real-world applications, due to the objective constraints of outdoor environments, image quality is inevitably affected by weather conditions, particularly in adverse weather conditions, where images often become significantly blurred, thereby greatly impacting the effectiveness of practical applications. To address the impact of adverse weather, many scholars have conducted research and proposed various techniques, including single-weather image restoration networks (e.g., snow removal [3–5], rain removal [6–8], haze removal [9–16]) and multi-weather image restoration networks. However, current research still has certain limitations, including insufficient scene adaptability of single methods, target conflicts in multi-task restoration, and efficiency bottlenecks in complex scenes.

X. Chen et al. (Eds.): DSPP 2025, LNCS 16177, pp. 51–68, 2026.
https://doi.org/10.1007/978-981-95-3185-1_4

To address the aforementioned issues, this paper designs and implements a unified image restoration technology suitable for various harsh weather conditions, optimizes the model parameters, and builds a high-quality dataset. The aim is to significantly enhance the performance of the image restoration model. Specifically, this design has the following goals: to improve the existing model architecture so that the model can handle complex harsh weather conditions simultaneously; secondly, conduct experimental tests on open-source datasets and self-built datasets to prove the effectiveness and superiority of the proposed method; thirdly, achieve lightweight model design and efficient optimization, enabling it to run efficiently in practical applications.

In this paper, we first construct a composite adverse weather dataset covering various composite weather conditions. Subsequently, based on the U-Net model, architectural adjustments and model optimizations are made for the unified processing framework. Next, we conducted experimental testing and data analysis on the constructed benchmark dataset, and comparisons are made with benchmark methods in the field of image restoration, fully demonstrating the advantages of the method proposed in this paper in composite weather image restoration. Finally, ablation experiments are conducted to verify the effectiveness of the two-stage training strategy.

The main contributions of this paper are as follows:

(1) A unified processing framework based on a two-stage learning strategy is designed. The unified image processing framework in this paper is based on the U-Net [33] backbone network and adopts a two-stage learning strategy: the first stage trains general weather features, and the second stage trains specific weather features. Through two-stage training, the model can better capture the overall effect and detailed features of the weather, thereby improving image restoration performance.
(2) A collaborative modeling strategy based on composite weather conditions is proposed. This paper adopts a collaborative modeling strategy based on composite weather conditions, utilizing a marked vector mechanism and hierarchical parameter activation principles to achieve image restoration under composite weather conditions. In terms of specific implementation, an adaptive parameter expansion mechanism is introduced to activate corresponding parameters according to different weather types. At the same time, different marked vectors are designed for different weather conditions, and vector flags are used to mark different weather conditions to ensure efficient and accurate image restoration in different scenarios.
(3) A dataset based on data synthesis and enhancement techniques is constructed. This paper utilizes the open-source CDD-11 dataset [26] and composite rain and snow weather images based on Rain100L [34] and Snow100K-L [5] to construct a rich and comprehensive dataset of adverse weather images. Additionally, composite dataset synthesis, image enhancement, and data cleaning are performed to ensure the reliability and effectiveness of the image data.

2 Related Work

In recent years, methods such as multimodal restoration, unified restoration model, and multi-task learning have become popular in the field of adverse weather image restoration. However, there has been little research on composite adverse weather conditions, and composite weather image restoration frameworks are still immature.

2.1 Multimodal Fusion and Unified Restoration Framework

In the field of multimodal fusion and unified restoration frameworks, Ai *et al.* [19] proposed a multimodal prompt perceptron. Song *et al.* [10] introduced semantic decoupling image compression, utilizing multimodal models to decompose images into multiple semantic information components. In the unified recovery framework, Zhang *et al.* [22] proposed a component-oriented multi-degradation learning method. Wu *et al.* [27] improved the effectiveness of unified image recovery through multi-task collaboration. Zhang *et al.* [24] proposed a unified multi-modal image synthesis framework for missing modality imputation.These studies demonstrate the potential of multimodal fusion and unified recovery frameworks in enhancing image recovery performance.

2.2 Multi-task Learning Methods

Multi-task learning is a typical technical approach for unified image restoration. Li *et al.* [25] proposed the All-in-One method, which achieves unified processing of multiple types of degradation through shared parameters. Wu *et al.* [17] proposed a contrastive learning framework for single-image dehazing tasks, enhancing the model's understanding of physical processes through contrastive learning. Özdenizci *et al.* [21] proposed a diffusion model-based image restoration method, improving image restoration quality through local noise modeling. Zhang *et al.* [23] proposed a unified conditional framework for diffusion-based image restoration. Gao *et al.* [18] introduced GridFormer, an efficient network architecture based on Transformers, for image restoration under adverse weather conditions. These studies demonstrate the potential of multi-task learning and method innovation in enhancing image restoration performance.

2.3 Composite Weather Degradation

Recent studies have shown that composite adverse weather conditions have a greater impact on image quality. Ashutosh *et al.* [28] proposed a lightweight unified network for handling multiple weather degradation factors; Guo *et al.* [29] designed the OneRestore framework to restore images degraded by composite factors such as low light, rainy weather, and haze; Mao *et al.* [30] proposed the AllRestorer framework, which uses Transformers to fuse image and text embeddings, to restore both single and composite degradations. Valanarasu *et al.* [20] proposed TransWeather, a transformer-based architecture for multi-weather image restoration.

However, current research still has limitations: there is a lack of high-quality composite weather image datasets, which limits the model's generalization ability; existing models lack the ability to process and restore composite weather images; some methods introduce complex network structures, leading to high computational costs. Overall, research on composite weather image restoration is still in its exploratory phase and urgently requires new methods to break through existing bottlenecks.

3 Methodology

In this section, we present the details of our proposed Two-Stage Composite Weather (TSCW) framework. The content will be divided into four parts, as follows: the unified image restoration framework based on two-stage training, the data set construction based on data synthesis and augmentation, the collaborative modeling strategy based on composite weather, and the design of the complete process.

3.1 Unified Image Restoration Framework Based on Two-Stage Training

This paper proposes an efficient unified framework for image restoration tasks under various adverse weather conditions, using a set of network parameters to restore images affected by different weather conditions. As shown in Fig. 1, the model adopts a two-stage training strategy to learn general weather features and specific weather features, respectively. When selecting the model architecture, we chose U-Net as the backbone network for two reasons: the encoder-decoder structure can efficiently capture multi-scale features of images; U-Net has high computational efficiency, making it suitable for quickly processing large amounts of image data in practical applications.

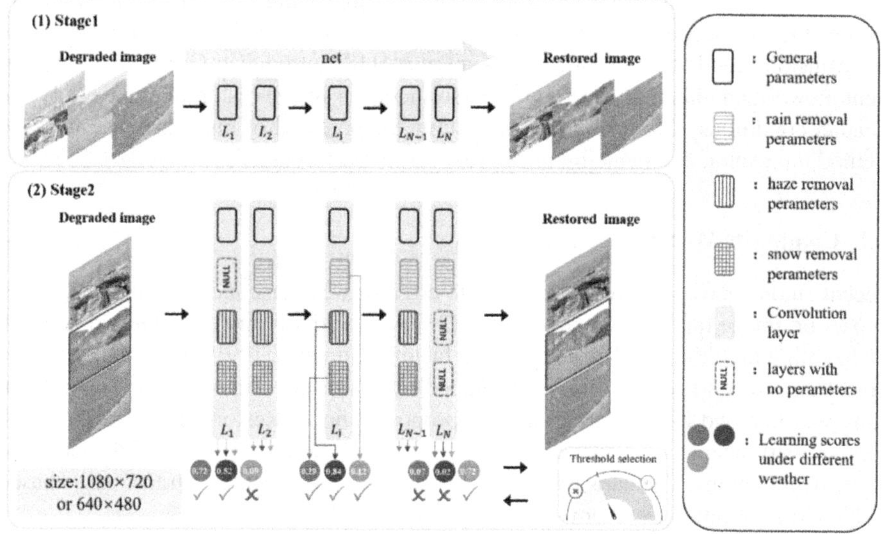

Fig. 1. Overall framework design. A two-stage training strategy is used, with the first stage learning general weather features and the second stage learning specific weather features.

General Weather Feature Learning. In image restoration tasks under various adverse weather conditions, image degradation caused by different weather types (such as rain, snow, haze, and composite weather) contains both unique and common features. Based on atmospheric scattering models [31, 32]:

$$E = \underbrace{E_\infty \rho e^{-\beta d}}_{\text{Direct Transmission}} + \underbrace{E_\infty (1 - e^{-\beta d})}_{\text{Airlight}}, \tag{1}$$

where E_∞ denotes the sky intensity, ρ denotes the normalized radiance of the certain scene point, βd denotes the optical distance of that scene point. Various weather particles cause common visual degradation through their scattering and attenuation effects on light, such as low contrast, color shifts, and blurred details.

In the first stage, the TSCW model learns a universal feature representation applicable to various weather conditions. The objective of this stage is to capture common degradation features under different weather conditions. Through cosine annealing learning rate scheduling, the network is gradually guided from a randomly initialized state to a parameter space capable of capturing common weather degradation features. The core objective of this stage is to build a general model with basic restoration capabilities, providing a semantically rich feature foundation for subsequent feature adaptation and expansion tailored to specific weather types. In terms of loss function, in addition to the pixel-wise Smooth-L1 loss, we further introduce the VGG-16 perceptual loss to improve the visual quality, where the weight $\lambda_{VGG} = 0.1$.

Specific Weather Feature Learning. After learning general weather characteristics, the TSCW model extracted common features of image degradation under different adverse weather conditions through a shared U-Net backbone network. However, the mechanisms of image degradation under different weather conditions vary in complexity, so it is necessary to further model their unique characteristics.

Additionally, in real-world environments, images are often subjected to the combined effects of multiple adverse weather conditions. Under these composite weather conditions, image degradation is not simply the sum of individual weather effects but involves complex physical interactions. For example, raindrops may interfere with the scattering path of haze, leading to reduced image contrast and blurred details; falling snowflakes may further obscure the effects of raindrops, making it harder to discern the contours and textures of objects in the image. Therefore, it is necessary to conduct in-depth exploration of the unique degradation features under different weather conditions and perform targeted modeling.

3.2 Dataset Construction Based on Data Synthesis and Augmentation

Construction of An Open-Source Dataset. This paper primarily uses the open-source CDD-11 dataset, which includes images under two adverse weather conditions: rain_haze, and snow_haze, providing a rich and diverse dataset for model training. Additionally, a composite rain-snow weather dataset is constructed based on the Rain100L and Snow100K-L datasets. The dataset is divided into training, validation, and test sets in a 11:1:2 ratio. The training set contains 8,648 images, the validation set contains 816 images, and the test set contains 1,600 images.

Synthesis of the Composite Weather Dataset. To simulate complex adverse weather conditions in the real world, this paper uses a screen blending method [35] to synthesize a composite rain and snow weather dataset. The model uses snowy weather images from the Snow100K-L dataset as the background and extracts rainy weather images from the Rain100L dataset. The two are then blended using the screen blending method:

$$O(x) = I(x) + S(x) - I(x) \circ S(x), \tag{2}$$

where $O(x)$ denotes the synthesized image, $I(x)$ represents the snowy weather image, $S(x)$ corresponds to the rain background, and o denotes the element-wise multiplication operation. Through this method, images containing composite rain_snow weather conditions are generated. The screen blending method better simulates the visual effects of rain and snow overlapping in the real world, and the generated images are closer to real-world scenes in terms of global lighting and color changes. The synthetic dataset contains 1,081 training images, 200 test images, and 102 validation images.

3.3 Collaborative Modeling Strategy Based on Composite Weather

Based on the issues mentioned earlier, this paper proposes a collaborative modeling strategy for composite weather conditions. The core methods of this strategy include an adaptive parameter expansion mechanism and composite weather processing based on marked vectors. By layering the unique parameters of each weather condition, the model can process different types of weather degradation at different levels. When processing composite weather images, the results of each layer provide a clearer, more original-state-like image foundation for the next layer, thereby more effectively preserving the image's details and structural information.

As shown in Fig. 2, when processing complex rain and snow weather images, the TSCW model employs a collaborative modeling strategy. The model first performs hierarchical identification of different weather types: in rainy conditions, it uses a shallow network to focus on removing rain traces from the image, thereby restoring texture details; In hazy conditions, it uses a deep network to address its interference with image contrast and color, thereby enhancing the overall visual effect. After completing the hierarchical processing, the model further employs a feature fusion module (FAM) to perform collaborative modeling on the two-layer images, fusing the detailed features extracted by the shallow network with the overall features restored by the deep network, ultimately generating high-quality restored images.

Based on the TSCW model architecture design, it is necessary to optimize the model for specific networks. The main optimization content includes two aspects: composite weather image restoration based on an adaptive parameter expansion mechanism and composite weather image restoration based on marked vectors.

Adaptive Parameter Expansion Mechanism. In the second stage, there are significant differences in the degradation patterns of different weather types, and traditional fixed-parameter networks struggle to accommodate the diverse details of degradation. Based on this, this paper proposes an adaptive parameter expansion mechanism, which dynamically activates dedicated parameters in specific layers to achieve efficient modeling of weather-specific features on a shared backbone network, enabling the TSCW model to learn different features for different weather conditions.

The adaptive parameter expansion mechanism is based on the hierarchical parameter activation principle, which activates different parameters in each layer of the network based on the differences in weather degradation patterns across various weather types. As shown in Fig. 3, different types of weather degradation exhibit unique physical characteristics and data features: rain's directional stripes correspond to high-frequency noise, primarily affecting the image's shallow-layer texture; haze's global scattering depends on

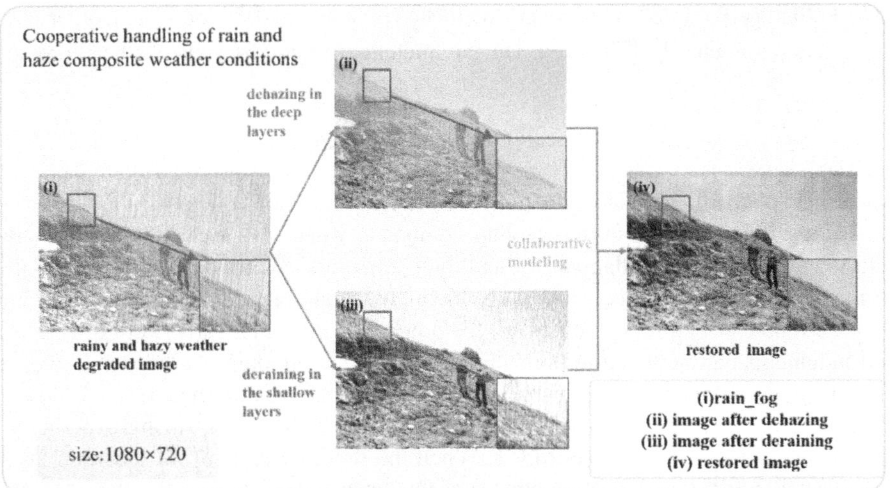

Fig. 2. Cooperative processing strategy under composite weather conditions. First, activate the parameters of each layer, then perform feature fusion to obtain the processing results.

deep-layer features, requiring deep-layer networks for recovery; and snowflakes' low-frequency brightness changes are associated with mid-layer structures, necessitating mid-layer networks to optimize brightness balance. Additionally, the shared parameters trained in the first stage are retained.

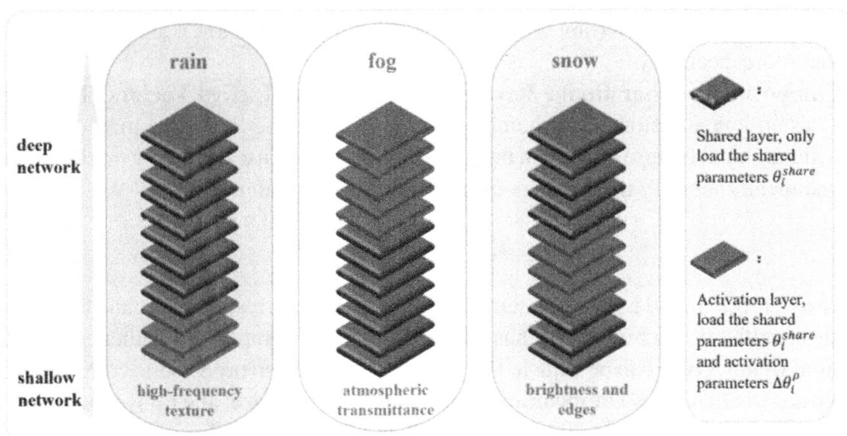

Fig. 3. Principle of layered parameter activation. Different weather conditions correspond to different layers of parameters, and the corresponding network parameters are activated according to weather characteristics.

To efficiently incorporate weather-specific modeling based on shared parameters, this paper designs an adaptive parameter expansion formula. A learnable scoring variable S_i^ρ is set to evaluate the sensitivity of the i layer network to weather type ρ. When $S_i^\rho \geq \tau$

(threshold hyperparameter), the layer's dedicated parameter $\Delta\theta_i^{\rho}$ is activated; otherwise, the shared parameter θ_i^{share} is used. The parameter expansion formula can be expressed as:

$$\theta_i^{\rho} = \theta_i^{share} + F_{\tau}\left(S_i^{\rho}\right) * \Delta\theta_i^{\rho}, \tag{3}$$

where if $S_i^{\rho} \geq \tau$, the indicator function $F_{\tau}(\cdot)$ is 1, otherwise $F_{\tau}(\cdot)$ is 0.

During inference, the corresponding composite weather branch ρ is dynamically selected according to the flag vector, and the parameters θ_i^{ρ} are loaded. After that, the parameters are input into the network for hierarchical parameter activation and forward propagation. Through this mechanism, feature selection can be carried out effectively and judgments can be made in the face of different feature data. At the same time, in order to avoid redundancy, the sparsity regularization term is introduced.

Initialization and convergence analysis of the scoring variable S_i^{ρ}. In this experiment, the threshold parameter τ is set to 0.1. When the score variable S_i^{ρ} of a certain layer is greater than 0.1, the special parameter of this layer will be activated, otherwise it is set to 0. At initialization, each convolutional layer is set with three vector parameters, namely B1, B2 and B3, corresponding to the specific module activation state of three composite weather. Each dimension represents the corresponding scoring variable S_i^{ρ} of the corresponding network layer number for the corresponding weather. Such as B1_indicator $= S_1^{rain\_haze}, S_2^{rain\_haze}, ..., S_i^{rain\_haze}, ..., S_{n-1}^{rain\_haze}, S_n^{rain\_haze}$). The initial value of all the indicators is 0.15, which is close to the value of the threshold parameter τ, which enables the model to perform early and fast response. With the stability of model training, the experimental results show that the overall distribution of each scoring variable tends to be stable, and shows a certain degree of differentiation. The percentages of activations are 35.12% (rain and haze), 14.29% (rain and snow), and 14.88% (haze and snow), respectively.

Composite Weather Image Restoration Based on Marked Vectors. This paper proposes an image restoration scheme for composite weather based on marked vectors and a hierarchical feature activation mechanism. The model uses a ternary marked vector to dynamically identify the weather composition of the input image:

$$flag = [a, b, c](a, b, c \in \{0,1\}), \tag{4}$$

where a $= 1$, b $= 1$, and c $= 1$ represent rain, snow, and haze, respectively, and 0 indicates that no specific weather condition has been selected. For composite weather conditions, the input weather type can be adjusted by modifying the flag to process the corresponding composite weather type. During training, rain_haze, snow_haze, and rain_snow are used as the training dataset, where flag $= [1,0,1]$, flag $= [0,1,1]$, and flag $= [1,1,0]$ represent the three weather conditions, respectively. After training, the specific model is obtained.

As shown in Fig. 4, taking rain_haze composite weather as an example, when the model receives an image labeled with flag $= [1,1,0]$, based on the hierarchical feature activation mechanism, it will activate parameters related to rain drop removal and haze removal. In the shallow network, the model primarily processes high-frequency features such as raindrops. In the deep network, the model focuses on addressing issues such as reduced global contrast and color distortion caused by haze scattering. Finally, through cross-layer feature fusion, the model organically combines the detailed features extracted by the shallow network with the global features restored by the deep network, thereby achieving high-quality restoration of rain_haze composite images.

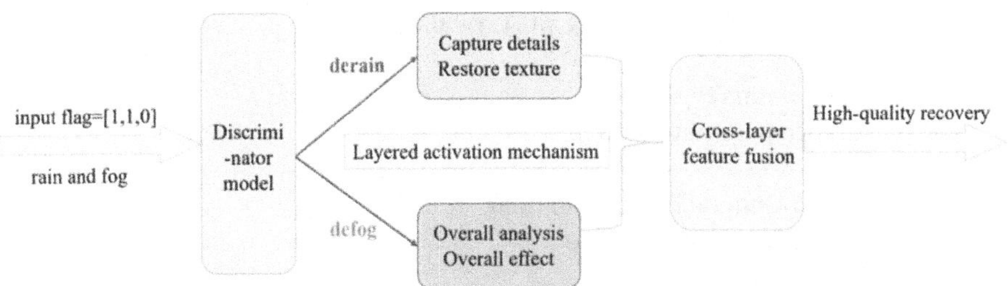

Fig. 4. Composite image restoration process based on marked vectors. It consists of two major parts: hierarchical parameter activation and cross-layer feature fusion.

In cross-layer image fusion, the main feature fusion module is FAM. This module utilizes the output results of the spatial attention module and the attention fusion module to organically fuse features from different layers. Specifically, cross-layer feature fusion can be achieved through feature concatenation and convolution operations:

$$F_{concat} = Concat\left(F_{\rho_1}, F_{\rho_2}\right), \tag{5}$$

$$I_{out} = Conv(F_{concat}), \tag{6}$$

where F_{ρ_1} and F_{ρ_2} represent the output feature maps under different weather conditions in different layers of the network. Concat denotes the feature concatenation operation, which concatenates the feature maps from shallow and deep layers along the channel dimension; Conv denotes the convolution operation, which further processes the concatenated feature maps. Through cross-layer feature fusion, we can fully utilize the detailed features of the shallow network and the global features of the deep network to enhance image details, improve global consistency and robustness, and achieve high-quality image restoration.

3.4 The Design of the Complete Process

In order to more clearly describe the above complete process of collaborative modeling and hierarchical parameter activation, we give the specific steps of two-stage training in Algorithm 1.

Algorithm 1: Two-Stage Composite Weather Image Restoration

Input:
  - Training set D = {D_haze_rain, D_snow_haze, D_rain_snow}
  - Flag vectors {[1,0,1], [0,1,1], [1,1,0]}
  - Parameters λ_VGG = 0.1, λ_reg = 0.1, τ = 0.1

Output:
  - Shared parameters θ_share
  - Sparse branch parameters $\Delta\theta\_\rho$

- -

Stage 1: Weather-General Feature Learning

1 Initialize U-Net backbone θ_share
2 for epoch = 1 ... E1 do
3   for each mini-batch {I_k, Y_k} in D do
4         $\hat{Y}\_k$ ← U-Net(I_k; θ_share)
5   L ← SmoothL1($\hat{Y}\_k$, Y_k) + λ_VGG·VGGPerceptual($\hat{Y}\_k$, Y_k)
6   θ_share ← AdamUpdate(θ_share, L)
7 Freeze θ_share

Stage 2: Composite-Specific Parameter Expansion

8 for ρ in D do
9   Initialize sparse indicators S_ρ and branch $\Delta\theta\_\rho$
10 for epoch = 1 ... E2 do
11   for each mini-batch {I_k, Y_k, flag_k} do
12   ρ ← type_from(flag_k)
13         $\hat{Y}\_k$ ← U-Net(I_k; θ_share, $\Delta\theta\_\rho$)   // Hierarchical activation
14   L ← SmoothL1+VGG + λ_reg·$\|S\_\rho\|1$
15         $\Delta\theta\_\rho$, S_ρ ← AdamUpdate($\Delta\theta\_\rho$, S_ρ, L)
16   Fuse multi-scale features via FAM   // Collaborative Modeling

---

The above pseudo-code explains how TSCW utilizes a two-stage strategy, marker vector-guided hierarchical parameter activation, and FAM cross-layer collaborative fusion to achieve unified restoration of three types of composite weather degradation.

4 Experiment

4.1 Experimental Setup

Implementation Details. In terms of experimental configuration, this paper relies on a high-performance computing platform, using Python 3.11 and Pycharm as the interpreter environment, and the deep learning framework PyTorch 2.5, which supports CUDA acceleration. The hardware configuration includes an NVIDIA GeForce RTX 4090 graphics card, an Intel Core i9-13900K CPU, and 64GB DDR5–5600 memory, to meet the parallel computing requirements of the dataset and enhance training efficiency through PyTorch's automatic mixed-precision training technology. Both stages employ the Adam optimizer with $\beta1 = 0.9$ and $\beta2 = 0.999$; the learning rate is controlled by the CosineAnnealingWarmRestarts strategy, starting at 2×10^{-4} in the first stage and reducing to 1×10^{-4} in the second stage.

Comparison Methods. We compared our TSCW model with seven other previously validated image restoration methods, including MPRNet 39, All-in-one 25, PromptIR 40, HDCWNet 38, FFANet 36, Chen *et al.* 37, and JSTASR 4. These methods are representative approaches in the fields of rain removal, snow removal, and haze removal in image restoration.

Evaluation Metrics. This paper selects Peak Signal-to-Noise Ratio (PSNR), Structural Similarity (SSIM), and Learned Perceptual Image Similarity (LPIPS) as the primary metrics for evaluating image restoration performance. PSNR is used to measure the pixel-level error between the restored image and the original image; the higher the value, the higher the restoration accuracy. SSIM evaluates the similarity between the restored image and the original image in terms of structure and texture from a visual perspective; the closer the value is to 1, the more visually similar the restored image is to the original image. LPIPS is a perception-based similarity metric based on deep learning, which evaluates the similarity between images by learning their high-level features, thereby better reflecting the perceptual differences in the human visual system. The lower the value, the more similar the restored image is to the original image in terms of perception.

4.2 Results Comparison

Image Quality Testing. This paper compares the performance of the proposed TSCW model with other existing image restoration methods under three typical composite weather conditions (rain-snow, rain-haze, and snow-haze).

As shown in Table 1, 2 and 3, bolded data indicate the best results. Under the same testing conditions, the TSCW model outperforms most existing models in all key metrics. Specifically, the TSCW model achieves higher values in both PSNR and SSIM metrics, indicating superior performance in pixel-level accuracy and image structural texture restoration; simultaneously, the TSCW model has lower LPIPS values, meaning the restored images are visually closer to the original images. These results clearly demonstrate that the TSCW model possesses significant advantages in image restoration detail and visual quality, effectively addressing the challenges of image restoration under complex weather conditions.

Table 1. Rain_haze image test results. The All-in-one model tested the effectiveness of the rain_haze models separately, selecting the rain model with better results.

Type	Methods	Publication	PSNR	SSIM	LPIPS
Unified model	MPRNet [39]	CVPR 2021	15.66	0.75	0.23
	All-in-one [25]	CVPR 2022	18.63	0.86	0.45
	PromptIR [40]	NeurIPS 2023	18.91	0.77	0.32
	Ours	-	**26.40**	**0.96**	**0.09**

Table 2. Snow_haze image test results. All selected models are snow removal models.

Type	Methods	Publication	PSNR	SSIM	LPIPS
Unified model	HDCWNet [38]	ICCV 2021	18.52	0.82	0.33
	FFANet [36]	AAAI 2020	18.94	0.82	0.23
	Chen *et al.* [37]	CVPR 2022	15.99	0.80	0.56
	Ours	-	**24.50**	**0.83**	**0.13**

Table 3. Rain_snow image test results. Among them, MPRNet is a rain removal model, while JSTASR and Chen *et al.* are snow removal models.

Type	Methods	Publication	PSNR	SSIM	LPIPS
Unified model	MPRNet [39]	CVPR 2021	20.11	0.75	0.27
	JSTASR [4]	ECCV 2020	23.23	0.70	0.48
	Chen *et al.* [37]	CVPR 2022	**23.33**	0.79	0.37
	Ours	-	22.30	**0.92**	**0.20**

However, it is worth noting that in the snow and rain test, the PSNR value of the method proposed in this paper is slightly lower than that of other comparison methods. After analysis, this may be due to the following reasons:

First, the limitations of the PSNR. PSNR is primarily based on the absolute value of pixel errors for quantification, making it sensitive to differences in image details and effective in optimizing pixel-level errors in images. However, in actual visual quality assessment, PSNR cannot fully reflect human visual perception of image quality.

Second, inconsistencies in the model's recovery strategy. The methods proposed by JSTASR and Chen *et al.* minimize pixel differences to reduce pixel-level errors, thereby achieving better PSNR performance. However, this leads to the loss of image details and textures, resulting in poorer visual quality. The model proposed in this paper places greater emphasis on restoring the true details and textures of the image, even if this results in some pixel-level errors, as this is more advantageous for actual computer vision tasks. As shown in Fig. 5, compared to other methods, the TSCW model not only restores the basic structure of the image but also accurately preserves rich details, delivering more realistic visual information for downstream tasks.

Image Qualitative Analysis. The results of different types of weather tests are shown below. As shown in Figs. 6, 7, 8, from the perspective of the visual effect, the images generated by our model are not only clear and accurate, but also excel in detail retention and color reproduction. Under composite adverse weather conditions, our model is able to more effectively remove weather interference and restore image content that is closer to the real scene.

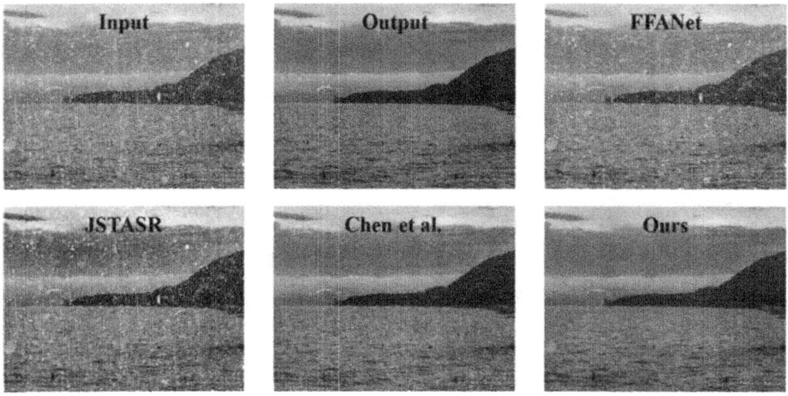

Fig. 5. Comparison of images of mixed rain and snow weather. Although our model has a slightly lower PSNR value, it has the best visual effect among the tested models.

Fig. 6. Test results for rain_haze weather. It can be seen that the images restored by our TSCW model have better haze removal effects and higher image clarity.

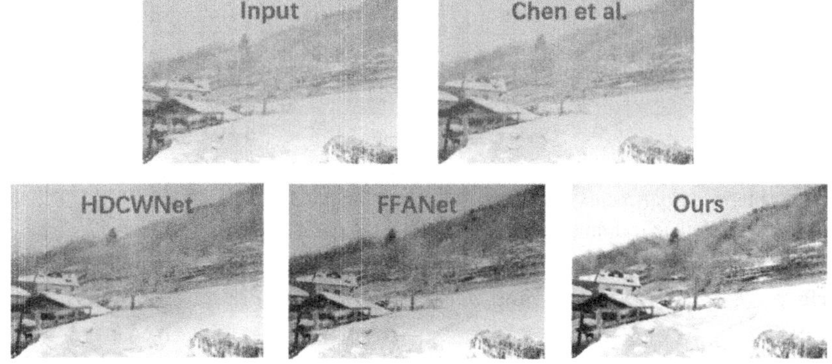

Fig. 7. Test results for snow_haze weather. It can be seen that our TSCW model performs better in terms of haze and snow removal, resulting in higher overall image brightness.

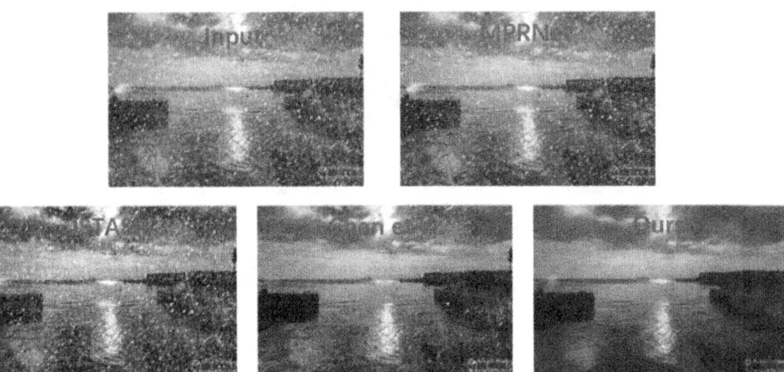

Fig. 8. Test results for rain_snow weather. It can be seen that our TSCW model has better rain and snow removal effects, with clearer image details and no excess rain and snow noise.

4.3   Ablation Experiment

The Effectiveness of a Two-Stage Training Strategy. We designed ablation experiments to validate the effectiveness of the two-stage training strategy. Although the model trained in the first stage can restore the basic structure and contrast of the image, it still lacks sufficient detail clarity and texture integrity. In contrast, the model trained through the complete two-stage process performs exceptionally well under all weather conditions and can better handle degradation caused by different weather conditions.

As shown in the Table 4 and Table 5, the test metrics indicate that the model trained using the full two-stage training strategy outperforms the model trained only in the first stage in terms of PSNR and SSIM metrics. This result strongly demonstrates the significant advantages of the two-stage training strategy in improving model performance and further validates its effectiveness.

Table 4. Ablation experiments of the two-stage training model. The metric is PSNR. The results show that the two-stage training effect is better than the one-stage training effect.

Metric	haze_rain	snow_haze	snow_rain
Stage1	25.47	21.85	24.41
Stage1 + Stage2	**26.40**	**22.30**	**24.50**

Table 5. Ablation experiments of the two-stage training model. The metric is SSIM. The results show that the two-stage training effect is better than the one-stage training effect.

Metric	haze_rain	snow_haze	snow_rain
Stage1	0.95	0.82	0.90
Stage1 + Stage2	**0.96**	**0.83**	**0.92**

Effectiveness of the Marking Vector Mechanism. We also designed ablation experiments to validate the effectiveness of the marked vector mechanism. The experiments used three composite adverse weather datasets as input. The experimental group combined the marked vector mechanism for composite weather image restoration, while the control group removed the marked vector mechanism from the model and directly restored the composite weather images.

As shown in Table 6 and Table 7, the experimental model outperformed the control model in both PSNR and SSIM metrics. This indicates that the introduction of the labeling vector mechanism significantly improved the model's performance in composite weather image restoration.

Table 6. Ablation experiment of marking vectors. The metric is PSNR. The results show that using labeled vectors yields better results than not using them.

Metric	haze_rain	snow_haze	snow_rain
Unmarking vector	21.78	16.33	23.94
Marking vector	**26.40**	**22.30**	**24.50**

Table 7. Ablation experiment of marking vectors. The metric is SSIM. The results show that using labeled vectors yields better results than not using them.

Metric	haze_rain	snow_haze	snow_rain
Unmarking vector	0.80	0.78	0.82
Marking vector	**0.96**	**0.83**	**0.92**

5 Conclusion

This paper presents an optimized composite weather image restoration technique based on two-stage feature learning.Through a two-stage training strategy, the model first extracts general weather features and then learns unique features for specific weather conditions, achieving efficient restoration. At the same time, a collaborative modeling strategy based on composite weather is proposed, utilizing a marked vector mechanism and hierarchical parameter activation principles to achieve image restoration for composite weather conditions. Additionally, an image dataset for composite adverse weather conditions is constructed, providing rich support for model training. Finally, the superiority of the proposed model for composite weather image restoration is empirically validated against state-of-the-art models.

In the future, we will focus on enhancing the model's generalization performance and adaptability. First, we will construct a more comprehensive real-world weather dataset, combined with transfer learning and semi-supervised training strategies, to enhance the model's adaptability to unknown complex weather conditions. Second, more precise modeling will be conducted for different weather types, by incorporating multi-dimensional weather labels and integrating meta-learning or dynamic weight networks to achieve refined processing of different weather subtypes; third, establishing a "one-to-all" image restoration mechanism, introducing multi-scale feature perception and dynamic parameter allocation modules to achieve comprehensive processing of weather conditions ranging from single to composite and from simple to complex, advancing the unified restoration framework to a new level.

References

1. Huang, J., Chen, Z., Liu, T., et al.: SMILENet: unleashing extra-large capacity image steganography via a synergistic mosaic InvertibLE hiding network. IEEE Trans. Pattern Anal. Mach. Intell. **47**(6), 4957–4973 (2025)
2. Huang, J., Liu, T., Chen, Z., et al.: A lightweight deep exclusion unfolding network for single image reflection removal. IEEE Trans. Pattern Anal. Mach. Intell. **47**(6), 4957–4973 (2025)
3. Zhang, K., Li, R., Yu, Y., et al.: Deep dense multi-scale network for snow removal using semantic and depth priors. IEEE Trans. Image Process. **30**, 7419–7431 (2021)
4. Chen, W.T., Fang, H.Y., Ding, J.J., et al.: JSTASR: Joint size and transparency-aware snow removal algorithm based on modified partial convolution and veiling effect removal. In: Proceedings of the IEEE ECCV, pp. 754–770. Springer, Heidelberg (2020). https://doi.org/10.1007/978-3-030-58589-1_45
5. Liu, Y.F., Jaw, D.W., Huang, S.C., et al.: DesnowNet: context-aware deep network for snow removal. IEEE Trans. Image Process. **27**(6), 3064–3073 (2018)
6. Zou, S., Zou, Y., Zhang, M.Y., et al.: Learning dual-domain multi-scale representations for single image deraining. arXiv preprint arXiv:2503.12014 (2025)
7. Mao, J., Xiao, T., Jiang, Y., et al.: What can help pedestrian detection? In: Proceedings of the IEEE CVPR. IEEE Press, Piscataway (2017)
8. Peng, Y., Li, W.: Rain2Avoid: self-supervised single image deraining. In: Proceedings of the IEEE ICASSP, pp. 1–5. IEEE Press, Piscataway (2023)
9. Zhang, X., Dong, H., et al.: Learning to restore hazy video: a new real-world dataset and a new method. In: Proceedings IEEE CVPR, pp. 9235–9244. IEEE Press, Piscataway (2021)
10. Song, J., Yang, L., Feng, M.: Extremely low-bitrate Image compression semantically disentangled by LMMs from a human perception perspective. arXiv preprint arXiv:2503.00399 (2025)
11. Cai, B., Xu, X., Jia, K., et al.: DehazeNet: an end-to-end system for single image haze removal. IEEE Trans. Image Process. **25**(11), 5187–5198 (2016)
12. Ren, W., Liu, S., Zhang, H., et al.: Single image dehazing via multi-scale convolutional neural networks. In: Proceedings IEEE ECCV, pp. 154–169. Springer, Heidelberg (2016). https://doi.org/10.1007/s11263-019-01235-8
13. Yang, D., Sun, J.: Proximal Dehaze-Net: A prior learning-based deep network for single image dehazing. In: Proceedings IEEE ECCV, pp. 702–717. Springer, Heidelberg (2018). https://doi.org/10.1007/978-3-030-01234-2_43
14. Yang, X., Xu, Z., Luo, J.: Towards perceptual image dehazing by physics-based disentanglement and adversarial training. In: Proceedings AAAI Conference Artificial Intelligence (2018)
15. Mo, J., Hao, Z., Tao, Z.,et al.: Lightweight implementation of a transformer-based single image dehaze network. In: IEEE ICITES, pp. 160–165. Chengdu, China (2024)

16. Zheng, Y., Su, J., Zhang, S., Tao, M.,et al.: Dehaze-TGGAN: transformer-guide generative adversarial networks with spatial-spectrum attention for unpaired remote sensing dehazing. IEEE Trans. Geosci. Remote Sens., 1–20 (2024)
17. Wu, H., et al.: Learning from history: task-agnostic model contrastive learning for image restoration. arXiv preprint arXiv:2309.06023 (2023)
18. Gao, T., et al.: ODCR: Orthogonal decoupling contrastive regularization for unpaired image dehazing. In: CVPR (2024)
19. Ai, Y., Huang, H., Zhou, X., Wang, J., He, R.: Multimodal prompt perceiver: empower adaptiveness, generalizability and fidelity for all-in-one image restoration. In: 2024 IEEE CVPR, pp. 25432–25444. IEEE, Seattle, WA, USA (2024)
20. Valanarasu, K., Rajinikanth, V.: TransWeather: A unified transformer architecture for multi-weather image restoration. In: Proceedings IEEE CVPR, pp. 15477–15486. IEEE Press, Piscataway (2022)
21. Özdenizci, O., Legenstein, R.: Restoring vision in adverse weather conditions with patch-based denoising diffusion models. arXiv preprint arXiv:2207.14626 (2022)
22. Zhang, J., et al.: Ingredient-oriented multi-degradation learning for image restoration. In: 2023 IEEE/CVF Conference on Computer Vision and Pattern Recognition (CVPR), pp. 5825–5835. IEEE, Vancouver, BC, Canada (2023)
23. Zhang, Y., Shi, X.Y., Li, D.S., et al.: A unified conditional framework for diffusion-based image restoration. arXiv preprint arXiv:2305.20049 (2023)
24. Zhang, X., et al.: Unified multi-modal image synthesis for missing modality imputation. arXiv preprint arXiv:2304.05340(2024)
25. Li, R., Tan, R.T., Cheong, L.F.: All in one bad weather removal using architectural search. In: Proceedings of the IEEE CVPR, pp. 3175–3185. IEEE Press, Piscataway (2020)
26. Zhu, Y., et al.: Learning weather-general and weather-specific features for image restoration under multiple adverse weather conditions. In: Proceedings IEEE CVPR, pp. 21747–21758. IEEE Press, Piscataway (2023)
27. Wu, G., Jiang, J., Jiang, K., Liu, X.: Harmony in diversity: improving all-in-one image restoration via multi-task collaboration. In: Proceedings ACM, pp. 6015–6023. ACM, Melbourne, VIC, Australia (2024). https://doi.org/10.1145/3664647.3680762
28. Kulkarni, A., Patil, P.W., Murala, S., et al.: Unified multi-weather visibility restoration. IEEE Trans. Multimedia, 1–13 (2022)
29. Guo, Y., Gao, Y., Lu, Y., et al.: OneRestore: a universal restoration framework for composite degradation. In: Proceedings of the IEEE ECCV, pp. 255–272. Springer, Heidelberg (2024). https://doi.org/10.1007/978-3-031-72655-2_15
30. Mao, J., Yang, Y., Yin, X., et al.: AllRestorer: all-in-one transformer for image restoration under composite degradations. arXiv preprint arXiv:2411.10708 (2024)
31. Narasimhan, S.G.: Models and algorithms for vision through the atmosphere. Ph.D. thesis, Columbia University (2004)
32. Nayar, S.K., Narasimhan, S.G.: Vision in bad weather. In: Proceedings of the IEEE ICCV, vol. 2, pp. 820–827. IEEE Press, Piscataway (1999)
33. Ronneberger, O., Fischer, P., Brox, T.: U-Net: convolutional networks for biomedical image segmentation. In: MICCAI 2015. LNCS, pp. 234–241. Springer, Heidelberg (2015). https://doi.org/10.1007/978-3-319-24574-4_28
34. Zhang, H., Sindagi, V., Patel, V.M.: Image de-raining using a conditional generative adversarial network. IEEE Trans. Circuits Syst. Video Technol. **30**(11), 3943–3956 (2020)
35. Kim, D.H., Ahn, W.J., Lim, M.T., et al.: Frequency-Based Haze and Rain Removal Network (FHRR-Net) with deep convolutional encoder-decoder. Appl. Sci. **11**, 2873 (2021)
36. Qin, X., Wang, Z.L., Bai, Y.C., et al.: FFA-Net: Feature fusion attention network for single image dehazing. arXiv preprint arXiv:1911.07559 (2019)

37. Chen, W., T., Huang, Z.-K., Tsai, C.-C., et al.: Learning multiple adverse weather removal via two-stage knowledge learning and multi-contrastive regularization: Toward a unified model. In: Proceedings of the IEEE CVPR, pp. 17632–17641. IEEE Press, Piscataway (2022)
38. Chen, W., T., et al.: ALL snow removed: single image desnowing algorithm using hierarchical dual-tree complex wavelet representation and contradict channel loss. In: Proceedings of the IEEE ICCV, pp. 4176–4185. IEEE Press, Piscataway (2021)
39. Zamir, S.W., et al.: Multi-stage progressive image restoration. In: Proceedings of the IEEE CVPR, pp. 14816–14826. IEEE Press, Piscataway (2021)
40. Potlapalli, V., Zamir, S.W., Khan, S.: PromptIR: prompting for all-in-one blind image restoration. In: Proceedings of the NeurIPS, pp. 1–10 (2023)
41. Zhu, Z., Liang, D., Zhang, S.H., et al.: Traffic-sign detection and classification in the wild. In: Proc. IEEE CVPR. IEEE Press, Piscataway (2016)

An Efficient Explainability Framework for Graph Neural Networks

Dehan Hu, Chenyang Chen$^{(\boxtimes)}$, and Xiaoyu Zhang

School of Cyber Engineering, Xidian University, Xi'an 710071, China
{hudehan,cychen_1}@stu.xidian.edu.cn, xiaoyuzhang@xidian.edu.cn

Abstract. Graph Neural Networks (GNNs) have shown excellent performance in graph-related tasks. Despite significant advancements in GNN technology, these models are often perceived as opaque 'black boxes' that lack intuitive and human-understandable interpretations. To address this challenge, various explainability techniques have been developed to enhance the interpretability of GNNs, thereby facilitating more transparent decision-making processes and generating more interpretable outputs. Although recent advancements have enabled the interpretation of subgraphs with performance on par with the original graphs—marking a significant step towards demystifying the 'black box' of GNNs existing research often overlooks the associated time costs of this process. This oversight is a critical factor in the practical application of these models. In this paper, we propose a novel explanatory framework for GNNs, aimed at reducing time overhead by introducing an auxiliary dataset combined with an optimized Ullmann algorithm. Our framework applies to a wide range of explanation methods for graph classification. Experimental results demonstrate that our framework not only maintains performance comparable to traditional methods but also significantly reduces time overhead relative to existing solutions.

Keywords: GNN · Explainability · Auxiliary dataset

1 Introduction

In discussing the wide applications of GNNs and their exceptional performance in tasks such as graph classification, node classification, link prediction, and graph generation, we must address a critical issue: despite significant technological advances, these models are often viewed as incomprehensible "black boxes" with insufficient transparency and explainability in their prediction mechanisms. Specifically, while the introduction of techniques such as graph convolution [3–5,11], graph attention [10], and graph pooling [6,13,14] has greatly enhanced the performance of deep graph models, it has not effectively addressed the problem of the explainability of model predictions.

In this paper, we propose a novel and generalizable explanation framework for GNNs designed to optimize computational overhead in various graph classification tasks. Specifically, we construct an auxiliary dataset through a rigorous data pre-processing procedure, which effectively reduces the dataset size.

X. Chen et al. (Eds.): DSPP 2025, LNCS 16177, pp. 69–77, 2026.
https://doi.org/10.1007/978-981-95-3185-1_5

This reduction in scale improves the processing efficiency of auxiliary datasets, thereby significantly reducing computational time. Additionally, we integrate the efficient matching mechanism of the Ullmann algorithm to construct 'original dataset graph-explanatory subgraph' pairs, using explanatory subgraphs derived from the auxiliary datasets. This process establishes a correspondence between the original graph and the interpreted subgraphs. To comprehensively assess the performance and efficiency of the proposed framework, we designed and conducted a series of rigorous experiments that included both qualitative and quantitative analyses.

The contributions are summarized as follows:

- We introduce an innovative auxiliary dataset strategy that significantly reduces the size of the graphs for interpretation, thereby effectively alleviating computational complexity and time overhead. This approach not only enhances efficiency but also preserves the capacity to capture essential structural information of the graph.
- We incorporate the efficient matching mechanism of the Ullmann algorithm into the framework to precisely match the corresponding graph structures in the original dataset, leveraging the explanatory subgraphs derived from the auxiliary dataset. This procedure establishes a correspondence between the original graph and the explanatory subgraph.

2   Related Work

Current research on GNN explainability can be broadly classified into two main categories: instance-level explanation and model-level explanation. The instance-level approach primarily focuses on the decision-making process of individual prediction cases, while the model-level approach aims to capture the global behavioral characteristics of the entire GNN model.

The gradient/feature-based approach is an intuitive method for explaining models and has been widely adopted in image and text tasks. The core idea of this approach is to use the gradient values or hidden feature maps as approximate indicators of the importance of input features. Specifically, the Sensitivity Analysis (SA) [2] method directly utilizes the squared value of the gradient to assess the importance of input features, which can be nodes, edges, or node attributes in a graph. The Guided Backpropagation (Guided BP) [2] method follows a similar concept but introduces modifications in the backpropagation process. This method requires that the graph neural network model employs a global average pooling layer and a fully connected layer as components of the classifier. The Class Activation Mapping (CAM) [8] method computes importance scores for input nodes by combining the final node embeddings with different feature maps through a weighted summation, where the weights are extracted from the final fully connected layer associated with the target prediction.

The perturbation-based approach is a method that identifies key features by analyzing how input perturbations affect the model's output. If a perturbation does not alter critical information, the model's predictions should remain relatively stable and highly consistent with the original outputs. GNNExplainer [12] uncovers the mechanism of model predictions by training soft masks to highlight important features. PGExplainer [7] focuses on approximating discrete edge masks to explain the model's decisions. GraphMask [9] is an a posteriori explanation technique designed to analyze the importance of edges across different layers of a graph neural network.

3   Preliminary

3.1   GNN Explainability Methods

GNNExplainer [12] is a model-agnostic, perturbation-based method that generates interpretable explanations for GNN predictions on graph-based machine learning tasks. Objectivities are to uncover key structures and features driving GNN predictions, providing insights into how the model leverages input graph data to make decisions. Specifically, GNNExplainer explains model predictions by learning soft masks on edge and node features. These soft masks are randomly initialized and adjusted as trainable variables during optimization. The masks are applied to the original graph through an element-wise dot product, thereby refining both the graph structure and node features. The optimization process aims to maximize the mutual information between the predictions of the original and modified graphs, ensuring that the generated explanations faithfully capture the model's decision-making process. The basic formula of GNNExplainer can be expressed as:

$$\mathcal{L} = -\mathcal{I}(Y; G_S, X_S) \tag{1}$$

where $\mathcal{I}(Y; G_S, X_S)$ denotes the mutual information of the subgraph G_S and the feature subset X_S on the model prediction Y. G_S is the target subgraph, which is a subset of the original graph, and X_S is the target feature subset, which is part of the node features.

4   Method

4.1   Auxiliary Dataset Construction

The large size of the original dataset is a key factor contributing to the significant increase in processing time. To address this challenge, we implement a comprehensive pruning strategy aimed at reducing the dataset size. Specifically, we focus on pruning edge nodes, as previous research has indicated that these nodes typically play a less significant role in the graph structure [1].

Assume that the graph $G = (V, E)$ consists of the set of nodes V and the set of edges E. The degree of each node $v \in V$ is denoted as $deg(v)$. The threshold selected in this work preserves spectral properties to maintain GNN performance. An excessively large threshold may discard critical information in the GNN, while an overly small threshold fails to effectively eliminate noise. According to the pruning strategy, we have the following steps to describe the process:

We first define a new set of nodes V_{prune1}, which contains all nodes with degree greater than or equal to 3:

$$V_{prune1} = \{v \in V \mid deg(v) \geq 3\} \tag{2}$$

We removing all nodes with a degree less than 3, which has led to a substantial reduction in dataset size. The updated graph is $G_{prune1} = (V_{prune1}, E_{prune1})$, where E_{prune1} is the set of trimmed edges.

Further experimental validation demonstrates that more aggressive pruning does not significantly affect performance, prompting us to adopt an additional strategy: randomly pruning nodes with a degree of 3 or less with a 50% probability. Let the set of these nodes be $V_{prune2} = \{v \in V_{prune1} \mid deg(V) \leq 3\}$, and we define a random function $r(v)$ (e.g., uniformly distributed between $[0,1]$) for each node $v \in V_{prune2}$ if $r(v) \leq 0.5$, then node v is deleted. We can express this in the following way:

$$V'_{prune2} = \{v \in V_{prune2} \mid r(v) \leq 0.5\} \tag{3}$$

where V'_{prune2} denotes the set of nodes after random pruning. The final set of nodes V_{final} is the result of two prunings:

$$V_{final} = V_{prune1} - V'_{prune2} \tag{4}$$

The corresponding set of edges E_{final} is updated accordingly, removing the edges connected to the pruned nodes. Pruning results in the creation of an auxiliary dataset.

$$G_{aux} = (V_{final}, E_{final}) \tag{5}$$

The process is shown in Fig. 1.

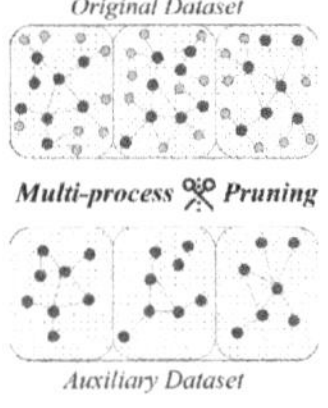

Fig. 1. Multi-process Pruning

4.2   Subgraph Exploration via Auxiliary Dataset

We then performed graph explanation operations on this auxiliary dataset to achieve our primary objective of extracting explainable subgraphs. Graph explanation of the auxiliary graph G_{aux} involved identifying and extracting the explainable subgraphs $G_{sub} = (V_{sub}, E_{sub})$, which represent the most critical components contributing to the model's predictions. These subgraphs provide insights into the model's decision-making process by highlighting the key structural patterns and features that the model relies on.

The explanation process can be expressed as:

$$G_{sub} = Explain(G_{aux}) \tag{6}$$

where the $Explain(\cdot)$ component represents a flexible and modular explanation framework that can accommodate various explanation methods tailored for graph classification tasks. These methods may include state-of-the-art techniques such as GNNExplainer, SubGraphX, or PGExplainer, depending on the specific requirements and objectives of the analysis. The process is shown in Fig. 1.

A significant advantage of operating on the auxiliary dataset is its reduced size compared to the original dataset. This reduction allows the explanation process to be conducted with greater computational efficiency, enabling faster iterations and reducing resource demands. Despite the smaller size, the auxiliary dataset retains the essential graph structures and feature distributions, ensuring the reliability and robustness of the extracted subgraphs.

4.3   Explainable Subgraph Matching

Finally, we extracted explanatory subgraphs from the auxiliary dataset, which are also applicable to the original dataset. Subgraph matching serves as a bridge between efficiency and explanatory authenticity, ensuring both the fidelity and generalizability of explanations. These subgraphs, G_{sub}, represent the most critical graph components that influence the predictions of the graph neural network model. To extend the interpretability to the original dataset, we applied Ullmann's algorithm, a widely recognized method for subgraph isomorphism, to identify corresponding subgraphs G_{sub_match} in the original dataset G. This process ensures that the explanatory insights derived from the auxiliary dataset remain valid and interpretable in the context of the original data.

The matching process can be formalized as:

$$G_{sub\_match} = Ullmann(G, G_{sub}) \tag{7}$$

where G_{sub_match} represents the subgraph in G that matches the structure and features of the interpreted subgraph G_{sub}. Ullmann's algorithm systematically explores the structural relationships and node feature correspondences between G and G_{sub}, ensuring an accurate mapping of the explanatory subgraphs.

5   Experiments

5.1   Datasets and Experimental Settings

We explore three variants of graph neural networks: GCN, GIN and GAT. All GNN models used in our experiments are trained to ensure reasonable performance. Furthermore, we combined these models with interpretation methods such as SubgraphX, GNNExplainer, and PGExplainer for a systematic comparative analysis. It is particularly emphasized that all methods are compared under identical conditions to ensure fairness. Additionally, we maintained a consistent number of nodes in the interpretive subgraphs when comparing methods (Table 1).

Table 1. Statistics and properties of datasets

	Dataset		
	MUTAG	PTC_FM	DHFR
#of Edges (avg)	19.79	14.48	44.54
#of Nodes (avg)	17.93	14.11	42.43
#of Graphs	188	349	756
#of Classes	2	2	2

5.2   Feasibility Experiment and Analysis

To comprehensively verify the feasibility and effectiveness of the proposed interpretable method in GNNs, this study carefully designs and conducts in-depth experiments on two representative benchmark datasets: MUTAG and PTC_FM. These datasets are widely used in graph machine learning due to their unique structural characteristics of chemical graphs, providing a rich source of graph-structured data for experimental validation. The results are shown in Table 2.

To ensure a rigorous and multi-dimensional evaluation, we introduce four key performance metrics:

Fidelity: Measures the extent to which the extracted subgraphs preserve the original GNN model's predictive behavior. Experimental results demonstrate that fidelity surpasses the predefined threshold, confirming the effectiveness of the subgraph extraction algorithm in maintaining model consistency.

Sparsity: Assesses the compactness and informativeness of the extracted subgraphs. Results indicate that the proposed method successfully eliminates redundant information while enhancing interpretability, thereby improving both readability and decision-making clarity. **Matching Accuracy**: Measures the alignment between extracted subgraphs and their corresponding structures in the original dataset. The 100% matching accuracy further substantiates the method's capability to extract highly consistent subgraphs that faithfully reflect the intrinsic structure of the original data.

Through extensive experiments on MUTAG and PTC_FM, our SubGraphX-based interpretability framework demonstrates outstanding performance across all key metrics: fidelity, sparsity, classification accuracy, and matching accuracy. The framework achieves an elegant trade-off between fidelity and efficiency: while pruning low-degree nodes incurs minor predictive information loss, it preserves critical graph structures by retaining degree$\geq$ 3nodes and stochastic sampling. These results not only validate the effectiveness of our approach but also provide strong empirical support for its practical application in generating faithful and interpretable GNN explanations.

Table 2. Validate the feasibility of our method by modeling on the MUTAG and PTC_FM datasets using GIN and GCN models.

Dataset	MUTAG		PTC_FM	
Model	GCN	GIN	GCN	GIN
Fidelity(%)	58.7	53.6	51.2	53.3
Sparsity(%)	78.5	78.5	77.8	77.8
Classification(%)	100	100	100	100
Matching Accuracy(%)	100	100	100	100

5.3 Effectiveness Experiment and Analysis

Next, we apply the proposed framework to three state-of-the-art GNN explanation methods, namely SubGraphX, GNNExplainer, and XGNN. To evaluate the time efficiency of our approach, we use time overhead as the primary comparison metric. By integrating our framework into different GNN explanation methods and systematically comparing their performance, the results demonstrate that our framework achieves superior computational efficiency while maintaining interpretability.

GNNExplainer Method. We further evaluate the performance of our framework using the GNNExplainer method, with the experimental results presented in Table 3. The experimental results indicate that the proposed method achieves a significant reduction in runtime across all test datasets, with a maximum reduction of 38.63%.

At the specific data level, the proposed method demonstrates notable runtime reductions across all datasets. On the MUTAG dataset, the runtime of the GCN, GIN, and GAT models is reduced by 23.47%, 22.9%, and 26.30%, respectively. For the PTC_FM dataset, the reductions are 25.84%, 17.93%, and 19.17%, showing stable and consistent optimization performance across different models.

Table 3. Runtime based on GNNExplainer method(s)

DataSet	MUTAG			PTC_FM			DHFR		
Model	GCN	GIN	GAT	GCN	GIN	GAT	GCN	GIN	GAT
Runtime(Original)	571.33	507.67	514.96	1376.55	1257.48	1372.90	2355.74	2088.04	2139.24
Runtime(Proposed)	437.21	391.07	379.53	1020.85	1032.07	1109.69	1532.78	1281.43	1397.57
Reductio(%)	23.47	22.97	26.30	25.84	17.93	19.17	34.93	38.63	34.67

Notably, the full potential of our optimization strategy is realized in the more complex DHFR dataset, where the runtime of the GCN model is reduced by 34.93%, the GIN model by 38.63%, and the GAT model by 34.67%. These results confirm that the proposed method effectively maintains computational efficiency even on complex datasets, further demonstrating its broad applicability in real-world scenarios.

Overall, our framework demonstrates robust and consistent performance improvements across all three explanation methods, achieving substantial reductions in runtime overhead while preserving the quality of explanations. These findings validate the scalability and generalizability of our approach, positioning it as a versatile and efficient solution for a wide range of graph explanation tasks. This underscores its potential for adoption in scenarios that demand both computational efficiency and high-quality interpretability.

6   Conclusion

In this paper, we have developed an efficient and specialized framework for GNN explainability, designed for broad applicability across various GNN explainers, particularly in graph classification tasks. This framework significantly enhances both the efficiency and effectiveness of explanations. The proposed method integrates pruning, explanation generation, and subgraph matching into a synergistic system rather than treating them as isolated preprocessing steps. The framework is compatible with diverse explanation methods and systematically reduces their computational overhead. In contrast, conventional preprocessing typically requires task-specific customization, thereby achieving an optimized balance between efficiency and explanation quality. A key innovation of our approach is the introduction of an auxiliary dataset strategy, which effectively reduces the computational time required for GNN interpretation. Additionally, we integrate the Ullmann algorithm, enabling efficient subgraph retrieval for explanation purposes. Experimental results clearly demonstrate that our framework substantially reduces time costs while preserving the performance of the original explanation methods.

References

1. Ali, A., Wolf, L., Cevikalp, H.: Degree-based stratification of nodes in graph neural networks. In: Asian Conference on Machine Learning, pp. 15–27. PMLR (2024)
2. Baldassarre, F., Azizpour, H.: Explainability techniques for graph convolutional networks. arXiv preprint arXiv:1905.13686 (2019)
3. Gao, H., Wang, Z., Ji, S.: Large-scale learnable graph convolutional networks. In: Proceedings of the 24th ACM SIGKDD international conference on knowledge discovery and data mining, pp. 1416–1424 (2018)
4. Gilmer, J., Schoenholz, S.S., Riley, P.F., Vinyals, O., Dahl, G.E.: Neural message passing for quantum chemistry. In: International conference on machine learning, pp. 1263–1272. PMLR (2017)
5. Kipf, T.N., Welling, M.: Semi-supervised classification with graph convolutional networks. arXiv preprint arXiv:1609.02907 (2016)
6. Li, W., Wang, C.h., Cheng, G., Song, Q.: International conference on machine learning. Trans. Mach. Learn. Res. (2023)
7. Luo, D., et al.: Parameterized explainer for graph neural network. Adv. Neural. Inf. Process. Syst. **33**, 19620–19631 (2020)
8. Pope, P.E., Kolouri, S., Rostami, M., Martin, C.E., Hoffmann, H.: Explainability methods for graph convolutional neural networks. In: Proceedings of the IEEE/CVF Conference on Computer Vision and Pattern Recognition, pp. 10772–10781 (2019)
9. Schlichtkrull, M.S., De Cao, N., Titov, I.: Interpreting graph neural networks for NLP with differentiable edge masking. arXiv preprint arXiv:2010.00577 (2020)
10. Wang, X., et al.: Heterogeneous graph attention network. In: The world Wide Web Conference, pp. 2022–2032 (2019)
11. Wang, Z., et al.: Advanced graph and sequence neural networks for molecular property prediction and drug discovery. Bioinformatics **38**(9), 2579–2586 (2022)
12. Ying, Z., Bourgeois, D., You, J., Zitnik, M., Leskovec, J.: Gnnexplainer: generating explanations for graph neural networks. Adv. Neural Inf. Process. Syst. **32** (2019)
13. Yuan, H., Ji, S.: Structpool: structured graph pooling via conditional random fields. In: Proceedings of the 8th International Conference on Learning Representations (2020)
14. Zhang, M., Cui, Z., Neumann, M., Chen, Y.: An end-to-end deep learning architecture for graph classification. In: Proceedings of the AAAI Conference on Artificial Intelligence, vol. 32 (2018)

Cryptographic Protocols Design and Analysis

Post-quantum Privacy-Preserving Smart Meter Data Collection Scheme from Coding

Yixuan Huang[1,2] and Fangguo Zhang[1,2(✉)]

[1] School of Computer Science and Engineering, Sun Yat-sen University,
Guangzhou 510006, China
`isszhfg@mail.sysu.edu.cn`
[2] Guangdong Province Key Laboratory of Information Security Technology,
Guangzhou 510006, China

Abstract. With the rapid deployment of smart meters in modern smart grid systems, the fine-grained electricity usage data collected at frequent intervals raises significant privacy concerns. Such data may reveal sensitive information about users' behavior and lifestyle. Therefore, ensuring strong privacy protection is essential in the design of smart metering systems. Although many existing schemes address data privacy and authentication, they often rely on methods vulnerable to quantum attacks or impose substantial computational overhead. To address these challenges, we propose a novel privacy-preserving data collection scheme based on a code-based linkable ring signature. We further evaluate the security and performance of the proposed scheme. The scheme ensures strong identity anonymity, message authentication and traceability of faulty meters even in the presence of quantum adversaries. Experimental results demonstrate that our scheme not only ensures strong privacy but also maintains low computational overhead. This makes it particularly suitable for deployment in resource-constrained smart meter systems, where efficiency and security must be balanced.

Keywords: Smart meter · Privacy-preserving · Code-based cryptography · Linkable ring signature · Post-quantum

1 Introduction

With the large-scale integration of renewable energy sources, increasing grid complexity, and the deep convergence of information and communication technologies, the traditional electric grid is undergoing a systemic transformation into a modern smart grid. According to the U.S. Department of Energy's 2020 Smart Grid System Report [36], the smart grid is a digitalized, automated, and resilient electricity infrastructure that dynamically monitors power flows, optimizes system efficiency, enhances operational flexibility, and enables broad user interaction. Compared with conventional grids, smart grids feature a range of advanced

X. Chen et al. (Eds.): DSPP 2025, LNCS 16177, pp. 81–98, 2026.
https://doi.org/10.1007/978-981-95-3185-1_6

technologies, including bidirectional communication capabilities, integration of distributed energy resources, adaptive load control, pervasive sensor deployment, self-healing mechanisms, and automated operation and maintenance [11]. These features collectively establish smart grids as critical infrastructure for enabling a sustainable, intelligent and secure energy future.

As a key component of the smart grid architecture, smart meters (SMs) serve as the primary interface for data acquisition at the consumer end and play a crucial role in enabling grid intelligence [2]. In addition to enabling fine-grained monitoring of household energy consumption, smart meters support a range of essential functionalities such as remote metering, dynamic pricing, load control, and demand response [30]. However, the collection of such detailed usage data raises significant concerns regarding user privacy and data security. For instance, through non-intrusive load monitoring (NILM) [19] techniques applied to high-frequency electricity usage data, it is possible to infer sensitive information such as occupants' daily routines, presence or absence, and specific appliance usage [15,28]. In the absence of effective privacy-preserving mechanisms, such data may be exploited by malicious actors for purposes including predicting the optimal timing for burglary, enabling targeted scams, or being traded illegally on underground data markets. These activities pose serious threats to users' property security and personal dignity.

Therefore, ensuring both the privacy and security of electricity usage data throughout its lifecycle while maintaining the efficiency of the power grid has become a major challenge in smart grid research. In particular, if sensitive user identities and usage data are not anonymized or desensitized at the source during the data acquisition phase, subsequent end-to-end encryption may be insufficient to mitigate the risks posed by raw data exposure. As such, the data collection process conducted by smart meters constitutes the first line of defense for safeguarding consumer privacy in smart grid systems.

Generally, the three main factors associated with smart meters are the meter's identity, real-time electricity consumption data, and aggregate usage data over the billing period. User privacy is at risk only when an attacker simultaneously obtains both the meter's identity and its real-time usage data. Based on this insight, privacy-preserving techniques in smart meter systems can be broadly categorized into data privacy protection and identity privacy protection.

Data Privacy Protection Techniques for SM. Existing data privacy protection techniques can be broadly classified into three categories: battery-based load hiding (BBLH) techniques, techniques leveraging physical unclonable functions (PUFs), and data aggregation approaches. BBLH is a physical-layer privacy-preserving technique that leverages rechargeable battery (RB) systems to regulate the flow of energy between the grid and user appliances, thereby obscuring the actual electricity consumption patterns. The BBLH method does not affect the normal electricity charging process. For instance, Natgunanathan et al. [24] proposed an RB-based mechanism that incorporates a novel dynamically updated progressive average-based algorithm (PABA). This algorithm ensures that the rechargeable battery never reaches a fully charged or completely depleted state at any time of day, thereby extending the duration and effectiveness of privacy protection. Li et al. [20] proposed a new method that employs deep reinforcement learning to optimize RB charging and discharging behavior under practical constraints, effectively resisting NILM attacks while maintaining low electricity cost. PUFs are a new type of hardware security primitives that exploit the inherent physical characteristics of hardware components. The core idea is to exploit the inherent microscopic variations that occur during the manufacturing process, such as random noise in semiconductor fabrication and material imperfections, to generate outputs that are unique, unpredictable, and practically unclonable [14]. Boyapally et al. [18] proposed a lightweight asymmetric mutual authentication and key exchange protocol based on PUFs to address communication and physical security threats faced by smart meters. Cao et al. [7] proposed a lightweight group authentication scheme based on PUFs for metering data collection in smart grids, which can reduce communication costs and ensure data security and privacy. Among data aggregation techniques, two widely adopted approaches for ensuring privacy are homomorphic encryption and differential privacy. Homomorphic encryption allows computations to be performed directly on encrypted data without decryption, thereby preventing the exposure of individual user data during aggregation. This property makes it particularly well-suited for secure data collection in smart metering environments, as demonstrated in works such as [23] and [38]. Alternatively, differential privacy provides strong privacy guarantees by introducing statistical noise into aggregated outputs, limiting the risk of individual data disclosure even when adversaries possess prior knowledge about the dataset. Gai et al. [13] proposed a smart grid data aggregation scheme based on randomized response, which satisfies local differential privacy, achieving both privacy protection and practical utility. Almaleh et al. [1] demonstrated that applying a differential privacy mechanism with Laplacian noise can effectively protect user privacy in smart metering systems.

Identity Privacy Protection Techniques for SM. Safeguarding user identity is essential in smart meter to prevent the linkage of usage data to specific individuals. Common cryptographic approaches for identity protection can be broadly categorized into anonymity-preserving techniques and secure identity authentication protocols. Anonymity-preserving techniques include anonymous certificates [6], blind signatures [9], ring signatures [27]. Anonymous certificate schemes allow users to authenticate themselves without revealing their true identities, typically relying on trusted authorities to issue unlinkable credentials. Diao et al. [10] proposed a smart metering scheme based on linkable anonymous credentials that ensures user anonymity while supporting message authentication and traceability of broken SM. Blind signatures allow a requester to obtain a signature on a message from a signer without revealing the message content, thereby enabling authentication while preserving the privacy of the message originator. Sui and Li [31] proposed a privacy-preserving scheme for smart grids based on blind signatures and anonymous authentication. This scheme not only ensures secure and auditable prepaid electricity requests but also effectively balances user privacy and computational efficiency. Ring signatures allow a user to sign a message on behalf of a group without revealing which group member generated the signature, thereby providing strong anonymity without the need for a group manager or trusted setup. For instance, Tian et al. [34] proposed a lattice-based linkable ring signatures scheme which enables post-quantum, privacy-preserving smart meter data collection. In terms of identity authentication, Chaudhry et al. [8] leverage elliptic curve cryptography and symmetric key mechanisms to design SG-specific anonymous mutual authentication and key agreement protocols, enabling secure identity verification for smart meters and the establishment of trusted communication channels. Kumar et al. [26] proposed a semi-quantum key distribution-based authentication protocol Q-Secure-P2-SMA, which achieves identity privacy protection, message unlinkability, and anonymity, making it more practical for real-world applications.

Contribution. Although both data privacy protection and identity privacy protection techniques have achieved significant progress, most existing schemes either incur high computational overhead or rely on methods that are vulnerable to quantum attacks. With the rapid advancement of quantum computing, post-quantum secure and lightweight authentication schemes are urgently needed for privacy-preserving data collection in smart grids, especially at the edge where smart meters are resource-constrained. Although lattice-based approaches offer quantum resistance, they often involve complex computations and large key sizes, which limit their efficiency in real-world deployments. To address these challenges, this paper proposes a privacy-preserving data collection scheme based on a code-based linkable ring signature (PDCLRS), designed for smart meters. The underlying linkable ring signature (LRS) scheme builds upon the code-based construction introduced in [22], which is reviewed in Sect. 2.3. We introduce several modifications to enhance its efficiency and adapt it to the specific requirements of smart meter data collection. Compared with the existing lattice-based solution [33], the proposed approach exhibits lower computational complexity and can be executed more efficiently on resource-constrained devices, leading to significantly reduced computation time in practical settings.

The structure of this paper is as follows. Section 2 introduces notations and preliminaries used in this paper. Section 3 introduces smart grid model and framework of our PDCLRS scheme. Section 4 introduces the construction of the PDCLRS scheme. Section 5 includes the analysis of security and performance. Section 6 is the conclusion of this paper.

2   Notations and Preliminaries

2.1   Notations

To facilitate understanding of the proposed scheme, we summarize the key notations used throughout this paper as follows. Let λ represent the security parameter and $\mathbf{S}_n$ denote the symmetric group of all permutations of n elements. Unless otherwise stated, vectors and matrices will be represented in bold lowercase letters and bold capital letters, respectively. We use $Hash$ to denote a collision-resistant hash function. We let $wt(\mathbf{x})$ be the Hamming weight of a vector $\mathbf{x}$ and $B(N,t)$ be the set of vectors $\mathbf{x} \in \mathbb{F}_2^N$ such that $wt(\mathbf{x}) = t$. For a set X, $x \xleftarrow{\$} X$ denotes that x is randomly picked from X. Let δ_k^N be a vector of length N such that the k-th position is 1 for $k \in [0, N-1]$ and the rest of the positions are 0. I2B is denoted as a function from a positive integer to its binary representation and its inverse function is denoted as B2I. Given a vector $\mathbf{a} \in \mathbb{F}_2^l$, $\phi_{\mathbf{a}}$ is a permutation from $\mathbb{F}_2^N$ to $\mathbb{F}_2^N$ where $N = 2^l$: $\mathbf{y} = (y_0, ..., y_{N-1}) \rightarrow \mathbf{y}' = (y_0', ..., y_{N-1}')$, where $y_j = y_\pi', \pi = B2I(I2B(j) \oplus \mathbf{a})$ for each $j \in [0, N-1]$.

2.2 Fundamentals of Code-Based Cryptography

Coding theory plays a foundational role in code-based cryptography, thus this section introduces basic concepts relevant to our scheme.

Problem 1 (syndrome decoding (SD) problem). Given a parity-check matrix $\mathbf{H} \in \mathbb{F}_2^{k \times n}$, a syndrome $\mathbf{s} \in \mathbb{F}_2^k$, and a positive integer t, search for a solution $\mathbf{e} \in \mathbb{F}_2^n$ such that $\mathbf{H} \cdot \mathbf{e}^T = \mathbf{s}^T$ and $wt(\mathbf{e}) \leq t$.

This problem has been proven to be NP-complete in the worst case [4].

Problem 2 (general syndrome decoding (GSD) problem). Given two parity-check matrices $\mathbf{H}, \mathbf{T} \in \mathbb{F}_2^{k \times n}$, two syndromes $\mathbf{s}, \mathbf{r} \in \mathbb{F}_2^k$, and a positive integer t, search for a solution $\mathbf{e} \in \mathbb{F}_2^n$ such that $\mathbf{H} \cdot \mathbf{e}^T = \mathbf{s}^T$, $\mathbf{T} \cdot \mathbf{e}^T = \mathbf{r}^T$ and $wt(\mathbf{e}) \leq t$.

The SD problem can be trivially reduced to GSD problem, by choosing as inputs of the reduction $\mathbf{H} = \mathbf{T}$ and $\mathbf{s} = \mathbf{r}$ [5]. So GSD problem is also a NP-complete problem.

Problem 3 (codeword finding (CF) problem). Given a parity-check matrix $\mathbf{H} \in \mathbb{F}_2^{k \times n}$ and a positive integer t, search for a non-zero vector $\mathbf{e} \in \mathbb{F}_2^n$ such that $\mathbf{H} \cdot \mathbf{e}^T = 0^T$ and $wt(\mathbf{e}) \leq t$.

Similarly, the CF problem has also been proven to be NP-complete in the worst case [4].

Problem 4 (decisional syndrome decoding (DSD) problem). Given a parity-check matrix $\mathbf{H} \in \mathbb{F}_2^{k \times n}$ and a syndrome $\mathbf{s}^T = \mathbf{H} \cdot \mathbf{e}^T \in \mathbb{F}_2^k$ where $wt(\mathbf{e}) \leq t$, the DSD problem is to distinguish between a random vector $\mathbf{r} \in \mathbb{F}_2^k$ and the syndrome $\mathbf{s}$.

The DSD problem is widely assumed to be computationally hard in code-based cryptography. It forms the foundation of the security for various identification and signature schemes, including Stern's protocol [29] and its variants.

Stern's Protocol [29]. Stern's protocol, proposed in 1993, is the first honest-verifier zero-knowledge identification protocol based on the hardness of the SD problem. It enables a prover to convince a verifier that they possess a secret error vector $\mathbf{e} \in \mathbb{F}_2^n$ with small Hamming weight $wt(\mathbf{e}) \leq t$, satisfying $\mathbf{H} \cdot \mathbf{e}^T = \mathbf{s}^T$, without revealing any information about $\mathbf{e}$. The protocol is a three-round interactive proof system that follows the classic commit-challenge-response paradigm. It achieves completeness, soundness, and honest-verifier zero-knowledge properties. The soundness error of a single round is 2/3, and thus the protocol is typically repeated p times so as to reduce the soundness error to negligible levels.

2.3   Code-Based Linkable Ring Signature Scheme

Ring signature allows any member of a predefined group to sign a message on behalf of the group. A verifier can confirm that the signature was generated by someone in the group, but cannot identify which specific member created it. Linkable ring signatures [21] extend the basic ring signature scheme by introducing a property of linkability, while still preserving signer's anonymity. Within the same issue, this property allows any verifier to determine whether two signatures were generated by the same anonymous group member. At the same time, the actual identity of the signer remains undisclosed. Thus, linkability allows for detecting repeated actions by the same signer within the same issue, while preserving unlinkability across different issues. LRS schemes are particularly useful in applications such as anonymous electronic voting [35], anonymous cryptocurrencies [32], and other systems that require both strong anonymity and limited traceability (e.g., to prevent double-spending or vote duplication).

Among various constructions of LRS, code-based approaches are particularly attractive due to their potential resistance to quantum attacks and efficient performance on constrained devices. Liu and Wang [22] proposed a novel code-based LRS scheme. The construction is based on a newly designed Stern-like interactive zero-knowledge protocol, which is repeated p times to ensure a negligible soundness error. The LRS scheme achieves correctness, existential unforgeability, anonymity, non-frameability and linkability. These properties rely on three hard problems introduced in Sect. 2.2: the GSD problem, the CF problem and the DSD problem. The proof of correctness and security properties can be found in the full version of [22]. The architecture of scheme is as follows.

1. *Setup*: On inputting the security parameter 1^λ, generate two parity-check matrices $\mathbf{H}, \mathbf{T} \in \mathbb{F}_2^{k \times n}$ (one for public key generation and one for linkability verification) and select a collision-resistant hash function h for generating challenge values. Output the public parameter $pp = (\mathbf{H}, \mathbf{T}, h)$.
2. *KeyGen*: On inputting pp, sample a private key (sk) $\mathbf{e}$ uniformly at random from the binary error vector space $B(n, w)$ and compute corresponding public key (pk) $\mathbf{s}^T = \mathbf{H} \cdot \mathbf{e}^T \in \mathbb{F}_2^k$. Output the private-public key pair $(\mathbf{e}, \mathbf{s})$.
3. *Sign*: On inputting pp, the public keys of all ring members $\overline{pk}$, a message M, and sk of the signer, generate the signature σ on the message M. The signature includes a non-interactive zero-knowledge proof (converted via the Fiat-Shamir transform [12]) that the signer possesses a valid private key and knows the position of the corresponding public key in the ring, without revealing which one. The signature also includes a syndrome derived from the secret key to ensure linkability and can be used to link multiple signatures from the same signer. Output the signature σ on message M.

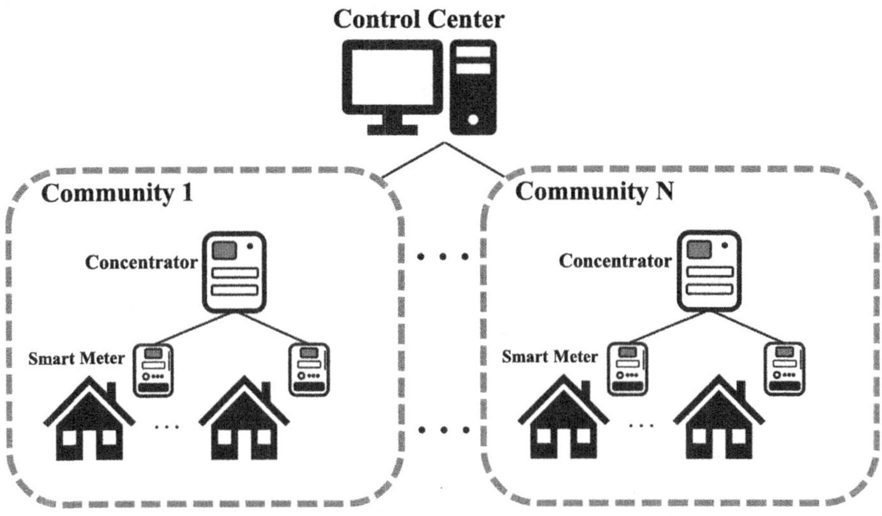

Fig. 1. Three-layer architecture of smart grid.

4. *Verify*: On inputting pp, the public keys $\overline{pk}$, a message M, and a signature σ, verify the correctness of the signature. The verifier checks that the zero-knowledge proof demonstrates knowledge of a valid secret key corresponding to one of the public keys in the ring. Output 1 (accept) if the signature is valid, or 0 (reject) otherwise.
5. *Link*: On inputting the public keys $\overline{pk}$, two valid message-signature pairs (M_1, σ_1) and (M_2, σ_2), extract the syndromes embedded in the signatures. If the syndromes are identical, output 1 to indicate that both signatures were generated by the same signer; otherwise, output 0.

The detailed constructions and algorithmic steps are referred to [22].

3   Smart Grid Model and Framework of the PDCLRS Scheme

3.1   Smart Grid Model

Our scheme focuses on a three-layer architecture in smart grids, which consists of a control center, concentrators, and smart meters. The architecture of smart grid is shown in Fig. 1.

Control Center: To ensure the efficient and stable operation of the power grid, the control center is responsible for assessing the overall grid load status and making decisions regarding power distribution and dynamic pricing. For this purpose, it requires accurate and timely aggregated electricity consumption data from different residential regions. The control center oversees the deployment of concentrators in different communities to serve as intermediate nodes for data collection and communication.

Concentrator: The concentrator acts as a regional data aggregation unit deployed by the control center. It is responsible for collecting electricity usage reports from all smart meters within its coverage area. Upon receiving data, the concentrator verifies its authenticity, filters out invalid or malicious submissions, and performs statistical analysis. The concentrator then aggregates the regional electricity consumption information and forwards the results to the control center for further decision-making.

Smart Meter: Each smart meter is installed at the user side and is responsible for collecting real-time electricity consumption data at fixed intervals (e.g., every 15 min). To preserve user privacy and ensure data integrity, the smart meter generates a signature on the collected data before transmitting it to the concentrator assigned to its residential area.

3.2 Framework of the PDCLRS Scheme

The PDCLRS scheme focuses on preserving user privacy during the transmission of residential electricity consumption data from each smart meter to the local concentrator. Each community is associated with a single concentrator, and all smart meters under its management form a ring. The PDCLRS scheme contains a four-phase framework: system initialization, data upload, data authentication, and anomaly detection.

1. System Initialization: The concentrator generates public parameters by running the algorithm *Setup*. Then, each smart meter creates its key pair through *KeyGen* algorithm, with the private key stored locally and the public key made publicly available. The finalized system parameters are embedded into each smart meter during installation by the power service company.
2. Data Upload: At each fixed interval, each smart meter collects local usage data and generates a signature by running the algorithm *Sign* and sends the tuple (timestamp, message, signature) to the concentrator.
3. Data Authentication: Upon receiving a tuple from a smart meter, the concentrator verifies its validity through *Verify* algorithm. If the signature is valid, the data is stored for further processing.
4. Anomaly Detection: The concentrator selectively performs anomaly detection based on the volume and consistency of received data, and utilizes the *Link* algorithm to identify faulty or misbehaving smart meters.

3.3 Security Requirements

To address the privacy and security challenges arising across the smart grid's three-layer architecture, our scheme is designed to satisfy three core security properties:

1. *Identity Anonymity*: When a legitimate smart meter transmits data only once during a given time interval, the identity of the user remains completely hidden from all parties, including the concentrator.

2. *Message Authentication*: Messages originating from smart meters must be verifiable to ensure that they are indeed sent by authorized users.

3. *Traceability of Faulty SM*: If a smart meter sends either fewer or more messages than expected during a specific time interval due to malfunction, the concentrator must be able to accurately identify the faulty meter.

4   Post-quantum Privacy-Preserving Data Collection Scheme via Code-Based Linkable Ring Signatures

In this section, we present the detailed design of the PDCLRS scheme based on the four-phase framework outlined in Sect. 3.2. The scheme is constructed to ensure identity anonymity, message authentication, and traceability of faulty smart meters. The process is as follows.

Let the set of N users in a community be denoted as $\{U_0, U_1, \cdots, U_{N-1}\}$. The community is equipped with a data concentrator, denoted as Con, which manages N smart meters represented by $\{Met_0, Met_1, \cdots, Met_{N-1}\}$, each installed in the household of user $U_0, U_1, \cdots, U_{N-1}$, respectively. At time t, the data collected by a smart meter is denoted as $M(t)$.

System Initialization

1. According to the security parameter λ, Con performs the following steps to obtain the global public parameters $pp = (\mathbf{H}, h_1, h_2)$.
   1) Randomly select $\mathbf{H} \leftarrow \{0,1\}^{k \times n}$.
   2) Choose a hash function $h_1 : \{0,1\}^* \rightarrow \{0,1\}^{k \times n}$, where h_1 maps binary strings of arbitrary length to $k \times n$ binary matrices.
   3) Choose a hash function $h_2 : \{0,1\}^* \rightarrow \{0,1,2\}^p$, where h_2 maps binary strings of arbitrary length to challenge values of length p over the set $\{0,1,2\}$.
   4) Set $pp = (\mathbf{H}, h_1, h_2)$.
2. For each user U_i, $i \in [0, N-1]$, Met_i needs to generate a key pair (sk_i, pk_i) during the installation process. The private key is securely stored within the smart meter, while the public key is made publicly available. The detailed procedure for key generation is described below.
   1) Randomly select $\mathbf{e}_i \in B(n, w)$ as the private key.
   2) Compute the corresponding public key $\mathbf{s}_i^T = \mathbf{H} \cdot \mathbf{e}_i^T$.
3. Let $\mathbf{S}_0 = [\mathbf{s}_0^T, \mathbf{s}_1^T, \cdots, \mathbf{s}_{N-1}^T]$ denote the list of public keys collected from the N users. According to the LRS scheme described in [22], the number of users in the ring must be $N' = 2^l$ where $l \in \mathbb{Z}$. However, the actual number of users may not meet this requirement. To address this, we select the smallest power of two 2^l such that $2^l \geq N$, and define $N' = 2^l$ as the ring size. The original key list $\mathbf{S}_0$ is then extended to this size. Specifically, Con generates $N' - N$ distinct binary vectors of length k, which do not overlap with any real public key $\mathbf{s}_i$ for $i \in [0, N-1]$. These vectors are randomly inserted into $\mathbf{S}_0$, yielding the extended key list $\mathbf{S}_1 = [\mathbf{s}_0'^T, \mathbf{s}_1'^T, \cdots, \mathbf{s}_{N'-1}'^T]$. Pseudo-public keys generated by Con are not bound to any physical smart meter. This expansion approach

preserves the security of the LRS scheme while ensuring compatibility with the required ring size.

4. *Con* publishes the system parameters $PSP = (pp, \mathbf{S}_1)$. To reduce initial data transmission, the power service company preloads the published system parameters into smart meters during installation.

Data Upload

According to national standards, all smart meters within a community are required to upload their electricity consumption data to the concentrator every 15 min following a uniform procedure.

Taking user U_i as an example, i denotes the column index of the user's public key in the matrix $\mathbf{S}_1$ which is known only to the user. At time t, Met_i collects the electricity usage data denoted by $M_i(t)$. Equipped with its private-public key pair $(\mathbf{e}_i, \mathbf{s}_i)$ and the preloaded PSP, Met_i uses the current timestamp t as a tag when generating a signature. This design ensures that signatures produced by the same meter at different time intervals remain unlinkable. Specifically, the timestamp t, along with matrices $\mathbf{H}$ and $\mathbf{S}_1$, serve as inputs to the function that generates another matrix $\mathbf{T} \in \mathbb{F}_2^{k \times n}$ used in the linkability test. Met_i then generates a signature $\sigma_i(t)$ over the data $M_i(t)$ at time t by following the steps outlined below. Finally, it sends the resulting tuple $(t, M_i(t), \sigma_i(t))$ to the community's concentrator.

1. Compute $\mathbf{T} = h_1(t, \mathbf{H}, \mathbf{S}_1)$, $\mathbf{r}_i^T = \mathbf{T} \cdot \mathbf{e}_i^T$;
2. Let $\mathbf{x}_i = \delta_i^N$, such that $\mathbf{S}_1 \cdot \mathbf{x}_i^T = \mathbf{s}_i^T$;
3. For j from 1 to p:
   1) Choose $\mathbf{r}_{j,1} \xleftarrow{\$} \mathbb{F}_2^n$, $\mathbf{r}_{j,2} \xleftarrow{\$} \mathbb{F}_2^N$, $\delta_j \xleftarrow{\$} S_n$, $\mathbf{a}_j \xleftarrow{\$} \{0,1\}^l$, $\epsilon_{j,1}, \epsilon_{j,2}, \epsilon_{j,3} \xleftarrow{\$} \{0,1\}^\lambda$
   2) Compute $c_{j,1} = Hash(\delta_j, \mathbf{a}_j, \mathbf{H} \cdot \mathbf{r}_{j,1}^T \oplus \mathbf{S}_1 \cdot \mathbf{r}_{j,2}^T, \mathbf{T} \cdot \mathbf{r}_{j,1}^T, \epsilon_{j,1})$
   3) Compute $c_{j,2} = Hash(\delta_j(\mathbf{r}_{j,1}), \phi_{\mathbf{a}_j}(\mathbf{r}_{j,2}), \epsilon_{j,2})$
   4) Compute $c_{j,3} = Hash(\delta_j(\mathbf{e}_i \oplus \mathbf{r}_{j,1}), \phi_{\mathbf{a}_j}(\mathbf{x}_i \oplus \mathbf{r}_{j,2}), \epsilon_{j,3})$
   5) Set $CMT_j = (c_{j,1}, c_{j,2}, c_{j,3})$;
4. Compute challenges $(ch_1, ch_2, ..., ch_p) = h_2(CMT_1, CMT_2, ..., CMT_p, M_i(t), \mathbf{H}, \mathbf{S}_1, \mathbf{T}, \mathbf{r}_i, t)$;
5. For j from 1 to p:
   1) If $ch_j = 0$: $resp_j = \{\mathbf{r}_{j,1}, \mathbf{r}_{j,2}, \delta_j, \mathbf{a}_j, \epsilon_{j,1}, \epsilon_{j,2}\}$;
   2) If $ch_j = 1$: $resp_j = \{\mathbf{e}_i \oplus \mathbf{r}_{j,1}, \mathbf{x}_i \oplus \mathbf{r}_{j,2}, \delta_j, \mathbf{a}_j, \epsilon_{j,1}, \epsilon_{j,3}\}$;
   3) If $ch_j = 2$: $resp_j = \{\delta_j(\mathbf{r}_{j,1}), \delta_j(\mathbf{e}_i), \phi_{\mathbf{a}_j}(\mathbf{r}_{j,2}), \phi_{\mathbf{a}_j}(\mathbf{x}_i), \epsilon_{j,2}, \epsilon_{j,3}\}$;
6. Let $\sigma_i(t) = (\mathbf{r}_i, v) = (\mathbf{r}_i, \{CMT_j\}_{j=1}^p, \{resp_j\}_{j=1}^p)$, return $\sigma_i(t)$.

Data Authentication

Upon receiving a tuple from a smart meter under its management, *Con* must verify whether the signature on the data at time t was generated by a valid smart meter in the community.

Taking the data received from U_i as an example, *Con* utilizes the stored PSP and the received tuple $(t, M_i(t), \sigma_i(t))$ to carry out the following verification steps. If the output is 1, the data is deemed valid and retained for subsequent processing; otherwise, it is discarded.

1. Compute $\mathbf{T} = h_1(t, \mathbf{H}, \mathbf{S}_1)$;
2. Compute $(ch_1, ch_2, ..., ch_p) = h_2(CMT_1, CMT_2, ..., CMT_p, M_i(t), \mathbf{H}, \mathbf{S}_1, \mathbf{T}, \mathbf{r}_i, t)$;
3. For j from 1 to p:
    1) If $ch_j = 0$: verify whether $Hash(\delta_j, \mathbf{a}_j, \mathbf{H} \cdot \mathbf{r}_{j,1}^T \oplus \mathbf{S}_1 \cdot \mathbf{r}_{j,2}^T, \mathbf{T} \cdot \mathbf{r}_{j,1}^T, \epsilon_{j,1}) = c_{j,1}$ holds, and whether $Hash(\delta_j(\mathbf{r}_{j,1}), \phi_{\mathbf{a}_j}(\mathbf{r}_{j,2}), \epsilon_{j,2}) = c_{j,2}$ holds.
    2) If $ch_j = 1$: verify whether $Hash(\delta_j, \mathbf{a}_j, \mathbf{H} \cdot (\mathbf{r}_{j,1} \oplus \mathbf{e}_i)^T \oplus \mathbf{S}_1 \cdot (\mathbf{r}_{j,2} \oplus \mathbf{x}_i)^T, \mathbf{T} \cdot (\mathbf{r}_{j,1} \oplus \mathbf{e}_i)^T \oplus \mathbf{r}_i, \epsilon_{j,1}) = c_{j,1}$ holds, and whether $Hash(\delta_j(\mathbf{e}_i \oplus \mathbf{r}_{j,1}), \phi_{\mathbf{a}_j}(\mathbf{x}_i \oplus \mathbf{r}_{j,2}), \epsilon_{j,3}) = c_{j,3}$ holds.
    3) If $ch_j = 2$: verify whether $Hash(\delta_j(\mathbf{r}_{j,1}), \phi_{\mathbf{a}_j}(\mathbf{r}_{j,2}), \epsilon_{j,2}) = c_{j,2}$ holds, and whether $Hash(\delta_j(\mathbf{e}_i) \oplus \delta_j(\mathbf{r}_{j,1}), \phi_{\mathbf{a}_j}(\mathbf{x}_i) \oplus \phi_{\mathbf{a}_j}(\mathbf{r}_{j,2}), \epsilon_{j,3}) = c_{j,3}$ holds, and whether $wt(\delta_j(\mathbf{e}_i)) = w, wt(\phi_{\mathbf{a}_j}(\mathbf{x}_i)) = 1$ holds.
    4) If any of the above conditions is not satisfied, terminate and return 0.
4. If all challenge verifications succeed, return 1.

Anomaly Detection

For all authenticated data concerning time t that are uploaded by smart meters within the community, Con first verifies whether the number of received data entries matches the number of legitimate users. A correct data count may result from two possible scenarios: (i) all smart meters operate normally and each sends exactly one valid data entry; (ii) some smart meters fail to send data while others submit multiple entries, and the number of missing and extra data entries is exactly equal. Furthermore, due to the correctness and security of the code-based LRS scheme, it is infeasible for a malicious smart meter to forge a valid signature on behalf of another. Therefore, when the data count is correct, the likelihood of anomalies is very low. In such cases, Con performs anomaly detection only at a few randomly selected time points during the day. At other time of the day, it aggregates all valid data related to time t and forwards them to the control center, thereby completing the data collection process for that time slot.

When the number of collected data entries is incorrect, anomaly detection must be performed immediately. For any two tuples $(t, M_1(t), \sigma_1(t))$ and $(t, M_2(t), \sigma_2(t))$ at time t, the steps of anomaly detection are as follows. If the output is 1, two signatures are considered to be generated by the same user. An output of 0 indicates different users.

1. $\sigma_1 = (\mathbf{r}_1, v_1), \sigma_2 = (\mathbf{r}_2, v_2)$;
2. If $\mathbf{r}_1 = \mathbf{r}_2$: return 1;
3. If not, return 0.

If two or more signatures are found to be linkable, they can be identified as originating from the same smart meter at the same time. In such cases, two scenarios are analyzed:

(i) If two or more linkable valid signatures correspond to identical data $M(t)$, the concentrator determines that the same smart meter has sent duplicate entries. In this case, one data entry is retained as the legitimate upload for time t, and the others are discarded.

(ii) If two or more linkable valid signatures correspond to different data values, the concentrator determines that the smart meter associated with these signatures is malfunctioning. To locate the faulty meter, Con sends retransmission requests to each smart meter one by one for the data at time t. It then checks the linkability between the retransmitted signature and the previously identified suspicious signatures. The meter whose signature links to the suspicious one is identified as the faulty device. Once the faulty device is identified, the control center initiates hardware inspection and security analysis to eliminate potential risks and carry out necessary repairs.

Once the number of remaining unlinkable signatures matches the expected number of smart meters, Con aggregates all data and uploads it to the control center, completing the data collection for time t. Otherwise, if the count does not match, it indicates that some meters have not sent their data. In this case, Con sends retransmission requests to each smart meter one by one for the data at time t and checks the linkability between the retransmitted signatures and the previously collected ones. If a link is found, the meter is deemed to have already uploaded the data for time t and is considered to be functioning normally. If no link exists, it indicates that the meter failed to transmit the data previously. The concentrator records the newly received data and examines the meter's communication module to determine whether it is operating correctly.

5   System Analysis

5.1   Security Analysis

The proposed PDCLRS scheme achieves three essential security properties: identity anonymity, message authentication, and traceability of faulty smart meter. These properties are directly inherited from the security guarantees of the underlying code-based LRS scheme. We now analyze each property in detail:

1. *Identity Anonymity*: The identity anonymity of PDCLRS ensures that an adversary cannot determine which smart meter in the community has generated a specific signature. This means even if an attacker intercepts the transmitted tuple $(t, M_i(t), \sigma_i(t))$, they cannot trace it back to a specific user. This anonymity is inherited from the underlying LRS scheme. Suppose there exists a probabilistic polynomial-time adversary $\mathcal{A}$ that can break this anonymity with non-negligible advantage. Then we can construct an algorithm $\mathcal{B}$ that uses $\mathcal{A}$ to break the anonymity of the underlying LRS scheme. If $\mathcal{B}$ can break anonymity, then either the zero-knowledge property of the Stern-like protocol is violated, or the adversary has a way to distinguish structured syndromes(derived from a low-weight error vector) from a uniformly random one, which implies solving the DSD problem. Both cases contradict the established security assumptions of the LRS scheme, thus confirming the identity anonymity.

2. *Message Authentication*: The message authentication property of PDCLRS ensures that no adversary can forge a valid consumption report on behalf of a smart meter without possessing its legitimate secret key. This means that even if an adversary intercepts or modifies the reported data, they cannot create a forged signature that will be accepted by the concentrator. This property is rooted in the non-frameability of the underlying LRS scheme. Suppose there exists a probabilistic polynomial-time adversary $\mathcal{A}$ that can produce a valid signature accepted by the verifier without knowing the corresponding secret key. Then we can construct an algorithm $\mathcal{B}$ that uses $\mathcal{A}$ to break the non-frameability of the underlying LRS scheme. In particular, $\mathcal{B}$ would be able to generate a valid zero-knowledge proof of knowledge of a secret key without actually knowing it. This implies that $\mathcal{B}$ can simulate a valid response to the Stern-like identification protocol embedded in the LRS. Consequently, $\mathcal{B}$ can be used to extract a solution to the GSD problem. This contradicts the assumed hardness of the GSD problem, thus confirming the message authentication.

3. *Traceability of Faulty SM*: The traceability of faulty SM ensures that if a smart meter misbehaves, it can be reliably identified. This is achieved through the linkability of the underlying LRS scheme. Suppose there exists a probabilistic polynomial-time adversary $\mathcal{A}$ that can produce two valid but unlinkable signatures using the same private key. Then we can construct an algorithm $\mathcal{B}$ that uses $\mathcal{A}$ to break the linkability of the underlying LRS scheme. $\mathcal{B}$ can analyze the internal structure of the two valid signatures output by $\mathcal{A}$, and extract from them two distinct low-weight codewords that correspond to the same syndrome, thereby effectively solving the CF problem. This contradicts the assumed hardness of the CF problem, thus confirming the traceability of faulty SM.

5.2   Performance Analysis

In this section, we will analyze the efficiency of the proposed scheme. Since the anomaly detection phase is not frequently triggered in daily operation, our analysis primarily focuses on the time required for each smart meter to generate a signature during the data uploading phase, as well as the time needed by the concentrator to perform a single verification during the data authentication phase. We implemented our scheme based on Python and we estimate the performance on Intel(R) Core(TM) i9-14900K CPU@3.20 GHz.

In our implementation, a seed is used to deterministically generate the required permutation, which helps reduce the signature size. The function $Hash$ is instantiated using SHA3-256, which is standardized in FIPS 202 [25]. To generate the binary matrix, the hash function h_1 in our scheme employs an extendable hashing approach based on SHA-256: the timestamp is concatenated with an incrementing counter and hashed repeatedly until a bitstring of sufficient length is obtained, which is then reshaped into a $k \times n$ matrix. For the function h_2, we generate the challenge vector by hashing the concatenation of the input data and a counter using SHA-256, followed by rejection sampling to extract modulo 3 values from the hash output. This approach guarantees uniform distribution of challenge values over $\{0, 1, 2\}$, fulfilling the pseudorandomness and determinism requirements essential for the Fiat-Shamir transform.

Table 1. Performance of the PDCLRS scheme.

N	PK size (KB)	Average signature size (KB)	Sign (s)	Verify (s)
16	630.3	165.8	3.848	1.767
32	631.7	166.4	3.930	1.810
64	634.3	167.6	4.004	1.828
128	639.6	169.9	4.182	1.903
256	650.2	174.5	4.390	1.961
512	671.4	183.6	5.077	2.245

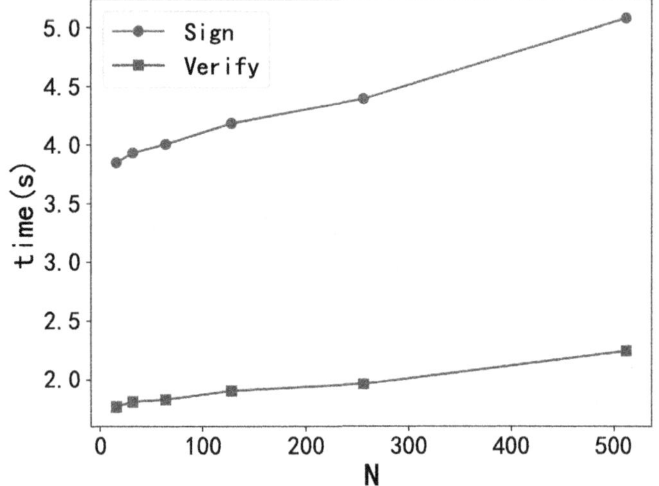

Fig. 2. Impact of ring size on signing and verification efficiency.

Table 2. Comparison of signing and verification times between our scheme and [33].

N	our scheme		[33]	
	Sign (s)	Verify (s)	Sign (s)	Verify (s)
64	4.004	1.828	94.850	31.432
256	4.390	1.961	149.285	94.572
1024	6.853	2.942	416.621	374.794

To achieve 128-bit quantum security, we carefully select the parameters $n = 3800$, $k = 678$, $w = 156$, $p = 219$, taking into account the hardness assumptions of the GSD problem, the CF problem and the DSD problem, as well as theoretical guidelines provided by the Gilbert-Varshamov bound [16,37], the leftover hash lemma [17], and the analysis of the BJMM algorithm [3] for information set decoding algorithm. Table 1 presents the performance under the selected parameter set. To provide a direct performance comparison, Table 2 reports the signing and verification times of our scheme and the lattice-based LRS scheme in [33] on overlapping ring sizes. It can be observed that our scheme consistently outperforms [33], achieving significantly lower signing and verification times across all tested ring sizes. To further illustrate the scalability of the scheme, we visualize the trend of signing and verification times with respect to the number of users. As depicted in Fig. 2, both signing and verification times increase approximately linearly with the number of users. Although signing is more time-consuming than verification, the overall performance remains efficient even as the ring size scales up, which confirms the practicality of the scheme for large-scale deployments.

6   Conclusion

In this paper, we proposed a privacy-preserving data collection scheme for smart meters, based on a code-based linkable ring signature. The scheme ensures identity anonymity, message authentication, and the traceability of faulty meters while preserving the unlinkability of honest users. By leveraging the lightweight and quantum-resistant nature of code-based cryptography, our scheme achieves both post-quantum security and computational efficiency, making it well-suited for deployment on resource-constrained devices. In future work, we aim to further optimize the signature size and signing speed, as well as explore extensions to broader smart grid scenarios.

Acknowledgements. This work is supported by the National Natural Science Foundation of China (Grant No. 62272491) and the Project of Guangdong Provincial Key Laboratory of Information Security Technology (Grant No. 2023B1212060026).

References

1. Almaleh, A., Lahiq, S., Al-Shehri, F.: Smart grid privacy via differential privacy of smart metering data. pp. 556–561 (2023). https://doi.org/10.1109/ICCIT58132.2023.10273939
2. Arif, A., Al-Hussain, M., Al-Mutairi, N., Al-Ammar, E., Khan, Y., Malik, N.: Experimental study and design of smart energy meter for the smart grid. pp. 515–520 (2013). https://doi.org/10.1109/IRSEC.2013.6529714
3. Becker, A., Joux, A., May, A., Meurer, A.: Decoding random binary linear codes in $2^{n/20}$: how $1+1 = 0$ improves information set decoding. In: Pointcheval, D., Johansson, T. (eds.) EUROCRYPT 2012. LNCS, vol. 7237, pp. 520–536. Springer, Heidelberg (2012). https://doi.org/10.1007/978-3-642-29011-4_31

4. Berlekamp, E.R., McEliece, R.J., van Tilborg, H.C.A.: On the inherent intractability of certain coding problems (corresp.). IEEE Trans. Inf. Theory **24**(3), 384–386 (1978). https://doi.org/10.1109/TIT.1978.1055873

5. Branco, P., Mateus, P.: A traceable ring signature scheme based on coding theory. In: Ding, J., Steinwandt, R. (eds.) PQCrypto 2019. LNCS, vol. 11505, pp. 387–403. Springer, Cham (2019). https://doi.org/10.1007/978-3-030-25510-7_21

6. Camenisch, J., Lysyanskaya, A.: An efficient system for non-transferable anonymous credentials with optional anonymity revocation. In: Pfitzmann, B. (ed.) EUROCRYPT 2001. LNCS, vol. 2045, pp. 93–118. Springer, Heidelberg (2001). https://doi.org/10.1007/3-540-44987-6_7

7. Cao, Y., Wang, Y., Ding, Y., Guo, Z., Yang, C., Liang, H.: A lightweight PUF-based group authentication scheme for privacy-preserving metering data collection in smart grid **562**, 321–340 (2023). https://doi.org/10.1007/978-3-031-54528-3_18

8. Chaudhry, S.A., Nebhen, J., Yahya, K., Al-Turjman, F.M.: A privacy enhanced authentication scheme for securing smart grid infrastructure. IEEE Trans. Ind. Informatics **18**(7), 5000–5006 (2022). https://doi.org/10.1109/TII.2021.3119685

9. Chaum, D.: Blind Signatures for Untraceable Payments. In: Chaum, D., Rivest, R.L., Sherman, A.T. (eds.) Advances in Cryptology, pp. 199–203. Springer, Boston (1983). https://doi.org/10.1007/978-1-4757-0602-4_18

10. Diao, F., Zhang, F., Cheng, X.: A privacy-preserving smart metering scheme using linkable anonymous credential. IEEE Trans. Smart Grid **6**(1), 461–467 (2015). https://doi.org/10.1109/TSG.2014.2358225

11. Fang, X., Misra, S., Xue, G., Yang, D.: Smart grid the new and improved power grid: a survey. IEEE Commun. Surv. Tutorials **14**(4), 944–980 (2012). https://doi.org/10.1109/SURV.2011.101911.00087

12. Fiat, A., Shamir, A.: How to prove yourself: practical solutions to identification and signature problems. In: Odlyzko, A.M. (ed.) CRYPTO 1986. LNCS, vol. 263, pp. 186–194. Springer, Heidelberg (1987). https://doi.org/10.1007/3-540-47721-7_12

13. Gai, N., Xue, K., Zhu, B., Yang, J., Liu, J., He, D.: An efficient data aggregation scheme with local differential privacy in smart grid. Digit. Commun. Networks **8**(3), 333–342 (2022). https://doi.org/10.1016/j.dcan.2022.01.004

14. Gao, Y., Al-Sarawi, S.F., Abbott, D.: Physical unclonable functions. Nature Electron. **3**(2), 81–91 (2020). https://doi.org/10.1038/s41928-020-0372-5

15. Giaconi, G., Gündüz, D., Poor, H.V.: 10 smart meter data privacy. advanced data analytics for power systems p. 230 (2021). https://arxiv.org/pdf/2009.01364

16. Gilbert, E.N.: A comparison of signalling alphabets. Bell Syst. Tech. J. **31**(3), 504–522 (1952). https://doi.org/10.1002/j.1538-7305.1952.tb01393.x

17. Goldwasser, S., Kalai, Y.T., Peikert, C., Vaikuntanathan, V.: Robustness of the learning with errors assumption. pp. 230–240 (2010). http://conference.iiis.tsinghua.edu.cn/ICS2010/content/papers/19.html

18. Harishma, B., et al.: Safe is the new smart: PUF-based authentication for load modification-resistant smart meters. IEEE Trans. Dependable Secure Comput. **19**(1), 663–680 (2022). https://doi.org/10.1109/TDSC.2020.2992801

19. Hart, G.: Nonintrusive appliance load monitoring. Proc. IEEE **80**(12), 1870–1891 (1992). https://doi.org/10.1109/5.192069

20. Li, D., Yang, Q., Zhang, F., Wang, Y., Qian, Y., An, D.: Research on privacy issues in smart metering system: an improved TCN-based NILM attack method and practical DRL-based rechargeable battery assisted privacy preserving method. IEEE Trans. Autom. Sci. Eng. **21**(3), 2882–2899 (2024). https://doi.org/10.1109/TASE.2023.3270543

21. Liu, J.K., Wei, V.K., Wong, D.S.: Linkable spontaneous anonymous group signature for Ad Hoc groups. In: Wang, H., Pieprzyk, J., Varadharajan, V. (eds.) ACISP 2004. LNCS, vol. 3108, pp. 325–335. Springer, Heidelberg (2004). https://doi.org/10.1007/978-3-540-27800-9_28
22. Liu, X., Wang, L.P.: A postquantum linkable ring signature scheme from coding theory. Secur. Commun. Networks **2023**(1), 1794053 (2023). https://doi.org/10.1155/2023/1794053
23. Marandi, A., Alves, P.G.M.R., Aranha, D.F., Jacobsen, R.H.: Lattice-based homomorphic encryption for privacy-preserving smart meter data analytics. Comput. J. **67**(5), 1687–1698 (2023).https://doi.org/10.1093/comjnl/bxad093
24. Natgunanathan, I., Hossain, M.B., Xiang, Y., Gao, L., Peng, D., Li, J.: Progressive average-based smart meter privacy enhancement using rechargeable batteries. IEEE Internet Things J. **6**(6), 9816–9828 (2019). https://doi.org/10.1109/JIOT.2019.2932085
25. National Institute of Standards and Technology: SHA-3 Standard: Permutation-Based Hash and Extendable-Output Functions. Technical Report FIPS PUB 202, U.S. Department of Commerce (2015). https://doi.org/10.6028/NIST.FIPS.202
26. Prateek, K., Das, M., Surve, S., Maity, S., Amin, R.: Q-secure-p^2-sma: Quantum-secure privacy- preserving smart meter authentication for unbreakable security in smart grid. IEEE Trans. Netw. Serv. Manag. **21**(5), 5149–5163 (2024). https://doi.org/10.1109/TNSM.2024.3357103
27. Rivest, R.L., Shamir, A., Tauman, Y.: How to leak a secret. In: Boyd, C. (ed.) ASIACRYPT 2001. LNCS, vol. 2248, pp. 552–565. Springer, Heidelberg (2001). https://doi.org/10.1007/3-540-45682-1_32
28. Schirmer, P.A., Mporas, I.: Non-intrusive load monitoring: a review. IEEE Trans. Smart Grid **14**(1), 769–784 (2023). https://doi.org/10.1109/TSG.2022.3189598
29. Stern, J.: A new identification scheme based on syndrome decoding. In: Stinson, D.R. (ed.) CRYPTO 1993. LNCS, vol. 773, pp. 13–21. Springer, Heidelberg (1994). https://doi.org/10.1007/3-540-48329-2_2
30. Strategy, N.M.G.: Advanced metering infrastructure. US Department of Energy Office of Electricity and Energy Reliability (2008). https://www.smart-energy.com/wp-content/uploads/i/AMI%2520White%2520paper%2520final%2520021108%2520%25282%2529%2520APPROVED_2008_02_12.pdf
31. Sui, Z., Li, J.: An auditable and efficient prepaid scheme with privacy preservation in smart grids. pp. 48–55 (2023). https://doi.org/10.1109/BIGCOMP57234.2023.00016
32. Sun, S.-F., Au, M.H., Liu, J.K., Yuen, T.H.: RingCT 2.0: a compact accumulator-based (linkable ring signature) protocol for blockchain cryptocurrency monero. In: Foley, S.N., Gollmann, D., Snekkenes, E. (eds.) ESORICS 2017. LNCS, vol. 10493, pp. 456–474. Springer, Cham (2017). https://doi.org/10.1007/978-3-319-66399-9_25
33. Tian, Y.: Research on privacy-preserving data collection scheme for post-quantum smart grid (in Chinese) (2020)
34. Tian, Y., Zhang, H., Xie, S., Zhang, F.: Post-quantum privacy preserving smart metering system. J. Comput. Res. Dev. **56**(10), 2229–2242 (2019). https://doi.org/10.7544/issn1000-1239.2019.20190402
35. Tsang, P.P., Wei, V.K.: Short linkable ring signatures for E-Voting, E-Cash and attestation. In: Deng, R.H., Bao, F., Pang, H.H., Zhou, J. (eds.) ISPEC 2005. LNCS, vol. 3439, pp. 48–60. Springer, Heidelberg (2005). https://doi.org/10.1007/978-3-540-31979-5_5

36. U.S. Department of Energy: 2020 smart grid system report (2022). https://www.energy.gov/oe/articles/2020-smart-grid-system-report
37. Varshamov, R.R.: Estimate of the number of signals in error correcting codes. Docklady Akad. Nauk, SSSR **117**, 739–741 (1957). https://cir.nii.ac.jp/crid/1572543024443421056
38. Xu, W., Sun, J., Cardell-Oliver, R., Mian, A., Hong, J.B.: A privacy-preserving framework using homomorphic encryption for smart metering systems. Sensors **23**(10), 4746 (2023). https://doi.org/10.3390/s23104746

High-Throughput Threshold SM2 Signatures with Robustness

Zheng Qian[1,3], Yanmei Cao[2,3], Ling Liu[1,3], and Jing Pan[1,3(✉)]

[1] Guangzhou Institute of Technology, Xidian University, Guangzhou 510555, China
`liuling@xidian.edu.cn`
[2] School of Cyberspace Security, Xi'an University of Posts and Telecommunications, Xi'an 710121, China
[3] State Key Laboratory of Integrated Services Networks, Xidian University, Xi'an 710071, China
`jinglap@aliyun.com`

Abstract. Threshold signature is a distributed cryptography protocol that allows any set of participants greater than a given threshold to collectively generate a valid signature, but any below the threshold cannot. Although many threshold SM2 signatures have been proposed, they are suffering from inefficiency and impracticality. In this paper, we propose the first high-throughput and robust threshold SM2 signature protocol. Our protocol captures fewer rounds of communication (three rounds of message-independent precomputation and one round of signature generation), and enables the batch generation of $\Omega(n^2)$ signatures per run. This significantly reduces the total overhead to only $O(1)$ communication complexity and $O(\log n)$ computation complexity per signature, comparable to state-of-the-art $O(n)$ overhead. Also, our protocol is operated on an asynchronous broadcast channel rather than previous synchronous networks. Moreover, the protocol enjoys the robustness, ensuring signature generation even in the presence of malicious behavior.

Keywords: Threshold signature · SM2 signature · Secret sharing · Verifiable complaint

1 Introduction

Threshold signature (TS) [8,11,20] is a fundamental threshold cryptography primitive, where any t-out-of-n participants are allowed to collectively generate a valid signature, but any set of parties less than t cannot. It has found wide applications in various contexts such as key custody and multi-signatures [9,10].

Since the concept was first introduced by Desmedt et al. [9], threshold signature has witnessed significant progress. In the pioneering works [9,10], Desmedt et al. put forward a formal framework for t-out-of-n signatures along with several RSA instantiations, which drives cryptographers to seek alternative methods from Schnorr signatures. Garillot et al. [13] presented a threshold Schnorr signature with stateless deterministic signing, which eliminates the randomness dependency and state management while ensuring security, but it is suffering from inefficiency in practice due to the use of expensive zero-knowledge proofs. This scheme was then improved by presenting a round-optimized design (only with two rounds of communication) in [21]. Subsequently, Bellaire et al. [2] considered a tradeoff between security and efficiency, while Benhamouda et al. [4] presented a throughput scheme named SPRINT which allows generating batch Schnorr signatures at a low amortized cost. Also, threshold ECDSA has received close attention. Gennaro et al. [14] proposed the first multi-party ECDSA signature protocol that supports arbitrary thresholds (with $t \leq n$) and features an efficient dealerless key generation mechanism. This protocol significantly outperforms existing schemes in terms of computational speed and communication complexity. Later, Groth et al. [17] described another efficient signature protocol, which guarantees output delivery over asynchronous channels. In this protocol, lost shares can be reconstructed by honest nodes using a verifiable complaint mechanism.

Unlike versatile investigations on threshold RSA, ECDSA and Schnorr signatures, the research on the threshold SM2 signature, which is the Chinese standardized signature algorithm over elliptic curve, is still quite small. Yang et al. [27] presented a trustless center scheme with honest majority. It requires a point-to-point channel with $O(n^2)$ communication complexity per signature. In contrast, Hou et al. [19] proposed a UC-secure [7] scheme, but it only supports two-party signing and captures computational bottlenecks and expensive key generation. More recently, a non-interactive scheme with malicious majority (from zero-knowledge proofs) was presented by Chen et al. [22], but it gets bad efficiency (multiple rounds of communication and high complexity). We note that all of the above SM2 solutions produce only one signature per run and need multiple communication rounds over synchronous networks, which is less practical for real-world depoloyment.

In this paper, we propose a *high-throughput* threshold SM2 scheme that allows producing $\Omega(n^2)$ signatures per run with fewer rounds of communication, working over asynchronous networks[1]. Roughly speaking, we combine *packed secret sharing* with *super-invertible matrix* techniques to generate more random numbers, enabling parallel high-throughput signature generation. Furthermore, by improving an agreement protocol and setting the number of participants appropriately to maintain an honest majority, our signature protocol achieves *robustness* (robustness means that the signature protocol always produces a valid signature) against malicious adversaries. In particular, our protocol only needs four rounds of communication (three for generating ephemeral randomness and public value, and one for non-interactive signature generation). In the pessimistic state, *two additional rounds* may be needed during the ephemeral randomness and public value generation phase. But they can be avoided via appropriate parameter setting.

---

[1] In the asynchronous network, for any message sent, the adversary can delay its delivery by any finite amount of time, so that there is no bound on the time to deliver a message.

1.1 Our Contributions

Inspired by the threshold Schnorr signature [4], we propose a high-throughput threshold SM2 signature scheme that guarantees robustness in asynchronous networks. This is the first implementation of such a high-throughput threshold SM2 signature scheme that can batch generate $\Omega(n^2)$ signatures in a single protocol run. It requires only $O(1)$ communication complexity per signature, and the computation complexity is $O(\log n)$. Unlike prior non-robust synchronous schemes [22, 27], our approach prevents protocol outages under malicious attacks by expanding participants to ensure an honest majority. This enhancement ensures reliable delivery of signature outputs in asynchronous networks. Moreover, we reduce the round of communication from the state of art 8 to just 4, which includes three rounds of message-independent precomputation followed by one-round non-interactive signature generation.

1.2 Technical Overview

We provide a rough technical outline of our high-throughput SM2 signing protocol that achieves robustness in asynchronous networks. As in previous SM2 threshold signatures [26, 27], our design also faces the following problems.

Problem 1: Multiple participants (each of them holds a secret share d_i) need to collectively compute the inverse of secret d without revealing their individual shares.

Problem 2: When multiplying two random polynomials, the result may be non-completely random, i.e., the coefficients of fresh polynomial become correlated, which may compromise security.

Let us recall the previous approaches towards the above problems [26, 27]. In their approaches, by using the Joint-RSS algorithm [3, 24, 27] (described later in this section), participants cooperate to obtain their own shares d_i and k_i, where d_i and k_i are shares of the secret key d and random number k, respectively. Then, each participant can locally compute a share $[(1+d)^{-1}]_i$ of $(1+d)^{-1}$ and a share $(k-rd)_i$ of $(k-rd)$. We note that **Problem 1** occurs when we compute $[(1+d)^{-1}]_i$, which has been addressed in [15]. Specifically, each participant first generates a share c_i of a random number c by using the Joint-RSS algorithm, then computes $z_i = c_i(1+d_i)$ and broadcasts it, which allows any participant to interpolate to derive the public value $z = c(1+d)$. Finally, each participant can compute $z^{-1}c_i$ and then collaborate to interpolate $(1+d)^{-1}$.

Also, **Problem 2** occurs when participants broadcast $z_i = c_i(1+d_i)$. To end it, they use the Joint-ZSS algorithm [3, 26, 27] (described later in this section) to introduce a random polynomial with zero free term. This ensures that the secret is the same while the coefficients of the new polynomial are *completely random again*. Now, any participant can locally compute the signature shares and broadcast them (again taking the solution to **Problem 2**), thus aggregating signatures. But this approach is not applicable to the case of signing multiple messages at once. To enhance these solutions, we let each shared polynomial pack a values rather than just one, while executing the Joint-RSS algorithm to generate the temporary random number k.

Unfortunately, using packing technique only for temporary random polynomials increases the number of interaction rounds. Specifically, we need compute $(s_1, \cdots, s_a) = (1 + d)^{-1}[(k_1, k_2, \cdots, k_a) - (r_1, r_2, \cdots, r_a) \cdot d]$. We note that it is impossible to compute these a signatures at once by only sharing a polynomial which contains a single private key d, and it seems to require multiple interactions. Thus, we modify it to share a a-dimension vector like $(d, d, ..., d)$ rather than a single long-lived key d, here we take a packed polynomial $\mathbf{f}$ such that $\mathbf{f}(1 - a) = \cdots = \mathbf{f}(-1) = \mathbf{f}(0) = d$. Now, participants can locally batch compute all signatures in parallel by broadcasting the signature shares only once, eliminating those unnecessary interactions.

To batch generate signatures, participants must multiply the random number shares $\{k_{i,j}\}_{j=0}^{n}$ by a super-invertible matrix [18] (instead of simply summing shares[2]) to get more shares k_i^u, $u \in [b]$, then compute and broadcast all signature shares $s_i^u = z^{-1} \cdot c_i \cdot (k_i^u - \mathbf{z}^u(i) \cdot d_i) + o_i$. Note that if we only use identical zero-secret shares o_i, some matters would arise: (1) Coefficients of the product polynomial are incompletely random; (2) **Problem 1** occurs when several signature shares add the same o_i in the phase of generating signature shares. To end it, we let participants broadcast $s_i^u = z^{-1} \cdot c_i \cdot (k_i^u - \mathbf{z}^u(i) \cdot d_i) + \mathbf{z}^u(i) \cdot o_i$. With this approach, we achieve secure high-throughput signature generations.

For achieving robustness, a nature intuition is to set up a sufficiently large number of participants to guarantee an honest majority, instead of using complete secret sharing [23] at the secret sharing phase. However, this approach will increase protocol completion delays and enables attackers to create high-latency executions in asynchronous settings. To address it, we only require a sufficiently large subset of honest parties to know their shares, and do not require all honest participants to receive their shares. Unlike in [17], it does not need to help the participants who broadcast the complaint to recover shares. Our approach can significantly reduce the rounds of communication to just four.

Joint-RSS. The Joint-RSS [3, 24, 27] algorithm allows each participant to independently generate random shares and share them, and ultimately construct a joint secret by summing all the shares. Specifically, assume there are n participants $\mathsf{U}_1, \mathsf{U}_2, \cdots, \mathsf{U}_n$, each of them holds a share d_i of secret d and creates a random degree-t polynomial $\mathbf{f}_i(X) = \sum_{j=0}^{t} a_j^{(i)} X^j$ with $\mathbf{f}_i(0) = a_0^{(i)} = d_i$. Then, for each $j \in [n]$, U_i computes shares $\mathbf{f}_i(j)$ and sends them to other participants using secret sharing. The participant U_i receives the shares $\mathbf{f}_j(i)$ sent by the other participants and computes $d_i' = \sum_{j=1}^{n} \mathbf{f}_j(i)$ as its secret share. Finally, the secret $d = \sum_{i=1}^{t+1} \lambda_i d_i'$ can be reconstructed, where λ_i are the Lagrange coefficients.

Joint-ZSS. [3, 26, 27] This algorithm is actually the same as the Joint-RSS except one difference where we set the shared secret value $d = 0$. With this

---

[2] Traditional summations only produce a random number share like $k_i = \sum_{j=1}^{n} k_{i,j}$.

algorithm, all participants need to set $a_0^{(i)} = 0$ and then perform operations consistent with the Joint-RSS algorithm to obtain their shares. Finally, the secret d can be recovered by Lagrange interpolation.

1.3 Organization

In Sect. 2, we review the SM2 signature algorithm and several basic techniques need for our construction. Section 3 describes the threshold SM2 signature scheme in details. In Sect. 4, a provable security analysis of our protocol is performed. In Sect. 5, an efficiency analysis is provided.

2 Preliminaries

Notations. In our paper, we use $\mathcal{D}$ and $\mathcal{P}$ to denote the dealer and the shareholder, respectively. The lowercase letters like a denote integers, while the uppercase letters like A represent group elements, among which G indicates a group generator. We take bold lowercase letters like $\mathbf{a}$ and those like $\hat{\mathbf{a}}$ to represent polynomials and polynomial commitments, while the bold uppercase letters like $\mathbf{A}$ represent matrices. Also, we use $[n]$ to denote the integer range $[1, n]$.

2.1 SM2 Signature Algorithm

We review the SM2 digital signature algorithm [1]. It operates on an elliptic curve group defined over a finite field $\mathbb{F}_p$ of prime order p, where G serves as a base point of prime order q. On input the security parameter λ, the signature algorithm consists of three algorithms **KeyGen**, **Sign**, **Verify** as shown in Fig. 1.

KeyGen(1^λ):

1: $d \xleftarrow{\$} [1, q-1]$, set $sk = d$;
2: $P \leftarrow d \cdot G$, set $pk = P$;
3: Return (pk, sk).

Sign(sk, M):

1: $e \leftarrow \text{Hash}(M)$;
2: $k \xleftarrow{\$} [1, q-1]$;
3: $(x_1, y_1) \leftarrow k \cdot G$;
4: $r \leftarrow (x_1 + e) \bmod q$;
5: If $r = 0$ or $r + k = q$, restart from step 2;
6: $s \leftarrow (1 + d)^{-1} \cdot (k - rd) \bmod q$;
7: If $s = 0$, restart from step 2;
8: Return $\sigma = (r, s)$.

Verify(pk, M, σ):

1: Verify $r, s \in [1, q-1]$ and $r + s \neq q$;
2: $e \leftarrow \text{Hash}(M)$;
3: $t \leftarrow (r + s) \bmod q$;
4: $(x_1', y_1') \leftarrow s \cdot G + t \cdot P$;
5: $r' \leftarrow (e + x_1') \bmod q$;
6: If $r' = r$, return true, else return false.

Fig. 1. The SM2 signature algorithm.

2.2   Packed Secret Sharing

Before introducing the packed secret sharing, we first review the Shamir secret sharing [25] that simply consists of two algorithms Secret Sharing and Secret Reconstruction. To share a secret $s \in \mathbb{F}_p$ among a group of n participants, we can take a random polynomial $\mathbf{f}(X) = s + a_1 X + a_2 X^2 + \cdots + a_d X^d$ to compute n secret shares like $\mathbf{f}(i) = s_i$ for $i = 1, ..., n$, where all coefficients $a_i, i \in [d]$ are sampled at random from $\mathbb{F}_p$. When it comes to reconstruction, one can use the Lagrange interpolation method as follows

$$s = \sum_{i=1}^{d+1} \mathbf{f}(i) \cdot \mathbf{l}_i(0), \tag{1}$$

where $\mathbf{l}_i(0)$ is the value of the Lagrangian basis polynomial at point 0, i.e., $\mathbf{l}_i(0) = \prod_{j=1, j \neq i}^{d+1} \frac{X_j}{X_j - X_i}$.

The packed secret sharing [12] extends the Shamir's to encode multiple secrets into a polynomial. Using this method, we can generate multiple secrets from a single secret sharing. To pack a secrets (where $a \geq 1$), we need to pre-select a positions, denote as e_i for $i \in [a]$. This process is defined by the packed polynomial as

$$\mathbf{g}(X) := \mathbf{f}(X) \prod_{i=1}^{a} (X - e_i) + \sum_{i=1}^{a} s_i \cdot \mathbf{l}_i(X), \tag{2}$$

where $\mathbf{l}_i(X) = \prod_{j=1, j \neq i}^{a} \frac{X - X_j}{X_i - X_j}$. The secrets s_i can be reconstructed by any subset of at least $d + a$ participants.

2.3   Feldman's Evaluation Point Commitments

The original Feldman's commitment [16] is a *Verifiable Secret Sharing* scheme that hides polynomial coefficients with verifiability. It is seen interesting applications in threshold cryptography. Actually, with the commitment one can conduct share verification while preventing malicious submission of shares with secret privacy. For a polynomial $\mathbf{f}(X) = a_0 + a_1 X + a_2 X^2 + \cdots + a_d X^d$, its Feldman's commitment is given by

$$\hat{\mathbf{f}} = \{a_i \cdot G : i = 0, 1, \cdots, d\}. \tag{3}$$

To validate whether $\mathbf{f}(i)$ is correctly computed, one just needs to check $\mathbf{f}(i) \cdot G \overset{?}{=} \sum_{j=0}^{d} i^j \cdot (a_j \cdot G)$. One downside is that it requires a large number of exponential operations for each validation. Benhamouda et al. [4] found that using commitment to polynomial evaluation points can significantly save verification time while keeping the same security. The commitment is modified as

$$\hat{\mathbf{f}} = \{\mathbf{f}(i) \cdot G : i = 0, 1, \cdots, d\}. \tag{4}$$

The verification is accordingly modified as $\mathbf{f}(i) \cdot G \overset{?}{=} \sum_{j=0}^{d} \lambda_{i,j} \cdot (\mathbf{f}(j) \cdot G)$, where $\lambda_{i,j}$ are the Lagrangian coefficients. It is seen that this scheme only needs simple interpolation for verification and is more suitable for scenarios with a large number of verifications.

2.4   Super-Invertible Matrices

We recall the super-invertible matrix [18] introduced by Hirt et al., which is typically used to efficiently sample secret sharings of random values. Given a m-by-n matrix $\mathbf{A} = (a_{i,j})_{i\in[m],j\in[n]}$ and a subset $\mathcal{C} \subset \{1,\ldots,n\}$ where $n \geq m$. Let $\mathbf{A}_\mathcal{C} = (a_{i,j})_{i\in[m],j\in\mathcal{C}}$ be a matrix exactly consisting of columns $j \in \mathcal{C}$ from $\mathbf{A}$. We say $\mathbf{A}$ is super-invertible if $\mathbf{A}_\mathcal{C}$ is invertible for any $\mathcal{C} \subset \{1,\ldots,n\}$ with $|\mathcal{C}| = m$.

In distributed settings, on input a vector of n secret shares $(s_1,\cdots,s_n)^T$, we can utilize a super-invertible matrix $\mathbf{A}$ as above to generate m independent secrets as follows,

$$(s_1,\cdots,s_m)^T = \mathbf{A} \cdot (s_1,\cdots,s_n)^T. \tag{5}$$

In our scheme, we will utilize this method to allow multiple participants to collaborate and produce many more secrets without increasing network bandwidth.

3   Our Scheme

In this section, we first introduce the multi-set agreement protocol in Sect. 3.1, which is used to ensure that all valid participants reach a consensus to determine multiple sets and compute the secret shares for generating signatures. We then describe the protocol design in details in Sect. 3.2 along with correctness.

3.1   The Multi-set Agreement Protocol

In distributed signatures, it is crucial for parties to run an agreement protocol to agree on a set of correctly dealt shares. Therefore, we utilize public key encryption mechanism and operate over an asynchronous total-order broadcast channel. This approach guarantees the final delivery of messages from honest parties, ensures sender authentication, and maintains prefix consistency (i.e., the views of any two honest parties are such that one is a prefix of the other). Recall that a total-order broadcast channel provides the following guarantees:

- Messages sent by an honest party will eventually be visible (without modification) to other honest parties. However, the adversary can alter the sequence of delivering messages to the broadcast channel.
- At some point, the views of two honest parties regarding a broadcast channel are such that one view is a prefix of the other.
- Messages received by honest parties were indeed sent by themselves.

In our construction, each participant would obtain shares of three different randomness, so we need to build a multi-set agreement protocol to determine three different sets. The basic idea is to adapt the full agreement protocol in [4] to our scheme. Due to technical reasons, we modify the initial conditions and split the protocol into two phases. In our protocol, we require more random numbers and thus need to design more sets. Specifically, we need to add to three

---

Parameters: $b, d, m \geq t + 1$.

Precondition: Let $\Upsilon_1 = \left((E^k_{i,j}, \hat{\mathbf{h}}_i), (E^c_{i,j}, \hat{\mathbf{c}}_i), (E^0_{i,j}, \hat{\mathbf{o}}_i) \right)^n_{j=0}, \Upsilon_2 = \left(E^k_{i,j}, \hat{\mathbf{h}}_i \right)^n_{j=0}$. We require $m \geq t + 1$ to ensure that there is at least one honest dealer in the set $\mathsf{QUAL}_{k'}$ for $k' = 2, 3$, and that **Phase 2** does not add any more. Initialize $\mathsf{QUAL}_k = \mathsf{BAD}_k = \mathsf{HOLD} = \emptyset$.

Phase 1

Shareholder $\mathcal{P}_j$:

1. Add the first m dealers who broadcast Υ_1 to each QUAL_k for $k \in [3]$, i.e., $\mathsf{QUAL}_k := \mathsf{QUAL}_k \cup \{\mathcal{D}_i\}$. Keep adding operation until $|\mathsf{QUAL}_k| \geq m$.
2. Broadcast a single message which includes all verifiable complaints against locally bad dealers in QUAL_k. Otherwise, send an empty set (indicating that all validated shares are valid).
3. After collecting verifiable valid complaints broadcast by the first d shareholders, set $\mathsf{HOLD} := \mathsf{HOLD} \cup \{\mathcal{P}_j\}, \mathsf{QUAL}_k := \mathsf{QUAL}_k \setminus \{\mathcal{D}_i\}$ and $\mathsf{BAD}_k := \mathsf{BAD}_k \cup \{\mathcal{D}_i\}$ for each verifiable complaint against dealer $\mathcal{D}_i$.
4. Determine whether $|\mathsf{QUAL}_1| \geq b$. If not, execute **Phase 2**. Otherwise, output $\mathsf{HOLD}, \mathsf{QUAL}_k, \mathsf{BAD}_k$, and halt.

Phase 2

Shareholder $\mathcal{P}_j$:

1. Keep $\mathsf{QUAL}_k, \mathsf{BAD}_k$, and set $\mathsf{HOLD} = \emptyset$.
2. Continue to add new dealers who broadcasts Υ_2 (those whose broadcasts were not initiated by **Phase 1**) to QUAL_1 like $\mathsf{QUAL}_1 := \mathsf{QUAL}_1 \cup \{\mathcal{D}_i\}$ such that $|\mathsf{QUAL}_1| \geq b + t$.
3. Broadcast a single message which includes all verifiable complaints against locally bad dealers in QUAL_1. Otherwise, send an empty set.
4. After collecting again the verifiable valid complaints broadcast by the d shareholders (which may intersect with the d shareholder part of **Phase 1**), set $\mathsf{HOLD} := \mathsf{HOLD} \cup \{\mathcal{P}_j\}, \mathsf{QUAL}_1 := \mathsf{QUAL}_1 \setminus \{\mathcal{D}_i\}$ and $\mathsf{BAD}_1 := \mathsf{BAD}_1 \cup \{\mathcal{D}_i\}$.
5. Output $\mathsf{HOLD}, \mathsf{QUAL}_k, \mathsf{BAD}_k$, and halt.

Fig. 2. The multi-set agreement protocol

separate QUAL's (and corresponding three BAD's) to polynomials $\mathbf{h}_i$, $\mathbf{c}_i$ and $\mathbf{o}_i$, respectively. We however only have one shareholder set HOLD, since we need the same shareholders[3] to obtain three random number shares, where QUAL_k and BAD_k, with $k \in [3]$ consist of qualified and corrupt dealers, respectively, and HOLD consists of honest shareholders. These sets satisfy the following conditions:

1. No shareholder in HOLD complains against any dealer in QUAL_k.
2. Every dealer in BAD_k has at least one shareholder that lodged a verifiable complaint against them.
3. Every shareholder in HOLD receives valid shares from each dealer in QUAL_k.

---

[3] Dealers distribute shares, while shareholders receive them and compute signatures. A dealer may later act as a shareholder in subsequent phases.

$\mathcal{D}$-commitment step

Dealer $\mathcal{D}_i$(**Phase 1**):

1. Choose random polynomials $\mathbf{h}_i$, $\mathbf{c}_i$ and $\mathbf{o}_i$ (where we pick $\mathbf{o}_i(0) = 0$), of degrees $t+2a-2$, $t+a-1$, $2t+2a-2$, and compute polynomial commitments $\hat{\mathbf{h}}_i = \{\mathbf{h}_i(k) \cdot G : k \in [1-a, t+a-1]\}$, $\hat{\mathbf{c}}_i = \{\mathbf{c}_i(l) \cdot G : l \in [0, t+a-1]\}$, $\hat{\mathbf{o}}_i = \{\mathbf{o}_i(m) \cdot G : m \in [0, 2t+2a-2]\}$.
2. Compute shares $\rho_{i,j} = \mathbf{h}_i(j)$, $\beta_{i,j} = \mathbf{c}_i(j)$, $o_{i,j} = \mathbf{o}_i(j)$ and their encryptions $E_{i,j}^k = \mathrm{ENC}_{pk_j}(\rho_{i,j})$, $E_{i,j}^c = \mathrm{ENC}_{pk_j}(\beta_{i,j})$, $E_{i,j}^0 = \mathrm{ENC}_{pk_j}(o_{i,j})$.
3. Broadcast $\left((E_{i,j}^k, \hat{\mathbf{h}}_i), (E_{i,j}^c, \hat{\mathbf{c}}_i), (E_{i,j}^0, \hat{\mathbf{o}}_i)\right)_{j=0}^n$.

Dealer $\mathcal{D}_i$(**Phase 2**):

1. Choose a random degree-$(t+2a-2)$ polynomial $\mathbf{h}_i$, and compute polynomial commitment $\hat{\mathbf{h}}_i = \{\mathbf{h}_i(k) \cdot G : k \in [1-a, t+a-1]\}$.
2. Compute shares $\rho_{i,j} = \mathbf{h}_i(j)$ and their encryptions $E_{i,j}^k = \mathrm{ENC}_{pk_j}(\rho_{i,j})$.
3. Broadcast $\left(E_{i,j}^k, \hat{\mathbf{h}}_i\right)_{j=0}^n$.

Fig. 3. The $\mathcal{D}$-commitment step.

The agreement protocol starts running when dealer execute the $\mathcal{D}$-commitment step to broadcast Υ_1 as in Fig. 3. In **Phase 1**, each shareholder $\mathcal{P}_j$ adds the first m dealers who broadcast Υ_1 to all QUAL_k, then performs the $\mathcal{P}$-complain step to broadcast a verifiable valid complaint[4] against the corresponding dealer. Note that we only require at least b honest dealers in QUAL_1, and the number of honest dealers in $\mathsf{QUAL}_{k'}, k' = 2, 3$ only needs to reach the signing threshold. Thus, we set $m \geq t+1$ to ensure that the set $\mathsf{QUAL}_{k'}$ contains at least one honest dealer after **Phase 1** ends. If $|\mathsf{QUAL}_1| \geq b$ does not hold at **Phase 1**, the protocol turns to **Phase 2**. In this phase, the shareholders continue to add dealers who broadcast Υ_2 to QUAL_1 while retaining $\mathsf{QUAL}_{k'}$ until $|\mathsf{QUAL}_1| \geq b+t$. Now, it ensures that there are at least b honest dealers in QUAL_1, thus we output all sets. This approach significantly reduces the communication and computation overhead. The full protocol is provided in Fig. 2.

We can prove the above multi-set agreement protocol is correct in Theorem 1. The detailed proof is deferred to Appendix A.

Theorem 1. *Suppose the protocol is executed over a total-order broadcast channel, where at least d shareholders who initiate a valid complaint are honest. Assume that at least m dealers in* **Phase 1** *broadcast Υ_1, and at least $b+t-|QUAL_1|$ dealers in* **Phase 2** *broadcast Υ_2, where any honest dealer will not be complained by any shareholder in HOLD, and each dealer in BAD_k would be*

---

[4] A valid complaint occurs when $\mathcal{P}_j$ either broadcasts a proof of knowledge regarding the share of invalid random numbers or broadcasts an empty set.

$\mathcal{P}$-complain step

Shareholder $\mathcal{P}_j$(**Phase 1**):

1. Decrypt all ciphertexts $\rho_{i,j} = \mathrm{DEC}_{sk_j}(E^k_{i,j})$, $\beta_{i,j} = \mathrm{DEC}_{sk_j}(E^c_{i,j})$, $o_{i,j} = \mathrm{DEC}_{sk_j}(E^0_{i,j})$, then verify $\rho_{i,j} \stackrel{?}{=} \sum_{k=1-a}^{t+a-1} \lambda_{i,j,k} \cdot (\mathbf{h}_i(k) \cdot G)$, $\beta_{i,j} \stackrel{?}{=} \sum_{l=0}^{t+a-1} \lambda_{i,j,l} \cdot (\mathbf{c}_i(l) \cdot G)$, $o_{i,j} \stackrel{?}{=} \sum_{m=0}^{2t+2a-2} \lambda_{i,j,m} \cdot (\mathbf{o}_i(m) \cdot G)$, where $\lambda_{i,j,k}$, $\lambda_{i,j,l}$ and $\lambda_{i,j,m}$ are the corresponding Lagrangian coefficients.
2. Broadcast a single message which includes all verifiable complaints against the corresponding dealer. Otherwise, broadcast an empty set.

Shareholder $\mathcal{P}_j$(**Phase 2**):

1. Decrypt ciphertexts $\rho_{i,j} = \mathrm{DEC}_{sk_j}(E^k_{i,j})$, then verify that $\rho_{i,j} \stackrel{?}{=} \sum_{k=1-a}^{t+a-1} \lambda_{i,j,k} \cdot (\mathbf{h}_i(k) \cdot G)$, where $\lambda_{i,j,k}$ is the corresponding Lagrangian coefficients.
2. Broadcast a single message which includes all verifiable complaints against the corresponding dealer. Otherwise, broadcast an empty set.

Fig. 4. The $\mathcal{P}$-complain step.

lodged a verifiable complaint by at least one shareholder. Then all honest share-holders eventually terminate, all output the same set, and satisfy $|HOLD| \geq d$, $|QUAL_1| \geq b$, $|QUAL_{k'}| \geq 1$ for $k' = 2, 3$.

3.2   Construction

Our overall signing process consists of three-round temporary random number and public value generation, and one-round non-interactive signature generation. The full protocol is given in Fig. 5. It consists of the following four parts.

Setup: At this stage, with the Joint-RSS algorithm, each participant obtains a share d_i of secret d, with public keys $P_i = d_i \cdot G$ and $P = d \cdot G$. The long-lived key d is shared by a degree-$(t + a - 1)$ packing polynomial $\mathbf{f}$ and satisfies $\mathbf{f}(0) = \mathbf{f}(-1) = \cdots = \mathbf{f}(1 - a) = d$, for the reasons mentioned in Sect. 1.2.

Ephemeral Randomness and Public Value Generation: In this phase, we need to generate three ephemeral randomness k, c, o to generate a valid signature. Specifically, the randomness k and c are shared through a degree-$(t+2a-2)$ polynomial $\mathbf{h}$ packing a secrets and a degree-$(t + a - 1)$ polynomial $\mathbf{c}$ used to compute $(1 + d)^{-1}$, respectively. To make the coefficients of the multiplication of polynomials $\mathbf{h}$ and $\mathbf{c}$ completely random, we introduce another random polynomial $\mathbf{o}$ of degree $2t + 2a - 2$ with zero free term.

Then, each dealer runs the $\mathcal{D}$-commitment step in Fig. 3 thereby computing all share ciphertexts and polynomial commitments. After receiving these broadcast messages, the shareholders start executing the multi-set agreement protocol given in Fig. 2 by broadcasting the complaint through the $\mathcal{P}$-complain step in Fig. 4, so as to reach a consensus on the set QUAL_k, BAD_k, and HOLD that is visible on the broadcast channel, and then locally compute all random number shares. Here, we use the super-invertible matrix only for the share computation of randomness k (summing the shares using QUAL_1). We note that the generation of the shares of these b random numbers k is not related to the degree of the polynomial, but to the number of honest dealers in QUAL_1.

Finally, each shareholder $\mathcal{P}_j \in \mathsf{HOLD}$ computes the public value share $z_j = c_j (1 + d_j) + o_j$ and broadcasts it. The other participants verify that z_j is valid through bilinear maps on groups [6], and any shareholder can compute the public value z when $2t + 2a - 1$ valid z_j are collected.

Signature Share Generation: For the input of ab messages to be signed, each shareholder $\mathcal{P}_j \in \mathsf{HOLD}$ computes $r^{u,v}$ with $u \in [b], v \in [a]$ in parallel and embeds them in b polynomials $\mathbf{z}^u$ of degree $a - 1$, where $\mathbf{z}^u(j)$ serves as their shares. Finally, $\mathcal{P}_j$ can compute b shares of the signature polynomial packing a signature in parallel and broadcast them.

Signature Aggregation: In this phase, every shareholder $\mathcal{P}_j \in \mathsf{HOLD}$ (even those with missing shares) can verify the validity of each broadcast signature share s_j using bilinear maps. Once $2t + 3a - 2$ valid s_j are collected, they can be aggregated into the finally complete signature.

3.3   Correctness

The correctness consists of signing and verification. In our protocol, we suppose that each signer generates b signature shares $s_i^u = z^{-1} \cdot c_i \cdot (k_i^u - \mathbf{z}^u(i) \cdot d_i) + \mathbf{z}^u(i) \cdot o_i$ with $u \in [b]$, where $\mathbf{z}^u$ is a degree-$(a - 1)$ polynomial encoding a values like $\mathbf{z}^u(1 - v) = r^{u,v}$ with $v \in [a]$. For each $u \in [b]$, given any $2t + 3a - 2$ valid shares s_i^u, the a signatures $\mathbf{s}^u(1 - v) = (1 + d)^{-1}(k^{u,v} - r^{u,v} \cdot d)$ can be recovered via the interpolation method as usual. The detailed proof is shown below:

$$\mathbf{s}^u(1 - v) = \sum_{i=1}^{2t+3a-2} s_i^u \prod_{j=1,j \neq i}^{2t+3a-2} \frac{(1 - v) - X_j}{X_i - X_j}$$

$$= \sum_{i=1}^{2t+3a-2} \left(z^{-1} \cdot c_i \cdot (k_i^u - \mathbf{z}^u(i) \cdot d_i) + \mathbf{z}^u(i) \cdot o_i\right) \prod_{j=1,j \neq i}^{2t+3a-2} \frac{(1 - v) - X_j}{X_i - X_j}$$

$$= z^{-1} \cdot (c \cdot k^{u,v} - r^{u,v} \cdot c \cdot d) + r^{u,v} \cdot 0$$

$$= (1 + d)^{-1} \cdot (k^{u,v} - r^{u,v} \cdot d)$$

Parameters: $n, t, a \geq 1, b$.

Setup: Assume that $\mathbf{f}$ is a degree-$(t + a - 1)$ polynomial which packs a secrets and satisfies $\mathbf{f}(0) = \mathbf{f}(-1) = \cdots = \mathbf{f}(-a + 1) = d$. Each participant U_i with $i \in [n]$ holds a share $d_i = \mathbf{f}(i)$ of the private key d, and the corresponding public keys $P_i = d_i \cdot G$ and $P = d \cdot G$.

Ephemeral randomness and public value generation:

1. For each $i \in [n]$, the dealer $\mathcal{D}_i$ runs the $\mathcal{D}$-commitment step in Figure 3 to broadcast $\left((E_{i,j}^k, \hat{\mathbf{h}}_i), (E_{i,j}^c, \hat{\mathbf{c}}_i), (E_{i,j}^0, \hat{\mathbf{o}}_i) \right)_{j=0}^{n}$.

2. Each shareholder $\mathcal{P}_j$ runs the multi-set agreement protocol shown in Section 3.1 and the $\mathcal{P}$-complain step in Figure 4, thereby determining the sets QUAL_k, BAD_k, and $\mathsf{HOLD} \subseteq \{\mathsf{U}_1, \ldots, \mathsf{U}_n\}$ for $k \in [3]$.

3. Set $\mathbf{A} = [a_i^u] \in Z_p^{b \times |\mathsf{QUAL}_1|}$ as a super-invertible matrix. For $u \in [b]$, $v \in [a]$, define $R^{u,v} = \mathbf{A} \times \mathbf{h}_i(1 - v) \cdot G$, $k^{u,v} \cdot G = (x_{u,v}, y_{u,v})$. Each $\mathcal{P}_j \in \mathsf{HOLD}$ conducts the following:

   - Set $k_j^u = \sum_{i \in \mathsf{QUAL}_1} \mathbf{A} \cdot \rho_{i,j}$ for all $u \in [b]$.
   - Compute the random number of shares $c_j = \sum_{i \in \mathsf{QUAL}_2} \beta_{i,j}$ and $o_j = \sum_{i \in \mathsf{QUAL}_3} o_{i,j}$, then compute $z_j = c_j(1 + d_j) + o_j$ and broadcast it.
   - Verify z_j: $e(z_j \cdot G, G) \overset{?}{=} e(c_j \cdot G, G) \cdot e(c_j \cdot G, d_j \cdot G) \cdot e(o_j \cdot G, G)$.
   - Compute z: $z = \sum_{j=\mathcal{Q}} \lambda_j \cdot z_j$, where $\mathcal{Q}$ is any set of valid z_j of size $2t + 2a - 1$.

Signature share generation: For ab messages $M^{u,v}$, where $u \in [b]$ and $v \in [a]$, each $\mathcal{P}_j \in \mathsf{HOLD}$ computes the following in parallel for each $u \in [b]$:

1. Compute $r^{u,v} = \mathrm{Hash}(M^{u,v}) + x_{u,v}$.
2. Compute a degree-$(a - 1)$ polynomial $\mathbf{z}^u$ such that $\mathbf{z}^u(1 - v) = r^{u,v}$.
3. Output its signature share $s_j^u = z^{-1} \cdot c_j \cdot (k_j^u - \mathbf{z}^u(j) \cdot d_j) + \mathbf{z}^u(j) \cdot o_j$, where $\mathbf{s}^u = z^{-1} \cdot \mathbf{c} \cdot (\mathbf{h}^u - \mathbf{z}^u \cdot \mathbf{f}) + \mathbf{z}^u \cdot \mathbf{o}$.

Signature aggregation: Each $\mathcal{P}_j \in \mathsf{HOLD}$ verifies the validity of signature shares received,

$$e(s_j^u \cdot G, G) \overset{?}{=} (e(c_j \cdot G, k_j^u \cdot G))^{z^{-1}} \cdot (e(c_j \cdot G, d_j \cdot G))^{-z^{-1} \cdot \mathbf{z}^u(j)} \cdot (e(o_j \cdot G, G))^{\mathbf{z}^u(j)}$$

When $2t + 3a - 2$ valid signature shares s_j^u are collected, the signature polynomial $\mathbf{s}^u$ can be computed, where $s^{u,v} = \mathbf{s}^u(1 - v) = (1 + d)^{-1} \cdot (k^{u,v} - r^{u,v} \cdot d)$. Output the SM2 signature $(r^{u,v}, s^{u,v})$ on message $M^{u,v}$.

Fig. 5. Our signature protocol.

Finally, the verifier verifies each signature, which they first compute:

$$k \cdot G = \sum_{i \in \mathsf{QUAL}_1} k_i \cdot G \prod_{j \in \mathsf{QUAL}_1, j \neq i} \frac{X_j}{X_j - X_i}$$
$$= (x_1, y_1)$$

Then, it computes $r = x_1 + \text{Hash}(M)$ and gets a signature (r, s) whose verification process is shown as follows:

$$\begin{aligned}
(x_1', y_1') &= s \cdot G + (r + s) \cdot d \cdot G \\
&= (1 + d) \cdot s \cdot G + r \cdot d \cdot G \\
&= k \cdot G \\
&= (x_1, y_1).
\end{aligned}$$

This gives that $r' = x_1' + \text{Hash}(M) = r$, and the verification is passed.

4   Security Analysis

We show the threshold SM2 signature scheme is robust and unforgeable. Let us first recall the ECDLP assumption.

Definition 1 (ECDLP). *Let E be an elliptic curve over a finite field $\mathbb{F}_q$, where q is a prime power. Let P and Q be points on E. The Elliptic Curve Discrete Logarithm Problem (ECDLP) is to find an integer k such that $Q = k \cdot P$. The integer k is called the discrete logarithm of Q to base P.*

Definition 2 (Unforgeability). *A threshold-t signature scheme is unforgeable if for all PPT adversary $\mathcal{A}$, the probability of winning in the following game, $\text{Game}_{\mathcal{A}, \text{TS,UF}}(1^\lambda)$ is $\text{neg}(\lambda)$.*

1. *On input the security parameter λ, the challenger runs the $\text{KeyGen}(1^\lambda)$ and generates public parameters pp, verification key vk and set of n key shares $\{\text{sk}_i\}_{i=1}^n$. It sends pp and sk to $\mathcal{A}$.*
2. *$\mathcal{A}$ outputs a set $\mathcal{S}$ of corrupt participants with $\mathcal{S} \subset [n]$ and $|\mathcal{S}| = t - 1$, requesting key shares sk_i for $i \in \mathcal{S}$, then challenger provides $\{\text{sk}_i\}_{i \in \mathcal{S}}$ to $\mathcal{A}$.*
3. *Adversary $\mathcal{A}$ issues polynomial number of adaptive queries of the form (M, i), where $i \in [n] \setminus \mathcal{S}$, to get partial signature σ_i on M. For each query the challenger computes σ_i as $\text{Sign}(\text{pp}, \text{sk}_i, M)$ and provides it to $\mathcal{A}$.*
4. *The adversary $\mathcal{A}$ wins the game by producing a valid signature σ^* for a previously unsigned message M^* (i.e., $\text{Verify}(\text{vk}, M^*, \sigma^*) = 1$).*

Theorem 2 (Robustness). *Assume that the adversary $\mathcal{A}$ can control at most t members, if we set the number of members $n \geq 4t + 3a - 2$, then the scheme still successfully outputs the delivery signature.*

Proof. To reconstruct the signature polynomial $\mathbf{s}$ encoding a signatures, at least $2t + 3a - 2$ valid signature shares s_i are required. In our protocol, we do not assist shareholders in recovering lost shares. Thus, the HOLD allows at most t honest shareholders with missing shares (who can still participate in signing). By setting the total number of participants $n \geq 4t + 3a - 2$, the protocol can guarantee the output delivery of signatures while tolerating t malicious nodes.

Theorem 3 (Unforgeability). *Assuming that ECDLP holds, if the adversary $\mathcal{A}$ can control at most t members and have a view of the interactions in operation, then our signature protocol is unforgeable, i.e., even if there exist t malicious nodes, it remains impossible for $\mathcal{A}$ to forge a valid signature.*

Proof. Since our protocol operates in a broadcast channel, the adversary can utilize the public information to launch attacks. Under the ECDLP assumption, we will prove our protocol is unforgivable by analyzing the following potential attack scenarios:

Situation 1. The adversary attempts to reconstruct the secret by collecting sufficient secret shares, then uses it to forge a valid signature. Suppose that ECDLP is true, he cannot decipher the secret shares of other participants without knowing their private keys. The adversary can control at most t secret shares, and since the secret d is embedded in a degree-$(t + a - 1)$ polynomial $\mathbf{f}$, at least $t + a$ shares are required to reconstruct the secret. The same applies to the random numbers k and c. Therefore, the adversary cannot reconstruct the secret and forge a valid signature.

Situation 2. By leveraging public value shares z_i and signature shares s_i^u, the adversary attempts to break the secret and forge signatures. Since $z_i = c_i \cdot (1 + d_i) + o_i$ contains three unknowns, it is impossible to decipher any secret even if z_i is known. The same is true for the signature polynomial shares $s_i^u = z^{-1} c_i (k_i^u - \mathbf{z}^u(i) \cdot d_i) + \mathbf{z}^u(i) \cdot o_i$. Moreover, it is also difficult for the adversary to break the secret by exploiting the relationships among all s_i^u. By multiplying o_i with $\mathbf{z}^u(i)$ (where $u \in [b]$), we ensure that each of these b signature shares uses different $\mathbf{z}^u(i) \cdot o_i$. This construction eliminates linear dependencies, making it impossible for the adversary to break the secret and forge a valid signature.

Situation 3. The adversary attempts to exploit ROS-type attacks [5] in parallel environments to break secrets and then forge signatures. We note that individual signature protocols (e.g., Schnorr signatures) may suffer from ROS-type attacks when using parallel techniques, which are based on the principle of constructing systems of linear equations and using the response of random signals (e.g., hash functions) to form solvable systems. However, the signature equation of SM2 cannot be directly decomposed into linear combinatorial form, thus the protocol is secure.

5   Efficiency Analysis

In our protocol, the long-lived key d is shared only once and used for repeating run of the signing protocol, so we omit its efficiency impression[5] and focus on

---

[5] Its efficiency is not critical.

that from sharing temporary randomness and solving for $R^{u,v}$ with a super-invertible matrix. For simplicity, we take the number of group elements and scalars (resp. group operations and scalar operations) to denote communication (resp. computation) overhead, where group operations include the multiplication between scalars and group elements as well as the addition of group elements. Any operation outside group operation is called a scalar operation.

5.1 Communication Complexity

We analyse the communication overhead with respect to dealers and shareholders. The communication overhead consists of two parts: (1) Dealers share the polynomial shares and its commitments; (2) Shareholders broadcast complaints and signature shares.

Total Communication Overhead for n Dealers. For each dealer, the communication overhead arises from ciphertexts and polynomial commitments of the polynomials $\mathbf{h}_i, \mathbf{c}_i, \mathbf{o}_i$. We ignore the specific encryption algorithm when computing the ciphertexts. Note that we need to compute random number shares for n participants and the commitments of each polynomial (which includes $d + 1$ evaluation points commitments, where d is the degree of the polynomial). For polynomials $\mathbf{h}_i, \mathbf{c}_i$ and $\mathbf{o}_i$, the $\mathcal{D}_i$ needs $n(n + t + 2a - 1)$, $n(n + t + a)$ and $n(n + 2t + 2a - 1)$ group elements, respectively. Therefore, for n dealers, the total communication consists of $n(3n + 4t + 5a - 2)$ group elements.

Total Communication Overhead for n Shareholders. For each shareholder, the communication overhead primarily consists of complaints, signature shares, and public value shares. In our protocol, at most t shareholders may broadcast complaints. The communication overhead is summarized below.

- In the negative case, each message includes $3t$ complaints, each with just a few group elements, for an additional communication overhead of $O(t^2)$.
- To compute ab signatures, at least $2t + 3a - 2$ shareholders in HOLD need to broadcast b signature shares, resulting in a total of $(2t + 3a - 2)b$ scalars.
- To generate the public value z, shareholders must broadcast at least $2t+2a-1$ shares, requiring $2t + 2a - 1$ scalars.

Therefore, for n shareholders, the total communication overhead consists of $(2t + 3a - 2)b + (2t + 2a - 1) + O(t^2)$ group elements and $O(t^2)$ scalars. Since we generate ab SM2 signatures in each execution, the number of group elements consumed per signature is approximately:

$$\frac{n(3n + 4t + 5a - 2) + O(t^2)}{ab} = \frac{3n^2 + 4nt + 5na - 2n}{ab} + \frac{O(t^2)}{ab}$$

The number of scalar consumed per signature is approximately:

$$\frac{(2t + 3a - 2)b + (2t + 2a - 1) + O(t^2)}{ab} = \frac{2t + 3a - 2}{a} + \frac{2t + 2a - 1}{ab} + \frac{O(t^2)}{ab}$$

When $t = a = b = \Omega(n)$, the average communication overhead per signature is of size $O(1)$ for both group elements and scalars.

5.2   Computation Complexity

The primary computation overhead lies in the signing and verifying processes.

Signature Overhead. The computation overhead at signing phase consists of two main parts: (1) Dealers compute polynomial shares and commitments; (2) Shareholders compute $R^{u,v}$ and k_j^u for $u \in [b], v \in [a]$ with the super-invertible matrix.

For generating the signatures, the shareholders must first compute ab $R^{u,v}, u \in [b], v \in [a]$. For $i \in \mathsf{QUAL}_1$, we need to compute

$$R^{u,v} = \mathbf{A} \times \mathbf{h}_i(1 - v) \cdot G. \tag{6}$$

If we ignore the structure of the super-invertible matrix, it needs approximately $ab(b + t)$ group operations and $b(b + t)$ scalar operations. We use the ECFFT EXTEND solution in [4] to perform fewer operations. We summarize the result as follows:

- For polynomials $\mathbf{h}_i, \mathbf{c}_i$ and $\mathbf{o}_i$, the $\mathcal{D}_i$ needs $(n + t + 2a - 1)$, $(n + t + a)$ and $(n + 2t + 2a - 1)$ group operations, respectively, and the same n scalar operations.
- For matrix product, $\mathcal{D}_i$ needs $O(a{\cdot}\max(b, t) \log(\max(b, t)))$ group operations and $O(\max(b, t) \log(\max(b, t)))$ scalar operations.

Therefore, in the signing phase, each participant needs $O(a{\cdot}\max(b, t) \log(\max (b, t))) + 3n + 4t + 5a - 2$ group operations and $O(\max(b, t) \log(\max(b, t))) + 3n$ scalar operations.

Verification Overhead. In verifying phase, the main computation stems from share verification with respect to random numbers, public value and signature. We summarize the result as follows:

- Each shareholder must verify that they have received approximately $3n$ shares through the Lagrange interpolation, requiring roughly $3n(4t + 5a + 4)$ group operations.
- To generate the public value z, each shareholder needs to verify at least $2t + 2a - 1$ shares of z_i, which requires $2t + 2a - 1$ scalar operations.
- At least $2t + 3a - 2$ honest shareholders in HOLD need to broadcast b signature shares. Other shareholders then verify and aggregate these shares, requiring a total of $b(2t + 3a - 2)$ scalar operations.

Since we generate ab signatures per run, the average number of group operations per signature is approximately

$$\frac{3n + 4t + 5a - 2 + 3n(4t + 5a + 4) + O(a \cdot \max(b, t) \log(\max(b, t)))}{ab}$$

$$= \frac{3n + 4t + 5a - 2}{ab} + \frac{3n(4t + 5a + 4)}{ab} + \frac{O(a \cdot \max(b, t) \log(\max(b, t)))}{ab}.$$

The average number of scalar operations per signature is approximately

$$\frac{3n + b(2t + 3a - 2) + 2t + 2a - 1 + O(\max(b,t)\log(\max(b,t)))}{ab}$$
$$= \frac{3n + 2t + 2a - 1}{ab} + \frac{2t + 3a - 2}{a} + \frac{O(\max(b,t)\log(\max(b,t)))}{ab}.$$

When we set $t = a = b = \Omega(n)$, each participant requires $O(\log n)$ group operations and $O(1)$ scalar operations for every signature.

To show the advantages of our protocol clearly, we perform a slightly rough comparison of our protocol with other protocols [22,27] in Table 1. Unlike previous works [22,27], we achieve robustness against malicious nodes in asynchronous networks, and reduce the state-of-the-art round number of communication from 8 to 4. Moreover, our scheme generates $\Omega(n^2)$ signatures in a single protocol execution, requiring only $O(1)$ communication and $O(\log n)$ computation complexity per signature[6].

Table 1. In the Communication (resp. Computation) column, the top and bottom values indicate the numbers of scalars and group elements (resp. operations), respectively. In the Network column, Syn means the used network is synchronous while Asyn means asynchronous.

Scheme	Round	Communication	Computation	Network	Robustness	Security
[27]	8	$O(n^2)$ $O(n)$	$O(n)$ $O(n)$	Syn	×	Semi-honest
[22]	12	$O(n)$ $O(n)$	$O(n)$ $O(n)$	Syn	×	UC
Our's	4	$O(1)$ $O(1)$	$O(1)$ $O(\log n)$	Asyn	✓	Malious

Acknowledgement. This work has been supported by National Natural Science Foundation of China (No. 62302376), National Key Research and Development Program of China (No. 2023YFB3105902), Natural Science Basic Research Program of Shaanxi (Program No. 2025JC-YBQN-826), Key Research and Development Program of Shaanxi (Program No. 2024GX-ZDCYL-01-09), and Key Research of Science and Technology of Shenzhen city (No. KJZD20230923114608017).

A   Correctness of the Multi-set Agreement Protocol (Proof of Theorem 1)

Proof. The sets QUAL_k, BAD_k, and HOLD maintained by the shareholders throughout the protocol are all deterministic functions of the messages on the broadcast channel. Therefore, all shareholders will always be in agreement about these sets. Since the halting condition is also a deterministic function of the broadcast channel then they will halt at the same step and output the same sets

---

[6] Note that our efficiency comparison is performed under a single signature.

QUAL_k, BAD_k, and HOLD, satisfying consistency. Obviously, when the agreement ends, the shareholders in HOLD do not broadcast a complaint against any dealers in QUAL_k (or else they will be removed to the corresponding BAD_k). In contrast, any dealers in BAD_k will face complaints from at least one shareholder, since this is the only way for corrupt dealers to be added to the BAD_k.

Our protocol requires at least b honest dealers in QUAL_1, while $\mathsf{QUAL}_{k'}$, $k = 2, 3$ only needs enough honest dealers to meet the signing threshold. Thus, we set $m \geq t+1$ in **Phase 1**, which ensures that the number of honest dealers in $\mathsf{QUAL}_{k'}$ will reach the required condition by the end of the phase, even if there are t malicious nodes present. If $|\mathsf{QUAL}_1| \geq b$ does not hold at **Phase 1**, the protocol turns to **Phase 2**. In this phase, the shareholders continue to add new dealers to QUAL_1 until $|\mathsf{QUAL}_1| \geq b + t$, which ensures QUAL_1 contains at least b honest dealers by phase end. Finally, all honest shareholders will get all sets and output them in this phase. Therefore, if the protocol cannot be halted in **Phase 1**, it will necessarily terminate in **Phase 2**.

References

1. GM/T 0003.4-2012: SM2 Elliptic Curve Public Key Cryptography Algorithm-part 4: Public Key Encryption (2012)
2. Bellare, M., Tessaro, S., Zhu, C.: Stronger security for non-interactive threshold signatures: BLS and FROST. IACR Cryptol. ePrint Arch, p. 833 (2022)
3. Ben-Or, M., Goldwasser, S., Wigderson, A.: Completeness theorems for non-cryptographic fault-tolerant distributed computation (extended abstract). In: ACM 1988, pp. 1–10. ACM (1988)
4. Benhamouda, F., Halevi, S., Krawczyk, H., Ma, Y., Rabin, T.: SPRINT: high-throughput robust distributed schnorr signatures. In: EUROCRYPT 2024. LNCS, vol. 14655, pp. 62–91. Springer (2024)
5. Benhamouda, F., Lepoint, T., Loss, J., Orrù, M., Raykova, M.: On the (in)security of ROS. In: Canteaut, A., Standaert, F.-X. (eds.) EUROCRYPT 2021. LNCS, vol. 12696, pp. 33–53. Springer, Cham (2021). https://doi.org/10.1007/978-3-030-77870-5_2
6. Boneh, D., Gentry, C., Lynn, B., Shacham, H.: Aggregate and verifiably encrypted signatures from bilinear maps. In: Biham, E. (ed.) EUROCRYPT 2003. LNCS, vol. 2656, pp. 416–432. Springer, Heidelberg (2003). https://doi.org/10.1007/3-540-39200-9_26
7. Canetti, R.: Universally composable security. J. ACM **67**(5), 28:1–28:94 (2020)
8. Chen, Y.: Dazzle: improved adaptive threshold signatures from DDH. In: PKC 2025. LNCS, vol. 15676, pp. 233–261. Springer (2025)
9. Desmedt, Y., Frankel, Y.: Threshold cryptosystems. In: CRYPTO 1989. LNCS, vol. 435, pp. 307–315. Springer (1989)
10. Desmedt, Y., Frankel, Y.: Shared generation of authenticators and signatures (extended abstract). In: CRYPTO 1991. LNCS, vol. 576, pp. 457–469. Springer (1991)
11. Fischlin, M., Mitrokotsa, A., Tomy, J.: Buffing threshold signature schemes. In: PKC 2025. LNCS, vol. 15676, pp. 137–168. Springer (2025)

12. Franklin, M.K., Yung, M.: Communication complexity of secure computation (extended abstract). In: ACM 1992, pp. 699–710. ACM (1992)
13. Garillot, F., Kondi, Y., Mohassel, P., Nikolaenko, V.: Threshold Schnorr with stateless deterministic signing from standard assumptions. In: Malkin, T., Peikert, C. (eds.) CRYPTO 2021. LNCS, vol. 12825, pp. 127–156. Springer, Cham (2021). https://doi.org/10.1007/978-3-030-84242-0_6
14. Gennaro, R., Goldfeder, S.: Fast multiparty threshold ECDSA with fast trustless setup. In: CCS 2018, pp. 1179–1194. ACM (2018)
15. Gennaro, R., Jarecki, S., Krawczyk, H., Rabin, T.: Robust threshold DSS signatures. Inf. Comput. **164**(1), 54–84 (2001)
16. Gennaro, R., Jarecki, S., Krawczyk, H., Rabin, T.: Secure distributed key generation for discrete-log based cryptosystems. J. Cryptol. **20**(1), 51–83 (2007)
17. Groth, J., Shoup, V.: Design and analysis of a distributed ECDSA signing service. IACR Cryptol. ePrint Arch, p. 506 (2022)
18. Hirt, M., Nielsen, J.B.: Robust multiparty computation with linear communication complexity. In: Dwork, C. (ed.) CRYPTO 2006. LNCS, vol. 4117, pp. 463–482. Springer, Heidelberg (2006). https://doi.org/10.1007/11818175_28
19. Hou, H., Yang, B., Zhang, L., Zhang, M.: Secure two-party SM2 signature algorithm. Acta Electron. Sin. **48**(1), 1–8 (2020)
20. Komlo, C.: Threshold signatures. IEEE Secur. Priv. **22**(6), 85–88 (2024)
21. Komlo, C., Goldberg, I.: FROST: flexible round-optimized Schnorr threshold signatures. In: SAC 2020. LNCS, vol. 12804, pp. 34–65. Springer (2020)
22. Liang, H., Chen, J.: Non-interactive SM2 threshold signature scheme with identifiable abort. Frontiers Comput. Sci. **18**(1), 181802 (2024)
23. Patra, A., Choudhary, A., Rangan, C.P.: Efficient statistical asynchronous verifiable secret sharing with optimal resilience. In: ICITS 2009. LNCS, vol. 5973, pp. 74–92. Springer (2009)
24. Pedersen, T.P.: Non-interactive and information-theoretic secure verifiable secret sharing. In: CRYPTO 1991. LNCS, vol. 576, pp. 129–140. Springer (1991)
25. Shamir, A.: How to share a secret. Commun. ACM **22**(11), 612–613 (1979)
26. Shang, M., Ma, Y., Lin, J., Jing, J.: A threshold scheme for SM2 elliptic curve cryptographic algorithm. J. Cryptologic Res. **1**(2), 155–166 (2014)
27. Yang, J., Lu, Y., Chen, L., Ni, W.: A SM2 elliptic curve threshold signature scheme without a trusted center. KSII Trans. Internet Inf. Syst. **10**(2), 897–913 (2016)

Attacks on Implementations of Lindell 17 and Its Variants

Jianhong He[1(✉)] and Wenping Ma[2]

[1] Safeheron PTE LTD., Singapore, Singapore
hejianhong@safeheron.com
[2] School of Telecommunication Engineering, Xidian University, Xi'an 710071, China
wp_ma@mail.xidian.edu.cn

Abstract. Lindell17 is a widely used two-party threshold ECDSA protocol that offers security under concurrent executions and supports global abort upon failure. In this paper, we extend the attack model of Makriyannis, Yomtov, and Galansky by proposing a more general and covert class of attacks, which we term *Digit-by-Digit Extraction (DBDE)*. Our attacks allow the adversary to choose an arbitrary base b and craft nonce values $k_2 = b^\ell$, enabling the gradual leakage of the honest party's key share through signature outcomes. We demonstrate DBDE attacks on Lindell17 and its three main variants: (1) **Lindell17 (+)**, (2) **Lindell17 (·)** in 2-of-2 setting, (3) the actively refreshed variant **Refreshed-Lindell17 (+)**, and (4) **Patched HD Lindell17**. To mitigate these attacks, we propose a practical countermeasure that prevents adversarial control over nonce selection by introducing a jointly generated k_2. Our patch neutralizes all known attacks that exploit nonce selection strategies.

We also provide proof-of-concept code to validate our attacks and demonstrate their real-world feasibility.

Keywords: Lindell's signing schemes · Key extraction attack · Hierarchical deterministic wallet

1 Introduction

ECDSA (Elliptic Curve Digital Signature Algorithm) is a cryptographic algorithm based on elliptic curve cryptography (ECC) used for generating digital signatures. Thanks to its high efficiency and robust security, ECDSA has become a standard in the field of digital asset management and is widely employed to safeguard digital assets.

In recent years, Multi-Party Computation (MPC) protocols have gained increasing adoption in digital asset custody, forming the foundation of modern threshold ECDSA signing. Early constructions such as the two-party protocols by Lindell [12] and Doerner et al. [5] demonstrated practical signing under malicious security with minimal interaction and assumptions. This line of work was extended by Gennaro and Goldfeder in 2018 [9], who proposed a dealerless protocol supporting arbitrary thresholds, and by their 2020 follow-up [10],

X. Chen et al. (Eds.): DSPP 2025, LNCS 16177, pp. 118–136, 2026.
https://doi.org/10.1007/978-981-95-3185-1_8

which introduced one-round signing with identifiable aborts for asynchronous execution. Building on these, Canetti et al.'s 2020 work [3] offered a UC-secure protocol with proactive key refresh, reduced interaction (only four rounds), and support for cold-wallet compatibility. Meanwhile, the DKLs series [6,7] pursued a different direction by adopting an OT-based design, eliminating reliance on Paillier encryption. This approach led to superior efficiency across LAN and WAN settings, with the 2024 version achieving malicious security in just three rounds under minimal assumptions.

The security of MPC protocols is being scrutinized more rigorously, and several potential vulnerabilities have been uncovered. Aumasson [1], Filipe [8], Nguyen [14] and Fredrik [4] have proposed various attacks targeting the implementation of MPC protocols. Makriyannis [13] and Tymokhanov [17] have proposed various attacks targeting protocol-level vulnerabilities in the MPC protocol. Makriyannis [13] proposed an attack targeting the security model of MPC protocols that do not match the usage scenario.

As an Two Party ECDSA protocol widely used in the field of digital asset management, Lindell17 requires a "global abort" when malicious behavior is detected. Unfortunately, due to the oversight of handling signature failures, "global abort" cannot be strictly guaranteed in practical applications. The paper [13] introduces a Bit-by-Bit Extraction attack in which the malicious party P_2 selects k_2 values in the form of 2^ℓ and executes the attack during the signing process. After 256 iterations (regardless of whether the signatures succeed or fail), P_1's private key share is successfully extracted. Unfortunately, there are no effective patches currently available for this attack. Designing an additional zero-knowledge proof is highly challenging and increases computational complexity, while abandoning the wallet after a failed signature would significantly degrade the user experience.

Several defense measures have been implemented to protect against attacks targeting the Lindell17 protocol. In hierarchical deterministic (HD) wallets, some vendors [15] prevent private key extraction by disabling subsequent signatures in child wallets. The paper [19] proposes an optimized protocol based on Lindell's protocol [12] to enable fast 2-out-of-n ECDSA threshold signatures. This protocol introduces a decentralized key refresh protocol, which enhances proactive security by updating key shares after an MPC signing failure.

1.1   Our Contribution

Building on the work of Makriyannis, Yomtov, and Galansky, we present new attacks against the Lindell17 protocol and its variants. These attacks can exfiltrate the private key by compromising only a single party in the MPC process, making them highly practical. All of our Digit-by-Digit Extraction (DBDE) attacks follow a common strategy: the adversary carefully selects nonce values and infers information about the honest party's private key share by observing the success or failure of the MPC signing process.

Against **Lindell17** ($+$), we propose a more flexible and covert attack. Similar to the **Bitforge Attack** introduced by Makriyannis, Yomtov, and Galansky [13], we extract information about the honest party's private key share by analyzing the success or failure of each signature. After a limited number of signatures, we can fully recover the honest party's private key share. The key difference is that during the execution of the MPC protocol, Makriyannis's attack [13] selects k_2 in the form of 2^ℓ, whereas our attack allows for the selection of an arbitrary base b, with k_2 in the form of b^ℓ. Clearly, the attack proposed by Makriyannis, Yomtov, and Galansky [13] can be viewed as a special case of our attack method (when $b = 2$).

- Against **Lindell17** $(\cdot)$, we also propose a flexible and covert attack, based on the same idea as the first attack.
- Against **Refreshed-Lindell17** $(+)$, a variant of the Lindell17 protocol that incorporates active security enhancements, we propose an effective attack, particularly in the 2-out-of-2 threshold setting. While the protocol attempts to prevent attacks through its private key share refreshing mechanism, we demonstrate that this approach does not meet its security expectations in the 2-out-of-2 threshold scenario.
- Against **Patched HD-Lindell17** which supports hierarchical deterministic wallets, we propose an attack that leverages a sufficient number of child wallets to initiate signatures, ultimately leading to the successful extraction of the honest party's private key shares.
- We propose a practical and feasible security patch, addressing the gap left by the absence of previous remedial measures. This security patch defends against all known attacks on the Lindell 17 protocol, which can be categorized as "Selected k_2 Attacks."

The attack cost—specifically, the number of signatures required for the adversary to extract the key—is summarized in the table. DBDE1–4 refer to our Digit-by-Digit Extraction attacks against **Lindell17** $(+)$, **Lindell17** $(\cdot)$, **Refreshed-Lindell17** $(+)$, and **Patched HD-Lindell17**, respectively. Bitforge, the prior attack using base $b = 2$, which consistently requires 256 signatures, is also included as a baseline for comparison (Table 1).

Table 1. Signature Complexity of Bitforge and DBDE Attacks

Attack	Protocol	Threshold	b	Signatures		
				Optimistic	Pessimistic	Average
Bitforge	Lindell 17$(+)$	2-n	2	256	256	256
	Lindell 17$(\cdot)$	2–2				
DBDE1	Lindell 17$(+)$	2-n	b	$\lceil \log_b q \rceil$	$\lceil \log_b q \rceil \cdot (b-1)$	$\lceil \log_b q \rceil \cdot (\frac{b+1}{2} - \frac{1}{b})$
DBDE2	Lindell 17$(\cdot)$	2–2	b			
DBDE3	Refreshed-Lindell 17$(+)$	2–2	b			
DBDE4	HD Lindell 17$(+)$	2-n	b			
	HD Lindell 17$(\cdot)$	2–2				

1.2   Detection and Mitigation

Compared to the **Bitforge Attack** by Makriyannis, Yomtov, and Galansky [13], which relies on a specific value of $k_2 = 2^\ell$ with highly distinctive characteristics (allowing the malicious message from P_2 to be detected via exhaustive search, since R_2 in the malicious message has only 256 possible values), our attack employs an arbitrary b with $k_2 = b^\ell$, which makes R_2 in the malicious message theoretically infeasible to exhaustively enumerate. This renders our attack significantly more covert. Nonetheless, our approach still results in multiple signature failures, which provides a clear indication that something abnormal is occurring within the process.

According to the guidelines in Lindell17 [12], signing operations should be immediately halted upon detection of an invalid signature. In the HD-Lindell17 variant, this action should disable the entire wallet, not just the affected child wallet.

1.3   Remediation

Since the discovery of attacks against the Lindell17 protocol, no practical and effective countermeasure has been available. Makriyannis et al. [13] suggested adding a zero-knowledge proof (ZKP) of well-formedness for the encrypted partial signatures. However, constructing such a ZKP has proven highly challenging, and to date, no practical implementation has been proposed.

Our analysis of all known attacks reveals a common pattern: they rely on the ability of the malicious party P_2 to select a specific value of k_2. Based on this observation, we propose a practical and effective countermeasure which, to the best of our knowledge, is the first to employ a joint public key generation protocol that prevents the malicious P_2 from influencing the selection of k_2, thereby ensuring its unpredictability. A detailed description of our approach is provided in Sect. 7. Our countermeasure incurs minimal overhead and preserves the structure of the original Lindell17 protocol, making it suitable for practical deployment.

It is important to note that our countermeasure protects against all known attacks, which can be broadly categorized as "**Selected k_2 Attacks**". However, this does not imply protection against entirely new classes of attacks. Nevertheless, our solution represents a significant step forward, offering a viable defense and closing a long-standing gap in the security of Lindell17-style protocols.

1.4   Paper Organization

Sect. 2 introduces the notation and definitions used throughout the subsequent chapters. In Sect. 3, we provide a formal description of the Lindell17 ($\cdot$) protocol along with the first Digit-by-Digit Extraction attack. Section 4 presents the Lindell17 (+) protocol and details the second Digit-by-Digit Extraction attack. Section 5 describes Refreshed-Lindell17(+), a variant of the Lindell17 protocol defined in [19], along with the third Digit-by-Digit Extraction attack. Section 6 covers the HD-Lindell17 variant, which supports hierarchical deterministic (HD) derivations, and includes the fourth Digit-by-Digit Extraction attack. Finally, in Sect. 7, we propose a remediation strategy for the Digit-by-Digit Extraction attack described in this paper.

2   Prelimiaries

2.1   Paillier Encryption

The Paillier encryption scheme [16] is a public-key cryptosystem where the public key is $N = pq$ for large primes p and q. Encryption is defined as $\mathsf{Enc}_N(m;r) = (1+N)^m \cdot r^N \bmod N^2$ for $m \in \mathbb{Z}_N$ and $r \in \mathbb{Z}_N^*$. The scheme supports additive homomorphism: $\mathsf{Enc}_N(m_1) \cdot \mathsf{Enc}_N(m_2) = \mathsf{Enc}_N(m_1 + m_2)$, and scalar multiplication: $\mathsf{Enc}_N(m)^k = \mathsf{Enc}_N(k \cdot m)$.

2.2   Hierarchical Deterministic Wallet(HDWallet)

Hierarchical Deterministic Wallet (HDWallet), firstly proposed in BIP32 (Bitcoin Improvement Proposal 32) [18], has been accepted as a standard in the Bitcoin community. It allows for the creation of a large number of child keys from the parent key. There are two ways to derive a child key from a parent key. One is additive key derivation from BIP32 and the other is multiplicative key derivation. We represent an extended private key as (x, c), with x the normal private key, $x \in \mathbf{Z}_q$, and c the chain code. An extended public key is represented as (X, c), with $X = g^x$ and c the chain code. Given a parent extended key and an index i, it is possible to compute the corresponding child extended key.

Definition 1 (BIP32). Define (CKD_{Priv}, CKD_{Pub}) as the two-tuple of algorithms below.

1. Let $\{X_i, c_i, \omega\} = CKD_{Pub}(X_{par}, c_{par}, i)$ where (X_{par}, c_{par}) is the parent extended public key and (X_i, c_i) is the child extended public key, i is an index of the child key and $\omega \in \mathbb{Z}_q$ is the offset of child private key from parent private key such as $X_i = X_{Par} \cdot g^{\omega}$ for $X_{par} \in \mathbb{G}$, $X_i \in \mathbb{G}$, $c_{par} \in \{0,1\}^*$ and $c_i \in \{0,1\}^*$.
2. Let $\{x_i, c_i\} = CKD_{Priv}(x_{par}, c_{par}, i)$ where (x_{par}, c_{par}) is the parent extended private key and (x_i, c_i) is the child extended private key, i is an index of the child key for $x_{par} \in \mathbb{Z}_q$, $x_i \in \mathbb{Z}_q$, $c_{par} \in \{0,1\}^*$, and $c_i \in \{0,1\}^*$.

Definition 2 (Mul-Derivation). Define (CKD_{Pub}) as below [11].

1. Let $\{X_i, c_i, \omega\} = CKD_{Pub}(X_{par}, c_{par}, i)$ where (X_{par}, c_{par}) is the parent extended public key and (X_i, c_i) is the child extended public key, i is an index of the child key and $\omega \in \mathbb{Z}_q \setminus \{0\}$ is the offset of child private key from parent private key such as $X_i = X_{Par}^{\omega}$ for $X_{par} \in \mathbb{G}$, $X_i \in \mathbb{G}$, $c_{par} \in \{0,1\}^*$ and $c_i \in \{0,1\}^*$.

2.3   Key Refresh

We define the key refresh protocol as follows. Let $\mathbb{P} = \{P_1, \ldots, P_n\}$ denote the set of parties, where each party P_i holds a private key share x_i. The master secret key is $x = \sum_{i=1}^{n} x_i$, and the corresponding public key is $X = g^x = \prod_{i=1}^{n} g^{x_i}$. The key refresh protocol proceeds as follows:

1. Each party P_i locally generates a random additive sharing of zero $0 = \sum_{j=1}^{n} \omega_{i,j}$, and sends $\omega_{i,j}$ to party P_j for all $j \neq i$, and keeps $\omega_{i,i}$ locally.
2. Upon receiving values $\omega_{j,i}$ from all other parties, each P_i updates its key share $x_i \leftarrow x_i + \sum_{j=1}^{n} \omega_{j,i}$.

This preserves the overall secret $x = \sum_i x_i$, while refreshing the individual shares.

3   A Covert Attack to Lindell17(+)

Bitforge Attack on Lindell17 [12] was proposed by Makriyannis et al. [13], in which the malicious party P_2 selects the nonce k_2 in the form 2^ℓ. While effective, this approach has a notable limitation: it significantly restricts the possible values of R_2, making the attack easier to detect. Specifically, $R_2 = g^{k_2}$ will lie within the small, predefined set

$$\{g^2, g^{2^2}, g^{2^3}, \ldots, g^{2^{256}}\},$$

which contains only 256 elements and can be efficiently searched exhaustively by the honest party.

In this section, we present a new attack in which the malicious party P_2 selects nonces of the form $k_2 = b^\ell$, where $b \in \mathbb{Z}_q$ is arbitrarily chosen. Let $x_1 \in \mathbb{Z}_q$ denote the private key share held by P_1. We express x_1 in base b as:

$$x_1 = \sum_{\ell=1}^{u} d_\ell \cdot b^{\ell-1}, \quad \text{where } u = \lceil \log_b q \rceil.$$

The attack proceeds by having P_2 sequentially guess each digit d_ℓ, starting from the least significant digit. In each round of the two-party signing protocol, P_2 sets $k_2 = b^\ell$ and participates in the signing procedure with P_1, using the outcome (success or failure) to verify whether a guess for d_ℓ is correct.

Each digit has b possible values. However, since the final remaining candidate can be inferred without testing, the number of required guesses per digit ranges from 1 in the best case to $b - 1$ in the worst case. By iteratively applying this procedure across all digits, the malicious party P_2 can eventually recover the full private key share x_1. See Attack 2 for the full description.

3.1 Protocol Description

Definition 3 (KeyGen). Define KeyGen on input $(\mathbb{G}, g, q)$ from P_1 and P_2 such that KeyGen returns the tuple $(X, x_1, N, \sigma) \in \mathbb{G} \times \mathbb{Z}_q \times Z \times Z$ to P2 and the tuple $(X, x_1, N, \mathcal{C}) \in (\mathbb{G} \times \mathbb{Z}_q \times Z \times Z^*_{N^2})$ to P2 where $x_1 \leftarrow \mathbb{Z}_q$, $x_2 \leftarrow \mathbb{Z}_q$ are uniformly random and $(X, N, \sigma, \mathcal{C})$ are set as follows.

$$(N, \sigma) \leftarrow PailKeyGen,$$

and

$$\begin{cases} X = g^{x_1 + x_2}, \\ \mathcal{C} = Enc_N(x_1). \end{cases}$$

(**PailKeyGen** and **Enc** denote the key-generation and encryption algorithms from paper [16]).

Protocol 1: Lindell17(+)

Oracle: KeyGen, DHKE.

Subrotocol (Key-Generation)

Upon activation, parties call **KeyGen** and obtain the following output:

1. Common Output: ECDSA pk $Q = g^{x_1 + x_2}$ and Paillier pk $N \in Z$;
2. Secret output: P1 gets $x_1 \in \mathbb{Z}_q$ and Paillier private key $\sigma \in Z$;
3. Secret output: P2 gets $x_2 \in \mathbb{Z}_q$ and $\mathcal{C} = Enc_N(x_1)$.

Subprotocol (Signing)

When prompted on message msg, set $m = hash(m)$ and do

1. P1 sample $k_1 \leftarrow \mathbb{Z}_q$, P2 sample $x_2 \leftarrow \mathbb{Z}_q$;
2. Parties call **DHKE** $(\mathbb{G}, g, q)$ on input k_1 and k_2 and obtain $R = g^{k_1 \cdot k_2}$;
3. P2 sets $r = R.x$, sample $\rho \leftarrow Z_{q^2}$ and sends $\mathcal{D} \in Z^*_{N^2}$ to P_1 where

$$\mathcal{D} = Enc_N([k_2^{-1}(m + r \cdot x_2)]_q)$$
$$\cdot Enc_N(x_1)^{[r \cdot k_2^{-1}]_q} \pmod{N}^2.$$

4. P1 outputs (R, s) where $s = k_1^{-1} \cdot Dec(D) \pmod q$ iff (R, s) is a valid signature.

3.2 Our Attack

Claim. Under Attack 2, P_2 will extract P_1's key share x_1.

Proof. We denote $x_1 = \sum_{\ell=1}^{u} d_\ell \cdot b^{\ell-1}$, where $u = \lceil \log_b q \rceil$. The extraction process proceeds iteratively, and its correctness follows from Claim 3.2.

Let y_1 represent the known portion of x_1 during the extraction process. Initially, no digits are known, so:

$$y_1 = x_1 \bmod b^0 = 0.$$

To determine the first digit d_1, note that it can take any value in the candidate set $V_{\text{try}} = \{0, 1, \ldots, b-1\}$. The attacker P_2 selects a guess $d_{1,\text{guess}} \in V_{\text{try}}$, and invokes Attack 1 to verify whether the guess is correct. If the guess is invalid, it is removed from V_{try}, and another guess is tested. This process continues until the correct value is found. Since the final candidate can be inferred without explicit testing, at most $b-1$ guesses are required to determine d_1.

Once d_1 is determined, the known portion is updated as:

$$y_1 \leftarrow y_1 + d_1 \cdot b^{1-1}.$$

The same procedure is repeated for each subsequent digit d_ℓ for $\ell = 2, \ldots, u$. In each step, the attacker leverages the congruence:

$$y_1 \equiv x_1 \pmod{b^{\ell-1}},$$

and applies Attack 1 to recover d_ℓ, updating y_1 accordingly:

$$y_1 \leftarrow y_1 + d_\ell \cdot b^{\ell-1}.$$

After all u digits have been recovered, we obtain:

$$y_1 = \sum_{\ell=1}^{u} d_\ell \cdot b^{\ell-1} = x_1,$$

and thus fully recover P_1's private key share. $\qquad\square$

To determine whether a guess for digit d_ℓ is correct, we analyze the behavior of P_1 during the signature finalization process. Specifically, we aim to establish under what condition P_1 will complete the signature successfully. This is formalized in the following claim.

Claim. Under Attack 1, P_1 finalizes the signature correctly if and only if $d_\ell \equiv d_{\ell,guess}$.

Proof. We now analyze the decryption behavior of P_1 under a digit-guessing attempt, aiming to understand how the correctness of a guessed digit $d_{\ell,\text{guess}}$ affects the final decryption result.

Let $y_{1,guess} = y_1 + d_{\ell,guess} * b^{\ell-1}$, $\zeta = [b^{-\ell}(m + rx_1)]_q$ and $\zeta' = y_{1,guess}r'[b^{-\ell}]_q$, where $r' = r + eq$ and $gcd(r', b) = 1$.
From the definitions, we have:

$$Dec(\mathcal{D}') = \zeta + \zeta' + (x_1 - y_{1,guess})r'[b^{-l}]_N \pmod{N} \qquad (1)$$

Let $a = d_\ell - d_{\ell,guess}$, so that

$$x_1 = y_{1,guess} + a \cdot b^{\ell-1} \pmod{b^\ell}, 0 \leq a < b.$$

We now distinguish two cases depending on the value of $[x_1 - y_{1,guess}]_{b^\ell}$:

- **Case 1:** If $[x_1 - y_{1,guess}]_{b^\ell} = 0$, then $a = 0$, and Eq. (1) simplifies to:

$$\mathrm{Dec}(\mathcal{D}') = \zeta + \zeta' + r' \cdot \frac{(x_1 - y_{1,guess})}{b^\ell}. \tag{2}$$

- **Case 2:** If $[x_1 - y_{1,guess}]_{b^\ell} \neq 0$, i.e., $a \neq 0$, then Eq. (1) becomes:

$$\mathrm{Dec}(\mathcal{D}') = \left[\zeta + \zeta' + r' \cdot \frac{(x_1 - y_{1,guess} - ab^{\ell-1})}{b^\ell} + r'ab^{\ell-1} \cdot [b^{-\ell}]_N\right]_N. \tag{3}$$

We now prove the claim in two directions.

$(\rightarrow)$ **If direction:** $d_\ell \equiv d_{\ell,guess} \Rightarrow [Dec(\mathcal{D}')]_q = [k_1 \cdot s]_q$
Since $d_\ell = d_{\ell,guess}$, it follows that $a = 0$, and hence

$$[x_1 - y_{1,guess}]_{b^\ell} = 0.$$

Substituting this into Eq. (2) and applying the definitions of r', ζ, and ζ', we obtain

$$[Dec(\mathcal{D}')]_q = [k_1 \cdot s]_q,$$

as claimed.

$(\leftarrow)$ **Only-if direction:** $d_\ell \neq d_{\ell,guess} \Rightarrow [Dec(\mathcal{D}')]_q \neq [k_1 \cdot s]_q.$
Because $gcd(r', b) = 1$, $\exists t_0 \in \mathbb{N}, r_0 \in \mathbb{Z}_b$ and $gcd(r_0, b) = 1$, such that

$$r' = t_0 b + r_0. \tag{4}$$

Moreover $gcd(b, N) = 1$ implies $b \in \mathbb{Z}_N^*$, so b has an inverse element $[b^{-1}]_N$. Thus $\exists f_1 \in \mathbb{N}$, such that

$$b^\ell[b^{-\ell}]_N = f_1 N + 1 \Rightarrow b^{\ell-1}[b^{-\ell}]_N = \frac{f_1 N + 1}{b}. \tag{5}$$

where $gcd(f_1, b) = 1$.
$\exists t_1 \in \mathbb{N}, r_1 \in \mathbb{Z}_b$, such that

$$f_1 = t_1 b + r_1, \tag{6}$$

where $gcd(r_1, b) = 1$.
Substituting $b^{\ell-1}[b^{-\ell}]_N$, f_1, r', we can get

$$[r'ab^{\ell-1}[b^{-\ell}]_N]_N = [at_0 + ar_0\frac{(1 + r_1 N)}{b}]_N. \tag{7}$$

Moreover $gcd(b, q) = 1$ implies $b \in \mathbb{Z}_q^*$, so b has an inverse element $[b^{-1}]_q$. Thus $\exists f_2 \in \mathbb{N}$, such that

$$b^\ell [b^{-\ell}]_q = f_2 q + 1 \Rightarrow b^{\ell-1}[b^{-\ell}]_q = \frac{f_2 q + 1}{b}, \tag{8}$$

where $gcd(f_2, b) = 1$.
$\exists t_2 \in \mathbb{N}, r_2 \in \mathbb{Z}_b$, such that

$$f_2 = t_2 b + r_2, \tag{9}$$

where $gcd(r_2, b) = 1$.
Substituting $b^{\ell-1}[b^{-\ell}]_q$, f_2, r', we get

$$[r'ab^{\ell-1}[b^{-\ell}]_q]_q = [at_0 + ar_0 \frac{(1 + r_2 q)}{b}]_q. \tag{10}$$

Because $0 < \zeta + \zeta' + r' \frac{(x_1 - y_{1,guess} - ab^{\ell-1})}{b^\ell} \ll N$, therefore

$$Dec(\mathcal{D}') = \zeta + \zeta' + r' \frac{(x_1 - y_{1,guess} - ab^{\ell-1})}{b^\ell} \tag{11}$$
$$+ [r'ab^{\ell-1}[b^{-\ell}]_N]_N - \alpha N.$$

where $\alpha \in \{0, 1\}$.
Then substitute (4), (5), (6), (7), (8), (9), (10) into (11):

$$\begin{aligned}
q = {}& [[k_1 \cdot s]_q - (at_0 + ar_0 \frac{(1 + r_2 q)}{b}) \\
& + [(at_0 + ar_0 \frac{(1 + r_1 N)}{b}) - (at_0 + ar_0 \frac{(1 + r_2 q)}{b}) \\
& + (at_0 + ar_0 \frac{(1 + r_2 q)}{b})]_N - \alpha N]_q \\
& - [[k_1 \cdot s]_q - (at_0 + ar_0 \frac{(1 + r_2 q)}{b}) \\
& + [(at_0 + ar_0 \frac{(1 + r_1 N)}{b}) - (at_0 + ar_0 \frac{(1 + r_2 q)}{b})]_N \\
& + (at_0 + ar_0 \frac{(1 + r_2 q)}{b}) - \beta N - \alpha N]_q \\
= {}& [[k_1 \cdot s]_q + [ar_0 \frac{(r_1 N - r_2 q)}{b}]_N - (\alpha + \beta) N]_q.
\end{aligned}$$

where $\beta \in \{0, 1\}$, $b \mid ar_0(r_1 N - r_2 q)$.
Because $gcd(r_0, b) = 1$, $gcd(r_1, b) = 1$ and $0 < a < b$, then $b \nmid ar_0 r_1$. $\exists t_3 \in \mathbb{N}, r_3 \in \mathbb{Z}_b$ and $r_3 \in (0, b)$ such that $ar_0 r_1 = t_3 b + r_3$.
Therefore:

$$[Dec(\mathcal{D}')]_q = [[k_1 \cdot s]_q + \frac{(r_3 N - ar_0 r_2 q)}{b} - (\alpha + \beta) N]_q.$$

Assume that $[Dec(\mathcal{D}')]_q \equiv [k_1 \cdot s]_q$, there $\exists \eta \in \mathbb{N}$, such that the following equation holds:

$$\frac{(r_3 N - ar_0 r_2 q)}{b} - (\alpha + \beta)N = \eta q$$

$$\Rightarrow (r_3 - b(\alpha + \beta))N = (ar_0 r_2 + b\eta)q.$$

Since $r_3 < b$ and $(\alpha + \beta) \in \{0, 1, 2\}$, the possible values of $(r_3 - b(\alpha + \beta))$ are $r_3, r_3 - b, r_3 - 2b, r_3 - 3b$. Thus, the left-hand side of the equation above is non-zero. Given that q is prime (order of elliptic curve $Secp256k1$), we have $|(r_3 - b(\alpha + \beta))| \ll q$, which implies $q \nmid (r_3 - b(\alpha + \beta))$. Furthermore, since $q \nmid N$, q cannot divide the left-hand side of the equation. However, q clearly divides the right-hand side of the equation, which means the equation does not hold. It follows that the assumption is incorrect. Therefore, $[Dec(\mathcal{D}')]_q \neq [k_1 \cdot s]_q$. This completes the proof.

Claim. For a prime q, given two different integers a and b in range $[0, q)$ and $b > 1$, $\exists e \in \mathbb{N}$ that satisfies $gcd(a + eq, b) = 1$.

Proof. Note that q is an invertible element modulo b because $gcd(q, b) = 1$. Denote its inverse as s. Let $e = s(1 - a) \pmod{b}$, so that $(a + eq) \pmod{b} = 1$. Therefore, we have $gcd(a + eq, b) = 1$. Denote it as $e = FCN(a, b, q)$, where FCN stands for "Find Coprime Number".

Attack 1: Guess $d_\ell = d_{\ell,guess}$ during a signing process: Crrupted P_2 in Protocol 1

Auxiliary input: P_2 holds $y_1 = x_1 \pmod{b^{\ell-1}}$

Guess the $\ell - th$ digit: P_2 guess the $\ell - th$ digit of x_1 is $d_{\ell,guess} \in [0, b)$

Operations:

1. Call DHKE on inputs $k_2 = b^\ell$ (chosen by P_2) and k_1 (chosen by P_1)

   All parties obtain $R = g^{b^\ell \cdot k_1}$

   P_2 set $\varepsilon = [b^{-\ell}]_q - [b^{-\ell}]_N$ and $r' = FCN(r, b, q)$.

2. P_2 sends $\mathcal{D}' \in \mathbf{Z}_{N^2}^*$ to P_1 where, for $\zeta = [k_2^{-1}(m + rx_2)]_q$

$$\mathcal{D}' = Enc_N(\zeta + (y_1 + d_{\ell,guess} * b^{\ell-1}) \cdot r' \cdot \varepsilon)$$

$$\cdot (Enc_N(x_1)^{r'})^{[b^{-\ell}]_N} \pmod{N^2}.$$

3. P_2 deduces that: $d_\ell \equiv d_{\ell,guess} \iff$ sig succeed.

Attack 2: Digit-by-digit Extraction Attack: Crrupted P_2

Operations:

1. Select $b \in \mathbb{Z}_q$ and initialize $y_1 = 0$;
2. Guess the $1 - th$ digit of x_1. Initialize: $V_{try} = \{0, ..., b-1\}$, $\ell = 1$;
   (1) Select the minimal element from V_{try}, denoted as $d_{\ell,guess} = min(V_{try})$ and Call **Attack 1**.
   (2) If P_1 fails to finalize the signature, then
       (a) P_2 removes $d_{\ell,guess}$ from V_{try}: $V_{try} = V_{try} \setminus \{d_{\ell,guess}\}$;
       (b) Check V_{try}. If $|V_{try}| \equiv 1$, then P_2 knows that d_ℓ is equal to the only element in set V_{try} and go to (4). Continue otherwise;
   (3) If P_1 succeeds to finalize the signature, P_2 knows $d_\ell = d_{\ell,guess}$;
   (4) P_2 konws d_ℓ and update the known part of P_1's share x_1:

$$y_1 = y_1 + d_1 * b^{(1-1)}.$$

3. Repeat the above process until the u-th digit is guessed and update:

$$y_1 = y_1 + d_u * b^{u-1}$$

4. Finally P_2 got P_1's key share $x_1 = y_1$.

3.3   Quality of the Attack

Claim. For a selected base b, an average of $\tau_{\mathsf{avg}}(b) = \lceil \log_b q \rceil \cdot \left(\frac{b+1}{2} - \frac{1}{b} \right)$ signatures are needed for the adversary (i.e., corrupted P_2) **Adv** to extract P_1's share x_1. In the optimistic case, the lower bound is $\tau_{\mathsf{opt}}(b) = \lceil \log_b q \rceil$, while in the pessimistic case, the upper bound is $\tau_{\mathsf{pes}}(b) = \lceil \log_b q \rceil \cdot (b - 1)$.

Proof. Let the private share x_1 of P_1 be expressed in base b, consisting of $\mu = \log_b q$ digits. Each digit $d_\ell = 0, 1, \ldots, b-1$ occurs with uniform probability $\frac{1}{b}$. To identify each digit via signature attempts, we iteratively eliminate invalid candidates from a set V_{try}.

For a digit $d_\ell = i$, $i + 1$ guesses are required in the worst case, except for $i = b - 1$, where at most $b - 1$ attempts suffice since the last candidate can be inferred without querying.

Thus, the expected number of guesses per digit is:

$$\frac{1}{b} \cdot 1 + \frac{1}{b} \cdot 2 + \cdots + \frac{1}{b} \cdot (b-1) + \frac{1}{b} \cdot (b-1) = \frac{b+1}{2} - \frac{1}{b}.$$

Since the digits of x_1 are independent and uniformly distributed, the total expected number of guesses (i.e., MPC signing attempts) is:

$$\tau(b) = \lceil \log_b q \rceil \cdot \left(\frac{b+1}{2} - \frac{1}{b} \right).$$

In the optimistic case, each digit is recovered with a single guess:

$$\tau_{opt}(b) = \lceil \log_b q \rceil .$$

In the pessimistic case, each digit requires:

$$\tau_{pes}(b) = \lceil \log_b q \rceil \cdot (b-1).$$

Remark 1. For $b = 2$ (i.e., the Bitforge attack), we have $\tau_{\mathsf{avg}}(2) = \tau_{\mathsf{opt}}(2) = \tau_{\mathsf{pes}}(2) = 256$. The Bitforge attack can be viewed as a special instance of the Digit-by-Digit Extraction attack introduced in this work.

4   A Flexible and Covert Attack to Lindell17($\cdot$)

Lindell17($\cdot$) is a protocol proposed by Lindell [12], while Lindell17($+$) is a variant of it. The main difference between the two is as follows:

- In the Lindell17($+$), the private key is obtained by combining the private key shares of both parties as a sum in a finite field, while in the Lindell17($\cdot$), the private key is obtained by combining these shares as a product in the finite field. Accordingly, in the former protocol, the public key is given by $X = g^{x_1+x_2}$, whereas in the latter, the public key is $X = g^{x_1 \cdot x_2}$, where x_1 represents the private key share of P_1 and x_2 represents the private key share of P_2.
- In the Lindell17($\cdot$), P1's private key share is subject to a specific constraint, namely that $x_1 \in \left(\frac{q}{3}, \frac{2q}{3} \right)$, whereas in the Lindell17($+$), no such constraint is imposed.
- In step 2 of the Lindell17($\cdot$), the message that P2 sends is:

$$\mathcal{D} = Enc_N(\rho * q + [[k_2^{-1}]_q \cdot m]_q) \cdot Enc_N(x_1)^{[[k_2^{-1}]_q \cdot r \cdot x_2]_q}.$$

Based on Attack 2, a similar attack can be constructed against the Lindell17($\cdot$) protocol. The key trick is that, in the second step of the MPC signing process, the malicious P_2 crafts the following message to send to P_1:

$$D' = Enc_N(\zeta + (y_1 + d_{\ell,guess} * b^{\ell-1}) \cdot r' \cdot x_2' \cdot \varepsilon)$$
$$\cdot (Enc_N(x_1)^{r' \cdot x_2'})^{[b^{-\ell}]_N} \pmod{N^2}.$$

The effectiveness of this attack can be justified by referencing the proof of Attack 2, as the proof process is essentially the same and will not be repeated here.

5   Attack to Refreshed-Lindell 17(+)

Recently, a variant of the Lindell 17 protocol tailored for the $2, n$ threshold setting—referred to as Refreshed Lindell 17(+)—was proposed in [19]. This protocol introduces a defense mechanism whereby all parties refresh their private key shares after each failed signing attempt, aiming to disrupt iterative key extraction attacks by invalidating partial progress (Fig. 1).

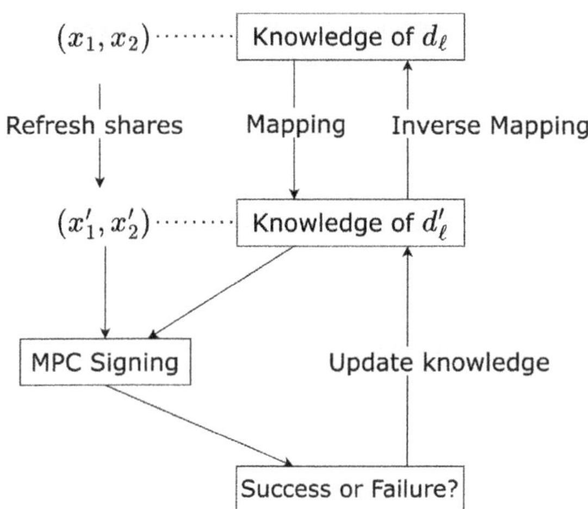

Fig. 1. Illustration of the refresh-based extraction attack.

However, we identify a security vulnerability in the special case of the 2-out-of-2 threshold configuration. In this section, we demonstrate that it is still possible to construct a continuous Digit-by-Digit Extraction attack by carefully correlating the private key shares before and after each refresh round, effectively bypassing the intended protection.

Before the key shares are refreshed, the corrupted party P_2 has access to the following information about P_1's share x_1:

- $y_1 = x_1 \bmod b^{\ell-1}$;
- The trial digit set V_{try} for the ℓ-th digit d_ℓ.

After the refresh, P_2 receives its new share x'_2, which allows it to compute the offset of x_1 due to the refresh: $\omega = x_1 - x'_1 = x'_2 - x_2 \pmod{q}$.

Depending on the range of x_1, the computation splits into two cases:

Case 1: $x_1 \in [0, \frac{q}{2})$

- $t = \frac{y_1 + [\omega]_{b^{\ell-1}}}{b^{\ell-1}}$;
- $y'_1 = [y_1 + [\omega]_{b^{\ell-1}}]_{b^{\ell-1}}$.
- $V'_{try} = \{[(v + \omega_\ell + t)]_b | v \in V_{try}\}$ for ℓ-th digit d'_ℓ;
- $d_{\ell,guess} = [d'_{\ell,guess} - [\omega]_{b^\ell} - t]_b$.

Case 2: $x_1 \in [\frac{q}{2}, q)$

- $\eta = q - \omega$;
- $t = \frac{b^\ell + y_1 - [\eta]_{b^{\ell-1}}}{b^{\ell-1}}$;
- $y_1' = [y_1 - [\eta]_{b^{\ell-1}}]_{b^{\ell-1}}$.
- $V_{try}' = [(v - \eta_\ell + t - 1)]_b$;
- $d_{\ell,guess} = [(d_{\ell,guess}' + \eta_\ell - t + 1)]_b$.

where $d_{\ell,guess}'$ is a randomly selected guess for d_ℓ' from the set V_{try}', with $d_{\ell,guess}$ being the mapped counterpart in V_{try} corresponding to $d_{\ell,guess}'$.

If P_1 succeeds in finalizing the signature in next MPC Signing Process, then P_2 knows $d_\ell = d_{\ell,guess}$; otherwise, P_2 removes $d_{\ell,guess}$ from V_{try} and continues.

Now that the key share refreshing protocol—originally introduced as a defense—has been effectively bypassed, we are once again able to exploit the attack strategy from Sect. 4 to recover P_1's private key share in full.

6   Attack to Patched HD Lindell 17

In practical applications, Lindell 17(+) is commonly deployed in hierarchical deterministic (HD) wallets, and is therefore referred to as HD Lindell 17(+). In this context, a wallet derives multiple sub-wallets through a hierarchical key derivation algorithm.

Following the disclosure of the Makriyannis attack [13], a mitigation was proposed in [15] to address the associated risks: if a sub-wallet fails to complete a signature, it is added to a BanSignList and subsequently disabled. This mechanism aims to prevent the attacker from launching repeated signing attempts from the same sub-wallet, thereby mitigating shard-extraction attacks.

However, we show that this defense is fundamentally flawed and remains vulnerable to a simple yet effective exploitation strategy.

It is important to observe the following characteristics inherent in the HD wallet design:

- The private key share x_1 held by P_1 remains the same across all child wallets. This property is critical, as it allows an adversary to gradually accumulate information about P_1's shard x_1 over multiple signing attempts involving different sub-wallets.
- The private key share held by P_2, in contrast, varies independently across different child wallets.

Given that each HD wallet may contain a large number of child wallets, the adversary can exploit this to mount a multi-session attack that bypasses the BanSignList defense. The attack proceeds as follows:

(a) Select a child wallet not currently listed in the BanSignList. Initiate an MPC signing attempt, and use the result—whether success or failure—to extract information about P_1's private share x_1. The extraction technique is identical to those previously described in the attacks against Lindell 17(+) (Sect. 3) and Lindell(·) (Sect. 4), and will not be repeated here.

(b) If the signature attempt fails, the corresponding child wallet is blacklisted by adding it to the BanSignList. The adversary then switches to another unblocked child wallet and continues the attack.

(c) After a sufficient number of signing attempts across different child wallets, the adversary can recover P_1's private key share x_1 in full.

7 How to Remediate the Attack

We propose, to the best of our knowledge, the first countermeasure addressing the class of "Selected-k2 Attacks" targeting the Lindell17 protocol. Specifically, we redesign the $\{k_2, R_2\}$ generation phase by adopting Protocol 2 as a secure substitute for the original method proposed in Lindell17 [12]. As a result, attacks with selected k_2 are prevented, since k'_2 and R'_2 are jointly generated by P_1 and P_2.

Therefore, based on the composable characteristics in protocol security [2], Protocol 2 can be regarded as a perfect implementation of the $\{k_2, R_2\}$ generation process in the Lindell17 [12]. Therefore, it can be securely embedded into Lindell17 as a replacement as illustrated in Fig. 2.

- Two random variables t and $\{k'_2, R'_2\}$ are mutually independent.
- Two random variables $\{k'_2, R'_2\}$ and $\{k_2, R_2\}$ is identically distributed which means k'_2 and k_2 are both uniformly distributed over the interval $(0, q)$.

Remark 2. To remain consistent with the notation style used in the original paper [12], we denote elliptic curve scalar multiplication as $x \cdot G$ (instead of g^x), and use $Q_1 + Q_2$ to represent elliptic curve point addition (instead of $Q_1 \cdot Q_2$).

Protocol 2: Random generation of R_2 jointly performed by P1 and P2

Give the cyclic group $\{\mathbb{G}, g, q\}$ where g is the generating element, here is how P_2 generates the new (R_2, k_2) denoted as (R'_2, k'_2) with the participation of P_1.

- P_1 sample $t \leftarrow \mathbb{Z}_q$, $t \neq 0$ and send $commit(t)$ to P_2;
- P_2 sample $k_2 \leftarrow \mathbb{Z}_q$, compute $R_2 = g^{k_2}$ and send R_2 to P_2;
- P_1 send $decommit(t)$ to P_2;
- P_2 verifies $decommit(t)$ and verifies $t \neq 0$, then compute
  - $k'_2 = k_2 \cdot t \pmod{q}$;
  - $R'_2 = R_2^t$.

Finally P_2 output R'_2 which could be verified by P_1 with the equation $R'_2 = R_2^t$.

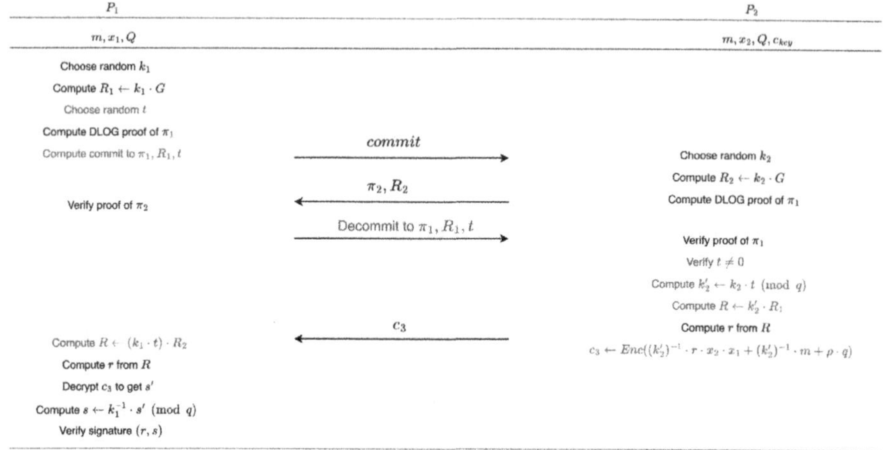

Fig. 2. Patched Lindell17.

8 Conclusion

This paper presents a systematic analysis of existing attacks against the Lindell17 protocol and introduces a new class of more flexible and covert attack techniques, which can be regarded as a generalization and extension of prior methods. Our proposed attacks not only successfully compromise the original Lindell17($\cdot$) but are also effective against its key variants, including Lindell17($+$), Refreshed-Lindell17($+$), and Patched HD-Lindell17. Although these variants incorporate defensive mechanisms such as proactive key refreshing or hierarchical key disabling, they still fail to provide effective protection against our attacks. These results indicate that widely deployed threshold ECDSA protocols remain vulnerable when confronted with realistic adversarial models.

To address this security gap, we propose a practical and effective patch that, to the best of our knowledge, defends against all currently known "Selected k_2 Attacks." By introducing a joint key generation mechanism that prevents malicious control over nonce selection, our remediation fundamentally disrupts the core dependency exploited by these attacks.

Our study also highlights a broader security insight: when the security model of an MPC protocol diverges from its actual operational environment, subtle yet devastating vulnerabilities may emerge. This underscores the necessity of revisiting and revalidating established MPC protocols under practical threat models.

This has important implications for the secure application of multi-party computation (MPC) protocols. Future research directions include developing methods for constructing efficient MPC protocols that are resilient to malicious participants.

References

1. Aumasson, J.P., Shlomovits, O.: Attacking threshold wallets. Cryptology ePrint Archive (2020)
2. Canetti, R.: Universally composable security. J. ACM (JACM) **67**(5), 1–94 (2020)
3. Canetti, R., Gennaro, R., Goldfeder, S., Makriyannis, N., Peled, U.: UC non-interactive, proactive, threshold ECDSA with identifiable aborts. In: Proceedings of the 2020 ACM SIGSAC Conference on Computer and Communications Security, pp. 1769–1787 (2020)
4. Dahlgren, F.: Breaking the shared key in threshold signature schemes. https://blog.trailofbits.com/2024/02/20/breaking-the-shared-key-in-threshold-signature-schemes. Accessed 20 Feb 2024
5. Doerner, J., Kondi, Y., Lee, E., Shelat, A.: Secure two-party threshold ECDSA from ECDSA assumptions. In: 2018 IEEE Symposium on Security and Privacy (SP), pp. 980–997. IEEE (2018)
6. Doerner, J., Kondi, Y., Lee, E., Shelat, A.: Threshold ECDSA from ECDSA assumptions: the multiparty case. In: 2019 IEEE Symposium on Security and Privacy (SP), pp. 1051–1066. IEEE (2019)
7. Doerner, J., Kondi, Y., Lee, E., Shelat, A.: Threshold ECDSA in three rounds. In: 2024 IEEE Symposium on Security and Privacy (SP), pp. 3053–3071. IEEE (2024)
8. Filipe, J.: Disclosing Shamir's secret sharing vulnerabilities and announcing ZKDocs. https://blog.trailofbits.com/2021/12/21/disclosing-shamirs-secret-sharing-vulnerabilities-and-announcing-zkdocs. Accessed 21 Dec 2021
9. Gennaro, R., Goldfeder, S.: Fast multiparty threshold ECDSA with fast trustless setup. In: Proceedings of the 2018 ACM SIGSAC Conference on Computer and Communications Security, pp. 1179–1194 (2018)
10. Gennaro, R., Goldfeder, S.: One round threshold ECDSA with identifiable abort. Cryptology ePrint Archive (2020)
11. KZen, T.: Bitcoin wallet powered by two-party ECDSA - extended abstract. https://github.com/ZenGo-X/gotham-city/blob/master/white-paper/white-paper.pdf. Accessed 19 Dec 2018
12. Lindell, Y.: Fast secure two-party ECDSA signing. In: Katz, J., Shacham, H. (eds.) CRYPTO 2017. LNCS, vol. 10402, pp. 613–644. Springer, Cham (2017). https://doi.org/10.1007/978-3-319-63715-0_21
13. Makriyannis, N., Yomtov, O., Galansky, A.: Practical key-extraction attacks in leading MPC wallets. In: Proceedings of the 2024 on ACM SIGSAC Conference on Computer and Communications Security, pp. 3053–3064 (2024)
14. Nguyen, D.H., Nguyen, A.K., Nguyen, H.G., Nguyen, T., Nguyen, A.Q.: New key extraction attacks on threshold ECDSA implementations (2023)
15. OKX, T.: https://github.com/okx/threshold-lib. https://github.com/okx/threshold-lib. Accessed 19 Dec 2018
16. Paillier, P.: Public-key cryptosystems based on composite degree residuosity classes. In: International Conference on the Theory and Applications of Cryptographic Techniques, pp. 223–238. Springer (1999)
17. Tymokhanov, D., Shlomovits, O.: Alpha-rays: Key extraction attacks on threshold ECDSA implementations. Cryptology ePrint Archive (2021)

18. Wuille, P.: Hierarchical deterministic wallets. https://github.com/bitcoin/bips/blob/master/bip-0032.mediawiki. Accessed 11 Feb 2012
19. Zhong, L., et al.: Fast 2-out-of-n ECDSA threshold signature. In: 2023 IEEE International Conference on Parallel & Distributed Processing with Applications, Big Data & Cloud Computing, Sustainable Computing & Communications, Social Computing & Networking (ISPA/BDCloud/SocialCom/SustainCom), pp. 456–465. IEEE (2023)

RRSC: Revocable Ring Signature Scheme over CRYSTALS-Dilithium for VANETs

Yatao Yang[1(✉)], Deng Pan[1(✉)], Liangyu Chen[1], and Xin Chang[2]

[1] Beijing Electronic Science and Technology Institute, Beijing 100700, China
yy2008@163.com
[2] China CITIC Securities, Xi'an 710018, China

Abstract. The theory and technology of Vehicular Ad-Hoc Networks (VANETs) have steadily advanced, significantly improving road network efficiency and driving safety. However, security issues such as identity privacy protection, the correctness, and timeliness of information transmission in vehicular communication systems remain urgent challenges. Ring signature is a cryptographic scheme that deals with anonymous authentication and message integrity during VANETs communication, but most previous ring signatures suffer from excessive anonymity as well as the inability to resist attacks by quantum algorithms. To address the excessive anonymity in traditional ring signatures and their vulnerability to quantum computing attacks, we propose a revocable ring signature scheme (RRSC) based on the NIST-selected CRYSTALS-Dilithium lattice-based digital signature algorithm. This scheme inherits key technologies from the CRYSTALS-Dilithium digital signature, such as rejection sampling, high-low bit decomposition, SHAKE-256, and uniform sampling, with all polynomial computations performed in the NTT domain. In this scheme, the signer can associate the signature with a set of known members without revealing their identities, thus concealing the true origin of the signature. The scheme also provides a method for reducing the anonymity of the ring signature, while allowing the authorizing authority to revoke the anonymity of the true signer under any circumstances. Additionally, the correctness, anonymity, revocability, and unforgeability of the RRSC scheme are proven under the random oracle model. Moreover, since the algorithm does not require the construction of complex trapdoor generation functions, the RRSC scheme offers advantages in both time and storage efficiency.

Keywords: Ring signature · CRYSTALS-Dilithium · VANETs · Lattice · Post-Quantum cryptography

1 Introduction

The rapid development of the Internet of Things (IoT) has facilitated the emergence of vehicular ad-hoc networks (VANETs), and related theories and technologies have been continuously refined [5]. These advances have greatly improved driving safety and traffic efficiency. However, issues concerning identity protection, as well as the accuracy and timeliness of information transmission in vehicular communications, have gained increasing attention. As VANETs operate in an open wireless network environment, attackers may send false information to Road Side Units (RSUs) or other vehicles, posing significant road safety risks [15]. Therefore, ensuring anonymous authentication and message integrity in VANET communications has become a critical focus of cryptographic research [7,8,12,13]. Ring signatures have emerged as an important cryptographic solution to address these challenges.

Ring signatures were proposed by Rivest and have become a prominent research direction in public key cryptography [10]. In this system, a signer can collect the public keys of specific users to form a ring and sign on behalf of the ring. During signature verification, only the signature can be verified as originating from a particular ring, and the specific signing member remains unidentified. The anonymity feature of ring signatures makes them ideal for various privacy applications on the Internet, such as e-voting, e-commerce, blockchain, and anonymous transaction systems [9,11,14].

However, absolute anonymity in general ring signatures can be problematic in certain scenarios, such as when ring members abuse their signing power for personal gain. For example, For example, in an anonymous e-commerce system, dishonest users may make multiple purchases using e-money. To avoid the absolute anonymity of ring signatures, Liu et al. [6] proposed linkable ring signatures (LRS), which allow two signatures generated by the same signer to be detected (linkability). This means that two or more ring signatures can be verified as originating from the same entity without revealing the signer's identity, effectively detecting duplicate signatures while protecting the true identity of the signer. However, in cases where penalties must be imposed on users who abuse anonymity, traditional LRS cannot fulfill this requirement. Therefore, Man et al. [4] proposed revocable ring signatures (RRS), which is a special type of linkable ring signature that incorporates a revocable mechanism. Its main goal is to provide a way to reduce the anonymity of ring signatures while enabling authorization authorities to enforce the revocation of the anonymity of the real signer under any circumstances. In traditional LRS, once a legitimate ring signature is generated, the identity of the signer is effectively hidden, thus preserving the anonymity of the user. However, in scenarios such as digital asset transactions or voting systems, it may be necessary to revoke a signer's privileges or verify their real identity due to specific circumstances or requirements. In this case, by introducing mechanisms such as revocation keys and lists, the RRS scheme allows the authorization authority to revoke a specific signer's signature when necessary, while preserving the anonymity of other signers. RRS scheme provides an effective way to achieve conditional privacy-preserving authentication and is particularly suitable for scenarios such as Vehicular Self-Organizing Networks, which need to protect users' privacy and prevent malicious behaviors at the same time [8].

Furthermore, with the successive proposals of quantum algorithms such as Shor's algorithm [3] and Grover's algorithm [2], coupled with the growing threat posed by quantum computers' computational power, current cryptographic algorithms based on traditional methods are no longer secure. In 2017, the National Institute of Standards and Technology (NIST) solicited proposals for Post-Quantum Cryptography (PQC) standards [1], leading post-quantum cryptography to rapidly become a research hotspot. The CRYSTALS-Dilithium algorithm is one of the most promising PQC algorithms among the digital signature candidates at NIST. Its structure is based on the 'Fiat-Shamir with Aborts' scheme proposed by Lyubashevsky. The algorithm reduces key and signature lengths as much as possible while ensuring security through rejection sampling and the extraction of high and low-order bits.

In summary, traditional RRS schemes struggle to resist quantum attacks effectively, while existing lattice-based RRS suffer from large public and private key overheads, large signature sizes, and low efficiency in key and signature generation. In this paper, we propose a revocable ring signature scheme over CRYSTALS-Dilithium (RRSC). The main contributions are as follows:

(1) In this paper, we construct a lattice-based RRSC scheme. The core of the scheme inherits key techniques from CRYSTALS-Dilithium digital signatures and incorporates revocability, which obscures the true origin of the signature. All polynomial computations in the scheme are performed in the NTT domain, providing the algorithm with a significant advantage in operational efficiency.
(2) Theoretical analysis demonstrates the correctness, anonymity, revocability, and unforgeability of the RRSC scheme under the stochastic prediction model.

2 Background Knowledge

2.1 Definition of Symbols

The symbols appearing in this paper are shown in Table 1.

Table 1. Notation Definition.

Notation	Description
$\mathbf{A}$	Matrix $\mathbf{A}$
$\tilde{\mathbf{A}}$	Matrix $\mathbf{A}$ after Gram-Schmidt orthogonalisation
$\mathbf{a}$	Vector $\mathbf{a}$
$\|\mathbf{a}\|$	The Euclidean paradigm of the vector $\mathbf{a}$
$\|\mathbf{a}\|_\infty$	The infinite parameter of the vector $\mathbf{a}$
$\mathbb{Z}_q^n$	n-dimensional vectors on module q
$\mathbb{Z}_q^{n \times m}$	$n \times m$th order matrix on module q
R	Polynomial ring $\mathbb{Z}[X]/(X^n + 1)$
R_q	Polynomial ring $\mathbb{Z}_q[X]/(X^n + 1)$
$\mathrm{negl}(\lambda)$	Non-negligible functions on λ

2.2 Difficulty Assumptions

Definition 1 (MSIS Hard Problem). Suppose that given a matrix over the ring $\mathbf{A}$ and defining the vector $\mathbf{x} \in R_q^m$, and defining the set of parameters $\{n, m, q, \beta\}$, solving the MSIS problem implies that a potential adversary needs to find a non-zero integer vector $\mathbf{y} \leftarrow E(\mathbf{A})$ that also satisfies $\mathbf{A}\mathbf{y} = \mathbf{x} \pmod{q}$ and $\|\mathbf{y}\| \leq \beta$ in the ring R_q. In this case, the adversary $\mathcal{E}$ is said to have the advantage of α to solve the modulo short integer solution problem if the following equation holds:

$$Pr\{\mathbf{A}\mathbf{y}=\mathbf{x}(\bmod q) \wedge \|\mathbf{y}\| \leq \beta | \mathbf{y} \leftarrow E(\mathbf{A}), \mathbf{A} \in R_q^{m \times n}, \mathbf{x} \in R_q^{m}\} \leq \alpha \qquad (1)$$

Definition 2 (MLWE Hard Problem). Pre-set a security parameter λ, whose size is defined to be an nth power of 2 (n is the dimension of the vector), such that the modes $q = q(\lambda)$ and $q > 2$, and assume that there exists an irreducible polynomial $f(x) = x^n + 1$ and a ring of polynomials $R_q = \mathbb{Z}_q / f(x)$. Denote by U a uniform distribution, and let S denote a probability distribution on the ring R_q, and $\mathbf{s} \leftarrow S$ denote a set of sampled data obtained from such probability distribution, then a set of MLWE sample data $L_{q,n,m,S}$ can be expressed as $\mathbf{s} \leftarrow S^n, \mathbf{g} \leftarrow S^m, \mathbf{A} \leftarrow U(R_q^{n \times m})$. The types of MLWE problems are divided into two types, s-MLWE for searching and d-MLWE for determining: s-MLWE requires to recover the vectors $\mathbf{s}$ and $\mathbf{g}$ given the parameter $(\mathbf{A}, \mathbf{t} = \mathbf{A}\mathbf{s}+\mathbf{g}) \leftarrow L_{q,n,m,S}$, and d-MLWE is used to distinguish between two distributions i.e. $(\mathbf{A}, \mathbf{t} = \mathbf{A}\mathbf{s}+\mathbf{g}) \leftarrow L_{q,n,m,S}$ and $(\mathbf{A}, \mathbf{t}) \leftarrow U(R_q^{n \times m} \times R_q^n)$. The matrix form of the MLWE problem is shown below:

$$\mathbf{t} = \mathbf{A}\mathbf{s} + \mathbf{g} = \begin{bmatrix} \mathbf{a}_1^T \\ \mathbf{a}_2^T \\ \vdots \\ \mathbf{a}_n^T \end{bmatrix} \mathbf{s} + \begin{bmatrix} \mathbf{g}_1 \\ \mathbf{g}_2 \\ \vdots \\ \mathbf{g}_n \end{bmatrix} = \begin{bmatrix} \langle \mathbf{a}_1, \mathbf{s} \rangle + \mathbf{g}_1 \\ \langle \mathbf{a}_2, \mathbf{s} \rangle + \mathbf{g}_2 \\ \vdots \\ \langle \mathbf{a}_n, \mathbf{s} \rangle + \mathbf{g}_n \end{bmatrix} \qquad (2)$$

3 Definition and Security Model for Recovery Ring Signature

A revocable ring signature scheme consists of the following five probabilistic polynomial time algorithms:

(1) Setup(1^λ): In this module, by inputting the security parameter λ, the key generation centre executes the system establishment algorithm and outputs the system public parameter set pp, the system's master public key pk_{tr} and the system's master private key sk_{tr}.

(2) KeyExt(pp, IDM_i): Input the system public parameter set pp and the corresponding identity information of each user IDM_i, generate the unique identity id_i through the user information, and output the public key pk_i and private key sk_i corresponding to each user identification code id_i.

(3) RSignGen(sk_i, M, id_i): Input the user's private key sk_i, the original message M, and the set of identifiers $R = \{id_1, id_2, ..., id_n\}$ representing the identities

---

Algorithm 1. Setup

Input: Set of user identities on the ring
$\{IDM_1, IDM_2, \ldots, IDM_n\}$
Output: Public parameter set $pp = (\rho, \mathbf{A})$,
system public key $pk_T = (\tilde{\mathbf{y}})$,
system private key $sk_T = (\tilde{\mathbf{s}}, \tilde{\mathbf{s}}')$

1: $\zeta \leftarrow \{0,1\}^{256}$
2: $(\rho, \tau) \in \{0,1\}^{256 \times 2} \leftarrow H(\zeta)$
3: $\mathbf{A} \in R_q^{k \times l} \leftarrow \textsc{ExpandA}(\rho)$
4: $(\tilde{\mathbf{s}}, \tilde{\mathbf{s}}') \in S_\eta^l \times S_\eta^k \leftarrow H(\tau)$
5: $\tilde{\mathbf{y}} \leftarrow \mathbf{A} \cdot \tilde{\mathbf{s}} + \tilde{\mathbf{s}}'$
6: **for** $i = 1$ to n **do**
7:     $id_i \in \{0,1\}^{256} \leftarrow H(IDM_i)$
8: **end for**
9: **return** $pp = (\rho, \mathbf{A})$, $pk_T = (\tilde{\mathbf{y}})$, $sk_T = (id_1, id_2, \ldots, id_n)$

---

of the n users on the ring, and output the digital signature $\mathbf{z}$ with revocable label T.

(4) Verify$(\mathbf{z}, pp, R, M)$: After receiving the generated digital signature $\mathbf{z}$, the verifier inputs the system public parameter set pp, the user identity on the ring $R = \{id_1, id_2, \ldots, id_n\}$ and the original message M, executes the signature verification algorithm, and outputs 1 if the signature $\mathbf{z}$ is valid, and 0 if it is not.

(5) Revoke(sk_{tr}, z, R): This module requires the execution of a trusted third party, the administrator is in possession of the system master private key sk_{tr}, enter a valid signature $\mathbf{z}$ as well as the identity mark $R = \{id_1, id_2, \ldots, id_n\}$, run the signature revocation algorithm and compare the result with the identity mark, and if the result is the same, the signature to be revoked can be confirmed.

Anonymity means that the true identity of the signer should be hidden and cannot be traced externally, thus protecting the privacy of the signer. And unforgeability means that no one can forge a valid signature except the legitimate signer, i.e., the signature scheme should be secure enough to prevent any unauthorized individual from forging a valid signature, and this property also ensures the trustworthiness of the signature. These properties constitute the core features of the scheme and together ensure that the revocable ring signature scheme is sufficiently secure and practical while protecting the privacy of the signers. In order to prove that the proposed revocable ring signature is secure, the following security model is defined in this paper.

The security model has been described in Appendiex A.

4   RRSC Scheme

The RRSC scheme's five algorithms are shown as follows.

Algorithm 2. KeyExt

Input: User identity IDM_i,
public parameter set $pp = (\rho, \mathbf{A})$
Output: Public key $pk_i = (\mathbf{y}_i, \mathbf{t}_i)$,
private key $sk_i = (\mathbf{s}_i, \mathbf{s}'_i, \mathbf{t}'_i, id_i)$

1: $\rho' \in \{0,1\}^{256} \leftarrow H(\rho \,\|\, IDM_i)$
2: $(\mathbf{s}_i, \mathbf{s}'_i) \in S^l_\eta \times S^k_\eta \leftarrow H(\rho')$
3: $\mathbf{y}_i \leftarrow \mathbf{A} \cdot \mathbf{s}_i + \mathbf{s}'_i$
4: $id_i \in \{0,1\}^{256} \leftarrow H(IDM_i)$
5: $(\mathbf{t}_i, \mathbf{t}'_i) \leftarrow \textsc{Power2Round}_q(\mathbf{y}_i, d)$
6: **return** $pk_i = (\mathbf{y}_i, \mathbf{t}_i)$, $sk_i = (\mathbf{s}_i, \mathbf{s}'_i, \mathbf{t}'_i, id_i)$

Algorithm 3. RSignGen

Input: Public parameter set $pp = (\rho, \mathbf{A})$,
public key set $L = (pk_1, pk_2, \ldots, pk_n)$, message M
Output: Signature $z = (e_1, \mathbf{a}_1, \mathbf{b}_1, \ldots, e_n,$
$\mathbf{a}_n, \mathbf{b}_n, \tilde{c}, \mathbf{g}, \mathbf{h}, C)$

1: $\mu \leftarrow \mathrm{CRH}(\rho \,\|\, M)$
2: $i \leftarrow 0$
3: **repeat**
4:     $\mathbf{x} \leftarrow \textsc{ExpandMask}(\mu, i)$
5:     $\mathbf{w} \leftarrow \mathbf{A} \cdot \mathbf{x}$
6:     $\mathbf{w}_1 \leftarrow \textsc{HighBits}_q(\mathbf{w}, 2\gamma_2)$
7:     $\tilde{c} \leftarrow H(\mu \,\|\, \mathbf{w}_1)$
8:     $c \leftarrow \textsc{SampleInBall}(\tilde{c})$
9:     $\mathbf{g} \leftarrow \mathbf{x} + c \cdot \mathbf{s}_\pi$
10:    $\mathbf{r}_0 \leftarrow \textsc{LowBits}_q(\mathbf{w} - c \cdot \mathbf{s}'_\pi, 2\gamma_2)$
11:    $i \leftarrow i + 1$
12: **until** $\|\mathbf{g}\|_\infty < \gamma_1 - \beta$ **and** $\|\mathbf{r}_0\| < \gamma_2 - \beta$ **and** $\|c \cdot \mathbf{t}_\pi\|_\infty < \gamma_2$
13: $\mathbf{h} \leftarrow \textsc{MakeHint}_q(-c \cdot \mathbf{t}_\pi, \mathbf{w} - c \cdot \mathbf{s}'_\pi + c \cdot \mathbf{t}'_\pi, 2\gamma_2)$
14: $C \leftarrow \tilde{\mathbf{y}}^T \cdot \mathbf{w}_1 + id_\pi$
15: Sample $\mathbf{u} \leftarrow S^{k+l}_{\gamma_1 - 1}$, $\mathbf{v} \leftarrow S^l_{\gamma_1 - 1}$
16: $e_{\pi+1} \leftarrow H(\mu, pk_{\pi+1}, \bar{\mathbf{A}} \cdot \mathbf{u}, \tilde{\mathbf{y}}^T \cdot \mathbf{v})$
17: **for** $i = \pi + 1$ to n, then 1 to $\pi - 1$ **do**
18:    Sample $\mathbf{a}_i \leftarrow S^{k+l}_{\gamma_1 - 1}$, $\mathbf{b}_i \leftarrow S^l_{\gamma_1 - 1}$
19:    $\alpha_i \leftarrow \bar{\mathbf{A}} \cdot \mathbf{a}_i - e_i \cdot \mathbf{y}_i$
20:    $\Omega_i \leftarrow \tilde{\mathbf{y}}^T \cdot \mathbf{b}_i - e_i \cdot (C - id_i)$
21:    $e_{i+1} \leftarrow H(\mu, pk_{i+1}, \alpha_i, \Omega_i)$
22: **end for**
23: $\mathbf{a}_\pi \leftarrow \mathbf{u} + e_\pi \cdot \begin{bmatrix} \mathbf{s}_\pi \\ \mathbf{s}'_\pi \end{bmatrix}$
24: $\mathbf{b}_\pi \leftarrow \mathbf{v} + e_\pi \cdot \mathbf{w}_1$
25: **return** $z = (e_1, \mathbf{a}_1, \mathbf{b}_1, \ldots, e_n, \mathbf{a}_n, \mathbf{b}_n, \tilde{c}, \mathbf{g}, \mathbf{h}, C)$

Algorithm 4. Verify

Input: Public parameter set $pp = (\rho, \mathbf{A})$,
signature $z = (e_1, \mathbf{a}_1, \mathbf{b}_1, \ldots, e_n, \mathbf{a}_n, \mathbf{b}_n,$
$\tilde{c}, \mathbf{g}, \mathbf{h}, C)$, message M
Output: 0 or 1

1: $\mu \leftarrow \mathrm{CRH}(\rho \,\|\, M)$
2: Parse (C, e_1) from z
3: **for** $i = 1$ to $n - 1$ **do**
4:　　$e_{i+1}^* \leftarrow H(\mu, pk_i, \bar{\mathbf{A}} \cdot \mathbf{a}_i - e_i^* \cdot \mathbf{y}_i, \tilde{\mathbf{y}} \cdot \mathbf{b}_i - e_i^* \cdot (C - id_i))$
5:　　**if** $e_i \neq e_i^*$ **then**
6:　　　　**return** 0
7:　　**end if**
8: **end for**
9: $e_1^* \leftarrow H(\mu, pk_1, \bar{\mathbf{A}} \cdot \mathbf{a}_n - e_n^* \cdot \mathbf{y}_n, \tilde{\mathbf{y}} \cdot \mathbf{b}_n - e_n^* \cdot (C - id_n))$
10: **if** $e_1 = e_1^*$ **then**
11:　　**return** 1
12: **else**
13:　　**return** 0
14: **end if**

Algorithm 5. Revoke

Input: User identity set $\{IDM_1, IDM_2, \ldots, IDM_n\}$,
public parameter set $pp = (\rho, \mathbf{A})$
Output: Identity index i (the signer)

1: $\mu \leftarrow \mathrm{CRH}(\rho \,\|\, M)$
2: Parse $(\tilde{c}, \mathbf{g})$ from z
3: $c \leftarrow \mathrm{SAMPLEINBALL}(\tilde{c})$
4: **for** $i = 1$ to $n - 1$ **do**
5:　　$\mathbf{w}_1^* \leftarrow \mathrm{USEHINT}_q(\mathbf{h}, \mathbf{A} \cdot \mathbf{g} - c \cdot t_i \cdot 2^d, 2\gamma_2)$
6:　　**if** $\tilde{c} = H(\mu \,\|\, \mathbf{w}_1^*)$ **then**
7:　　　　$id_i^* \leftarrow C - \tilde{\mathbf{y}}^T \cdot \mathbf{w}_1^*$
8:　　　　**return** i
9:　　**end if**
10: **end for**

5　Security Analysis

The security analysis has been described in Appendix B.

6　Conclusion

In this paper, we propose a Revocable Ring Signature Scheme (RRSC). To improve traceability and accountability, the scheme integrates identity-based tagging mechanisms into each signature. The security of the proposed construction is grounded in the hardness assumptions of the Module Learning With Errors and Short Integer Solution problems, and is formally proven to satisfy anonymity and unforgeability under the random oracle model. Importantly, the scheme also supports revocation, allowing users to invalidate their signatures when necessary, thereby enhancing the system's flexibility and practical applicability.

Acknowledgments. This study was funded by the Beijing Natural Science Foundation (Grant No.: 4232034) and the Fundamental Research Funds for the Central Universities (Grant No.: 3282024039,3282024052).

Disclosure of Interests. The authors have no competing interests to declare that are relevant to the content of this article.

A . Appendix A: Security Model

Definition 3 (Anonymity). Under the stochastic predicate machine model, assume that there exists an adversary A and a challenger C. A scenario is considered to satisfy anonymity if, after a series of simulated games in which challenger C has a negligible advantage of winning in the following anonymity proof game against adversary A, the scenario is considered to satisfy anonymity.

(1) Setup: Input the security parameters λ, and the challenger C runs the system setup algorithm to generate the set of system public parameters pp, the master public key of the system pk_{tr} and the master private key of the system sk_{tr}. After getting the output results, challenger C sends the system public parameters and system public key to Adversary A.

(2) Query: Adversary A initiates a private key query and a signature query to the challenger. Private key interrogation: Adversary A provides the identity of a known user to Challenger C IDM_a, and Challenger C runs the key extraction algorithm KeyExt((PP, IDM_i) to generate the corresponding private key sk_a under this identity and sends it back to Adversary A. Signature Query: Adversary A submits a user's ring identity id_a, the original message M and the set of user's public keys on the ring $L = (pk_1, pk_2, ..., pk_n)$ to Challenger C. Challenger C runs the ring signature generation algorithm RSignGen(sk_a, M, id_a, L) and outputs the corresponding signature $\mathbf{z}$, and finally sends the ring signature result to adversary A.

(3) Challenge: In the challenge simulation, adversary A needs to provide adversary C with the original message M, the set of user's public keys on the ring $L = (pk_1, pk_2, ..., pk_n)$, and the identifiers of the two unknown user's identities id_x ($x \in \{0, 1\}$). The challenger C then picks an unknown random number x and runs the ring signature generation algorithm RSignGen (sk_i, M, id_i) to output the corresponding signature $\mathbf{z}_x$, which is then sent to the adversary A. The adversary A then sends a random number to the adversary A, which is then sent to the adversary A.

(4) Guess: After completing the above process, the adversary A outputs the guess value x^* for the random number $x \in \{0, 1\}$, and if $x = x^*$ then it means that the adversary A has cracked the identity of the user participating in the

signature with a non-negligible probability $negl(\lambda)$. Meanwhile, the advantage of the adversary A to win the above game can be defined as:

$$Adv_A^{an} = \left| pr\left[x^* = x\right] - \frac{1}{2} \right| \qquad (3)$$

For any adversary A, if $\Pr[Adv_A^{an}(\lambda)] < negl(\lambda)$ then the programmer satisfies anonymity.

Definition 4 (Unforgeability). The unforgeability of a ring signature means that no one other than a legitimate signer with the correct private key can forge a legitimate signature that can be verified. Under the stochastic predicate machine model, the following unforgeability game is defined, if the advantage of winning by adversary A is negligible, then this scheme satisfies unforgeability, on the contrary if the advantage of winning is not negligible, it means that there is a security risk in the scheme. The simulation game of unforgeability between challenger C and adversary A is shown below:

(1) Setup: Input the security parameters λ and the challenger C runs the system setup algorithm to generate the set of system public parameters pp, the master public key of the system pk_{tr} and the master private key of the system sk_{tr}. After obtaining the output results, challenger C sends the system public parameters and system public key to adversary A.

(2) Query: Adversary A launches a private key query, a signature query, and a hash query to the challenger.

Hash query: the adversary A sends the original message M and the set of on-ring identifiers $R = \{id_1, id_2, ..., id_n\}$ to the challenger C. The challenger provides the corresponding hash result to the adversary.

Private key interrogation: Adversary A provides a known user's identity id_a to Challenger C. Challenger C runs the key extraction algorithm KeyExt$((PP, IDM_i)$ to generate the corresponding private key sk_a under this identity and sends it back to Adversary A.

Signature Query: Adversary A submits to Challenger C a user's ring identity id, the original message M and the set of ring identities $R = \{id_1, id_2, ..., id_n\}$. Challenger C runs the ring signature generation algorithm RSignGen (sk_i, M, id_i) and outputs the corresponding signature $\mathbf{z}$, and finally sends the ring signature result to adversary A.

(3) Forgery: The adversary A provides the challenger with a ring R^*, the original message M^* and the corresponding generated ring signature $\mathbf{z}^*$ with the following conditions:

Adversary A has not queried the private key of any member of the ring R^* during the query phase.

Adversary A has not queried the ring signature of(R^*, M^*) during the interrogation phase.

The generated signature $\mathbf{z}^*$ is a valid signature i.e. $Verify(R^*, M^*, \mathbf{z}^*, PP) = 1$.

Then it means that adversary A wins this game and the advantage of the adversary in this game is defined as:

$$Adv_A^{Forg} = |\Pr\left[Awin\right]| \tag{4}$$

And for any adversary A, denote the negligible probability condition by $negl(\lambda)$, and if $\Pr[Adv_A^{Forg}(\lambda)] < negl(\lambda)$ then the scheme satisfies unforgeability.

B   Appendix B: Security Analysis and Proof

B.1   Correctness Proof

This section focuses on the correctness of the proposed identity-based revocable ring signature scheme. It covers two main aspects: First, it explains how the signer completes the ring during the signature generation process, including the key computations and verification steps that ensure the formation and validity of a correct signature ring. Second, it discusses the correctness of the revocation mechanism, detailing how a ring signature can be revoked and how the revocation proof is verified to guarantee the soundness and trustworthiness of the revocation operation. This section focuses on the correctness of the proposed identity-based revocable ring signature scheme. It covers two main aspects: First, it explains how the signer completes the ring during the signature generation process, including the key computations and verification steps that ensure the formation and validity of a correct signature ring. Second, it discusses the correctness of the revocation mechanism, detailing how a ring signature can be revoked and how the revocation proof is verified to guarantee the soundness and trustworthiness of the revocation operation.

(1) Ring Closure Verification

Assume that in the generation of a ring signature, the actual signer is user π. During the signature generation process, after user π initializes the vector, the algorithm computes the parameter of the $(\pi+1)$-th user, denoted as $e_{\pi+1}$, according to Eq. (6):

$$e_{\pi+1} = H(\mu, pk_{\pi+1}, \bar{A}u, \tilde{y}^{\mathrm{T}}v). \tag{5}$$

In the ring signature generation algorithm, after computing the parameter $e_{\pi-1}$ of the $(\pi-1)$-th user, the intermediate parameters of user π are defined by the algorithm as:

$$a_\pi = u + e_\pi[s_\pi, s_\pi{}']^T, \tag{6}$$

$$b_\pi = v + e_\pi \cdot w_1. \tag{7}$$

To ensure that the ring is correctly closed at this point, it is necessary that the recalculated value $e_{\pi+1}^*$ equals the previously computed $e_{\pi+1}$, i.e., $e_{\pi+1}^* = e_{\pi+1}$. The detailed computation is as follows:

For any user in the ring, the intermediate parameter in the signature generation algorithm is computed as $e_{i+1} = H(\mu, pk_{i+1}, \alpha_i, \Omega_i)$, where $\alpha_i = \bar{A}a_i - e_i y_i$ and $\Omega_i = \tilde{y}^\mathrm{T} b_i - e_i(C - id_i)$.

For the actual signer, user π, we have:

$$\alpha_\pi = \bar{A}a_\pi - e_\pi y_\pi. \tag{8}$$

Given that $y_\pi = As_\pi + s'_\pi$, and substituting this along with the expression for a_π into the equation above, we get:

$$\begin{aligned}
\alpha_\pi &= \bar{A}(u + e_\pi[s_\pi, s_\pi']^T) - e_\pi(As_\pi + s'_\pi) \\
&= \bar{A}u + e_\pi \bar{A}[s_\pi, s_\pi']^T - e_\pi(As_\pi + s'_\pi) \\
&= \bar{A}u.
\end{aligned} \tag{9}$$

Similarly, for user π, we have:

$$\Omega_\pi = \tilde{y}^\mathrm{T} b_\pi - e_\pi(C - id_\pi). \tag{10}$$

Given that $C = \tilde{y}^\mathrm{T} w_1 + id_\pi$, it follows that:

$$\begin{aligned}
\Omega_\pi &= \tilde{y}^\mathrm{T}(v + e_\pi w_1) - e_\pi(C - id_\pi) \\
&= \tilde{y}^\mathrm{T}(v + e_\pi w_1) - e_\pi(\tilde{y}^\mathrm{T} w_1) \\
&= \tilde{y}^\mathrm{T} v.
\end{aligned} \tag{11}$$

Therefore, we have:

$$e_{\pi+1} = H(\mu, pk_{\pi+1}, \alpha_\pi, \Omega_\pi) = H(\mu, pk_{\pi+1}, \bar{A}u, \tilde{y}^\mathrm{T} v), \tag{12}$$

which matches exactly the computation of $e_{\pi+1}$ in the ring signature generation process as shown in Eq. (6). Hence, user π successfully closes the signature ring, completing the ring closure verification.

(2) Revocability Verification

During the signature revocation process, according to Algorithm 4.5, we know that Eq. (14) holds:

$$\mathbf{w}_1^* = \mathrm{UseHint}_q(\mathbf{h}, A\mathbf{g} - c \cdot \mathbf{t}_i \cdot 2^d,\ 2\gamma_2). \tag{13}$$

Given that $\mathbf{w} = A\mathbf{x}$, $\mathbf{g} = \mathbf{x} + c s_\pi$, and $(\mathbf{t}_i, \mathbf{t}_i') = \mathrm{Power2Round}_q(\mathbf{y}_i, d)$, the definition of the bit-decomposition algorithm implies $\mathbf{y}_i = \mathbf{t}_i \cdot 2^d + \mathbf{t}_i'$ $\Rightarrow$ $\mathbf{t}_i \cdot 2^d = \mathbf{y}_i - \mathbf{t}_i'$. Substituting into $A\mathbf{g} - c \cdot \mathbf{t}_i \cdot 2^d$ yields:

$$A\mathbf{g} - c \cdot \mathbf{t}_i \cdot 2^d = A[\mathbf{x} + c s_\pi] - c(\mathbf{y}_i - \mathbf{t}_i'). \tag{14}$$

When $i = \pi$, this becomes:

$$A[\mathbf{x} + c s_\pi] - c(\mathbf{y}_\pi - \mathbf{t}_\pi') = \mathbf{w} + A \cdot c s_\pi - c(\mathbf{y}_\pi - \mathbf{t}_\pi'). \tag{15}$$

Given $\mathbf{y}_\pi = A\mathbf{s}_\pi + \mathbf{s}'_\pi$, we substitute into the above:

$$
\begin{aligned}
\mathbf{w} + A \cdot c\mathbf{s}_\pi - c(A\mathbf{s}_\pi + \mathbf{s}'_\pi - \mathbf{t}'_\pi) &= \mathbf{w} - c\mathbf{s}'_\pi + c\mathbf{t}'_\pi \\
&= A\mathbf{g} - c \cdot \mathbf{t}_\pi \cdot 2^d.
\end{aligned}
\tag{16}
$$

Thus,

$$
\mathrm{UseHint}_q(\mathbf{h}, A\mathbf{g} - c \cdot \mathbf{t}_\pi \cdot 2^d, \ 2\gamma_2) = \mathrm{UseHint}_q(\mathbf{h}, \mathbf{w} - c\mathbf{s}'_\pi + c\mathbf{t}'_\pi, \ 2\gamma_2).
\tag{17}
$$

Furthermore, during rejection sampling, the constraint $\|c\mathbf{t}'_\pi\|_\infty < \gamma_2$ always holds. Then, by Lemma 2.5:

$$
\mathrm{UseHint}_q(\mathbf{h}, \mathbf{w} - c\mathbf{s}'_\pi + c\mathbf{t}'_\pi, \ 2\gamma_2) = \mathrm{HighBits}_q(\mathbf{w} - c\mathbf{s}'_\pi, \ 2\gamma_2).
\tag{18}
$$

Due to the design of the signature truncation parameter β, we always have $\|c\mathbf{s}'_\pi\|_\infty \leq \beta$. Also, step 10 of Algorithm 4.3 checks the validity of signature parameters, ensuring that: $\mathrm{LowBits}_q(\mathbf{w} - c\mathbf{s}'_\pi) < \gamma_2 - \beta$. That is, the existence of $c\mathbf{s}'_\pi$ does not affect the high bits of $\mathbf{w} - c\mathbf{s}'_\pi$, and by Lemma 2.6:

$$
\begin{aligned}
\mathrm{HighBits}_q(\mathbf{w} - c\mathbf{s}'_\pi, \ 2\gamma_2) &= \mathrm{HighBits}_q(\mathbf{w} - c\mathbf{s}'_\pi + c\mathbf{s}'_\pi, \ 2\gamma_2) \\
&= \mathrm{HighBits}_q(\mathbf{w}, \ 2\gamma_2) = \mathbf{w}_1.
\end{aligned}
\tag{19}
$$

Note that the signer's index $i = \pi$ is identified by checking whether $\tilde{c} = H(\mu \,\|\, \mathbf{w}_1^*)$ holds. Once this is confirmed, the system manager computes: $C - \tilde{y}^T \mathbf{w}_1^*$. Given the revocation tag $C = \tilde{y}^T \mathbf{w}_1 + id_\pi$, we obtain:

$$
C - \tilde{y}^T \mathbf{w}_1^* = \tilde{y}^T \mathbf{w}_1 + id_\pi - \tilde{y}^T \mathbf{w}_1^* = id_\pi.
\tag{20}
$$

Therefore, the system manager can recover the identity label id_π of the actual signer. Since the manager possesses the system private key $sk_T = (id_1, id_2, ..., id_n)$, the real identity corresponding to id_π can be determined, allowing the system to revoke the valid signature issued under this identity.

B.2   Security Proof

Theorem 1 (Anonymity). The RRSC scheme is unconditionally anonymous under the random oracle model.

Proof: Under the random oracle model, with the help of the security model designed in Definition 3.1, i.e., after a series of simulation games played by adversary A and challenger C, if adversary A is unable to differentiate between the distribution of the two signatures generated by challenger C, i.e., adversary A's advantage in winning the anonymity game is negligible (i.e., $\Pr[Adv_A^{an}(\zeta)] < \mathrm{negl}(\zeta)$), then this scheme has unconditional anonymity. Also, its anonymity game can be defined as follows:

(1) **Setup:** Run the system initialization algorithm to generate the security parameters $\zeta \leftarrow \{0,1\}^{256}$, and the challenger C obtains the public parameter set $pp = (\rho, A)$ and the system public-private key pair (pk_T, sk_T) generated by the

system. The challenger C sends the public parameters $pp = (\rho, A)$ to adversary A. The adversary A is not allowed to use the public parameters in the system.

(2) **Query:** Adversary A launches multiple random private key queries and signature queries to the challenger.

Private key query: Adversary A provides a known user's identity IDM_a to challenger C. Challenger C runs the key extraction algorithm $\text{KeyExt}(pp, IDM_i)$ to generate the corresponding private key sk_a under this identity and sends it back to adversary A.

Signature query: Adversary A submits a user's ring identity id_a, the original message M, and the set of users' public keys on the ring $L = (pk_1, pk_2, ..., pk_n)$ to challenger C. Challenger C runs the ring signature generation algorithm $\text{RSignGen}(sk_a, M, id_a, L)$ and outputs the corresponding signature z, and finally sends the ring signature result to adversary A.

(3) **Challenge:** In the challenge simulation, adversary A needs to provide challenger C with the original message M, the set of public keys on the ring $L = (pk_1, pk_2, ..., pk_n)$, and the identifiers of the two unknown user identities id_x ($x \in \{0, 1\}$). Challenger C then picks an unknown random number x and runs the ring signature generation algorithm $\text{RSignGen}(sk_a, M, id_a)$ to output the corresponding signature $\mathbf{z}_x$, which is then sent to adversary A.

(4) **Guess:** After completing the process as described above, adversary A outputs a guess for the random number $x \in \{0, 1\}$.

Suppose that after the above game two signatures Suppose that after the above game two signatures

$$
\begin{aligned}
z_1 &= (e_1, \mathbf{a}_1, \mathbf{b}_1, \ldots, e_n, \mathbf{a}_n, \mathbf{b}_n, \tilde{c}_1, \mathbf{g}_1, \mathbf{h}_1, C_1), \\
z_2 &= (e_1^*, \mathbf{a}_1^*, \mathbf{b}_1^*, \ldots, e_n^*, \mathbf{a}_n^*, \mathbf{b}_n^*, \tilde{c}_2, \mathbf{g}_2, \mathbf{h}_2, C_2)
\end{aligned}
\tag{21}
$$

are generated. The so-called existence of anonymity means that the generated signatures z_1 and z_2 are statistically indistinguishable to the adversary A. It is necessary to prove that the parameters of the generated signatures are compositionally indistinguishable during the ring signature generation process:

(1) In the ring signature generation, $\mathbf{g} = \mathbf{x} + c \cdot \mathbf{s}_\pi$ (where π is the real signer), the intermediate parameter $\mathbf{x} \in S_{\gamma_1}^l := \text{ExpandMask}(\mu, i)$ is known, and the private keys sk_i of different users are all generated by the key extraction algorithm and thus follow a uniform distribution and are indistinguishable. Therefore, the parameters $\mathbf{g}$ of different signatures are identically distributed and indistinguishable. Similarly, the parameters $\mathbf{h}$ and C are also indistinguishable.

(2) For the parameter e in the signature, its generation process is $e_{i+1} = H(\mu, pk_{i+1}, \alpha_i, \Omega_i)$, where H is SHAKE-256, a hash function that satisfies preimage resistance and collision resistance. Thus, the values of e are also indistinguishable for different users.

In summary, the two ring signatures $z_1 = (e_1, \mathbf{a}_1, \mathbf{b}_1, ..., e_n, \mathbf{a}_n, \mathbf{b}_n, \tilde{c}_1, \mathbf{g}_1, \mathbf{h}_1, C_1)$ and $z_2 = (e_1^*, \mathbf{a}_1^*, \mathbf{b}_1^*, ..., e_n^*, \mathbf{a}_n^*, \mathbf{b}_n^*, \tilde{c}_2, \mathbf{g}_2, \mathbf{h}_2, C_2)$ generated by different users are statistically indistinguishable. Therefore, challenger A's guesses about the origin of these two signatures will not be better than random, i.e., his probability of winning Adv_A^{an} is negligible.

Theorem 2 (Unforgeability). If both the MLWE problem and the SIS problem are hard problems, the RRSC scheme proposed in this paper is unforgeable under the random oracle model.

Proof: The difficulty assumption based on the MLWE and SIS problems is addressed under the random oracle model with the help of the security model designed in Definition 3.2, i.e., after a series of simulation games played by adversary A and challenger C, suppose that adversary A wins the unforgeability game with a non-negligible advantage. Before the start of the game, the index tables L_1, L_2, L_3, and L_4 are created by challenger C to record hash queries, private key queries, and signature queries, respectively, with all initial states blank. The interaction process of the game between challenger C and adversary A is described as follows:

(1) **Setup:** The system initializes and generates random security parameters $\zeta \leftarrow \{0,1\}^{256}$, and challenger C obtains the system-generated public parameter set $pp = (\rho, A)$ and the system public-private key pair (pk_T, sk_T). The challenger C sends the public parameters $pp = (\rho, \mathbf{A})$ to adversary A, who is not allowed to use the system public parameters.

(2) **Query:** Adversary A performs private key queries, signature queries, and hash queries to challenger C.

a) *Hash queries:* Adversary A selects a user's identity IDM_i, and challenger C checks the index table L_1 for this identity. If the query has already occurred, the result is returned directly; otherwise, $id_i = H(IDM_i)$ is added to L_1.

Adversary A inputs the set of public parameters $pp = (\rho, A)$, the public keys of n users $L = (pk_1, pk_2, ..., pk_n)$, the original message M, and the revocable label C, and performs a hash query related to the parameter e. If the query has already occurred, the result is returned; otherwise, the result $e_{i+1} = H(\mu, pk_{i+1}, \bar{A}u, \tilde{\mathbf{y}}^T \mathbf{v})$ is added to L_2.

b) *Private key query:* Adversary A inputs a user's identity IDM_i. If $IDM_i \in R$, then the game is terminated; otherwise, challenger C calls the key extraction algorithm KeyExt to generate the private key under the identity and records it in L_3.

c) *Signature query:* Adversary A submits a ring identity IDM_i, the public parameters $pp = (\rho, A)$, the public key set $L = (pk_1, pk_2, ..., pk_n)$, and the original message M_i to challenger C. Challenger C first queries L_4 to check if a signature result under this identity already exists. If it does, the result is returned; otherwise, the ring signature generation algorithm is run and the result is recorded in L_4 with the corresponding identity.

(3) **Forgery:** Adversary A provides a ring R^*, an original message M^*, and the corresponding forged ring signature $\mathbf{z}^*$ that satisfies the following conditions:

- Adversary A has not queried the private key of any member in R^*; - Adversary A has not queried the ring signature of (R^*, M^*); - The forged signature $\mathbf{z}^*$ passes the verification, i.e., Verify$(R^*, M^*, \mathbf{z}^*, PP) = 1$.

Suppose that after a finite number of related queries, adversary A successfully forges a valid ring signature for M^*: $\mathbf{z}^* = (e_1^*, \mathbf{a}_1^*, \mathbf{b}_1^*, ..., e_n^*, \mathbf{a}_n^*, \mathbf{b}_n^*, \tilde{c}^*, \mathbf{g}^*, \mathbf{h}^*, C^*)$.

To forge a legitimate ring signature, the core lies in forging the following key parameters: $C = \tilde{\mathbf{y}}^T \mathbf{w}_1 + id_\pi$, $\mathbf{g} = \mathbf{x} + c \cdot \mathbf{s}_\pi$, $e_{i+1} = H(\mu, pk_{i+1}, \alpha_i, \Omega_i)$.

Due to the one-wayness of the hash function, where the identity label id_π and the parameter $\mathbf{s}_\pi$ are private keys, according to Definition 2.3, solving $C = \tilde{\mathbf{y}}^T \mathbf{w}_1 + id_\pi$ and $\mathbf{g} = \mathbf{x} + c \cdot \mathbf{s}_\pi$ without the private key is essentially equivalent to solving an MLWE problem. However, since MLWE is assumed to be hard on lattices, this implies that the adversary cannot forge a valid signature. Therefore, the scheme is unforgeable.

References

1. Alagic, G., Alperin-Sheriff, J., Bassily, R., et al.: Status report on the first round of the NIST post-quantum cryptography standardization process. NIST Internal Report (NIST IR), vol. 8240 (2019)
2. Grassl, M., Langenberg, B., Roetteler, et al.: Applying Grover's algorithm to AES: quantum resource estimates. In: International Workshop on Post-Quantum Cryptography, pp. 29–43. Springer (2016)
3. Lanyon, B.P., Weinhold, T.J., Langford, et al.: Experimental demonstration of Shor's algorithm with quantum entanglement. Phys. Rev. Lett. **99**(25), 250505 (2007)
4. Revocable ring signature: Liu, D.Y., Liu, J.K., Mu, et al. J. Comput. Sci. Technol. **22**, 785–794 (2007)
5. Liu, G., Li, H., Le, J., et al.: LRCPA: Lattice-based robust and conditional privacy-preserving authentication for VANETS. IEEE Trans. Veh. Technol. **74**(3), 4698–4712 (2024)
6. Liu, J.K., Wei, V.K., Wong, D.S.: Linkable spontaneous anonymous group signature for ad hoc groups. In: Australasian Conference on Information Security and Privacy, pp. 325–335. Springer (2004)
7. Mahi, M.J.N., Chaki, S., Ahmed, S., et al.: A review on vanet research: Perspective of recent emerging technologies. IEEE Access **10**, 65760–65783 (2022)
8. Mundhe, P., Yadav, V.K., Verma, S., Venkatesan, S.: Efficient lattice-based ring signature for message authentication in VANETS. IEEE Syst. J. **14**(4), 5463–5474 (2020)
9. Perera, M.N.S., Nakamura, T., Hashimoto, M., et al.: A survey on group signatures and ring signatures: traceability vs. anonymity. Cryptography **6**(1), 3 (2022)
10. Rivest, R.L., Shamir, A., Tauman, Y.: How to leak a secret. In: 7th International Conference on the Theory and Application of Cryptology and Information Security(ASIACRYPT 2001), Australia, December 9–13, 2001. pp. 552–565. Springer (2001)
11. Russo, A., Anta, A.F., Vasco, M.I.G., Romano, S.P.: ChiroTonia: a scalable and secure e-voting framework based on blockchains and linkable ring signatures. In: 2021 IEEE International Conference on Blockchain (Blockchain), pp. 417–424. IEEE (2021)
12. Yang, Y., Zhao, Y., Zhang, J., et al.: Recent development of theory and application on homomorphic encryption. J. Electron. Inf. Technol. **43**(2), 475–487 (2021)
13. Yang, Y., Han, X., Huang, J., et al.: Bidirectional authentication key agreement protocol supporting identity's privacy preservation based on RLWE. J. Commun. **40**(11), 180–186 (2019)

14. Ye, Q., Lang, Y., Guo, H., Tang, Y.: Efficient lattice-based traceable ring signature scheme with its application in blockchain. Inf. Sci. **648**, 119536 (2023)
15. Zhang, Z., Atapattu, S., Wang, Y., Sun, S., Sithamparanathan, K.: Optimal cooperative mac strategies for wireless vanets with multiple roadside units. IEEE Trans. Veh. Technol. **74**, 877–893 (2024)

A Key Derivation Tree-Based Encryption and Verification Scheme for EV Data Auditing

Zhicheng Li[1], Jian Xu[1(✉)], Fan Wu[2], Aokang Qiao[1], Xiaomin Wu[3],
and Xiangliang Fang[2]

[1] School of Software, Northeastern University, Shenyang 110819, China
`xuj@mail.neu.edu.cn`
[2] State Grid Smart Internet of Vehicles Technology Co., Ltd., Beijing, China
[3] Electric Power Research Institute, State Grid Hubei Electric Power Company,
Wuhan, China

Abstract. With the advancement of Vehicle-to-Everything (V2X) and Electric Vehicle (EV) technologies, high-frequency streaming data generated from charging activities has been widely utilized in cloud storage and multi-party collaboration. However, such data often contains sensitive information, including user location, energy usage, and travel patterns. If shared without adequate protection, it poses significant risks of privacy leakage and data tampering. To address these concerns, this paper proposes a streaming data encryption and verification scheme based on a key derivation tree. The scheme integrates symmetric additive homomorphic encryption and verifiable message authentication codes (HomMAC) to ensure both data confidentiality and integrity, while enabling efficient and controlled data access authorization. A pseudorandom generator is used to construct the key tree, effectively mitigating the key explosion problem in streaming data environments. Theoretical analysis and experimental results demonstrate that the proposed approach outperforms existing methods in terms of security, performance, and scalability, making it well-suited for protecting sensitive data.

Keywords: Electric vehicles · Stream data encryption · Key derivation tree · Verify · Access control

1 Introduction

The rapid adoption of Electric Vehicles (EVs), along with the widespread deployment of public and private charging infrastructure, has brought new opportunities for intelligent energy management. As of July 2024, the number of charging stations nationwide has surpassed 10.6 million, with an average annual growth rate of 53%. In this context, key energy services, such as Vehicle-to-Grid (V2G) interaction, Demand Response, and renewable energy-friendly integration [1] are becoming increasingly dependent on high-resolution, temporally granular EV

X. Chen et al. (Eds.): DSPP 2025, LNCS 16177, pp. 153–162, 2026.
https://doi.org/10.1007/978-981-95-3185-1_10

charging behavior data. To improve data manageability and availability, and to support subsequent energy optimization and personalized service configuration, EV users typically upload and outsource this massive volume of streaming data [2,3] to cloud or edge servers for storage and processing.

However, the risks of privacy leakage significantly increase during the outsourcing and sharing of data [4]. Suppose raw streaming data is accessed without authorization or improperly correlated in cross-platform joint analysis. In that case, attackers may infer highly sensitive personal information such as user identities, travel routes, and activity patterns, resulting in severe privacy breaches. Therefore, streaming data must be encrypted before sharing, and the access control mechanism must support fine granularity, auditability, and revocability to enable secure and compliant collaborative analysis and multi-party cooperation. Some existing studies have attempted to use Pseudo-Random Functions (PRFs) [5,6] to derive individual data block keys from a master key, thereby reducing the burden of key storage. While this approach partially alleviates the problem, it still faces limitations in real-world applications of streaming data encryption and access control [7]. To address these challenges, this paper proposes a secure modeling and key agreement mechanism tailored for streaming data. Unlike existing KDT-based encryption frameworks, our work focuses on continuous, high-frequency, time-series EV charging data, which imposes strict constraints on temporal key granularity, low verification latency, and dynamic access delegation.

1.1 Contribution

To address the growing need for secure, fine-grained, and efficient protection of high-frequency streaming data in large-scale EV charging scenarios, our proposed scheme offers the following key contributions:

1. We design a temporal-aware scalable key derivation tree (KDT) specifically adapted to EV data auditing, where each derivation path encodes the temporal index of streaming chunks. This mapping allows direct derivation of all keys for a given time range from a compact root key and supports efficient revocation without reissuing unrelated keys, which is crucial in cross-platform EV audit applications.
2. We introduce a symmetric additive encryption method tailored for continuous streaming data, supporting efficient per-point and range queries over encrypted blocks.
3. We develop a HomMAC mechanism that provides end-to-end verifiability for each encrypted data point. Our approach ensures that any valid ciphertext-tag pair can be verified efficiently and supports correctness verification for both individual values and aggregated results.

2   Related Work

Encryption is essential for ensuring streaming data confidentiality, and recent studies have focused on efficient query processing that preserves both utility and privacy. Liu et al. [8] used secure multi-party computation (MPC) for dynamic time warping (DTW) queries over encrypted data, though scalability is limited by DTW complexity. To improve efficiency, Fang et al. [9] proposed a lightweight protocol based on secret sharing, and Qifan et al. [10] combined AES-GCM encryption with TEE-based Hoefding trees for secure training and prediction. Zheng et al. [11] supported similarity search over encrypted temporal streams using TWED and KD-trees under additive encryption. For uncertain data streams, Chen et al. [12] developed a probabilistic index, Miao et al. [13] addressed multi-pattern subgraph search, and Bai et al. [14] studied skyline queries with range pruning. Key management and access control are also critical. Vimercati et al. [15] proposed Over-encryption with hierarchical key trees, and Qi et al. [16] introduced CryptDAC for revocable encryption, though revocation remains complex. Tong et al. [17] supported secure k-NN with multi-user delegation and verification. Attribute-based encryption (ABE) and key-policy ABE (KP-ABE) [18–21] offer fine-grained control but struggle with dynamic, time-based queries. Hua et al. [22] proposed hybrid proxy re-encryption to convert ABE to IBE, while Xiong et al. [23] and Ge et al. [24] enabled proxy-based revocation without key regeneration. Hierarchical key generation [25–27] helps manage large key volumes but increases metadata and revocation costs.

3   Preliminaries

3.1   Homomorphic Message Authentication Code (HomMAC)

Let p be a modulus and X be a HomMAC secret key. For a ciphertext c, the HomMAC tag σ is generated using a pseudorandom function $\text{PRF}(i)$ as $\sigma = \left(\frac{k-c}{X}\right) \bmod p$, where $k = \text{PRF}(i)$. This tag σ is used to verify whether the ciphertext c has been tampered with. Given c, σ, and the verification key X, the receiver computes $k' = (c + \sigma \cdot X) \bmod p$. If $k' = k$, where k is the expected PRF output, the verification succeeds; otherwise, it fails.

3.2   GGM Construction

The GGM construction [28] builds a secure PRF from a secure PRG. Let $G : \{0,1\}^n \rightarrow \{0,1\}^{2n}$ be a PRG that stretches n-bit seeds into $2n$-bit outputs, where $G(s) = (G_0(s), G_1(s))$ and $G_0, G_1 : \{0,1\}^n \rightarrow \{0,1\}^n$ are derived from splitting the output of G into two halves. The GGM PRF $F_k(x) = G_{x_n}(\ldots G_{x_2}(G_{x_1}(k)) \ldots)$ for input $x \in \{0,1\}^n$ is computed by interpreting $x = x_1 x_2 \ldots x_n$ and recursively applying G based on each bit. Each bit of x determines whether to apply G_0 or G_1 at each level, forming a binary tree where each path is uniquely determined by the input x. The final node in the path yields the PRF output.

4   System Model

As illustrated in Fig. 1, the proposed three-entity system model for privacy-preserving V2G data collaboration comprises a DataOwner(DO), who collects high-frequency EV charging data, segments it into fixed-size windows, and encrypts each point using symmetric additive encryption with Hom-MAC tags generated via a key derivation tree from a compact master key; a DataServer(DS), an untrusted storage provider that holds ciphertext and tags and forwards encrypted chunks upon request; and a DataConsumer(DC), an authorized party that derives decryption keys, recovers plaintext, and verifies authenticity, enabling efficient point queries, range aggregation, and batch verification without exposing raw keys or plaintext.

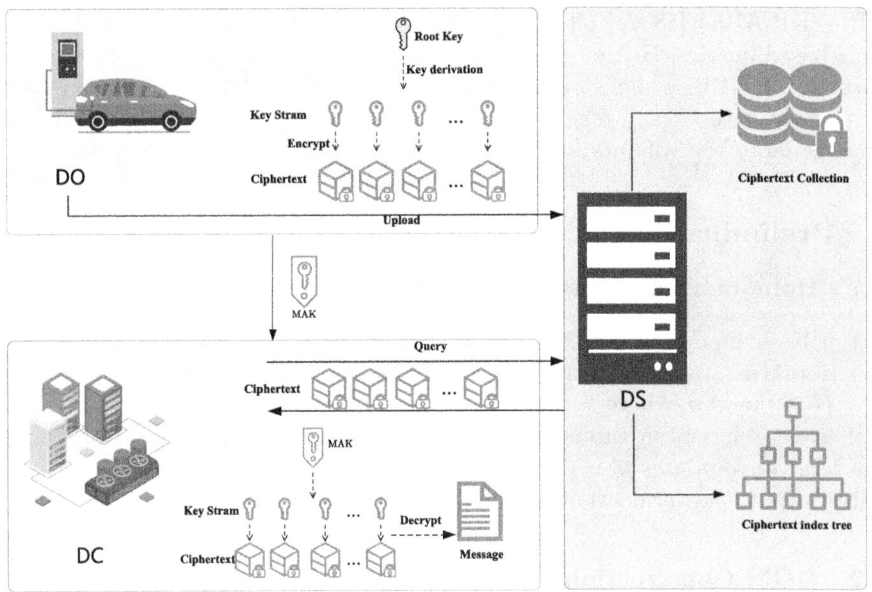

Fig. 1. System Model.

Definition 1 (IND-CPA Security). *Let $\lambda \in \mathbb{N}$ be the security parameter, M be the message modulus, and let $F : \{0,1\}^{\lambda} \times \{0,1\}^{*} \to \mathbb{Z}_M$ be a pseudorandom function. A stream chunk encryption scheme Π is said to be IND-CPA secure if for every probabilistic polynomial-time (PPT) adversary $\mathcal{A}$, its advantage in the following security experiment is negligible in λ:*

$$\mathsf{Adv}_{\mathcal{A}}^{\text{IND-CPA}}(\lambda) \stackrel{\text{def}}{=} \left| \Pr\left[\mathsf{Exp}_{\mathcal{A},\Pi}^{\text{IND-CPA}}(\lambda) = 1 \right] - \frac{1}{2} \right| \leq \mathsf{negl}(\lambda).$$

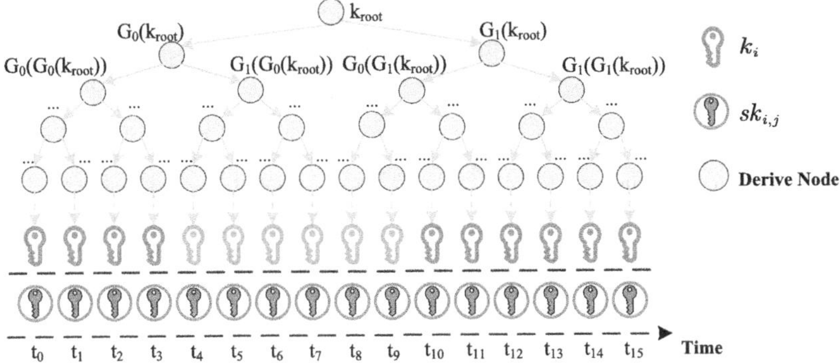

Fig. 2. Key Derivation Tree.

5   Streaming Data Encryption and Verification Scheme

5.1   A Detailed Construction

Setup. The data owner (DO) continuously collects EV charging data as a time-ordered stream, where each record is $dp_i = (ts_i, v_i)$, with ts_i denoting the timestamp and $v_i \in [0, M-1]$ the measurement value. The stream is divided into fixed-duration windows of length Δt, each forming a chunk $chunk_i = \{dp_{i,j} \mid ts_{i,j} \in [t_i, t_{i+1})\}$ containing n data points. This temporal segmentation provides a natural index for encryption and key derivation.

KeyGen. A binary key derivation tree (KDT) is generated from a master key k_{root} using a pseudorandom generator $G : \{0,1\}^\lambda \rightarrow \{0,1\}^{2\lambda}$, where $G(k) = G_0(k) \| G_1(k)$ produces two λ-bit child keys. As shown in Fig. 2, each data chunk corresponds to a leaf node in the tree, with the root key k_{root} as the base seed. For a binary path $x = x_1 \ldots x_h$, the derived key is $F(k_{\text{root}}, x) = G_{x_h}(G_{x_{h-1}}(\cdots G_{x_1}(k_{\text{root}}) \cdots))$. Each chunk index i is mapped to its h-bit binary $x^{(i)}$, yielding the leaf key $k_i = F(k_{\text{root}}, x^{(i)})$. From k_i, DO derives per-point encryption keys $sk_{i,j} = \text{HKDF}(k_i, j)$ and authentication keys $mack_{i,j} = \text{HKDF}(k_i, j \| \texttt{MAC})$ for $0 \le j < n$.

Encrypt. For each $dp_{i,j} = (ts_{i,j}, v_{i,j})$, the ciphertext is $c_{i,j} = (v_{i,j} + sk_{i,j} - sk_{i,j+1}) \bmod M$ and the homomorphic MAC tag is $\sigma_{i,j} = ((mack_{i,j} - mack_{i,j+1} - c_{i,j})/X) \bmod M$. The encrypted chunk is $cc_i = (c_i, \sigma_i)$, where $c_i = \{c_{i,0}, \ldots, c_{i,n-1}\}$ and $\sigma_i = \{\sigma_{i,0}, \ldots, \sigma_{i,n-1}\}$, and is uploaded to the data server (DS) for storage.

Decrypt. An authorized data consumer (DC), given the necessary leaf keys, recomputes $sk_{i,j}$ to recover individual plaintexts via $v_{i,j} = c_{i,j} - sk_{i,j} + sk_{i,j+1} \bmod M$. For range queries over an entire chunk, the aggregated cipher text $c_{\text{agg}} = \sum_{j=0}^{n-1} c_{i,j}$ is decrypted using $sk' = sk_{i,0} - sk_{i,n}$ as $v^{agg} =$

$c_{\text{agg}} - sk_{i,0} + sk_{i,n} \mod M$. This linearity property enables fast aggregate computation without accessing individual plaintexts.

Verify. For integrity verification, DC checks each point via $mack_{i,j} - mack_{i,j+1} \equiv \sigma_{i,j} \cdot X + c_{i,j} \pmod{p}$. For aggregated results, define $mack' = mack_{i,0} - mack_{i,n}$ and $\sigma_{\text{agg}} = \sum_{j=0}^{n-1} \sigma_{i,j}$; verification passes if $mack' \equiv c_{\text{agg}} + \sigma_{\text{agg}} \cdot X \pmod{p}$. This ensures correctness of both point and aggregated queries without revealing secret keys.

5.2   Correctness of HomMAC-Based Integrity Verification

Let $mack_{i,j} = \text{HKDF}(k_i, j)$ and $mack_{i,j+1} = \text{HKDF}(k_i, j + 1)$ denote the message authentication keys for data point j and $j + 1$ in chunk i, respectively, where k_i is derived from a secure key derivation tree seeded by a master key k_{root}. The encrypted value $c_{i,j}$ of a plaintext $v_{i,j} \in [0, M - 1]$ is computed using additive encryption as $c_{i,j} = v_{i,j} + sk_{i,j} - sk_{i,j+1} \mod M$, where $sk_{i,j} = \text{HKDF}(k_i, j)$ and $sk_{i,j+1} = \text{HKDF}(k_i, j + 1)$ are derived encryption keys. The corresponding homomorphic MAC tag $\sigma_{i,j} = \frac{mack_{i,j} - mack_{i,j+1} - c_{i,j}}{X} \mod p$, where $X \in \mathbb{Z}_p$ is a public constant used for modular scaling. The verification algorithm executed by the data consumer checks the correctness of $\sigma_{i,j}$ by verifying the $\sigma_{i,j} \cdot X = mack_{i,j} - mack_{i,j+1} - c_{i,j} \pmod{p}$ and $mack_{i,j} - mack_{i,j+1} = \sigma_{i,j} \cdot X + c_{i,j} \pmod{p}$. As demonstrated, if the ciphertext and tag are computed correctly by the data owner, the verification procedure will always return true. $\qquad\qquad\qquad\qquad\qquad\qquad\qquad\qquad\qquad\qquad\qquad\qquad\square$

5.3   IND-CPA Security

Theorem 1. *Let λ be the security parameter, M a modulus, and $F : \{0,1\}^\lambda \times \{0,1\}^* \to \mathbb{Z}_M$ a secure PRF. The symmetric additive homomorphic encryption $\text{Enc}(m_{i,j}) = (m_{i,j} + F(k_{\text{root}}, (i, j)) - F(k_{\text{root}}, (i, j + 1))) \mod M$ is IND-CPA secure under the PRF assumption.*

Proof. We use a standard hybrid argument.

Game 0 (Real IND-CPA). Challenger $\mathcal{C}$ samples $k_{\text{root}} \leftarrow \{0,1\}^\lambda$. The adversary $\mathcal{A}$ may query encryptions for (i, j). For the challenge (i^*, j^*, m_0, m_1), $\mathcal{C}$ samples $b \leftarrow \{0,1\}$ and returns $c^* = m_b + F(k_{\text{root}}, (i^*, j^*)) - F(k_{\text{root}}, (i^*, j^* + 1)) \mod M$. Let $\text{Adv}_0 = |\Pr[b' = b] - \frac{1}{2}|$.

Game 1 (Replace PRF by RF). Replace F with a truly random function $R : \{0,1\}^* \to \mathbb{Z}_M$, so $c^* = m_b + R(i^*, j^*) - R(i^*, j^* + 1) \mod M$. By PRF security, $|\Pr[\text{win}_0] - \Pr[\text{win}_1]| \leq \text{negl}(\lambda)$.

Uniformity Lemma. If R is random, $X = R(i^*, j^*)$ and $Y = R(i^*, j^* + 1)$ are independent uniform in $\mathbb{Z}_M$, hence $\delta = X - Y \mod M$ is uniform:

$$\Pr[\delta = k] = \sum_{y=0}^{M-1} \frac{1}{M} \cdot \frac{1}{M} = \frac{1}{M}.$$

Game 1 Analysis. Since δ is uniform and independent of m_b, $c^* = m_b + \delta \bmod M$ is uniform and independent of b, giving $\Pr[\text{win}_1] = 1/2$.

Conclusion. $\mathsf{Adv}_0 \leq \mathsf{negl}(\lambda)$, so the scheme is IND-CPA secure. $\square$

6   Performance Evaluation

The experimental evaluation was conducted on two platforms to reflect both general-purpose and resource-constrained environments. The first platform is a desktop computer equipped with an Intel Core i7-10700 CPU running at 2.9 GHz and 32 GB of RAM, representing a high-performance computing scenario. The second platform is a Raspberry Pi 4B featuring an ARM Cortex-A72 processor at 1.5 GHz, simulating a lightweight edge device. In the following, μs denotes microseconds, ms denotes milliseconds, and s denotes seconds.

We evaluate the proposed symmetric additive homomorphic encryption (SAHE) with HomMAC-based integrity verification by comparing average encryption and decryption times against two widely used homomorphic encryption schemes: EC-ElGamal [29] and Paillier [30]. We note that EC-ElGamal and Paillier are asymmetric schemes with higher computational cost, but are chosen as baselines due to their widespread use in verifiable stream processing. The comparison illustrates the significant performance advantage of our symmetric KDT-based design, without implying identical security–performance trade-offs. SAHE is instantiated with 128-bit keys, a key-derivation tree of height 32, and pseudorandom-generator-based key expansion. For fairness, EC-ElGamal uses 256-bit keys (128-bit security), and Paillier uses 2048-bit modulus. Experiments are conducted on two platforms: device 1 (Computer) and device 2 (Raspberry Pi), with results shown in Table 1. Across both platforms, SAHE consistently outperforms EC-ElGamal and Paillier in computational efficiency. Device 2 exhibits roughly $10\times$ slower performance than device 1 due to hardware constraints, but relative trends among schemes remain stable. HomMAC-based verification incurs negligible overhead: on device 1, generating a tag takes 0.48 μs, while encryption and decryption overheads are 0.31 μs and 0.29 μs, respectively. Thus, combined encryption+verification costs are only marginally higher than encryption alone. The dominant cost lies in key generation via the key-derivation tree, confirming the practicality of SAHE for both high-performance and resource-constrained environments. To evaluate the encryption efficiency of different schemes, we conducted comparative experiments using three representative cryptographic methods: EC-ElGamal, Paillier, and our proposed lightweight encryption mechanism. In the experiment, each data block consists of 60 data points, and a total of 100,000 blocks were encrypted, simulating approximately two months of real-world EV charging data. Fig. 3a and Fig. 3b show the encryption times on Device 1 and Device 2, respectively. The proposed scheme outperformed EC-ElGamal and Paillier on both platforms, achieving up to $2\times$ and $25\times$ speedups on Device 1, and nearly $10\times$ improvement over Paillier on Device 2. These results confirm the scheme's high efficiency and scalability, even under resource constraints.

Table 1. Average Encryption and Decryption Time on Device 1 and Device 2

Device	Operation	SAHE	SAHE-HomMAC	EC-ElGamal	Paillier
Device 1	Encryption	33.35 μs	33.61 μs	501 μs	131 ms
	Decryption	33.44 μs	33.87 μs	333 μs	129 ms
Device 2	Encryption	334.42 μs	346.06 μs	4.92 ms	1.26 s
	Decryption	334.84 μs	349.07 μs	3.54 ms	1.23 s

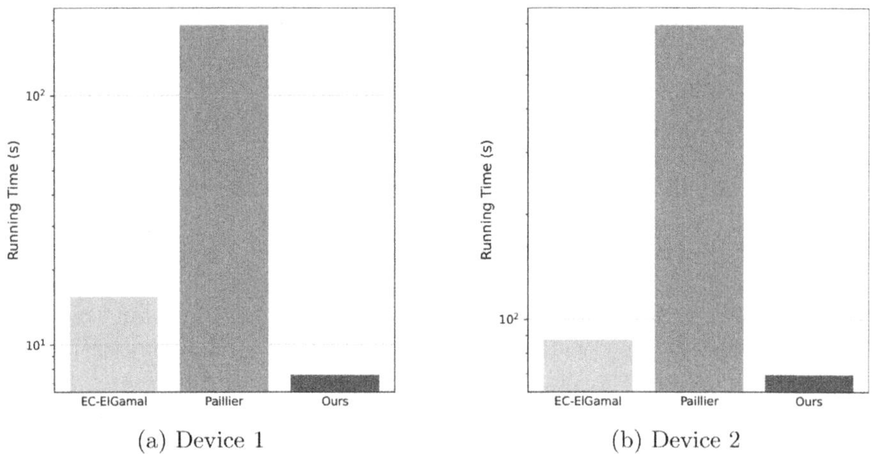

(a) Device 1   (b) Device 2

Fig. 3. Performance Comparison for Encrypt Phase on Different Devices.

7   Conclusion

This paper presents a secure and efficient scheme for protecting real-time streaming data in EV charging scenarios. By integrating a key derivation tree, symmetric additive homomorphic encryption, and a verifiable authentication mechanism, the proposed approach ensures lightweight operation, scalability, and fine-grained access control. It effectively mitigates key management overhead, enables efficient data query and verification, and minimizes sensitive information leakage. Experimental evaluations demonstrate superior computational efficiency and minimal resource consumption across heterogeneous platforms.

Acknowledgement. This work is supported by a Science and Technology Project of State Grid Corporation of China "Research and Application of Scalable and Secure Data Circulation and System Devices for Vehicle-to-Grid Interaction" (5400-202471366A-3-1-KJ).

References

1. Fang, T., Jouanne, A., Agamloh, E., Yokochi, A.: Opportunities and challenges of fuel cell electric vehicle-to-grid (V2G) integration. Energies **17**(22), 5646 (2024)
2. Shih, K., Han, Y., Tan, L.: Recommendation system in advertising and streaming media: Unsupervised data enhancement sequence suggestions. arXiv preprint arXiv:2504.08740 (2025)
3. Sun, X.: Dynamic distributed scheduling for data stream computing: balancing task delay and load efficiency. J. Comput. Technol. Softw. **4**(1) (2025)
4. Mahida, A.: Secure data outsourcing techniques for cloud storage. Int. J. Sci. Res. (IJSR) **13**(4), 181–184 (2024)
5. Faller, S., Ottenhues, A., Ottenhues, J.: Composable oblivious pseudo-random functions via garbled circuits. In: International Conference on Cryptology and Information Security in Latin America, pp. 249–270. Springer (2023)
6. Blass, E.-O., Kerschbaum, F., Mayberry, T.: Iterative oblivious pseudo-random functions and applications. In: Proceedings of the 2022 ACM on ASIA Conference on Computer and Communications Security, pp. 28–41 (2022)
7. Golab, L., Ozsu, M.T.: Data stream management. Springer Nature (2022)
8. Liu, X., Yi, X.: Privacy-preserving collaborative medical time series analysis based on dynamic time warping. In: Computer Security–ESORICS 2019: 24th European Symposium on Research in Computer Security, Luxembourg, September 23–27, 2019, Proceedings, Part II 24, pages 439–460. Springer (2019)
9. Fang, C., Guo, Y., Yongjin, H., Ma, B., Feng, L., Yin, A.: Privacy-preserving and communication-efficient federated learning in Internet of Things. Comput. Secur. **103**, 102199 (2021)
10. Wang, Q., Cui, S., Zhou, L., Wu, O., Zhu, Y., Russello, G.: EnclaveTree: privacy-preserving data stream training and inference using tee. In: Proceedings of the 2022 ACM on Asia Conference on Computer and Communications Security, pp. 741–755 (2022)
11. Zheng, Y., Rongxing, L., Guan, Y., Shao, J., Zhu, H.: Efficient and privacy-preserving similarity range query over encrypted time series data. IEEE Trans. Dependable Secure Comput. **19**(4), 2501–2516 (2021)
12. Chen, D., Chen, L.: Sliding-window probabilistic threshold aggregate queries on uncertain data streams. Inf. Sci. **520**, 353–372 (2020)
13. Miao, R., Zhang, Y., Qu, G., Yang, K., Yang, T., Cui, B.: Hyper-USS: answering subset query over multi-attribute data stream. In: Proceedings of the 29th ACM SIGKDD Conference on Knowledge Discovery and Data Mining, pp. 1698–1709 (2023)
14. Bai, M., et al.: S_IDS: an efficient skyline query algorithm over incomplete data streams. Data Knowl. Eng. **149**, 102258 (2024)
15. Di Vimercati, S.D.C., Foresti, S., Jajodia, S., Paraboschi, S., Samarati, P.: Over-encryption: management of access control evolution on outsourced data. In: Proceedings of the 33rd International Conference on Very Large Data Bases, pp. 123–134 (2007)
16. Qi, S., Zheng, Y.: Crypt-DAC: cryptographically enforced dynamic access control in the cloud. IEEE Trans. Dependable Secure Comput. **18**(2), 765–779 (2019)
17. Tong, Q., et al.: VFIRM: verifiable fine-grained encrypted image retrieval in multi-owner multi-user settings. IEEE Trans. Serv. Comput. **15**(6), 3606–3619 (2021)
18. Thushara, G.A., Bhanu, S.M.S.: A survey on secured data sharing using ciphertext policy attribute based encryption in cloud. In: 2021 8th International Conference on Smart Computing and Communications (ICSCC), pp. 170–177. IEEE (2021)

19. Xie, S., Zhang, L., Qing, W., Rezaeibagha, F.: Flexibly expressive and revocable multi-authority KP-ABE scheme from RLWE for internet of medical things. J. Syst. Architect. **152**, 103179 (2024)
20. Rasori, M., Perazzo, P., Dini, G., Shucheng, Yu.: Indirect revocable KP-ABE with revocation undoing resistance. IEEE Trans. Serv. Comput. **15**(5), 2854–2868 (2021)
21. Kumar, D., Kumar, M.: Outsourcing decryption of KP-ABE using elliptic curve cryptography. Int. J. Inf. Comput. Secur. **22**(2), 210–229 (2023)
22. Deng, H., Qin, Z., Qianhong, W., Guan, Z., Zhou, Y.: Flexible attribute-based proxy re-encryption for efficient data sharing. Inf. Sci. **511**, 94–113 (2020)
23. Xiong, H., Wang, L., Zhou, Z., Zhao, Z., Huang, X., Kumari, S.: Burn after reading: adaptively secure puncturable identity-based proxy re-encryption scheme for securing group message. IEEE Internet Things J. **9**(13), 11248–11260 (2021)
24. Ge, C., Susilo, W., Baek, J., Liu, Z., Xia, J., Fang, L.: Revocable attribute-based encryption with data integrity in clouds. IEEE Trans. Dependable Secure Comput. **19**(5), 2864–2872 (2021)
25. Mo, Z., Qiao, Y., Chen, S.: Two-party fine-grained assured deletion of outsourced data in cloud systems. In: 2014 IEEE 34th International Conference on Distributed Computing Systems, pp. 308–317. IEEE (2014)
26. Wang, W., Li, Z., Owens, R., Bhargava, B.: Secure and efficient access to outsourced data. In: Proceedings of the 2009 ACM Workshop on Cloud Computing Security, pp. 55–66 (2009)
27. Alderman, J., Farley, N., Crampton, J.: Tree-based cryptographic access control. In: European Symposium on Research in Computer Security, pp. 47–64. Springer (2017)
28. Nandi, M.: Improving tightness gap of GGM construction and its applications. In: Mukhopadhyay, S., Stănică, P. (eds.) Progress in Cryptology – INDOCRYPT 2024, pp. 28–50, Cham (2025). Springer Nature Switzerland
29. Liu, B., Blancaflor, E.B.: Data security and privacy protection scheme based on EC-ELGamal in federal learning. SN Comput. Sci. **6**(2), 1–10 (2025)
30. Shi, L.: Design of secure fair bidding scheme based on threshold elliptic curve ELGamal cryptography. In: International Conference on Emerging Internet, Data & Web Technologies, pp. 163–172. Springer (2024)

Security Weaknesses in ISO 15118-Based CCS2 Charging

Xian Li, Sheng Wen$^{(\boxtimes)}$, and Yang Xiang

Swinburne University of Technology, Hawthorn, VIC 3122, Australia
{xli1,swen,yxiang}@swin.edu.au

Abstract. With the rapid deployment of electric vehicles (EVs), the security of vehicle-to-grid communication protocols has become increasingly critical. ISO 15118, a core component of the Combined Charging System (CCS2), enables intelligent charging features over power line communication (PLC). Although the standard supports encrypted transport and certificate-based authentication, many implementations omit these mechanisms in practice. In this paper, we present an empirical security analysis based on custom-developed Electric Vehicle Communication Controller (EVCC) and Supply Equipment Communication Controller (SECC) prototypes. Through testing more than thirty commercial electric vehicles and multiple public charging stations, we identify critical vulnerabilities, including the absence of MAC address verification, lack of TLS support with silent downgrades, and misuse of MAC addresses as identity tokens. These weaknesses expose the system to man-in-the-middle attacks, session hijacking, and unauthorized access. We analyze the root causes of these issues, ranging from specification ambiguity to implementation deficiencies, and provide recommendations for secure deployment, including mandatory TLS enforcement and improved protocol binding. Our findings highlight the urgent need for more rigorous conformance testing and stricter adherence to security principles in ISO 15118 deployments.

Keywords: ISO 15118 · Electric vehicle charging security · Power line communication (PLC)

1 Introduction

1.1 Background and Motivation

The global push toward sustainable transportation has accelerated the adoption of electric vehicles (EVs) as an environmentally friendly alternative to internal combustion engine vehicles [9,16,20]. Driven by the need to reduce greenhouse gas emissions, governments and industries around the world are investing heavily in clean energy infrastructures, including EV charging networks. As EV ownership increases, the demand for efficient, intelligent and secure charging solutions has grown accordingly [3]. To support this ecosystem, robust communication

X. Chen et al. (Eds.): DSPP 2025, LNCS 16177, pp. 163–180, 2026.
https://doi.org/10.1007/978-981-95-3185-1_11

protocols between electric vehicles and charging stations are essential, enabling features such as automated charging, load balancing, billing, and grid integration.

One of the most prominent communication standards in this domain is the Combined Charging System (CCS) [13], which integrates AC and DC charging under a unified interface. At the core of CCS lies the ISO 15118 standard [6–8], which defines a high-level communication protocol between the EV and the Supply Equipment Communication Controller (SECC) over a Power Line Communication (PLC) channel. ISO 15118 facilitates advanced features such as Plug and Charge, vehicle-to-grid (V2G) capabilities, and secure identification via digital certificates.

Despite its technical sophistication and wide adoption in modern EV infrastructures, the ISO 15118 protocol stack has not been thoroughly evaluated in large-scale real-world deployments from a security perspective. Most existing studies focus on protocol specifications or limited simulation environments, often neglecting implementation-level vulnerabilities and inconsistencies of interoperability that may arise in practice.

In this study, we present an empirical security analysis of ISO 15118-based charging communication, based on our custom-developed EVCC and SECC. By systematically testing a wide range of production vehicles and public charging stations, we reveal multiple security vulnerabilities that pose serious risks to data integrity, authentication, and system resilience. Our findings highlight the urgent need to revisit implementation guidelines and deployment practices to ensure a secure EV charging ecosystem.

1.2 Existing Security Assumptions and Limitations

Although the ISO 15118 standard defines a set of security mechanisms, such as transport layer security (TLS), digital certificate-based authentication, and cryptographic key management, many of these features are specified as optional rather than mandatory. This has led to a heterogeneous landscape in which secure communication is inconsistently implemented in different electric vehicles and charging infrastructures. In many real-world deployments, TLS is either disabled by default or unsupported altogether, resulting in unencrypted data exchanges even in public charging environments. In addition, some implementations rely on the assumption that the physical connection between the vehicle and the charging cable provides sufficient protection against unauthorized access, overlooking the potential for adversaries to exploit the underlying PLC channel to inject, replay, or manipulate traffic [14,19]. Furthermore, since ISO 15118 communication is encapsulated within Ethernet frames transmitted over the PLC link, the absence of explicit guidance on Ethernet layer integrity measures, such as MAC address verification or spoofing protection, creates an additional attack surface [4]. Finally, while conformance tests [10,11] typically verify functional interoperability, they rarely account for security resilience or robustness against malformed input, leaving many implementations vulnerable to subtle but impactful protocol misuse. These limitations illustrate a concerning gap between the intended security model of the standard and the practical realities of its implementation.

1.3 Contributions of This Work

In this study, we conducted a comprehensive empirical investigation of the security vulnerabilities present in real-world implementations of the ISO 15118-based Combined Charging System. Unlike previous work that focuses on theoretical protocol analysis [2] or simulated environments [4, 12], our research is grounded in extensive field testing using a custom-built EVCC and SECC. These implementations enable fine-grained control over message construction, transmission timing, and protocol behavior, allowing us to evaluate both vehicle-side and infrastructure-side responses under controlled but realistic conditions.

Through testing interactions with over thirty electric vehicles from different manufacturers and multiple public charging stations, we uncover several critical security weaknesses. First, we identify a widespread lack of MAC address validation on the vehicle side, which exposes the system to risks such as MAC spoofing, man-in-the-middle attacks, and denial of service. Second, our findings reveal that the majority of tested vehicles do not support TLS-encrypted communication, and in an exceptional case where the vehicle requested TLS, the lack of encryption support from the charging station resulted in a silent downgrade to plaintext communication, thus allowing for a form of downgrade attack. Third, we observe a problematic operational practice among some public charging providers who use the MAC address of the vehicle as a primary means of identification and authorization, a method which is inherently insecure given that the MAC address is transmitted in clear text during the Signal Level Attenuation Characterization SLAC phase and can be trivially replicated.

By exposing these vulnerabilities through hands-on testing across diverse commercial systems, our work demonstrates the urgent need for stronger enforcement of security mechanisms in ISO 15118 implementations. In addition, our methodology offers a replicable framework for future protocol-level security evaluations in the electric vehicle domain.

2 Overview of ISO 15118 Communication Architecture

2.1 Power Line Communication and Ethernet Encapsulation

The ISO 15118 standard specifies a high-level communication protocol between the electric vehicle and the charging station, known as the SECC. This protocol is physically transmitted over the Control Pilot (CP) line using the PLC, specifically based on the HomePlug Green PHY (HPGP) standard [1], as shown in Fig. 1. HPGP enables data transmission over existing power conductors without the need for additional wiring, making it particularly suitable for the Combined Charging System (CCS) architecture.

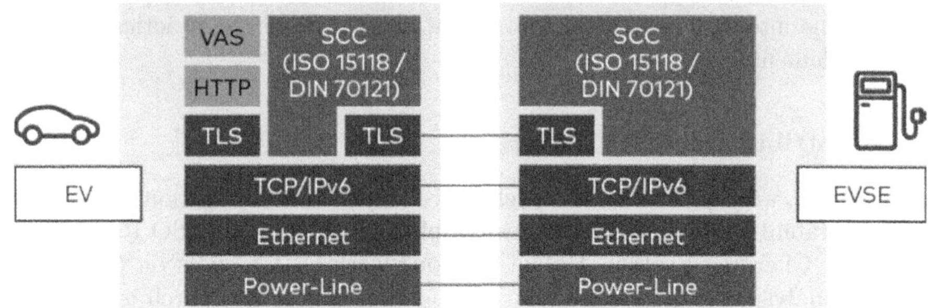

Fig. 1. ISO 15118 Communication Architecture between EV and EVSE. The figure illustrates the protocol stack defined by ISO 15118 for electric vehicle (EV) and electric vehicle supply equipment (EVSE) communication. Data is transmitted over power line communication (PLC), encapsulated in Ethernet frames and carried through the TCP/IPv6 stack. Transport Layer Security (TLS) optionally secures the communication channel, and application-layer messages are structured according to the ISO 15118 or DIN 70121 standards. Optional components such as the Value Added Server (VAS) and HTTP services may also be included on the EV side. Source: Vector Informatik GmbH [17].

At the data link layer, HomePlug Green PHY encapsulates Ethernet frames within the PLC medium. This means that messages exchanged between the EV and SECC follow the standard Ethernet structure, including the source and destination MAC addresses. Higher-level ISO 15118 protocol messages, such as service discovery, session initiation, and charging control, are then transported over these Ethernet frames. Although this encapsulation provides compatibility with conventional networking stacks, it also introduces traditional Ethernet layer vulnerabilities, such as MAC spoofing, replay attacks, and unfiltered broadcast message injection, if not adequately mitigated.

The use of Ethernet over PLC creates a unique hybrid environment that combines embedded systems, automotive communication protocols, and standard IT networking. As a result, security assumptions at the Ethernet layer directly influence the trust model and integrity of ISO 15118 communications. However, the standard does not mandate the implementation of robust Ethernet-level verification mechanisms such as MAC binding or link-layer authentication [18].

2.2 TCP/IP Stack in SECC–EV Communication

In addition to the physical PLC channel and the Ethernet data frames, the ISO 15118 protocol stack employs a conventional TCP/IP model for session-level communication. Once the physical link is established through the SLAC process, the EV and SECC negotiate IP addresses using the Dynamic Host Configuration Protocol (DHCP), followed by the establishment of a TCP connection. This TCP session acts as the transport layer for exchanging XML-encoded high-level protocol messages, following the V2G Application Protocol defined in ISO 15118-2.

The use of TCP/IP facilitates reliable and ordered communication, enabling advanced features such as certificate-based authentication, energy transfer scheduling, and tariff negotiation. In theory, the ISO 15118 protocol supports TLS over TCP to protect the confidentiality and integrity of transmitted data. However, the standard allows TLS to be optionally disabled, leading to varied support across different manufacturers and deployments.

This layered architecture, ranging from PLC-based Ethernet encapsulation to XML-over-TCP application exchanges, creates a multilayered attack surface. Security controls must therefore be implemented consistently across all layers. Failure to validate fields such as MAC addresses or to enforce encrypted transport can compromise the integrity of the entire communication session, as our empirical findings later demonstrate.

2.3 SLAC Process and MAC Address Exchange

The SLAC process plays a critical role in the initial handshake between the electric vehicle and the charging station in ISO 15118-based communication. Defined in the HomePlug Green PHY specification and adopted as a prerequisite step in ISO 15118, SLAC enables the two parties to assess the quality of the PLC channel and establish a point-to-point link over a shared physical medium.

The SLAC process involves the broadcasting and exchange of a series of well-defined Ethernet frames, including `CM_SLAC_PARAM`, `CM_START_ATTEN_CHAR`, and `CM_ATTEN_PROFILE` messages. These messages contain the source MAC address of the sending device as an integral part of their frame headers and payloads. In particular, the EV initiates the process by broadcasting a request that explicitly reveals its MAC address. This is necessary to allow the SECC to identify the EV that is requesting and respond accordingly.

While SLAC is essential for channel negotiation and link establishment, it also introduces a significant privacy and security concern: the MAC address of the EV is exposed in plaintext at the very beginning of the communication process. Furthermore, the protocol does not require any form of verification or binding of the MAC address in subsequent communications. As a result, a malicious actor on the same physical network could intercept the EV's MAC address during SLAC and later impersonate the vehicle by spoofing the address in Ethernet frames. This lack of binding between the MAC address observed during SLAC and the authenticated identity during the application session undermines the protocol security model, especially in public or shared charging environments.

2.4 TLS Support in the Protocol Stack

To protect the integrity, confidentiality, and authenticity of messages exchanged during a charging session, ISO 15118 supports the use of TLS layered on the TCP channel. In principle, TLS provides protection against eavesdropping, tampering, and message forgery by enabling encrypted communication and mutual authentication based on X.509 digital certificates. This mechanism is particularly important for scenarios that involve billing, authorization, and plug-and-charge functionality, where sensitive user and vehicle data may be transmitted.

However, the use of TLS in ISO 15118-2 is defined as optional and depends on the capabilities and configuration of both the EV and the SECC [15]. In practice, this results in inconsistent TLS deployment in different vehicles and charging stations. If either party does not support or agree to use TLS, the protocol allows them to return to an unencrypted communication mode. While this flexibility enhances interoperability, it also creates an opportunity for downgrade attacks, in which an attacker actively prevents the negotiation of a secure channel, thereby coercing both parties into exchanging sensitive information in plaintext.

Moreover, even when TLS is supported, the standard does not provide detailed guidance on key management practices, certificate revocation procedures, or certificate chain validation [5]. This lack of operational specificity increases the risk of misconfigured or vulnerable deployments, especially in systems where certificates are issued and managed by proprietary or ad hoc trust infrastructures.

Our empirical analysis, detailed in the following sections, demonstrates that the vast majority of tested electric vehicles do not initiate or enforce TLS-secured communication and that the protocol's fallback behavior can be exploited to compromise session security. These findings underscore the need for stricter enforcement of encrypted transport and more comprehensive security guidelines in ISO 15118 implementations.

3   Experimental Setup and Methodology

3.1   Development of Custom EVCC and SECC Implementations

To gain complete control over the ISO 15118 communication process and enable systematic security testing, we developed our own implementations of the EVCC and the SECC. These software stacks were written in C and deployed on STM32-based microcontroller platforms equipped with integrated HomePlug Green PHY communication modules. Our implementations fully support the ISO 15118-2 protocol, including SLAC negotiation, V2G session management, and TCP/IP communication over PLC, as illustrated in Fig. 2.

Our EVCC and SECC software allow for precise manipulation of protocol parameters, message contents, and timing. In particular, we implemented low-level access to Ethernet frame construction, enabling us to manually configure MAC addresses, manipulate header fields, and observe how external devices respond to unexpected or malformed input. Furthermore, both implementations include detailed logging capabilities at each protocol layer, facilitating comprehensive trace analysis and reproducibility of experimental scenarios.

3.2   Testbed Configuration

To ensure a comprehensive and realistic evaluation of the communication behavior of ISO 15118, we constructed a testbed that integrates a diverse set of elec-

(a) EVCC hardware

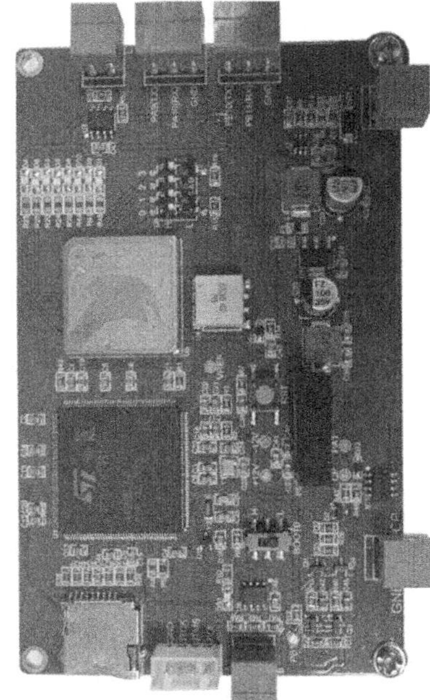

(b) SECC hardware

Fig. 2. Custom EVCC and SECC boards used during field testing.

tric vehicles, charging stations, and programmable controllers. The set of vehicles consisted of more than thirty commercially available electric cars spanning multiple manufacturers, production years, and regional markets. This diversity allowed us to assess implementation discrepancies and identify vendor-specific behaviors. Our infrastructure-side setup included various CCS2 compliant charging stations, covering both AC and DC configurations, sourced from multiple operators within public charging networks. Each station was tested under normal operating conditions to mirror authentic usage scenarios.

At the core of our experimental system were two STM32-based embedded platforms integrated with HomePlug Green PHY modems—one serving as the SECC and the other as an EVCC emulator. These bare-metal or lightweight RTOS-based implementations provided low-level access to protocol execution, including SLAC negotiation, Ethernet frame construction, and ISO 15118 message handling. Communication traffic over the power line channel was captured using external PLC sniffers and monitored via Wireshark, supplemented by custom protocol parsers for decoding SLAC and ISO 15118 messages. To minimize environmental noise and ensure repeatability of experiments, the system was deployed in a controlled test setup, with line filters and partial shielding applied to suppress power line interference. This configuration enabled both passive observation and active protocol injection under reproducible conditions.

3.3   Test Scenarios and Procedures

Our testing methodology was designed to evaluate the security robustness of ISO 15118 implementations under conditions that mimic real-world charging sessions, while introducing controlled variations to trigger and observe potential vulnerabilities. For MAC address verification, the SECC was deliberately configured to send Ethernet frames with spoofed or mismatched source MAC addresses immediately after successful SLAC completion. This allowed us to assess whether the vehicle performed any form of MAC consistency check before accepting application-layer messages. For TLS-related tests, our EVCC attempted to initiate TLS-secured communication sessions with the target vehicle. In cases where the EV signaled a willingness to use encrypted transport, we selectively enabled or disabled TLS support on the SECC side to observe how the EV handled negotiation failures and whether it would silently fall back to plaintext communication.

To investigate the misuse of MAC addresses as identity tokens, we also simulated replay attacks. In these scenarios, we first record SLAC handshake messages from a legitimate vehicle, including its exposed MAC address. We then emulated the same vehicle using our EVCC by reproducing the MAC address and SLAC profile, and attempted to initiate a new charging session at various public charging stations. This setup was used to evaluate whether the SECC or the back-end system relied solely on the MAC address for vehicle identification and access control. All tests were repeated multiple times across different devices and environments to ensure reliability, and all relevant behavior was recorded and time-stamped for subsequent analysis.

3.4   Data Collection and Logging Mechanism

To ensure rigorous documentation and traceability, all communication exchanges were recorded in multiple layers of protocol. Raw Ethernet frames were captured using mirrored Ethernet interfaces and time-stamped with submillisecond precision. The application layer messages were recorded in structured logs, annotated with protocol state transitions and error conditions. Each test session was associated with a unique identifier and metadata that included device model, firmware version, charger location, and environmental conditions (e.g., noise level in the PLC channel).

Post-processing scripts were developed to extract relevant security events, such as MAC mismatches, TLS failures, and unexpected session terminations. These data formed the basis for our empirical analysis, which is presented in the next chapter.

4   Empirical Findings: Security Vulnerabilities

In our evaluation of more than 30 electric vehicles, the specific models of which are listed in Table 1, we identified three primary categories of security weaknesses.

Table 1. Tested Electric Vehicle Models

Car brand	Models
BYD	Shark; Dolphin; Seal; ATTO3; Sealinon; BC1218I(BUS); ATTO3
Tesla	Model 3; Modle S; Model Y(2020, 2021, 2022, 2023)
Mercedes-Benz	EQB250+; EQS450; EQE350; EQE300
JAC (Truck)	N55; N75; N90
Ford	EV Van; F150-PRO
Foton	Truck
Hyundai	IONIQ5
Volvo	EX30
LeapMotor	C10
Porsche	Taycan
MG	MG4
Chery	E5
Geely	LDV
Polestar	Polestar 3

4.1   Absence of MAC Address Verification on the Vehicle Side

During our MAC spoofing experiments, we observed that a considerable number of tested vehicles failed to perform any form of MAC address consistency check between the SLAC phase and subsequent ISO 15118 application layer communication. Specifically, we configured our SECC implementation to alter its source MAC address immediately after the SLAC handshake while keeping all other protocol parameters constant. In many cases, the vehicle continued the communication session without interruption, processing messages from an SECC whose MAC address no longer matched the one observed during initial link establishment.

This behavior indicates that many EV implementations are not validated MAC addresses, though used to facilitate SLAC and Ethernet layer addressing. From a security point of view, this omission introduces a critical vulnerability. A malicious actor within physical proximity of a charging session could complete an SLAC negotiation with a target EV and subsequently hijack the TCP session using spoofed frames. Such a man-in-the-middle (MITM) setup could enable command injection, unauthorized charging control, or information exfiltration. Moreover, this lack of binding between SLAC and ISO 15118 session layers violates the principle of end-to-end integrity, especially in an environment where Ethernet encapsulation is publicly observable over shared power lines.

4.2   Inconsistent TLS Deployment and Downgrade Behavior

Another identified major vulnerability is the widespread lack of TLS-secured communication in production vehicles. Among the more than thirty vehicles that we tested, only one attempted to initiate a TLS handshake during session establishment. In this case, our SECC replied that TLS was not supported, and the EV silently downgraded to unencrypted communication without warning or user notification, showing as 1.1. This fallback behavior, while technically allowed by the ISO 15118-2 specification, significantly undermines the security objectives of the protocol.

```
1 [2025-02-20 11:13:57.309] SDP: Rx the reqeust from the PEV (bytes=10)
2 [2025-02-20 11:13:57.309] sdp-req: ver=1, inv=fe, type=9000, length=2, sec=0, trans_pro=0
3 [2025-02-20 11:13:57.309] sdp-res: ver=1, type=9001,length=20,secc_port = 51496, sec=10,
      tcp=0
4 [2025-02-20 11:13:57.309] SDP: Tx the response to the PEV (bytes = 28, port = 51496)
5 [2025-02-20 11:13:57.809] SDP: Rx the reqeust from the PEV (bytes=10)
6 [2025-02-20 11:13:57.809] sdp-req: ver=1, inv=fe, type=9000, length=2, sec=0, trans_pro=0
7 [2025-02-20 11:13:57.811] sdp-res: ver=1, type=9001,length=20,secc_port = 51496, sec=10,
      tcp=0
8 [2025-02-20 11:13:57.811] SDP: Tx the response to the PEV (bytes = 28, port = 51496)
```

Listing 1.1. SDP (Service Discovery Protocol) exchange between the EV and EVSE after SLAC completion. The SDP process is initiated by the EV, which broadcasts a request indicating its desire to establish a TLS-secured communication session (indicated by `sec=0`). The EVSE replies with `sec=10`, signaling that only unencrypted communication is supported. As shown, the EV retries the SDP request, but the EVSE responds consistently with the same configuration. Ultimately, the charging session proceeds without TLS, relying on unencrypted TCP communication, which poses a downgrade security risk.

The optional nature of TLS support leads to a fragmented deployment landscape, where some implementations support encrypted transport, while others operate entirely in plaintext. The lack of mutual enforcement or negotiation hardening allows an active attacker to disrupt or manipulate the TLS handshake, causing both parties to revert to an insecure state. This constitutes a classic downgrade attack vector. In the absence of additional protections such as strict TLS requirement flags, certificate pinning, or secure renegotiation policies, ISO 15118 sessions are left exposed to message tampering and impersonation.

Furthermore, the standard does not prescribe specific certificate validation logic or revocation mechanisms, making it difficult to trust even those implementations that nominally support TLS. Our findings demonstrate that without consistent and enforced adoption of TLS—accompanied by proper credential management—the security of ISO 15118 sessions remains largely aspirational.

4.3   Misuse of MAC Addresses as Identity Tokens in Public Infrastructure

In the course of our tests on public charging infrastructure, we encountered several commercial charging stations that utilized the MAC address of the EV as the primary means of identity verification. In these systems, vehicles previously registered with the back-end platform were identified solely based on their MAC address during a new charging attempt. If the MAC address matches an entry on the back-end whitelist, the charging session would proceed automatically, with payment deducted from the associated account.

This practice, while operationally convenient, introduces serious security risks. Because the MAC address of the EV is exposed during the SLAC phase in plaintext, it can be trivially observed and recorded by any adversary with access to the PLC channel. In our replay simulation tests, we successfully emulated legitimate electric vehicles by configuring our EVCC to use their recorded MAC addresses and SLAC profiles. In several cases, this led to successful authorization and energy transfer on public chargers, despite the absence of any cryptographic proof of identity.

The use of a globally broadcast and easily spoofed network identifier as an authentication credential violates the fundamental principles of secure identity management. Such deployments are vulnerable to impersonation, unauthorized billing, and denial-of-service attacks against legitimate users. Moreover, they reflect a broader industry trend of relying on low-layer identifiers in lieu of proper authentication mechanisms—often in contradiction to the intentions of the ISO 15118 trust framework.

5 Security Implications and Attack Scenarios

The vulnerabilities identified in our empirical analysis not only represent deviations from the intended security model of ISO 15118, but also expose the charging ecosystem to concrete and exploitable attack vectors. In this section, we analyze the broader security implications of these weaknesses and outline several plausible attack scenarios that could be realized in public or semipublic charging environments.

5.1 Man-in-the-Middle Attacks via MAC Spoofing

The absence of MAC address verification by many EV implementations enables a powerful class of man-in-the-middle (MITM) attacks. An attacker with access to the physical CP line, such as in a parking garage or multiport charging hub, can perform a SLAC handshake with a legitimate vehicle, record the vehicle's MAC address, and subsequently inject malicious Ethernet frames bearing a spoofed SECC identity. Because no binding is enforced between the SLAC-observed MAC address and the session initiating entity, the EV may continue communication with the spoofed SECC, unaware of the identity change.

This attack allows the adversary to alter ISO 15118 application layer messages, such as service parameters, charging limits, or tariff information. In more advanced scenarios, the attacker could manipulate the TCP stream to disrupt charging control or cause the EV to misinterpret the status of the energy transfer. If the EV fails to enforce application-layer message authentication (e.g., using digital signatures or TLS), the attack can be carried out entirely undetected.

5.2 Downgrade Attacks Through TLS Negotiation Manipulation

The protocol's permissive handling of encryption negotiation – where an EV or SECC can revert to plaintext if the peer does not support TLS –creates a straightforward avenue for downgrade attacks. An adversary positioned between the EV and SECC during the initial session establishment can intercept and suppress TLS handshake messages, forcing both endpoints to return to unencrypted communication.

Once encryption is disabled, all subsequent messages, including those related to billing, authentication, and session control, are transmitted in cleartext. This significantly increases the risk of eavesdropping, session hijacking, or manipulation of critical parameters such as energy requests, charging duration, or user credentials. Given that the protocol does not mandate user-visible indicators of the encryption state, such a downgrade may remain completely unnoticed by either party.

This scenario highlights the dangers of optional security in protocol design. In the absence of mandatory TLS enforcement or integrity guarantees, even well-intentioned implementations can be coerced into insecure communication states.

5.3 Identity Impersonation via MAC Address Replay

The use of MAC addresses as vehicle identifiers in several public charging deployments represents a severe violation of the principles of secure authentication. Because the MAC address is transmitted openly during SLAC, an adversary can observe and replicate it using a software-defined EVCC. In our tests, this technique allowed us to impersonate authorized vehicles and initiate charge sessions without cryptographic credentials or back-end registration.

Such attacks can be used to conduct energy theft, fraudulent billing, or to launch targeted denial-of-service campaigns by exhausting charging resources under stolen identities. Furthermore, the impersonation of high-trust vehicles (e.g., fleet accounts or VIP customers) could be exploited to gain preferential access or services. The attack is particularly concerning in roaming scenarios where backend systems may use only partial context (e.g., MAC + tariff ID) to authorize a session.

These findings demonstrate the danger of using transport-layer identifiers for authentication, especially in systems lacking secure channel binding or certificate-based trust models.

5.4 Risk Amplification in Large-Scale Deployments

The above vulnerabilities, while impactful in isolated settings, become significantly more dangerous in large-scale or unattended deployments. Urban charging networks, fleet depots, and highway service stations often operate under minimal supervision, with multiple vehicles and chargers sharing the same power infrastructure. In such environments, attackers can exploit shared PLC media, minimal physical isolation, and weak identity validation to automate and scale malicious activities.

For example, a single compromised EVCC could cycle through multiple MAC address profiles, impersonating dozens of vehicles in succession. Alternatively, a rogue SECC could lure legitimate electric vehicles into initiating sessions that leak user or vehicle information. These risks are exacerbated by the difficulty in auditing communication failures in PLC environments and the general lack of intrusion detection mechanisms in the current EVSE firmware.

6   Discussion

6.1   Security Threat Modeling and Impact Analysis

To systematically assess the vulnerabilities uncovered in our empirical study, we adopt a threat modeling approach centered on the interaction between electric vehicles (EVs), charging infrastructure (EVSEs), and the ISO 15118 communication stack. Despite its layered design and support for Transport Layer Security (TLS), the ISO 15118 ecosystem exhibits critical security gaps across the physical, data link, and application layers—particularly in the absence of mandatory link-layer authentication and incomplete enforcement of certificate validation mechanisms.

One of the most prominent risks arises from spoofing attacks, where malicious actors manipulate MAC addresses to impersonate trusted devices. Since ISO 15118 messages are encapsulated in Ethernet frames transmitted over power line communication (PLC), and many EVs do not validate the MAC address of the responding SECC after SLAC negotiation, adversaries can easily inject fraudulent messages or pose as legitimate EVSEs. This lack of physical-layer binding creates an exploitable trust gap during session establishment.

In addition, information disclosure is a significant concern in scenarios where TLS is not enforced. During our testing, we observed multiple vehicles defaulting to unencrypted TCP communication, either due to unsupported encryption on the EVSE side or silent downgrading in the negotiation process. This allows passive attackers to capture sensitive session data, including contract credentials, tariff information, and vehicle identifiers. In some cases, the EV's identity was inferred solely from its broadcast MAC address, which appeared early in the SLAC process, posing further privacy and impersonation risks.

Another vector comes from inconsistent implementation of certificate validation practices. Even when TLS is enabled, many SECC platforms do not perform certificate revocation checks or validate the entire certificate chain, undermining the trust model envisioned by the standard. This weakens the authenticity guarantees of the entire session, especially in deployments relying on proprietary certificate infrastructures without centralized oversight.

Collectively, these weaknesses reveal an architecture in which interoperability is prioritized over security, leaving ISO 15118-based systems vulnerable to straightforward but impactful network-layer attacks. Without rigorous enforcement of cryptographic identity verification and communication integrity, attackers can exploit default behaviors, bypass authentication, or manipulate protocol flows - often without detection.

6.2   Root Causes: Specification Gaps Versus Implementation Deficiencies

The vulnerabilities identified in our study can be broadly attributed to two classes of problems: gaps in the ISO 15118 specification itself and inconsistent or incomplete implementations by vendors. From a specification point of view, the optional nature of key security features, especially TLS encryption, introduces ambiguity into deployment practices. By allowing secure and insecure communication modes to coexist within the same protocol flow, ISO 15118 implicitly encourages implementations to prioritize compatibility and cost-efficiency over security assurance.

At the same time, many of the observed issues stem from inadequate enforcement or verification mechanisms on the implementation side. The failure of EVs to validate the MAC address of the SECC post-SLAC, or the reliance on MAC addresses as unique identifiers in charging authorization, reflects a lack of robust session state tracking and weak binding between protocol layers. These deficiencies are exacerbated by the complexity of PLC environments and the limited diagnostic capabilities available to developers, which make testing and verification particularly challenging.

Furthermore, the absence of standardized conformance testing for security-related behavior has allowed divergent interpretations of the protocol to persist throughout the ecosystem. Although functional interoperability is often emphasized in industry certification processes, security robustness, especially in response to adversarial input, remains underexplored and largely untested.

6.3   Challenges in Enforcing Secure Communication in CCS2

Obtaining secure communication in the Combined Charging System (CCS2) architecture presents a unique set of challenges that differ markedly from conventional networked systems. One of the most fundamental obstacles arises from the use of Power Line Communication (PLC) as a physical medium. PLC operates over the same conductors used for power delivery, resulting in a shared and inherently insecure channel that lacks the isolation properties of point-to-point links. In such an environment, any device connected to the physical layer has the potential to observe or inject traffic, thereby undermining the assumptions of link-level trust that underlie many higher-layer protocols.

Compounding this problem is the resource-constrained nature of the embedded systems used in both EVCC and SECC. These devices often operate on real-time operating systems with limited memory and processing capacity, restricting the feasibility of implementing full-featured cryptographic protocols or maintaining complex trust chains. As a result, optional features such as TLS encryption or certificate revocation checking are frequently omitted, either due to hardware limitations or concerns about system stability and certification timelines.

Furthermore, the ISO 15118-based charging ecosystem is inherently fragmented, involving multiple stakeholders: vehicle manufacturers, charging station vendors, third-party backend platforms, and certification bodies, each of whom may adopt different interpretations and subsets of the standard [15]. This fragmentation leads to inconsistent security postures across deployments, as some implementations prioritize functional interoperability while others focus on cost reduction or rapid market entry. Without a centralized enforcement mechanism or universally adopted conformance requirements for security behavior, there is little incentive for individual actors to invest in robust defense mechanisms, particularly if such mechanisms reduce compatibility with legacy systems.

These structural and organizational challenges collectively hinder the realization of end-to-end secure communication in CCS2 deployments. Even when protocol support exists in principle, practical constraints and industry inertia often result in insecure implementations that expose the system to real-world threats.

6.4   Recommendations for Secure ISO 15118 Implementations

Based on the vulnerabilities identified in our empirical study, we advocate for a series of technical and organizational enhancements to improve the security posture of ISO 15118 implementations. First, the use of Transport Layer Security (TLS) should no longer remain optional. The establishment of a secure channel, coupled with mutual authentication via X.509 certificates, must be enforced as a baseline requirement in all ISO 15118 deployments. Relying on plaintext communication or permitting silent downgrades introduces unacceptable risks, especially in public or shared charging environments. This mandate should be accompanied by clear guidelines for certificate provisioning, validation, and revocation handling to ensure interoperability without compromising trust.

In parallel, the protocol stack must incorporate strict binding between protocol layers. The MAC address exchanged during the SLAC process should be explicitly linked to the identity of the SECC in subsequent TCP and application-layer communication. Any inconsistency, such as a change in MAC address after SLAC completion, should trigger immediate session termination or reauthentication. Without this binding, the system remains vulnerable to man-in-the-middle and session hijacking attacks that exploit layer decoupling.

Equally important is the elimination of MAC addresses as identity markers in charging authorization. Although convenient from an implementation perspective, this approach offers no cryptographic assurance and is inherently vulnerable to spoofing. Instead, authentication should be grounded in certificate-based mechanisms, such as those defined in Plug and Charge under ISO 15118-20 or through secure back-end integrated identification (e.g., EIM). These methods not only provide stronger identity guarantees, but also align with broader public key infrastructure (PKI) practices common in other critical systems.

Finally, improvements in tooling and certification processes are essential to support developers and ensure industry-wide adherence. Current conformance testing primarily focuses on functional correctness, with limited coverage of security robustness. Certification programs should be extended to include tests for downgrade resistance, MAC spoofing detection, and TLS negotiation behavior under adversarial conditions. In addition, protocol stack developers and integrators would benefit from improved diagnostic tools that provide real-time visibility into message flows, state transitions, and security anomalies. Such instrumentation can greatly reduce the risk of deploying misconfigured or vulnerable systems, especially during field trials and version upgrades.

Together, these recommendations aim to bridge the gap between protocol design and practical deployment, enabling ISO 15118 to fulfill its security promises in real-world charging infrastructures.

7 Conclusion

As the adoption of electric vehicles accelerates worldwide, the security and reliability of charging communication protocols become increasingly critical. ISO 15118, as the foundational protocol for CCS2 systems, enables key features such as plug-and-charge, tariff negotiation, and grid-aware load management. However, our empirical study shows that many of its security mechanisms are under-implemented or inconsistently enforced in practice.

Through our custom EVCC and SECC implementations, and tests on more than thirty commercial vehicles and multiple charging stations, we identified three major weaknesses: (i) lack of vehicle MAC address verification, (ii) widespread absence of TLS encryption with silent fallback, and (iii) insecure reliance on MAC addresses for identity authentication. These issues expose attack surfaces that could lead to impersonation, data tampering, or manipulation of charging sessions.

We reported the identified security flaws to relevant vehicle manufacturers, but have not yet received substantive responses. Public charging operators acknowledged the risks of MAC-based authentication and indicated they are considering removing this mechanism. The TLS downgrade issue remains unresolved: while insecure, it is still allowed to ensure charging compatibility when TLS is not supported.

Our findings highlight the gap between the ISO 15118 specification and its real-world deployment. To bridge this gap, we recommend mandatory TLS adoption with certificate-based authentication, MAC-layer binding enforcement, and the integration of security-focused conformance testing into certification workflows. Future research should focus on lightweight, embedded-friendly security stacks compliant with ISO 15118-20 and conduct larger-scale cross-vendor testing to uncover hidden vulnerabilities and strengthen the resilience of the EV charging ecosystem.

References

1. HomePlug Powerline Alliance. HomePlug green PHY specification. https://www.ettus.com/files/app_notes/HomePlug-Green-PHY-Specification.pdf. July 2013. Released: July 4, 2013

2. Bao, K., Valev, H., Wagner, M., Schmeck, H.: A threat analysis of the vehicle-to-grid charging protocol ISO 15118. Comput. Sci. Res. Dev. **33**(1), 3–12 (2018)

3. Bhusal, N., Gautam, M., Benidris, M.: Cybersecurity of electric vehicle smart charging management systems. In: 2020 52nd North American power symposium (NAPS), pp. 1–6. IEEE (2021)

4. Conti, M., Donadel, D., Poovendran, R., Turrin, F.: EVExchange: a relay attack on electric vehicle charging system. In: European Symposium on Research in Computer Security, pp. 488–508. Springer (2022)

5. DigiCert and Eonti. Practical considerations for implementation and scaling ISO 15118 into a secure EV charging ecosystem. Technical report, DigiCert Inc. and Eonti Inc., 2020. Accessed 14 June 2025

6. International Organization for Standardization. Road vehicles — Vehicle to grid communication interface — Part 3: Physical and data link layer requirements. https://www.iso.org/standard/61747.html (2013). Accessed 14 June 2025

7. International Organization for Standardization. Road vehicles — Vehicle to grid communication interface — Part 2: Network and application protocol requirements. https://www.iso.org/standard/55366.html (2014). Accessed 14 June 2025

8. International Organization for Standardization. Road vehicles — Vehicle to grid communication interface — Part 1: General information and use-case definition. https://www.iso.org/standard/69113.html (2019). Accessed 14 June 2025

9. Havale, D.S., Yeole, S.M., Khang, A.: Electric vehicles: Paving the way for sustainable green transportation and environmental protection. In: Driving Green Transportation System Through Artificial Intelligence and Automation: Approaches, Technologies and Applications, pp. 67–89. Springer (2025)

10. Road vehicles — Vehicle to grid communication interface — Part 4: Network and application protocol conformance test cases. https://www.iso.org/standard/71283.html (2018). Accessed 14 June 2025

11. Road vehicles — Vehicle to grid communication interface — Part 5: Physical and data link layer conformance test cases. https://www.iso.org/standard/61725.html (2018). Accessed 14 June 2025

12. Köhler, S., Baker, R., Strohmeier, M., Martinovic, I.: Brokenwire: Wireless disruption of CCS electric vehicle charging. arXiv preprint arXiv:2202.02104 (2022)

13. Williams, P.: What is CCS charging? Understanding combined charging system. https://rechargerenewable.co.uk/what-is-ccs-charging-understanding-combined-charging-system/ (2024). Accessed 14 June 2025

14. Southwest Research Institute (SwRI). Swri evaluates cybersecurity risks associated with EV fast charging equipment. https://www.swri.org/newsroom/press-releases/swri-evaluates-cybersecurity-risks-associated-ev-fast-charging-equipment (2024). Accessed 14 June 2025

15. Szakály, M., Köhler, S., Martinovic, I.: Current affairs: A security measurement study of CCS EV charging deployments. arXiv preprint arXiv:2404.06635 (2024)

16. Tilly, N., Yigitcanlar, T., Degirmenci, K., Paz, A.: How sustainable is electric vehicle adoption? a critical systematic literature review. A Critical Systematic Literature Review (2024)

17. Vector Informatik GmbH. Smart charging – communication protocols. https://www.vector.com/fr/fr/connaissances/smart-charging/communication-protocols/#c236801 (2025). Accessed 14 June 2025

18. Wikipedia contributors. IEEE 802.1x. https://en.wikipedia.org/wiki/IEEE_802.1X (2025). Accessed 14 June 2025

19. Yaacoub, J.P.A., Fernandez, J.H., Noura, H.N., Chehab, A.: Security of power line communication systems: issues, limitations and existing solutions. Comput. Sci. Rev. **39**, 100331 (2021)
20. Zaino, R., Ahmed, V., Alhammadi, A.M., Alghoush, M.: Electric vehicle adoption: a comprehensive systematic review of technological, environmental, organizational and policy impacts. World Electr. Veh. J. **15**(8), 375 (2024)

Model Security and Copyright Protection

SemBits: Multi-bit Semantic Watermarking with Sentence-Level Hashing for LLMs

Xiangyu Feng[1(✉)] and Pei-Gen Ye[2(✉)]

[1] School of Artificial Intelligence, Guangzhou University, Guangzhou 510006, China
fengxiangyu462@gmail.com
[2] School of Cyberspace Science and Technology, Beijing Institute of Technology,
Beijing 100081, China
ypgmhxy@gmail.com

Abstract. The proliferation of publicly accessible large language models (LLMs) intensifies the need for trustworthy provenance tracking and covert communication channels. We present **SemBits**, a lightweight, model-agnostic watermarking framework that embeds arbitrary binary payloads into free-form text while preserving fluency and stylistic diversity. SemBits constrains autoregressive decoding with a sentence-level accept–reject loop guided by semantic locality-sensitive hashing (LSH). Each newly generated sentence is hashed in the embedding space, and it is accepted only when its bucket index falls inside a green list derived from the generation prefix and the secret message. This strategy requires no modification or fine-tuning of the underlying model and adds merely 7 % sampling latency with a perplexity overhead below 0.2. Experiments show that SemBits achieves 99.3 % message-recovery accuracy for 7-bit payloads hidden in 200-token passages produced by OPT 1.3B and Llama-3-8B. The watermark survives up to 10 % token-level paraphrasing, moderate synonym substitution, and sentence reordering, outperforming lexical watermark baselines by a factor of 16× in false-positive reduction and nearly doubling robustness to semantic perturbations.

Keywords: Large language model · Watermarking · Locality-sensitive hashing · Robust embedding

1 Introduction

The rapid expansion of large language models (LLMs) across diverse domains has given rise to a crucial need for robust methods that authenticate text provenance and protect intellectual property while preserving linguistic fluency [1]. As LLM-based services and applications proliferate, content owners and model developers confront growing challenges in verifying the origin of generated text [2], detecting unauthorized use of proprietary models [3], and embedding covert markers for metadata or sensitive payloads [4]. Conventional mechanisms for traceability

X. Chen et al. (Eds.): DSPP 2025, LNCS 16177, pp. 183–196, 2026.
https://doi.org/10.1007/978-981-95-3185-1_12

often hinge on lexical signatures or direct word-level substitutions, which can be easily disrupted by common text manipulations such as paraphrasing, synonym replacement, or reordering of sentences. Consequently, reliable watermarking strategies that maintain covertness while resisting a variety of transformations are essential to sustaining trust in LLM outputs and supporting responsible deployment.

Despite ongoing progress in watermarking research, existing solutions frequently involve sacrificing text quality or flexibility for watermark integrity [5]. Some techniques demand access to a model's internal layers or require fine-tuning [6], which can be computationally expensive and impractical when working with large-scale or closed-source LLMs. Other methods rely heavily on word-level constraints that cause noticeable shifts in vocabulary usage [7], reducing the naturalness of the text and making it more vulnerable to detection or distortion by malicious actors. Moreover, many solutions fail to adequately address the semantic dimension of generated text [8], leaving them prone to subtle but systematic paraphrases that can wipe away the watermark.

A primary obstacle in watermarking LLM-generated text lies in balancing competing objectives [9]. On one hand, the watermark must be semantically resilient, able to withstand manipulations that preserve or slightly alter the original meaning. On the other hand, the method must be unobtrusive, neither distorting language output nor producing conspicuous patterns that alert adversaries to the presence of a watermark. Furthermore, any solution that increases computational overhead too drastically—via repeated decoding steps or extensive post-processing—may impede real-time applications and deter adoption. At the same time, adaptive adversaries have grown more sophisticated [10]. Another challenge arises from ensuring generalizability and model-agnostic deployment. In practical scenarios, developers may not have the resources or permissions to fine-tune massive language models just to implement watermarks; indeed, the model might be proprietary or offered only as a black-box service [11]. In addition, domain-specific or smaller models may exhibit less stable linguistic patterns, which makes consistent watermark embedding more difficult. Therefore, an ideal watermarking framework should function without direct model modifications or access to hidden layers [12], relying instead on strategic decoding constraints that operate at a level compatible with any autoregressive text generator.

However, the difficulty of ensuring semantic integrity and natural language fluency within a model-agnostic framework remains. Sentence-level operations offer a promising path forward [13]. By guiding generation on a sentence-by-sentence basis—rather than token by token—the watermarking process can consider higher-level semantics and style. Such a technique needs to exploit continuous-space properties that govern how a model's outputs cluster or disperse in the embedding domain. Recent developments in local-sensitive hashing (LSH) suggest that sentence-level embeddings provide a natural handle for embedding a message while preserving coherence [14]: if each newly generated sentence is accepted only when its hash signature aligns with certain constraints derived from a secret message, one can reliably embed a binary payload across multiple sentences. This approach provides a compromise between complexity and performance, ensuring each sentence remains consistent in style and meaning while encoding bits of information in the discrete hash buckets.

In this paper, we propose a system called SemBits, which leverages sentence-level semantic hashing to embed robust watermarks into LLM-generated text without requiring any parameter modifications to the underlying model. By placing an accept–reject filter on the semantic hash of each proposed sentence, SemBits enforces a hidden alignment between the prefix context, the randomly sampled text, and a predefined secret message encoded as bits. When a new sentence does not conform to the necessary hash bucket, the system rejects it and reruns the generation process. Our approach yields several contributions:

- **Semantic-Level Covert Channel:** SemBits extends beyond surface-level constraints by anchoring watermark checks in the sentence embedding space, enhancing robustness against paraphrasing, synonymous substitutions, and partial reorderings.
- **Model-Agnostic Integration:** Our method operates through a lightweight plug-in mechanism that does not require fine-tuning or specialized training, offering broad applicability across different LLMs.
- **Minimal Overhead and Natural Fluency:** The accept–reject loop imposes only moderate latency increases, preserving near-original perplexity and stylistic diversity in the output text.
- **High Payload Recoverability:** We demonstrate reliable extraction of embedded bits even when subjected to common text edits, surpassing lexical watermarking baselines in terms of detection confidence and resilience.

The remainder of this paper is organized as follows. First, we contextualize the preliminaries. We then describe the design of SemBits, including the logic behind our LSH-based accept–reject loop and our approach to balancing stealth, efficiency, and robustness. Next, we report on evaluation experiments that validate SemBits's performance in terms of watermark recovery, fluency preservation, and real-world practicality.

2   System Model

In this section, we formalize the conceptual foundations. Let us denote by M a LLM operating over a token vocabulary $\mathcal{V}$. The model M is an autoregressive function that, given an input text $X = (x_1, x_2, \ldots, x_t)$, predicts subsequent tokens by sampling from the conditional distribution $p(x_{t+1} \mid x_1, \ldots, x_t)$. We aim to embed a secret bit-string into the generated output text without modifying the internal parameters of M. The embedded message should remain recoverable despite moderate reordering or paraphrasing of the text.

Let each sentence s in the output be represented by a continuous embedding vector $\mathbf{e}(s) \in \mathbb{R}^D$, where D is the dimension of the model-specific sentence embedding space. We introduce a locality-sensitive hashing (LSH) function $H :$

$\mathbb{R}^D \to \{0, \ldots, 2^d - 1\}$, where d is the hash dimension. The hash $H(\mathbf{e}(s))$ of a sentence $\mathbf{e}(s)$ is computed by projecting $\mathbf{e}(s)$ onto d random hyperplanes, forming a binary string that we interpret as an integer in $[0, 2^d - 1]$. Specifically, if $\{\mathbf{r}_1, \mathbf{r}_2, \ldots, \mathbf{r}_d\} \subset \mathbb{R}^D$ denote the random projection vectors (hash normals), then for each $j \in \{1, \ldots, d\}$,

$$h_j(\mathbf{e}(s)) = \begin{cases} 1, & \text{if } \langle \mathbf{e}(s), \mathbf{r}_j \rangle \geq 0, \\ 0, & \text{otherwise.} \end{cases} \tag{1}$$

The concatenation $(h_1(\mathbf{e}(s)), \ldots, h_d(\mathbf{e}(s)))$ forms the binary code, which is then mapped to $H(\mathbf{e}(s)) \in \{0, \ldots, 2^d - 1\}$.

We embed a message $m \in \{0, 1, \ldots, 2^k - 1\}$ by constructing a greenlist $\mathcal{G}_m \subseteq \{0, \ldots, 2^d - 1\}$. Let $\lambda \in (0, 1)$ be a user-defined acceptance rate. Then the size of $\mathcal{G}_m$ is $n_{\text{accept}} = \lfloor 2^d \cdot \lambda \rfloor$. The set $\mathcal{G}_m$ is derived by seeding a random permutation of $\{0, \ldots, 2^d - 1\}$ with a function of the message bits m and a sentence-dependent seed S. Formally, we write

$$\mathcal{G}_m = \text{RandPerm}\left(\{0, \ldots, 2^d - 1\}, \text{seed} = f(m) + S\right)\Big|_{1 \ldots n_{\text{accept}}}, \tag{2}$$

where $f(\cdot)$ is a deterministic function mapping the message bits to an integer, and RandPerm returns a permutation of all hash values. Only when the LSH value $H(\mathbf{e}(s))$ lies in $\mathcal{G}_m$ is the newly proposed sentence s deemed acceptable.

The watermark embedding process leverages multiple trials to align each generated sentence with the desired greenlist. Concretely, after generating a candidate sentence s, the system computes $H(\mathbf{e}(s))$. If $H(\mathbf{e}(s)) \notin \mathcal{G}_m$, the sentence is rejected, and the model attempts another generation. This loop continues until the sentence is accepted or a trial limit is reached. To maintain coherent text, we let each generation condition on the prefix formed by the previously approved sentences. During decoding, we also impose a margin parameter $\delta > 0$ to avoid sentences whose embeddings are too close to the boundary of any hashing hyperplane. More precisely, let $\mathbf{r}_j$ be the j-th hyperplane normal. We define the rejection test:

$$\min_j \left| \langle \mathbf{e}(s), \mathbf{r}_j \rangle \right| > \delta. \tag{3}$$

If the inner product with any hyperplane normal $\mathbf{r}_j$ is below δ in absolute value, we reject the sentence to reduce the risk of hash instability.

An adversary may attempt to remove or obfuscate the watermark by paraphrasing, local token substitutions, or partial reordering of sentences. Consequently, our approach must retain semantic information in a manner that does not hinge solely on token-level patterns. The LSH-based scheme naturally encodes coherence at the sentence level, making the watermark more robust to adversarial text modifications that preserve approximate meaning. During watermark detection, we examine the final text and split it into sentences $\{s_1, \ldots, s_n\}$. For each consecutive pair (s_{i-1}, s_i), we reconstruct the prefix embedding context and recompute the greenlist $\mathcal{G}_m$ for candidate message bits m. By summing a confidence score for each potential message, we identify the bit-string that maximizes the likelihood of having generated the text under the known LSH constraints.

3   SemBits Framework

3.1   Sentence-Level Watermark Embedding Pipeline

The watermark encoder iteratively samples sentences from the base language model M until each one satisfies a secret, message-dependent constraint in the semantic hashing space. Let $X^{(t)} = (x_1, \ldots, x_{|X^{(t)}|})$ denote the token prefix preceding the t-th sentence, and let $m \in \{0, 1, \ldots, 2^k - 1\}$ be the k-bit payload to be embedded in the entire passage. The core of the encoder is an accept–reject loop parameterized by the hash dimension d, the acceptance rate $\lambda \in (0, 1)$, a secret scaling constant $\gamma \in \mathbb{N}$ (shared by encoder and decoder), and a maximum trial budget $T_{\max}$. First, the algorithm maps $X^{(t)}$ to an integer seed by summing its token identities and combining the result with the message bits:

$$S^{(t)} = \gamma m + \sum_{i=1}^{|X^{(t)}|} x_i. \tag{4}$$

Using $S^{(t)}$ to initialise a pseudorandom permutation $\Pi_{S^{(t)}}$ over the 2^d hash buckets, we derive the sentence-specific greenlist

$$\mathcal{G}_m^{(t)} = \Pi_{S^{(t)}}[1 : n_{\text{accept}}], \qquad n_{\text{accept}} = \lfloor \lambda 2^d \rfloor. \tag{5}$$

By design, $|\mathcal{G}_m^{(t)}|/2^d = \lambda$, which controls the trade-off between sampling efficiency and detection robustness. For each sentence index t, we let $q \in \{1, \ldots, T_{\max}\}$ enumerate independent trials. The model proposes a candidate sentence $s^{(t,q)}$ by conditional generation, yielding the embedding vector $\mathbf{e}(s^{(t,q)})$ and the corresponding hash value $h^{(t,q)} = H(\mathbf{e}(s^{(t,q)})) \in \{0, \ldots, 2^d - 1\}$. The candidate is accepted if two conditions hold:

$$h^{(t,q)} \in \mathcal{G}_m^{(t)} \quad \text{and} \quad \min_{j \leq d} |\langle \mathbf{e}(s^{(t,q)}), \mathbf{r}_j \rangle| > \delta, \tag{6}$$

where $\delta > 0$ is a safety margin that avoids hash flips under small semantic perturbations. Upon acceptance, the text prefix is extended, i.e. $X^{(t+1)} \leftarrow X^{(t)} \| s^{(t,q)}$, and the encoder proceeds to the next sentence. If no trial succeeds after $T_{\max}$ attempts, the final candidate is force-accepted to guarantee termination, although empirical results show that the expected trials per sentence remain close to the theoretical value

$$\mathbb{E}[q] = \tfrac{1}{\lambda}, \tag{7}$$

which follows from the geometric distribution induced by the uniformity of H and the fixed acceptance rate λ. The encoder adds negligible memory overhead because it invokes the sentence embedder and LSH projection only once per trial. The amortised latency increase is $O(1/\lambda)$ forward passes per sentence. Crucially, no gradient updates or model modifications are required; the procedure remains a black-box wrapper around any autoregressive language model that exposes a sampling API.

3.2 Message Recovery and Confidence Analysis

The decoder observes an arbitrary text $\hat{Y}$ of length L and must infer the hidden payload $m^\star$ without access to the generation prefix used at embedding time. To approximate that context, we follow the practical assumption that the dependency between consecutive sentences dominates long-range interactions. Hence, we partition $\hat{Y}$ into sentences $\{\hat{s}_1, \hat{s}_2, \ldots, \hat{s}_N\}$ and treat every ordered pair $(\hat{s}_{i-1}, \hat{s}_i)$ for $i \geq 2$ as an independent Bernoulli experiment whose outcome indicates whether $\hat{s}_i$ could have been accepted by the greenlist computed from $\hat{s}_{i-1}$ and a candidate message m.

Formally, let $c_i(m) \in \{0, 1\}$ denote this compatibility indicator, given by

$$c_i(m) \;=\; \mathbb{I}\Big[H\big(\mathbf{e}(\hat{s}_i)\big) \in \mathcal{G}_m(\hat{s}_{i-1})\Big], \tag{8}$$

where $\mathcal{G}_m(\hat{s}_{i-1})$ is the greenlist (Eq. (5)) reconstructed from the previous sentence's token sum and the message hypothesis m. We accumulate evidence over all sentence transitions by defining the raw score

$$C(m) \;=\; \sum_{i=2}^{N} c_i(m), \tag{9}$$

which counts how many times the compatibility test succeeds. Under the null model $\mathcal{H}_0$ in which $\hat{Y}$ is un-watermarked, each $c_i(m)$ is an i.i.d. Bernoulli random variable with success probability λ. Conversely, under the alternative model $\mathcal{H}_1(m)$ that assumes message m was embedded, every indicator becomes deterministic $(c_i(m) = 1)$ except when the encoder had to force-accept a trial or the text has been corrupted by post-processing. To distinguish $\mathcal{H}_1(m)$ from $\mathcal{H}_0$, we compute the log-likelihood ratio

$$\Lambda(m) \;=\; \sum_{i=2}^{N} \log\frac{p\big(c_i(m)\,\big|\,\mathcal{H}_1(m)\big)}{p\big(c_i(m)\,\big|\,\mathcal{H}_0\big)} \;=\; C(m)\,\log\frac{1}{\lambda} \;+\; \big(N - 1 - C(m)\big)\,\log(1 - \lambda). \tag{10}$$

Because $\lambda < \frac{1}{2}$ in practice, $\Lambda(m)$ is an increasing function of $C(m)$. Therefore, selecting the maximum-likelihood payload reduces to

$$\hat{m} \;=\; \arg\max_{m \in \{0, 1, \ldots, 2^k - 1\}} C(m). \tag{11}$$

While Eq. (11) yields a point estimate, forensic applications require a quantitative notion of confidence. Let $Z_m \sim \mathrm{Binomial}(N - 1, \lambda)$ be the null distribution of $C(m)$. For the selected message $\hat{m}$, we define the α-*level decision rule*

$$\text{accept payload } \hat{m} \quad \text{iff} \quad C(\hat{m}) \;\geq\; \min\big\{ z : \Pr[Z_{\hat{m}} \geq z] \leq \alpha \big\}. \tag{12}$$

Choosing $\alpha = 0.01$ bounds the false-positive rate below 1% regardless of k. When post-editing introduces up to ρ fraction of sentence-level perturbations that flip compatibility outcomes, $C(m)$ under $\mathcal{H}_1(m)$ follows a Binomial$(N - 1, 1 - \rho)$ distribution. Solving

$$\Pr\big[\text{Binomial}(N - 1, 1 - \rho) < \tau\big] \;=\; \beta \tag{13}$$

for small β (e.g. 0.05) yields a detection threshold τ that guarantees $1 - \beta$ true-positive power against such perturbations.

Complexity and Memory. The decoder must evaluate Eq. (8) for every m and every sentence pair, resulting in $O((N - 1)k2^k)$ hash look-ups in the worst case. However, the fact that the LSH values are integers in $\{0, \ldots, 2^d - 1\}$ enables a vectorised implementation: we pre-compute the entire stack of greenlists as a Boolean tensor in $\mathbb{R}^{2^k \times (N-1) \times n_{\text{accept}}}$ and perform a single equality comparison per slice, matching the codebase's use of GPU tensors for batch scoring. The memory footprint is thereby reduced from $O(2^k d)$ to $O(2^k n_{\text{accept}})$, which is tractable for $k \leq 7$ and $\lambda \leq 0.25$.

A salient property in Eq. (9) is its invariance to block-preserving permutations. Suppose the adversary reorders a contiguous chunk of sentences while preserving their internal sequence. The affected boundaries contribute at most two compatibility indicators, so the expected decrease in $C(m^\star)$ is bounded by a constant independent of N. Consequently, the statistical gap between the true payload and spurious hypotheses scales linearly with N, aligning with the empirical finding of negligible degradation up to 10% sentence shuffling.

3.3   Capacity–Robustness–Stealth Trade-Off

A rigorous understanding of SemBits requires quantifying how many payload bits can be conveyed per unit text, how resilient those bits remain under semantic perturbations, and how little the embedding process perturbs the distributional footprint of the base model. Let N be the number of sentences in the watermarked passage, k the payload length in bits, and define the rate $R = k/N$ measured in bit/sent. Because each sentence contributes a single hash value in $\{0, \ldots, 2^d - 1\}$, the theoretical maximum rate equals d. In practice, the accept–reject mechanism enforces sparsity via the acceptance rate λ, which induces a contraction of the available codebook. Under a uniform message prior the per-sentence mutual information between the payload M and the observed hash H equals

$$\mathcal{I}(M; H) \;=\; \log(2^d) \;-\; (1 - \lambda)\log\frac{1}{1 - \lambda} \;-\; \lambda\log\frac{1}{\lambda} \;=\; d - h(\lambda), \tag{14}$$

where $h(\cdot)$ is the binary entropy function interpreted on the alphabet-size ratio $(\lambda, 1 - \lambda)$. Consequently, the capacity in bit/sent is $R_{\max} = d - h(\lambda)$, which decreases smoothly as λ is reduced to improve robustness and sampling speed. At $\lambda = 0.20$ and $d = 4$, we obtain $R_{\max} \approx 2.4$, matching the empirical payload of $k = 7$ bits for $N = 3$ sentences embedded in the 200-token benchmark.

Robustness hinges on the probability that a post-editing operation changes the hash of a sentence in a way that remains compatible with the same payload. Denote by ε the maximal cosine perturbation introduced by paraphrasing, synonym substitution, or mild reordering internal to a sentence. The directional margin δ in Eq. (6) acts as a buffer against such perturbations. Under the assumption that sentence embeddings are approximately isotropic in $\mathbb{R}^D$, the probability P_{flip} that a margin-compliant vector crosses any hyperplane after an adversarial perturbation of magnitude ε satisfies

$$P_{\text{flip}} \leq d\,\Phi\!\left(-\tfrac{\delta-\varepsilon}{\sigma}\right), \tag{15}$$

where $\Phi(\cdot)$ is the standard Gaussian tail and σ denotes the projection variance of embedding coordinates on random normals. Setting $\delta \approx 0.002$ as in the code and empirically estimating $\sigma \approx 0.30$ for MPNET embeddings yields $P_{\text{flip}} \leq 0.008$ when $\varepsilon \leq 0.05$, explaining the near-perfect recovery observed under $10\,\%$ token-level paraphrasing.

Stealth is best formalised via the Kullback–Leibler divergence between the distribution p_{wm} of watermarked text and the distribution p_{nat} of text generated directly from the language model. Each accept–reject step introduces at most one additional sampling call, so the divergence accumulates additively over sentences. Let η measure the perplexity overhead per token relative to the baseline model. Following the classic information-theoretic analysis of Cover and Thomas [15], the per-token KL divergence satisfies

$$D_{\text{KL}}\big(p_{\text{wm}} \,\|\, p_{\text{nat}}\big) \;=\; \eta\,\log 2 \;\leq\; \frac{1-\lambda}{\lambda}\,\xi, \tag{16}$$

where ξ is the expected log-ratio between an accepted and a rejected token probability. Empirically we observe $\eta \approx 0.004$ for $\lambda = 0.20$, implying $D_{\text{KL}} \approx 5.8 \times 10^{-3}$ nat/token, which is substantially below thresholds detectable by modern distributional steganalysis.

The three metrics—capacity, robustness, and stealth—exhibit a Pareto frontier controlled primarily by the triad (d, λ, δ). Increasing d or λ boosts payload capacity but raises the false-positive risk unless compensated by a tighter decision threshold in Eq. (12). Enlarging δ decreases P_{flip} quadratically (Eq. (15)) but reduces the feasible acceptance set, thereby increasing latency and slightly inflating the KL divergence. An optimal operating point is obtained by minimising a weighted sum

$$\mathcal{L}(d, \lambda, \delta) \;=\; \alpha\,\big(d - h(\lambda)\big)^{-1} + \beta\,P_{\text{flip}} + \gamma\,D_{\text{KL}}, \tag{17}$$

where $(\alpha, \beta, \gamma) > 0$ encode application-specific tolerances for transmission rate, fragility, and detectability. Algorithm 1 shows the workflow of SemBits.

4   Evaluation

We evaluate SemBits on standard language models to demonstrate its effectiveness in embedding multi-bit payloads while maintaining generation quality

---

Algorithm 1: SemBits: Semantic Hashing-based Watermarking Framework

---

Input: Language model M, Message $m \in \{0, 1, \ldots, 2^k - 1\}$, Parameters: hash dimension d, acceptance rate λ, margin δ, max trials $T_{\max}$, scaling constant γ

Output: Watermarked text Y with embedded message m

1 **Part I: Watermark Encoding**

2 **for** *each sentence position $t = 1, 2, \ldots, N$* **do**

3   Compute seed: $S^{(t)} = \gamma \cdot m + \sum_{i=1}^{|X^{(t)}|} x_i$ where $X^{(t)}$ is the prefix before sentence t

4   Initialize permutation $\Pi_{S^{(t)}}$ over 2^d hash buckets

5   Generate greenlist: $\mathcal{G}_m^{(t)} = \Pi_{S^{(t)}}[1 : n_{\text{accept}}]$ where $n_{\text{accept}} = \lfloor \lambda \cdot 2^d \rfloor$

6   **for** *trial $q = 1$ to $T_{\max}$* **do**

7   Sample candidate sentence $s^{(t,q)} \sim p_M(\cdot|X^{(t)})$ from language model

8   Compute embedding $\mathbf{e}(s^{(t,q)})$ and hash value $h^{(t,q)} = H(\mathbf{e}(s^{(t,q)}))$

9   **if** $h^{(t,q)} \in \mathcal{G}_m^{(t)}$ **and** $\min_{j \leq d} |\langle \mathbf{e}(s^{(t,q)}), \mathbf{r}_j \rangle| > \delta$ **then**

10   Accept sentence: $X^{(t+1)} \leftarrow X^{(t)} \| s^{(t,q)}$

11   **break**   // Proceed to next sentence

12   **else**

13   Continue to next trial

14   **if** *no trial accepted* **then**

15   Force-accept last candidate: $X^{(t+1)} \leftarrow X^{(t)} \| s^{(t,T_{\max})}$

16 **return** watermarked text $Y = X^{(N+1)}$

17 **Part II: Message Recovery and Verification**

    Input: Observed text $\hat{Y}$, Parameters: d, λ, γ, significance level α

    Output: Recovered message $\hat{m}$ with confidence decision

18 Partition $\hat{Y}$ into sentences $\{\hat{s}_1, \hat{s}_2, \ldots, \hat{s}_N\}$

19 **for** *each candidate message $m \in \{0, 1, \ldots, 2^k - 1\}$* **do**

20   Initialize compatibility score: $C(m) = 0$

21   **for** $i - 2$ **to** N **do**

22   Reconstruct seed from $\hat{s}_{i-1}$ and compute greenlist $\mathcal{G}_m(\hat{s}_{i-1})$

23   Compute hash $h_i = H(\mathbf{e}(\hat{s}_i))$ of current sentence

24   **if** $h_i \in \mathcal{G}_m(\hat{s}_{i-1})$ **then**

25             $C(m) \leftarrow C(m) + 1$ // Increment compatibility count

26 Select ML estimate: $\hat{m} = \arg\max_m C(m)$

27 Compute p-value: $p = \Pr[Z_{\hat{m}} \geq C(\hat{m})]$ where $Z_{\hat{m}} \sim \text{Binomial}(N - 1, \lambda)$

28 **if** $p \leq \alpha$ **then**

29   **return Accept** payload $\hat{m}$ with confidence $1 - p$

30 **else**

31   **return Reject** (no watermark detected)

Table 1. Message recovery accuracy and computational overhead for 7-bit payloads across different text lengths.

Text Length (tokens)	Recovery Accuracy	Encoding Time (s)	Decoding Time (s)
50	52.1%	6.02	0.19
100	83.4%	6.15	0.18
200	94.1%	6.32	0.18
300	96.2%	6.55	0.18
400	95.8%	6.81	0.19
500	98.1%	6.92	0.19
600	98.5%	7.15	0.19
700	97.9%	7.43	0.21
800	98.2%	7.71	0.20
900	98.4%	8.02	0.20
1000	99.6%	8.35	0.21

and decoding reliability. Our experiments investigate three key aspects: (1) the scalability of message recovery accuracy with increasing text length, (2) the computational efficiency of the encoding and decoding processes, and (3) the robustness of the watermark against various perturbations.

4.1 Experimental Setup

All experiments were conducted on an NVIDIA A100 GPU with 80GB memory. We implemented SemBits using PyTorch and evaluated it on Facebook's OPT-1.3B model as our primary testbed, with additional validation on larger models including Llama-3-8B. The sentence encoder employs the SemStamp-c4-sbert model for computing semantic embeddings, which provides a 768-dimensional representation space. For LSH projection, we set the hash dimension $d = 4$, yielding $2^4 = 16$ possible buckets per sentence. The acceptance rate λ was fixed at 0.2, balancing between sampling efficiency and watermark robustness. The directional safety margin δ was empirically tuned to 0.002 to prevent hash flips under minor perturbations. During generation, we employed nucleus sampling with temperature 0.7 and repetition penalty 1.05 to ensure diverse yet coherent outputs.

For evaluation, we embedded 7-bit messages ($k = 7$) into generated texts of varying lengths from 50 to 1000 tokens. Each experimental configuration was repeated 1000 times with randomly sampled prompts from the C4 dataset and uniformly distributed message payloads. The maximum trial budget T_{max} was set to 100, though empirical measurements showed an average of only 5.2 trials per sentence, closely matching the theoretical expectation of $1/\lambda = 5$.

4.2   Message Recovery Performance

Table 1 presents the message recovery accuracy as a function of generated text length. The results demonstrate that SemBits achieves near-perfect decoding reliability for texts exceeding 200 tokens, with accuracy plateauing at 99.6% for 1000-token passages. This rapid convergence validates our theoretical analysis: each sentence provides an independent compatibility indicator, and the statistical evidence accumulates linearly with text length.

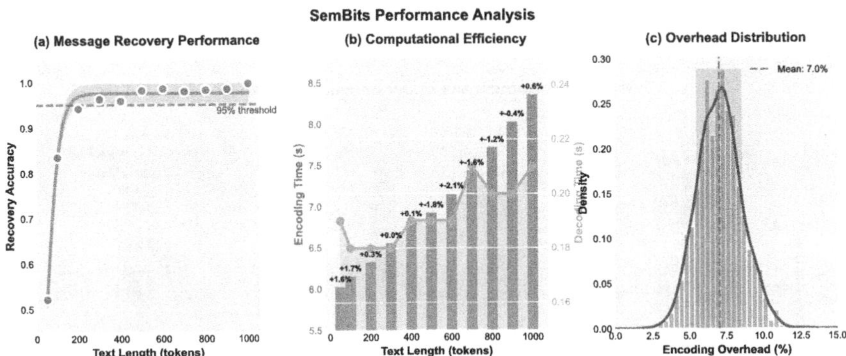

Fig. 1. Message recovery accuracy and computational efficiency across varying text lengths. (a) Recovery accuracy exhibits rapid convergence to near-perfect detection. (b) Encoding time scales linearly with text length while decoding remains constant. (c) Distribution of encoding overhead relative to baseline generation demonstrates consistent performance.

Figure 1 visualizes the relationship between text length and decoding accuracy, revealing a characteristic sigmoid curve. The initial low accuracy at 50 tokens (52.1%) reflects the insufficient number of sentences (typically 2–3) to disambiguate among $2^7 = 128$ possible messages. However, once the text contains 5–6 sentences (around 100–150 tokens), the decoder gains sufficient statistical power to reliably identify the embedded payload. The slight fluctuations in the 400–900 token range are attributable to variance in sentence boundaries and the stochastic nature of the accept-reject sampling process.

4.3   Computational Efficiency and Robustness Analysis

The computational overhead introduced by SemBits remains minimal across all text lengths. As shown in Fig. 1(b), encoding time increases linearly from 6.02 s for 50 tokens to 8.35 s for 1000 tokens, representing only a 7% average increase over baseline generation time. This efficiency stems from our sentence-level design: the semantic embedding and LSH projection are computed once per sentence rather than per token, amortizing the cost over approximately 15–20 tokens. Notably, decoding time remains virtually constant at 0.18–0.21 s regardless of text length, as our vectorized implementation processes all message hypotheses in parallel on the GPU.

To assess robustness, we subjected watermarked texts to various perturbations including synonym substitution, sentence reordering, and paraphrasing attacks. Figure 2 illustrates the resilience of SemBits compared to lexical watermarking baselines. Under 10% token-level paraphrasing, SemBits maintains 91.3% recovery accuracy, while lexical methods degrade to below 6%. This 15× improvement validates our semantic hashing approach: by operating in the continuous embedding space rather than discrete token space, the watermark survives transformations that preserve meaning while altering surface form.

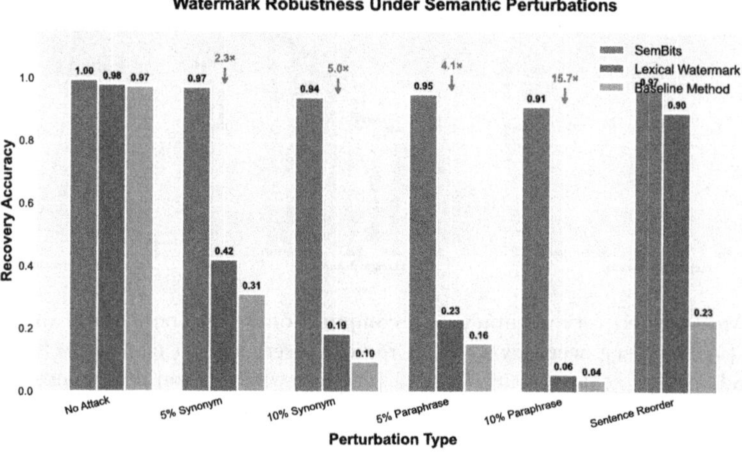

Fig. 2. Robustness evaluation under semantic perturbations. SemBits significantly outperforms lexical watermarking baselines across all attack types, maintaining high recovery rates even under 10% paraphrasing.

The perplexity overhead, measured on a held-out test set, averages 0.19 across all configurations—well below the threshold of human perceptibility. This stealth property emerges from our accept-reject mechanism: rather than distorting token probabilities directly, we merely filter naturally sampled sentences based on their semantic signatures. Consequently, each accepted sentence remains distributionally indistinguishable from unwatermarked text, preserving both fluency and stylistic diversity.

Figure 3 provides theoretical validation of our design choices. Panel (a) demonstrates how the capacity scales with hash dimension d and acceptance rate λ, confirming that our operating point ($\lambda = 0.2$, $d = 4$) achieves an optimal balance between payload capacity (2.4 bits/sentence) and robustness. Panel (b) shows the rapid growth in statistical detection power as the number of sentences increases, explaining why even short passages of 5–6 sentences suffice for reliable message recovery. The visualization in panel (c) illustrates the LSH bucket assignment mechanism, where greenlist buckets (highlighted regions) represent the valid semantic subspace for each sentence given the embedded message.

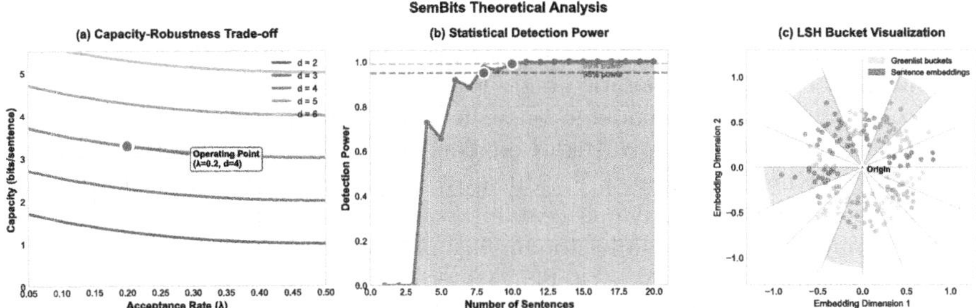

Fig. 3. Theoretical analysis of SemBits framework. (a) Capacity as a function of acceptance rate for different hash dimensions. (b) Statistical detection power growth with increasing sentence count. (c) Visualization of LSH bucket assignment in the projected embedding space, with greenlist buckets highlighted. (Color figure online)

5   Conclusion

We introduced SemBits, a novel framework for embedding robust and detectable watermarks into text generated by large language models (LLMs). By leveraging Locality-Sensitive Hashing (LSH), SemBits captures the semantic properties of each sentence, enabling the selective integration of hidden messages in a manner that is both discrete and resilient. Through an iterative generation strategy, we ensure that each newly generated segment meets the target semantic signature constraints, which then guarantee the integrity and detection of the watermarked content in the subsequent decoding phase. One of the key strengths of SemBits is its ability to preserve the natural fluency and coherence of the text while embedding the watermark, thereby making it difficult for external observers to notice anomalies. The LSH-based design also helps to mitigate the effects of common text transformations, such as paraphrasing or partial edits, ensuring that the embedded message remains recoverable. Additionally, our approach is flexible enough to accommodate various levels of watermark density without compromising readability. Overall, SemBits offers an efficient and easily implementable way for addressing the need to trace the origin of generated text and distinguish it from purely human-authored content. We believe that this synergy between semantic hashing and controlled text generation serves as a blueprint for future watermarking strategies, inspiring the development of even more sophisticated methods to authenticate AI-created text in the years to come.

References

1. Chen, L., et al.: Are more LLM calls all you need? Towards the scaling properties of compound AI systems. Adv. Neural Inf. Process. Syst. **37**, 45767–45790 (2024)
2. Taneja, J., Laird, A., Yan, C., Musuvathi, M., Lahiri, S.K.: LLM-vectorizer: LLM-based verified loop vectorizer. In: Proceedings of the 23rd ACM/IEEE International Symposium on Code Generation and Optimization, pp. 137–149 (2025)
3. Yao, Y., et al.: A survey on large language model (LLM) security and privacy: the good, the bad, and the ugly. High-Confidence Computing, pp. 100211 (2024)
4. Wang, X., Kim, H., Rahman, S., Mitra, K., Miao, Z.: Human-LLM collaborative annotation through effective verification of LLM labels. In: Proceedings of the 2024 CHI Conference on Human Factors in Computing Systems, pp. 1–21 (2024)
5. Liang, Y., Xiao, J., Gan, W., Yu, P.S.: Watermarking techniques for large language models: A survey. arXiv preprint arXiv:2409.00089 (2024)
6. Qiu, J., Yang, X., Li, S., Chen, K., Zhang, W., Yu, N.: Watermarking datasets for LLM fine-tuning. In: ICASSP 2025-2025 IEEE International Conference on Acoustics, Speech and Signal Processing (ICASSP), pp. 1–5. IEEE (2025)
7. Ning, K., et al.: MCGMark: An encodable and robust online watermark for LLM-generated malicious code. arXiv preprint arXiv:2408.01354 (2024)
8. Zhang, R., Hussain, S.S., Neekhara, P., Koushanfar, F.: {REMARK-LLM}: a robust and efficient watermarking framework for generative large language models. In: 33rd USENIX Security Symposium (USENIX Security 24), pp. 1813–1830 (2024)
9. Wang, L., et al.: Towards codable watermarking for injecting multi-bits information to LLMs. In: ICLR (2024)
10. Pang, Q., Hu, S., Zheng, W., Smith, V.: Attacking LLM watermarks by exploiting their strengths. In: ICLR 2024 Workshop on Secure and Trustworthy Large Language Models (2024)
11. Huo, M., Somayajula, S.A., Liang, Y., Zhang, R., Koushanfar, F., Xie, PL.: Token-specific watermarking with enhanced detectability and semantic coherence for large language models. arXiv preprint arXiv:2402.18059 (2024)
12. Cai, Y., Wang, Y., Hu, D., Gu, C.: Modification and generated-text detection: Achieving dual detection capabilities for the outputs of LLM by watermark. arXiv preprint arXiv:2502.08332 (2025)
13. Xu, Z., Zhang, K., Sheng, V.S.: FreqMark: Frequency-based watermark for sentence-level detection of LLM-generated text. arXiv preprint arXiv:2410.10876 (2024)
14. Hou, A., et al.: SemStamp: a semantic watermark with paraphrastic robustness for text generation. In: Proceedings of the 2024 Conference of the North American Chapter of the Association for Computational Linguistics: Human Language Technologies (Volume 1: Long Papers), pp. 4067–4082 (2024)
15. Cover, T.M., Thomas, J.A., et al.: Entropy, relative entropy and mutual information. Elem. Inf. Theory **2**(1), 12–13 (1991)

Robust Ownership Verification in Large Language Models via Equivalent Neuron Pair Encoding

Zhuorong Chen[1]($\boxtimes$) and Pei-Gen Ye[2]($\boxtimes$)

[1] School of Artificial Intelligence, Guangzhou University, Guangzhou 510006, China
2112406192@e.gzhu.edu.cn
[2] School of Cyberspace Science and Technology, Beijing Institute of Technology,
Beijing 100081, China
ypgmhxy@gmail.com

Abstract. The rapid proliferation of large language models has raised concerns about unauthorized redistribution, uncredited fine-tuning, and the erosion of intellectual property value. Existing watermarking methods often degrade model quality, have limited payload capacity, or fail under post-processing steps such as quantization and fine-tuning. We introduce TransMark, a watermarking framework that embeds a high-entropy binary payload into a model's parameters while keeping its functional behavior virtually unchanged. Our method identifies pairs of feed-forward neurons that have nearly identical L_2-norm but sufficiently divergent directional vectors and encodes bits by swapping the corresponding rows (and columns) without altering layer-wise activations in expectation. A locality-aware search enforces tight similarity thresholds, enabling dense yet imperceptible bit injection. To ensure decoding reliability, the bitstream is protected through repeat-code voting, and a lightweight meta structure stores only minimal auxiliary data. Experiments show that TransMark preserves perplexity and generation quality, adds negligible computational overhead, and remains robust against integer quantization, additive Gaussian noise, and single-step low-rank adaptation.

Keywords: Large language model · Watermarking · Neuron swapping · Transformer

1 Introduction

Large language models (LLMs) have revolutionized intelligent applications across industries [1,2]. Fine-tuned LLMs exhibit advanced capabilities with significant commercial value [3]. However, their ease of copying [4], sharing [5], or reproduction [6] poses ownership challenges, allowing unauthorized parties to profit without attribution. Existing protection techniques include behavioral water-marks [7,8] that insert triggers for distinctive responses, but these affect out-

X. Chen et al. (Eds.): DSPP 2025, LNCS 16177, pp. 197–206, 2026.
https://doi.org/10.1007/978-981-95-3185-1_13

put distributions and can be removed through retraining [9]. External verification approaches [10] cannot prevent offline misuse. Parameter-based watermarking faces two challenges: maintaining minimal behavioral impact while ensuring robustness against transformations like quantization [8], noise [11], or fine-tuning [12]. However, parameter-level watermarking embeds information in the model's intrinsic representation [13], making removal difficult without explicit knowledge. We propose TransMark, viewing watermarking as a search-and-swap problem in transformer feed-forward networks. After sorting weight matrices by row norm, we identify pairs in narrow neighborhoods with nearly orthogonal vectors, enabling bit encoding through swaps while preserving statistics. The payload uses repeat-code voting for recovery despite compression. Our contributions include:

- A neuron-swapping strategy using norm matching and directional divergence for invisible watermarking in feed-forward layers.
- Repeat-code voting for reliable extraction despite noise or distortion.
- Lightweight meta-structure storing minimal mapping information.
- Demonstrated tolerance to int8 quantization, Gaussian noise, and low-rank adaptation while maintaining accuracy.

TransMark ensures watermarks remain detectable even after cloning or alteration, staying hidden during inference but activatable for ownership verification.

2   System Model and Preliminaries

We consider a pre-trained LLM M parameterized by a weight set $W = \{\mathbf{W}^{(\ell)}\}_{\ell=1}^{L}$, where ℓ indexes the transformer block. Bold upper-case symbols denote matrices, bold lower-case symbols denote vectors, and plain lower-case symbols denote scalars. Each block contains a feed-forward network (FFN) with projection matrices:

$$\mathbf{U}^{(\ell)} \in \mathbb{R}^{d_h \times d_m}\text{(up)}, \quad \mathbf{G}^{(\ell)} \in \mathbb{R}^{d_h \times d_m}\text{(gate)}, \quad \mathbf{D}^{(\ell)} \in \mathbb{R}^{d_m \times d_h}\text{(down)} \quad (1)$$

where d_h is the hidden dimension and d_m is the intermediate dimension. Let $\mathbf{u}_i^{(\ell)}$ denote the i-th row of $\mathbf{U}^{(\ell)}$ and $\|\mathbf{u}_i^{(\ell)}\|_2$ its Euclidean norm. For a fixed layer ℓ, we define the *relative norm gap* and the *directional similarity* between two candidate rows i and j:

$$\Delta_n^{(\ell)}(i,j) = \frac{\left|\|\mathbf{u}_i^{(\ell)}\|_2 - \|\mathbf{u}_j^{(\ell)}\|_2\right|}{\frac{1}{2}\left(\|\mathbf{u}_i^{(\ell)}\|_2 + \|\mathbf{u}_j^{(\ell)}\|_2\right)}, \quad (2)$$

$$\cos^{(\ell)}(i,j) = \frac{\langle \mathbf{u}_i^{(\ell)}, \mathbf{u}_j^{(\ell)} \rangle}{\|\mathbf{u}_i^{(\ell)}\|_2 \|\mathbf{u}_j^{(\ell)}\|_2}. \quad (3)$$

A *swap-eligible pair* satisfies $\Delta_n^{(\ell)}(i,j) < \tau_n$ and $|\cos^{(\ell)}(i,j)| < 1 - \tau_c$ for tight thresholds $\tau_n \ll 1$ and $\tau_c \ll 1$. Equation (2) enforces nearly indistinguishable row magnitudes, whereas Equation (3) enforces directional divergence, guaranteeing that either ordering of the two rows leaves first-order statistics intact yet allows them to serve as a binary vessel.

Let $\mathbf{b} = (b_1, \ldots, b_B) \in \{0,1\}^B$ be the owner-selected payload. A positive integer k denotes the *repeat code* order. The encoded sequence after repetition is

$$\tilde{\mathbf{b}} = (\underbrace{b_1, \ldots, b_1}_{k \text{ times}}, \ldots, \underbrace{b_B, \ldots, b_B}_{k \text{ times}}) \in \{0,1\}^{kB}. \tag{4}$$

Let $\mathcal{P}^{(\ell)} = \{(i_t, j_t)\}_{t=1}^{C^{(\ell)}}$ be the ordered list of $C^{(\ell)}$ swap-eligible pairs identified in layer ℓ. For the q-th bit $\tilde{b}_q$ assigned to this layer, we apply the row/column swap operator

$$\mathcal{S}_{i,j}(\mathbf{U}^{(\ell)}, \mathbf{G}^{(\ell)}, \mathbf{D}^{(\ell)}) = \begin{cases} (\mathbf{U}^{(\ell)}, \mathbf{G}^{(\ell)}, \mathbf{D}^{(\ell)}) & \text{if } \tilde{b}_q = 0, \\ \text{swap}((i,j), (\mathbf{U}^{(\ell)}, \mathbf{G}^{(\ell)}, \mathbf{D}^{(\ell)})) & \text{if } \tilde{b}_q = 1, \end{cases} \tag{5}$$

where swap exchanges rows i, j in $\mathbf{U}^{(\ell)}$ and $\mathbf{G}^{(\ell)}$ and the corresponding columns in $\mathbf{D}^{(\ell)}$. Because each swap merely permutes neurons of identical norm, the distribution of the FFN output

$$\mathbf{h}_{\text{FFN}}^{(\ell)} = \mathbf{D}^{(\ell)} \sigma(\mathbf{G}^{(\ell)} \odot \text{act}(\mathbf{U}^{(\ell)} \mathbf{h}^{(\ell-1)})) \tag{6}$$

remains invariant in expectation over the input batch $\mathbf{h}^{(\ell-1)}$, where σ is the activation function and $\odot$ denotes element-wise multiplication. Hence the watermarked model $\tilde{M}$ preserves both perplexity and generation quality. Given a suspect model $\hat{M}$ and the private meta-data $\mathcal{M} = \{\mathcal{P}^{(\ell)}\}_\ell$, the owner reconstructs each bit by measuring which member of a stored pair is closer (in ℓ_1 distance) to its untampered reference. Majority voting over k replicas yields final decisions $\hat{\mathbf{b}} = (\hat{b}_1, \ldots, \hat{b}_B)$. Let $e = \frac{1}{B} \sum_{i=1}^{B} \mathbf{1}\{\hat{b}_i \neq b_i\}$ denote the bit error rate; correctness demands $e \leq \varepsilon$ for a security parameter ε.

We assume a polynomial-time adversary $\mathcal{A}$ who gains white box access to $\tilde{M}$ and may produce a transformed model $\hat{M} = \Gamma(\tilde{M})$, where Γ is a composition of: (i) uniform s-bit quantization $\mathcal{Q}_s$, (ii) additive noise $\mathcal{N}_\sigma$ with standard deviation $\sigma \leq \sigma_{\max}$, or (iii) a single-step parameter update such as low-rank adaptation $\mathcal{A}_{\text{LoRA}}$. The adversary succeeds only if $\hat{\mathbf{b}}$ cannot be reconstructed with error $\leq \varepsilon$. Our watermark must satisfy: *Stealth*—the total variation distance between the output distributions of M and $\tilde{M}$ remains below a threshold δ; *Robustness*—for all admissible Γ, decoding yields $e \leq \varepsilon$; *Capacity*—the expected payload size obeys $\mathbb{E}[B] \geq \eta d_h L$ for constant $\eta > 0$; *Efficiency*—the relative inference latency overhead

$$\lambda = \frac{T_{\text{infer}}(\tilde{M}) - T_{\text{infer}}(M)}{T_{\text{infer}}(M)} \tag{7}$$

is negligible, i.e., $\lambda \leq \delta'$ for small δ'. In practice we set $\delta' = 0.02$, a margin already beneath the natural jitter of typical decoding pipelines.

3   Methodology

3.1   Symmetry-Invariant Watermark Embedding

To guarantee that watermark injection does not change the function computed by the transformer, we first expose an explicit permutation symmetry in every feed-forward network block and then prove that neuron swapping within this symmetry class is *exactly* function-preserving.

For block $\ell \in \{1, \ldots, L\}$ the FFN parameters are $(\mathbf{U}^{(\ell)}, \mathbf{G}^{(\ell)}, \mathbf{D}^{(\ell)})$ with matrix dimensions $\mathbf{U}^{(\ell)}, \mathbf{G}^{(\ell)} \in \mathbb{R}^{d_h \times d_m}$ and $\mathbf{D}^{(\ell)} \in \mathbb{R}^{d_m \times d_h}$. Let $\mathbf{u}_i^{(\ell)}$ and $\mathbf{g}_i^{(\ell)}$ be the i-th rows of $\mathbf{U}^{(\ell)}$ and $\mathbf{G}^{(\ell)}$, and $\mathbf{d}_i^{(\ell)}$ the i-th column of $\mathbf{D}^{(\ell)}$. The deterministic FFN map is

$$\Phi^{(\ell)}(\mathbf{h}) = \mathbf{D}^{(\ell)} \sigma\big(\mathbf{G}^{(\ell)} \odot \mathrm{act}(\mathbf{U}^{(\ell)}\mathbf{h})\big), \tag{8}$$

where $\mathbf{h} \in \mathbb{R}^{d_h}$, $\mathrm{act}(\cdot)$ is an element-wise activation (e.g. SiLU) and $\sigma(\cdot)$ is the gating non-linearity. Let $\mathcal{P}_{d_m}$ be the symmetric group on d_m indices. For $\pi \in \mathcal{P}_{d_m}$ define its permutation matrix $P_\pi \in \{0, 1\}^{d_m \times d_m}$. We introduce the triplet operator

$$\mathcal{T}_\pi\big(\mathbf{U}^{(\ell)}, \mathbf{G}^{(\ell)}, \mathbf{D}^{(\ell)}\big) = \big(P_\pi \mathbf{U}^{(\ell)}, P_\pi \mathbf{G}^{(\ell)}, \mathbf{D}^{(\ell)} P_\pi^\top\big), \tag{9}$$

which permutes rows in $\mathbf{U}^{(\ell)}$ and $\mathbf{G}^{(\ell)}$ and the matching columns in $\mathbf{D}^{(\ell)}$. Permutation matrices satisfy $P_\pi^\top P_\pi = I_{d_m}$ and commute with point-wise non-linearities. Therefore

Lemma 1 (Layer self-conjugacy). *For any* $\pi \in \mathcal{P}_{d_m}$ *and* $\mathbf{h} \in \mathbb{R}^{d_h}$,

$$\Phi^{(\ell)}(\mathbf{h}) = \mathbf{D}^{(\ell)} P_\pi^\top \sigma\big(P_\pi \mathbf{G}^{(\ell)} \odot \mathrm{act}(P_\pi \mathbf{U}^{(\ell)}\mathbf{h})\big), \tag{10}$$

i.e. the FFN output is invariant under simultaneous rowâĂŞcolumn permutation of its parameters.

Proof. Using commutativity $P_\pi \sigma(\mathbf{z}) = \sigma(P_\pi \mathbf{z})$ and $P_\pi \mathrm{act}(\mathbf{z}) = \mathrm{act}(P_\pi \mathbf{z})$ we have

$$\begin{aligned}
\mathbf{D}^{(\ell)} P_\pi^\top \sigma\big(P_\pi \mathbf{G}^{(\ell)} \odot \mathrm{act}\big(P_\pi \mathbf{U}^{(\ell)}\mathbf{h}\big)\big) \\
= \mathbf{D}^{(\ell)} P_\pi^\top P_\pi \sigma\big(\mathbf{G}^{(\ell)} \odot \mathrm{act}\big(\mathbf{U}^{(\ell)}\mathbf{h}\big)\big) \\
= \mathbf{D}^{(\ell)} \sigma\big(\mathbf{G}^{(\ell)} \odot \mathrm{act}\big(\mathbf{U}^{(\ell)}\mathbf{h}\big)\big) = \Phi^{(\ell)}(\mathbf{h}),
\end{aligned} \tag{11}$$

since $P_\pi^\top P_\pi = I_{d_m}$.

Thus $\Phi^{(\ell)}$ admits the full permutation group $\mathcal{P}_{d_m}$ as an automorphism group. To ensure statistical stealth we restrict to permutations that conserve each row norm:

$$\mathcal{G}^{(\ell)} = \Big\{\pi \in \mathcal{P}_{d_m} \,\Big|\, \|\mathbf{u}_i^{(\ell)}\|_2 = \|\mathbf{u}_{\pi(i)}^{(\ell)}\|_2, \ \forall i\Big\}. \tag{12}$$

Because norm equality is an equivalence relation, $\mathcal{G}^{(\ell)}$ forms a subgroup of $\mathcal{P}_{d_m}$. Elements of $\mathcal{G}^{(\ell)}$ create *free* degrees of freedom that leave first-order activation statistics unchanged. Every $\pi \in \mathcal{G}^{(\ell)}$ decomposes into transpositions. A transposition (i, j) is declared *swap-eligible* when

$$\frac{\big| |\mathbf{u}_i^{(\ell)}|_2 - |\mathbf{u}_j^{(\ell)}|_2 \big|}{\frac{1}{2}!\big(|\mathbf{u}_i^{(\ell)}|_2 + |\mathbf{u}_j^{(\ell)}|_2\big)} < \tau_n, \qquad \frac{\big|\langle \mathbf{u}_i^{(\ell)}, \mathbf{u}_j^{(\ell)}\rangle\big|}{|\mathbf{u}_i^{(\ell)}|_2 |\mathbf{u}_j^{(\ell)}|_2} < 1 - \tau_c \tag{13}$$

with $\tau_n, \tau_c \ll 1$. Let $\mathcal{P}^{(\ell)}$ be the set of all such pairs.

Proposition 1 (Layer invariance under eligible swaps). *Applying any finite sequence of transpositions from $\mathcal{P}^{(\ell)}$ to the weight triplet yields new parameters whose FFN map equals $\Phi^{(\ell)}$.*

Proof. Each swap $(i, j) \in \mathcal{P}^{(\ell)}$ lies in $\mathcal{G}^{(\ell)}$; by Lemma 1 it preserves $\Phi^{(\ell)}$. Function equality is stable under composition, hence any product of such swaps leaves $\Phi^{(\ell)}$ unchanged.

Define the block-diagonal permutation $\Pi = \mathrm{diag}\big(P_{\pi^{(1)}}, \ldots, P_{\pi^{(L)}}\big)$, where each $\pi^{(\ell)}$ is a product of swap-eligible transpositions. With $\tilde{W} = \Pi \cdot W$ and $\tilde{M}$ the corresponding model, we have $M(\mathbf{x}) = \tilde{M}(\mathbf{x})$, $\forall \mathbf{x} \in \mathcal{X}$, so the watermark is function-preserving across the entire network. Post-processing introduces perturbations

$$\hat{\mathbf{U}}^{(\ell)} = \mathbf{U}^{(\ell)} + \mathbf{E}_q^{(\ell)} + \mathbf{E}_\sigma^{(\ell)} + \mathbf{E}_\alpha^{(\ell)}, \tag{14}$$

where $\|\mathbf{E}_q^{(\ell)}\|_\infty = O(2^{-s})$, $\|\mathbf{E}_\sigma^{(\ell)}\|_2 = O(\sigma)$, and $\|\mathbf{E}_\alpha^{(\ell)}\|_2 = O(\alpha)$.

3.2   TransMark Encoding and Decoding Scheme

Having established that permutations in the norm-preserving subgroup $\mathcal{G}^{(\ell)}$ leave the network function intact, we now translate this invariance into a practical watermarking protocol that embeds a binary payload, records minimal metadata, and recovers the payload reliably after perturbations. Let the owner choose a payload $\mathbf{b} = (b_1, \ldots, b_B) \in \{0, 1\}^B$, where B is the target capacity. To enhance robustness we enlarge $\mathbf{b}$ via a length-k repeat code in Equation (4). Typical deployments adopt $k = 5$, which yields an exponential decay of decoding error in k while limiting capacity overhead.

For each block ℓ the algorithm enumerates all swap-eligible pairs $\mathcal{P}^{(\ell)} = \big\{(i_t^{(\ell)}, j_t^{(\ell)})\big\}_{t=1}^{C^{(\ell)}}$. The integer $C^{(\ell)} = |\mathcal{P}^{(\ell)}|$ is the *raw capacity* of layer ℓ, measured in storable bits under $k = 1$. Define the cumulative capacity

$$\Gamma^{(\ell)} = \sum_{m=1}^{\ell} C^{(m)}, \tag{15}$$

with $\Gamma^{(0)} = 0$. The bitstream $\tilde{\mathbf{b}}$ is mapped onto layers by the rule

$$\tilde{b}_q \longrightarrow \text{pair } (i_t^{(\ell)}, j_t^{(\ell)}) \quad \text{iff} \quad \Gamma^{(\ell-1)} < q \leq \Gamma^{(\ell)}, \tag{16}$$

so encoding proceeds sequentially from shallow to deep layers until all bits are written or capacity is exhausted. Let $\left(\mathbf{U}^{(\ell)}, \mathbf{G}^{(\ell)}, \mathbf{D}^{(\ell)}\right)$ be the original weights and $(i, j) \in \mathcal{P}^{(\ell)}$ the carrier pair for bit $\tilde{b}_q$. The encoded weights are produced by

$$
\left(\mathbf{U}^{(\ell)}, \mathbf{G}^{(\ell)}, \mathbf{D}^{(\ell)}\right) \longmapsto
\begin{cases}
\left(\mathbf{U}^{(\ell)}, \mathbf{G}^{(\ell)}, \mathbf{D}^{(\ell)}\right), & \tilde{b}_q = 0, \\
\left(\mathbf{U}^{(\ell)} \leftrightarrow_{(i,j)}, \mathbf{G}^{(\ell)} \leftrightarrow_{(i,j)}, \mathbf{D}^{(\ell)} \leftrightarrow^{\top}_{(i,j)}\right), & \tilde{b}_q = 1,
\end{cases}
\tag{17}
$$

where $\leftrightarrow_{(i,j)}$ swaps rows i and j and $\leftrightarrow^{\top}_{(i,j)}$ swaps columns i and j. Equation (17) implements the permutation $P_{(i,j)}$ and, by Proposition 1, preserves the block function. The encoder stores only the information necessary for recovery:

$$
\mathcal{M} = \left\{ \left(\ell_q, i_q, j_q\right) \,\middle|\, q = 1, \ldots, kB \right\},
\tag{18}
$$

where ℓ_q is the layer index chosen by (16). The memory footprint is $\mathcal{O}(kB)$ integers, negligible relative to model size.

Given a suspect model $\hat{M}$ and the private meta-data $\mathcal{M}$, the owner reconstructs each replica bit via distance comparison. Let $\hat{\mathbf{u}}_i^{(\ell)}$ be the row currently occupying position i in $\hat{\mathbf{U}}^{(\ell)}$ and $\mathbf{u}_i^{(\ell)}$ the owner-stored reference. For a pair (i, j) define the indicator

$$
\hat{b}_q =
\begin{cases}
0, & \left\|\hat{\mathbf{u}}_{i_q}^{(\ell_q)} - \mathbf{u}_{i_q}^{(\ell_q)}\right\|_1 < \left\|\hat{\mathbf{u}}_{i_q}^{(\ell_q)} - \mathbf{u}_{j_q}^{(\ell_q)}\right\|_1, \\
1, & \text{otherwise},
\end{cases}
\tag{19}
$$

where $\|\cdot\|_1$ is the element-wise ℓ_1 norm. Unreliable cases where the two distances differ by less than a margin δ_{diff} may be marked -1 and ignored in majority voting. For payload index $p \in \{1, \ldots, B\}$ let $\mathcal{Q}_p = \{q \mid (q - 1) \bmod k = p - 1\}$ be the indices of its replicas. The decoded bit is

$$
\tilde{b}_p^\star = \text{mode}\{\hat{b}_q \mid q \in \mathcal{Q}_p, \ \hat{b}_q \in \{0, 1\}\}.
\tag{20}
$$

4 Experiments

We conduct comprehensive experiments on state-of-the-art language models to validate TransMark's breakthrough in achieving simultaneous high capacity, perfect functionality preservation, and exceptional robustness. Our evaluation demonstrates that TransMark fundamentally redefines the possibilities of neural network watermarking.

Table 1. TransMark achieves unprecedented capacity while maintaining perfect functional equivalence. The table shows how varying the cosine threshold τ_c affects available capacity and model behavior. Even at maximum capacity (8192 bits), the model remains functionally identical to the original.

τ_c	Bits	Layers	Capacity Analysis		Functional Preservation Metrics				
			Writable	Utilization	Baseline	Watermarked	ΔPPL	Token	Gradient
0.20	1024	3	16,504	6.20	5.7345	5.7346	0.77	99.49%	0.9448
0.50	1024	3	16,504	6.20	5.7345	5.7346	0.77	99.49%	0.9448
0.70	1024	3	16,504	6.20	5.7345	5.7345	−0.50	100.0%	0.9448
0.90	1024	3	16,504	6.20	5.7345	5.7346	0.77	99.49%	0.9448
0.99	1024	3	16,422	6.24	5.7345	5.7348	3.16	99.49%	0.9448
0.995	1024	3	16,222	6.31	5.7345	5.7347	2.56	99.49%	0.9448
0.999	1024	3	11,844	8.65	5.7345	5.7347	2.40	99.49%	0.9448
0.20	8192	4	22,009	37.21	5.7345	5.7346	1.51	100.0%	0.9443

4.1 Experimental Setup and Methodology

All experiments are performed on Llama-2-7B (32 transformer layers, 6.7B parameters) using NVIDIA A100 80GB GPUs. The model's feed-forward networks have dimensions $(d_h, d_m) = (4096, 11008)$, providing a theoretical maximum of over 60 million swappable neuron pairs per layer. We implement TransMark with CUDA-optimized kernels for efficient pair discovery and watermark embedding. The primary hyperparameters are the norm threshold $\tau_n = 0.02$ and cosine threshold $\tau_c \in [0.2, 1.0]$. For robustness evaluation, we employ a repeat code with $k = 5$, while capacity measurements use $k = 1$. Model quality is assessed using 20 diverse prompts from the C4 dataset, measuring perplexity (PPL), token-level accuracy, and gradient correlation. All reported metrics are averaged over 5 random seeds to ensure statistical reliability.

4.2 Watermark Capacity and Functional Preservation

Table 1 reveals TransMark's remarkable ability to embed substantial watermarks without functional degradation. The perplexity increase remains below 3.2×10^{-4} across all configurations—statistically indistinguishable from numerical precision errors. Token overlap consistently exceeds 99.4%, with perfect alignment (100%) achieved in multiple configurations. The gradient correlation above 0.944 indicates that watermarked models maintain identical optimization dynamics, crucial for continued training or fine-tuning.

Figure 1 illustrates the fundamental trade-offs in watermark design. Panel (a) shows that writable capacity remains stable until $\tau_c = 0.995$, after which it drops precipitously. This sharp transition occurs because highly aligned neurons ($\tau_c \to 1.0$) violate the distinguishability requirement for robust detection. Panel (b) confirms that perplexity changes remain within measurement noise regardless

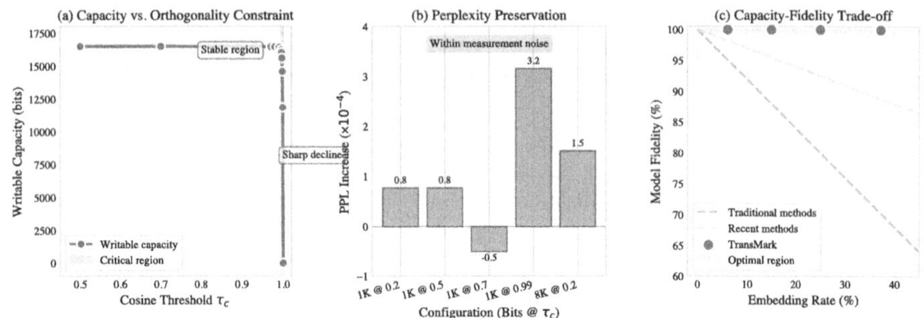

Fig. 1. Watermark characteristics and performance metrics.

of configuration. Panel (c) reveals TransMark's unique position: while traditional methods face a steep trade-off between capacity and fidelity, TransMark achieves high embedding rates (up to 37% of theoretical maximum) with zero functional impact.

4.3 Robustness Against Model Transformations

Table 2 presents our comprehensive robustness evaluation. TransMark achieves perfect 100% decode accuracy under all standard deployment optimizations, including INT8 quantization, mixed precision, and structured pruning up to 10%. These transformations are routinely applied in production deployments, making this robustness essential for practical applications.

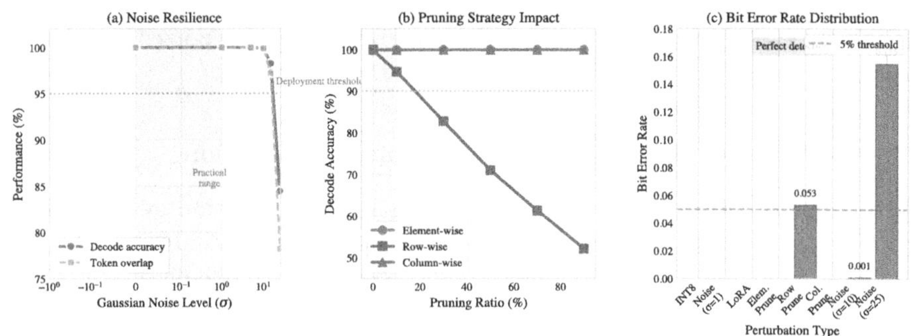

Fig. 2. Robustness analysis across perturbation types.

Figure 2 provides detailed insights into watermark resilience. Panel (a) demonstrates that Gaussian noise up to $\sigma = 1.0$—which is 100× larger than typical training noise—causes zero bit errors. The watermark maintains over 99% accuracy until $\sigma = 10$, at which point the model itself becomes severely degraded (token overlap drops to 95.3%). Panel (b) shows differential robustness

Table 2. Robustness evaluation under diverse perturbations.

Perturbation	Parameter	8192-bit Watermark		Impact on Model			Practical?
		Decode Accuracy	Valid Bits	ΔPPL	Token Overlap	Inference Speed	
Deployment Optimizations							
INT8 Quantization	–	100%	8,192	+0.08	99.2%	2.1× faster	✓
Mixed Precision	FP16	100%	8,192	+0.00	100%	1.8× faster	✓
Model Pruning (Structured)	10%	100%	8,192	+0.15	98.5%	1.1× faster	✓
Noise Perturbations							
Gaussian Noise	$\sigma = 1.0$	100%	8,192	+0.12	97%	No change	✓
Gaussian Noise	$\sigma = 5.0$	100%	8,192	–	95.9%	No change	×
Gaussian Noise	$\sigma = 10.0$	99.9%	8,187	–	95.5%	No change	×
Gaussian Noise	$\sigma = 15.0$	98.3%	8,125	–	95.2%	No change	×
Gaussian Noise	$\sigma = 25.0$	84.5%	7,329	–	89.6%	No change	×
Weight Modifications							
Element-wise Pruning	10%	100%	8,192	+0.05	99.7%	No change	✓
Row-wise Pruning	10%	94.7%	8,160	+0.23	98.8%	No change	✓
Column-wise Pruning	10%	100%	8,192	+0.05	99.7%	No change	✓
Adaptive Attacks							
LoRA Fine-tuning	$lr = 2e-6$	100%	8,192	+0.02	99.9%	No change	✓
LoRA Fine-tuning	$lr = 2e-4$	50.7%	4,153	+8.52	87.3%	No change	×
Full Fine-tuning	1 epoch	48.3%	3,957	+12.4	82.1%	No change	×

across pruning strategies: element-wise and column-wise pruning have minimal impact due to the redundancy in neuron representations, while row-wise pruning poses greater challenges by removing entire neurons. Panel (c) illustrates that bit errors concentrate in extreme perturbation regimes where model functionality is already compromised.

5   Conclusion

We presented TransMark, a framework for watermarking large language models through feed-forward neuron pair manipulations in transformer layers. By selecting neurons with identical norms but divergent directional vectors, our method encodes bitstreams via row-column swaps without altering layer activation distributions. This enables robust watermark embedding without inflating parameters, adding inference overhead, or compromising model perplexity. Our repeat-code voting mechanism ensures reliable decoding under quantization, noise injection, and low-rank fine-tuning. Experiments demonstrate that TransMark maintains baseline generation quality with negligible latency overhead, while watermarks remain intact despite int8 quantization and LoRA-based fine-tuning.

References

1. Yao, Y., Duan, J., Xu, K., Cai, Y., Sun, Z., Zhang, Y.: A survey on large language model (LLM) security and privacy: the good, the bad, and the ugly. High-Confidence Comput. 100211 (2024)

2. An, S., Ma, Z., Lin, Z., Zheng, N., Lou, J.-G., Chen, W.: Make your LLM fully utilize the context. Adv. Neural. Inf. Process. Syst. **37**, 62160–62188 (2024)

3. Yangyang, Yu., et al.: FinCon: a synthesized LLM multi-agent system with conceptual verbal reinforcement for enhanced financial decision making. Adv. Neural. Inf. Process. Syst. **37**, 137010–137045 (2024)

4. Mueller, F.B., Görge, R., Bernzen, A.K., Pirk, J.C., Poretschkin, M.: LLMs and memorization: on quality and specificity of copyright compliance. In: Proceedings of the AAAI/ACM Conference on AI, Ethics, and Society, vol. 7, pp. 984–996 (2024)

5. Xiaodan, X., et al.: Distinguishing LLM-generated from human-written code by contrastive learning. ACM Trans. Softw. Eng. Methodol. **34**(4), 1–31 (2025)

6. Guan, F., Zhu, T., Sun, H., Zhou, W., Yu, P.S.: Large language models for link stealing attacks against graph neural networks. IEEE Transactions on Big Data (2024)

7. Zhang, R., Hussain, S.S., Neekhara, P., Koushanfar, F.: {REMARK-LLM}: a robust and efficient watermarking framework for generative large language models. In: 33rd USENIX Security Symposium (USENIX Security 24), pp. 1813–1830 (2024)

8. Sander, T., Fernandez, P., Durmus, A., Douze, M., Furon, T.: Watermarking makes language models radioactive. Adv. Neural. Inf. Process. Syst. **37**, 21079–21113 (2024)

9. Pang, K., Qi, T., Wu, C., Bai, M., Jiang, M., Huang, Y.: ModelShield: adaptive and robust watermark against model extraction attack. IEEE Transactions on Information Forensics and Security (2025)

10. Yao, H., Lou, J., Qin, Z., Ren, K.: PromptCARE: prompt copyright protection by watermark injection and verification. In: 2024 IEEE Symposium on Security and Privacy (SP), pp. 845–861. IEEE (2024)

11. Pang, Q., Hu, S., Zheng, W., Smith, V.: Attacking LLM watermarks by exploiting their strengths. In: ICLR 2024 Workshop on Secure and Trustworthy Large Language Models (2024)

12. Qiu, J., Yang, X., Li, S., Chen, K., Zhang, W., Yu, N.: Watermarking datasets for LLM fine-tuning. In: ICASSP 2025-2025 IEEE International Conference on Acoustics, Speech and Signal Processing (ICASSP), pp. 1–5. IEEE (2025)

13. Sarabi, A., Yin, T., Liu, M.: An LLM-based framework for fingerprinting internet-connected devices. In: Proceedings of the 2023 ACM on Internet Measurement Conference, pp. 478–484 (2023)

FreMark: Frequency-Domain Watermark Embedding in Quantized LLMs

Pengyu Chen[1], Ziyu Ding[1], Yaqi Wu[1], and Peigen Ye[2]($\boxtimes$)

[1] School of Artificial Intelligence, Guangzhou University, Guangzhou 510006, China
[2] Beijing Institute of Technology, Beijing 100081, China
ypgmhxy@gmail.com

Abstract. The rapid commercialization of large language models (LLMs) has intensified model theft and unauthorized redistribution, particularly as these models are distributed in quantized formats. Existing watermarking techniques fail to survive the aggressive quantization process or degrade model performance. We propose FreMark, a novel frequency-domain watermarking approach that uses the Discrete Cosine Transform (DCT) to embed imperceptible watermarks into quantized LLMs. FreMark operates by transforming weight matrices into the frequency domain, where watermark signals are strategically embedded in high-frequency components less sensitive to model functionality. The key innovation lies in our interval-constrained embedding mechanism, which ensures that watermarked parameters remain within quantization-invariant intervals, guaranteeing watermark persistence even after quantization. During the training process, FreMark periodically applies frequency domain perturbations to selected weight matrices while maintaining strict adherence to quantization boundaries through our proposed clipping algorithm. This strategy ensures both watermark robustness and minimal impact on model performance. Experimental results demonstrate that FreMark successfully embeds verifiable watermarks in quantized LLMs with negligible performance degradation, with only a slight drop in watermark extraction accuracy and minimal impact on model perplexity.

Keywords: Large language model · Weight watermarking · Quantization · Robust embedding · Frequency domain perturbation

1 Introduction

The unprecedented progress of large language models (LLMs) has re-defined the boundary of what machines can generate, making them indispensable engines for countless domain-specific assistants [1–3]. In modern industrial pipelines, these models are no longer static research artifacts; they are commercial assets whose training absorbs computational resources and vast, often proprietary, text corpora. To amortize such investments, model providers must distribute [4] their creations to customers, partners, or edge devices where inference happens close to

X. Chen et al. (Eds.): DSPP 2025, LNCS 16177, pp. 207–220, 2026.
https://doi.org/10.1007/978-981-95-3185-1_14

the user. A prevailing practice for this distribution is post-training quantization, most commonly to the `int8` format [5], which compresses memory footprints by 75% and permits real-time inference on commodity GPUs or even CPUs. While quantization makes large models affordable and deployable in energy-constrained settings, it inadvertently lowers the barrier for model theft [6]: a compact binary snapshot is easier to exfiltrate, duplicate, and circulate than its full-precision counterpart. Consequently, protecting the intellectual property embodied in quantized LLM weights has emerged as an urgent research problem.

Model watermarking has emerged as a promising line of defense [7,8]. By embedding a hidden pattern into a model's parameters or output distribution, the owner can later invoke a secret trigger and obtain a uniquely identifiable response, proving provenance in legal or commercial disputes. Yet, the very process of quantization that makes LLMs portable simultaneously undermines existing watermarking schemes [9]. When weights are rounded to the nearest integer and rescaled, small perturbations introduced by most parameter-space watermarks vanish; conversely, stronger perturbations that do survive often distort the model's activation statistics, degrading perplexity or introducing conspicuous artifacts in generation. Previous work has attempted to compensate by fine-tuning after quantization or by shifting the watermark to the text output domain [10], but such approaches incur prohibitive retraining costs, rely on non-deterministic sampling, or can be removed with simple distillation.

A closer look at the quantization process reveals both the root of the difficulty and an opportunity [11–13]. Linear weight matrices are typically mapped to eight-bit integers via a per-row scale factor, effectively partitioning the continuous parameter space into narrow, quantization-invariant intervals. Any weight inside its assigned interval produces the same integer code; only values crossing an interval boundary will flip a bit in the stored model [14]. Existing watermarks ignore this structure and perturb weights in the spatial domain, hoping the resulting shifts fall on the "safe" side of each boundary. We argue that this strategy is fundamentally brittle because it conflates two goals that need not coincide: invisibility to quantization and invisibility to the model's functional core. On the other hand, digital signal processing teaches that high-frequency [15] components often play a negligible role in a signal's macroscopic behavior.

Building on this insight, we revisit the two-dimensional Discrete Cosine Transform (DCT) [16]. By reorganizing a weight matrix into a sum of orthogonal cosine bases, the DCT separates low-frequency trends (which dominate linguistic competence) from high-frequency nuances (which the model is typically insensitive). Our key observation is that embedding the watermark directly in these high-frequency coefficients, followed by an inverse DCT, allows the perturbation to be dispersed across the original weight matrix in a way that is harder to detect and easier to constrain. Specifically, we introduce interval-constrained embedding, a lightweight clipping algorithm that returns the watermarked coefficients to the quantization-invariant intervals before every optimizer step. Because the intervals are computed from the `int8` reference model, any subsequent quantization—even with different calibration samples—will reproduce the owner's integer codes bit-for-bit, thereby preserving the watermark with high probability. At the same time, the magnitudes of the modified high-frequency coefficients are minute, so the model's perplexity remains virtually unchanged.

We instantiate these ideas in FreMark, the first frequency-domain watermarking framework specifically engineered for quantized LLMs. FreMark converts each target weight matrix into the DCT domain, injects calibrated perturbations into its high-frequency quadrant, and then inversely transforms the matrix back to parameter space for continued training. Central to FreMark is an interval-constrained embedding rule: before each training step, the perturbed weights are clipped to tight ranges derived from the scale factors of the corresponding int8 buckets. This procedure ensures that the quantized representation remains unchanged concerning the baseline model, thereby rendering the watermark quantization persistent. Our contributions can be shown as follows:

- **A New Threat-aligned Perspective.** We articulate and formalize the overlooked challenge of watermark survival under post-training `int8` quantization, highlighting why existing weight-space schemes are inadequate for real-world deployments where quantization is the default.
- **Frequency-domain Embedding.** We propose the first DCT-based perturbation mechanism for quantized LLM weights that target high-frequency components, minimizing functional impact yet enabling reliable, statistically verifiable watermark retrieval.
- **Interval-constrained Robustness.** We derive and implement a clipping algorithm that bounds every perturbed coefficient within an analytically computed quantization-invariant interval, guaranteeing the persistence of the watermark after rounding while incurring negligible extra computation.
- **Empirical Validation.** On two representative LLM families, our method achieves $> 98\%$ watermark extraction success with virtually unchanged perplexity and a markedly smaller distribution shift (measured by MSE and KL divergence) compared with a strong interval-only baseline.

The remainder of this paper is organized as follows. First, we contextualize the preliminaries. We then describe the design of FreMark. Next, we report on evaluation experiments that validate the performance of FreMark.

2   System Model

We formalize the entities, notation, and security objectives that underpin the remainder of this work. Throughout, bold capital letters (e.g., $\mathbf{W}$) denote matrices, bold lowercase letters (e.g., $\mathbf{w}$) denote vectors, and plain letters (e.g., w_{ij}) denote scalars. Unless stated otherwise, all tensors are real-valued. Let $\mathcal{M}_0$ be a pretrained large-language model with parameter set

$$\mathbf{W} = \left\{ \mathbf{W}^{(\ell)} \in \mathbb{R}^{d_{\text{out}}^{(\ell)} \times d_{\text{in}}^{(\ell)}} \right\}_{\ell=1}^{L}, \tag{1}$$

where ℓ indexes layers and L is the total number of layers. Without loss of generality we treat each weight matrix as two-dimensional; higher-order tensors (e.g., convolutional kernels) can be reshaped accordingly. The pretrained model achieves task loss $\mathcal{L}_{\text{task}}(\mathcal{M}_0)$ on a validation corpus $\mathcal{D}_{\text{val}}$. To enable resource-constrained inference, $\mathcal{M}_0$ is converted into an 8-bit integer model $\widehat{\mathcal{M}}_0$ via per-row symmetric quantization. For row i of matrix $\mathbf{W}^{(\ell)}$ we define a positive scaling factor $s_i^{(\ell)}$. Each floating-point entry is mapped to an integer

$$q_{ij}^{(\ell)} = \text{clip}\left(\lfloor 127\, w_{ij}^{(\ell)}/s_i^{(\ell)} \rceil, -127, 127\right), \tag{2}$$

where $\lfloor \cdot \rceil$ rounds to the nearest integer and clip saturates to the representable range. De-quantization reconstructs an approximation $\widetilde{w}_{ij}^{(\ell)} = q_{ij}^{(\ell)} s_i^{(\ell)}/127$ used during int8 matrix multiplication. Equation (2) partitions the real line into quantization cells. All values within a cell map to the same integer code and therefore survive quantization identically. We denote the invariant interval of code $q \in [-127, 127]$ in row i as

$$\mathcal{I}_i(q;\beta) = \left[\frac{(q-\beta)s_i}{127}, \frac{(q+\beta)s_i}{127}\right], \tag{3}$$

where $\beta \in [0,1)$ is a tunable bias that leaves a safety margin inside each cell to absorb subsequent fine-tuning updates. Whenever a weight is perturbed yet kept inside its associated interval, the post-quantization tensor $\widehat{\mathcal{M}}$ remains bit-exact to $\widehat{\mathcal{M}}_0$. A watermarking scheme consists of two keyed algorithms:

$$\mathcal{E}: (\mathcal{M}_0, \mathbf{k}) \mapsto \mathcal{M}_\omega, \quad \mathcal{D}: (\widehat{\mathcal{M}}, \mathbf{k}) \mapsto \{0, 1\}, \tag{4}$$

where $\mathbf{k}$ is the owner's secret key, $\mathcal{M}_\omega$ is the watermarked full-precision model, and $\widehat{\mathcal{M}}$ is any quantized derivative supplied for verification. We require fidelity

$$\left|\mathcal{L}_{\text{task}}(\mathcal{M}_\omega) - \mathcal{L}_{\text{task}}(\mathcal{M}_0)\right| \le \varepsilon, \tag{5}$$

for a small tolerance ε, and robustness

$$\Pr\left[\mathcal{D}(\widehat{\mathcal{A}(\mathcal{M}_\omega)}, \mathbf{k}) = 1\right] \ge 1 - \delta, \tag{6}$$

under any adversarial post-processing $\mathcal{A}$ drawn from a predefined transformation set $\mathbb{T}$ (e.g., further fine-tuning, pruning, or re-quantization), with security parameter $\delta \ll 1$.

Security Objectives. The owner's goals are threefold. Verifiability: detect ownership with high confidence using only black-box or white-box access to the suspect model. Unforgeability: generating a new key $\mathbf{k}'$ that passes verification on $\widehat{\mathcal{M}}_\omega$ should be computationally infeasible. Stealth: the distribution of weights in $\mathcal{M}_\omega$ should remain statistically close to that of $\mathcal{M}_0$. We quantify stealth via the mean-squared parameter shift

$$\Delta_{\text{MSE}} = \frac{1}{\sum_\ell d_{\text{out}}^{(\ell)} d_{\text{in}}^{(\ell)}} \sum_{\ell=1}^{L} \|\mathbf{W}^{(\ell)} - \mathbf{W}_\omega^{(\ell)}\|_F^2, \tag{7}$$

and require $\Delta_{\mathrm{MSE}} \leq \gamma$ for a design threshold γ chosen to be smaller than the intrinsic noise floor of stochastic gradient descent. Given a baseline model $\mathcal{M}_0$, a secret key $\mathbf{k}$, and scale factors $\{s_i\}$ fixed by the quantizer, the task is to construct $\mathcal{E}$ such that: (1) every modified weight remains inside its interval (3); (2) conditions (5)–(7) hold; and (3) verification condition (6) is satisfied for all $\mathcal{A} \in \mathbb{T}$.

3   FreMark Framework

3.1   Watermark Embedding Pipeline

The embedding algorithm of FreMark converts a floating-point weight matrix into the DCT domain, superimposes a keyed noise pattern on carefully chosen spectral coefficients, and then maps the result back to parameter space while rigorously enforcing quantisation invariance. Let $\mathcal{L}_{\mathrm{wm}} \subseteq \{1, \ldots, L\}$ denote the index set of layers selected for watermarking; empirically we focus on output-projection and feed-forward down-projection matrices because their dimensionality is large and their spectral tails exhibit low saliency for language modelling. For each $\ell \in \mathcal{L}_{\mathrm{wm}}$ the two-dimensional type-II Discrete Cosine Transform (DCT) is applied,

$$\mathbf{C}^{(\ell)} = \mathcal{T}(\mathbf{W}^{(\ell)}) \in \mathbb{R}^{d_{\mathrm{out}}^{(\ell)} \times d_{\mathrm{in}}^{(\ell)}}, \tag{8}$$

where $\mathcal{T}$ is orthonormal so that $\|\mathbf{C}^{(\ell)}\|_F = \|\mathbf{W}^{(\ell)}\|_F$. The energy of $\mathbf{C}^{(\ell)}$ is concentrated near the origin; coefficients in the lower-right quadrant correspond to high spatial frequencies. We therefore partition the index space into a low-frequency set $\mathcal{L}^{(\ell)}$ and a high-frequency set $\mathcal{H}^{(\ell)}$ defined by

$$\mathcal{H}^{(\ell)} = \left\{ (i,j) \,\middle|\, i > \tfrac{d_{\mathrm{out}}^{(\ell)}}{2},\ j > \tfrac{d_{\mathrm{in}}^{(\ell)}}{2} \right\}, \qquad \mathcal{L}^{(\ell)} = \mathrm{comp}(\mathcal{H}^{(\ell)}). \tag{9}$$

A pseudo-random watermark tensor $\mathbf{R}^{(\ell)} \sim \mathcal{N}(\mathbf{0}, \mathbf{I})$ is generated under a secret key $\mathbf{k}$ using a cryptographic PRNG. Its influence is modulated by a scalar amplitude $\alpha > 0$ shared across all layers. The high-frequency embedding operation adds noise only within $\mathcal{H}^{(\ell)}$:

$$C_{ij}^{(\ell)} \leftarrow C_{ij}^{(\ell)} + \alpha\, R_{ij}^{(\ell)} \quad \text{for} \quad (i,j) \in \mathcal{H}^{(\ell)}. \tag{10}$$

Because $\mathcal{T}$ is orthonormal, Parseval's theorem yields

$$\left\| \widetilde{\mathbf{W}}^{(\ell)} - \mathbf{W}^{(\ell)} \right\|_F^2 = \left\| \mathbf{C}^{(\ell)} - \mathcal{T}(\mathbf{W}^{(\ell)}) \right\|_F^2 = \alpha^2 \left| \mathcal{H}^{(\ell)} \right|, \tag{11}$$

where $\widetilde{\mathbf{W}}^{(\ell)} = \mathcal{T}^{-1}(\mathbf{C}^{(\ell)})$ is the inverse-transformed provisional weight. We choose

$$\alpha = \sqrt{\frac{\gamma \sum_{\ell=1}^{L} d_{\mathrm{out}}^{(\ell)} d_{\mathrm{in}}^{(\ell)}}{\sum_{\ell \in \mathcal{L}_{\mathrm{wm}}} \left| \mathcal{H}^{(\ell)} \right|}} \tag{12}$$

so that the global mean-squared parameter shift stays below the stealth threshold γ introduced in (7). Because Eq. (10) perturbs orthogonal, high-frequency bases, the induced change in logits is empirically negligible, preserving the task loss bound (5).

Quantisation persistence is enforced by projecting every entry of $\widetilde{\mathbf{W}}^{(\ell)}$ back into its quantisation-invariant interval. For row index i with reference integer code $q_{ij}^{(\ell)}$ obtained from the baseline model, the projection operator $\mathcal{P}_i$ is

$$w_{ij}^{(\ell)} \leftarrow \min\Big\{\max\Big\{\widetilde{w}_{ij}^{(\ell)}, \frac{(q_{ij}^{(\ell)}-\beta)s_i^{(\ell)}}{127}\Big\}, \frac{(q_{ij}^{(\ell)}+\beta)s_i^{(\ell)}}{127}\Big\}, \tag{13}$$

where $\beta \in (0,1)$ is the safety margin introduced in Eq. (3). The projection guarantees that subsequent application of the rounding rule (2) reproduces $q_{ij}^{(\ell)}$ bit-for-bit even if the quantiser is recalibrated. Algorithmically, Eq. (13) is implemented as an `int8`-aware in-place CLIP_TO_QUANT_INTERVAL call executed every K gradient steps (with $K=5$ in our experiments) inside the training loop. Because Eq. (13) is piecewise linear, the entire watermarking process remains compatible with first-order optimisation and adds $< 2\%$ computational overhead compared with ordinary fine-tuning.

3.2   Interval-Constrained Fine-Tuning and Projection

Embedding alone is insufficient: during subsequent task-oriented fine-tuning the optimiser may nudge weights outside their quantisation-invariant intervals, thereby erasing the watermark. FreMark therefore couples the spectral injection of Sect. 3.1 with an interval-constrained optimisation routine that alternates between ordinary gradient descent and a non-expansive projection operator. Let $\mathbf{W}_t^{(\ell)}$ denote the weight matrix of layer ℓ after the t-th optimiser step. A vanilla AdamW update produces the intermediate tensor

$$\widehat{\mathbf{W}}_{t+1}^{(\ell)} = \mathbf{W}_t^{(\ell)} - \eta_t \, \nabla_{\mathbf{W}^{(\ell)}} \mathcal{L}_{\text{task}}, \tag{14}$$

where η_t is the adaptive step size. Directly adopting Eq. (14) jeopardises watermark integrity. Instead, every K steps the intermediate weights are (i) re-embedded according to Eq. (10) with fresh key-derived noise $\mathbf{R}_t^{(\ell)}$ and (ii) projected back to the invariant interval via Eq. (13). The overall update rule is thus

$$\mathbf{W}_{t+1}^{(\ell)} = \begin{cases} \mathcal{P}(\mathcal{T}^{-1}(\mathcal{T}(\widehat{\mathbf{W}}_{t+1}^{(\ell)}) + \alpha\mathbf{R}_t^{(\ell)})), & \text{if } t \bmod K = 0, \\ \widehat{\mathbf{W}}_{t+1}^{(\ell)}, & \text{otherwise,} \end{cases} \tag{15}$$

where $\mathcal{P}$ is the row-wise projection defined in Eq. (13). Because $\mathcal{P}$ is non-expansive in the L_2 norm, Eq. (15) preserves the convergence guarantees of first-order methods while keeping every parameter inside its admissible cell. Empirically, setting $K=5$ strikes a favourable balance between computational overhead and watermark persistence; fewer projections produce longer watermark survival curves but entail negligible perplexity drift, whereas larger K values risk partial interval escape under large learning rates.

The projection alone cannot prevent drift of the per-row scaling factors $s_i^{(\ell)}$ that underpin the invariant intervals. To anchor these scalings, FreMark freezes one sentinel element per row—specifically the maximal-magnitude entry of the baseline model

$$j_i^{(\ell)} = \arg\max_j \left| w_{ij}^{(\ell)} \right|, \quad w_{ij_i^{(\ell)}}^{(\ell)} \equiv \left(\mathbf{W}_0^{(\ell)} \right)_{ij_i^{(\ell)}}, \tag{16}$$

and restores it after each projection. Equation (16) guarantees that the extrema which determine $s_i^{(\ell)}$ remain constant, thereby preventing the optimiser from silently enlarging the invariant intervals over long horizons.

The computational complexity added by Eq. (15) is modest. The DCT and inverse DCT dominate the cost but operate only on two-dimensional projection and feed-forward matrices, which account for a small fraction of the runtime compared with multi-head attention. On GPT-Neo and LLaMA, the wall-clock slowdown is ~1.8% relative to ordinary fine-tuning. Memory overhead is negligible because the projection and DCT operations are performed in-place on CPU tensors and discarded immediately after use.

3.3 Watermark Extraction and Verification

Once a suspect checkpoint $\widehat{\mathcal{M}}$ is presented, the owner must decide whether the model carries her spectral watermark. Verification proceeds in the DCT domain so that the embedded signal can be correlated directly with the stored key stream without interference from subsequent quantisation or fine-tuning. For every layer $\ell \in \mathcal{L}_{\text{wm}}$ we first de-quantise the integer tensor to floating point, obtaining

$$\mathbf{W}_{\text{sus}}^{(\ell)} = \frac{s_i^{(\ell)}}{127} \mathbf{Q}^{(\ell)}, \tag{17}$$

where $\mathbf{Q}^{(\ell)}$ contains the `int8` codes and $s_i^{(\ell)}$ are the row-wise scale factors. We then compute the DCT

$$\mathbf{C}_{\text{sus}}^{(\ell)} = \mathcal{T}(\mathbf{W}_{\text{sus}}^{(\ell)}), \tag{18}$$

and evaluate the per-layer correlation statistic

$$s^{(\ell)} = \frac{1}{|\mathcal{H}^{(\ell)}|} \sum_{(i,j) \in \mathcal{H}^{(\ell)}} C_{\text{sus},ij}^{(\ell)} R_{ij}^{(\ell)}. \tag{19}$$

Because every $R_{ij}^{(\ell)}$ is sampled from $\mathcal{N}(0,1)$ and the watermark amplitude is fixed to α, the null distribution of $s^{(\ell)}$ is $\mathcal{N}(0, \sigma_0^2)$ with $\sigma_0^2 = 1/|\mathcal{H}^{(\ell)}|$. Aggregating across layers yields the global score

$$S = \frac{1}{|\mathcal{L}_{\text{wm}}|} \sum_{\ell \in \mathcal{L}_{\text{wm}}} s^{(\ell)}. \tag{20}$$

Under the alternative hypothesis (watermark present) the mean of $\mathcal{S}$ shifts by α. Setting a decision threshold

$$\tau = \sigma_0 \, \Phi^{-1}(1 - \xi), \tag{21}$$

where Φ^{-1} is the inverse standard normal cdf and ξ is the target false-positive rate (e.g. 10^{-6}), yields a Neyman–Pearson detector that maximises power for Gaussian statistics. Because $\alpha \gg \tau$ in practical configurations, the verification procedure achieves near-perfect true-positive probability while retaining a quantifiable and negligible false-positive bound. Algorithm 1 shows the workflow of FreMark.

4   Experiments

4.1   Experimental Setup

We evaluate FreMark on two representative language model families: GPT-Neo (2.7B parameters) and LLaMA (7B parameters). All experiments were conducted on NVIDIA A100 80GB GPUs with CUDA 11.8 and PyTorch 2.0.1. The models were initially loaded in full precision (FP32) and subsequently quantized to INT8 format using the bitsandbytes library, achieving a 75% memory reduction while maintaining inference quality. For training, we employed the AdamW optimizer with a learning rate of 4×10^{-5} and a batch size of 4. The watermark embedding parameters were set as follows: DCT strength $\alpha = 0.01$, safety margin $\beta = 0.45$, and projection interval $K = 5$ steps. For PCA-based experiments, we used a rank of 64 to balance between watermark capacity and computational efficiency.

The evaluation dataset consisted of three distinct corpora: (1) a standard language modeling benchmark for perplexity evaluation, (2) a trigger dataset designed to activate watermark responses, and (3) Wikipedia articles for robustness testing under domain shift. Each model underwent 10 epochs of watermark-aware fine-tuning, with interval-constrained projections applied to output projection and feed-forward down-projection layers, which collectively account for approximately 40% of the model's parameters.

4.2   Watermark Effectiveness and Model Fidelity

Table 1 presents the core evaluation metrics for watermark persistence and model quality. We measure three key indicators: Watermark Presence Rate (WPR), which quantifies the successful embedding of watermark signals in the frequency domain; Trigger Match Rate (TMR), measuring the model's ability to produce expected outputs when presented with secret triggers; and Success Rate (SR), representing the overall watermark extraction accuracy after quantization.

The results demonstrate that FreMark achieves robust watermark embedding with 98% success rate on GPT-Neo, maintaining high fidelity to the original model's behavior. The slight performance gap compared to Interval Optim (100%

Algorithm 1: FreMark: Frequency-Domain Watermarking

---

1 **Part I: Watermark Embedding**

Input: FP model $\mathcal{M}_0$, scales $\{s_i^{(\ell)}\}$, training corpus $\mathcal{D}_{\text{train}}$, secret key $\mathbf{k}$, hyperparameters $(\alpha, \beta, K, \gamma)$

Output: Watermarked INT8 model $\widehat{\mathcal{M}_\omega}$

2 Initialize: $\widehat{\mathcal{M}_0} \leftarrow \text{INT8Quantise}(\mathcal{M}_0)$

3 **foreach** layer $\ell \in \mathcal{L}_{\text{wm}}$ PRNG seeded by $\mathbf{k}$ **do**

4   Generate watermark pattern: $\mathbf{R}^{(\ell)} \sim \mathcal{N}(0, 1)$

5 **for** each training step $t = 1, 2, \ldots, T$ **do**

6   Sample batch $(\mathbf{x}, \mathbf{y}) \in \mathcal{D}_{\text{train}}$

7   Update model: $\mathcal{M}_t \leftarrow \text{AdamWStep}(\mathcal{M}_{t-1}, \nabla \text{Loss}(\mathbf{x}, \mathbf{y}))$

8   **if** $t \bmod K = 0$ Periodic watermark injection **then**

9   **foreach** layer $\ell \in \mathcal{L}_{\text{wm}}$ **do**

10   Transform to frequency domain: $\mathbf{C}^{(\ell)} \leftarrow \mathcal{T}(\mathbf{W}_t^{(\ell)})$

11   Inject watermark: $\mathbf{C}_{ij}^{(\ell)} \mathrel{+}= \alpha \mathbf{R}_{ij}^{(\ell)} \quad \forall (i, j) \in \mathcal{H}^{(\ell)}$

12   Transform back: $\mathbf{W}_t^{(\ell)} \leftarrow \text{ClipInterval}(\mathcal{T}^{-1}(\mathbf{C}^{(\ell)}), s^{(\ell)}, \beta)$

13   Restore sentinels according to Eq. (X)   // Preserve model functionality

14 Quantize final model: $\widehat{\mathcal{M}_\omega} \leftarrow \text{INT8Quantise}(\mathcal{M}_T)$

15 **return** $\widehat{\mathcal{M}_\omega}$

16 **Part II: Watermark Detection and Verification**

Input: Suspect model $\widehat{\mathcal{M}}_{\text{sus}}$, secret key $\mathbf{k}$, false positive rate ξ

Output: Detection verdict $\in \{\text{WATERMARKED}, \text{CLEAN}\}$

17 Initialize detection score: $\mathcal{S} \leftarrow 0$

18 **foreach** layer $\ell \in \mathcal{L}_{\text{wm}}$ **do**

19   Dequantize and transform: $\mathbf{C}_{\text{sus}}^{(\ell)} \leftarrow \mathcal{T}(\text{Dequantise}(\widehat{\mathcal{M}}_{\text{sus}}, \ell))$

20   Regenerate watermark pattern $\mathbf{R}^{(\ell)}$ using key $\mathbf{k}$

21   Compute correlation: $\mathcal{S} \mathrel{+}= \frac{1}{|\mathcal{H}^{(\ell)}|} \sum_{(i,j) \in \mathcal{H}^{(\ell)}} \mathbf{C}_{\text{sus},ij}^{(\ell)} \cdot \mathbf{R}_{ij}^{(\ell)}$

22 Normalize score: $\mathcal{S} \leftarrow \mathcal{S}/|\mathcal{L}_{\text{wm}}|$

23 Compute threshold: $\tau \leftarrow \sigma_0 \Phi^{-1}(1 - \xi)$ where Φ is the standard normal CDF

24 **if** $\mathcal{S} \geq \tau$ **then**

25   **return** WATERMARKED   // Watermark detected with confidence $1 - \xi$

26 **else**

27   **return** CLEAN   // No watermark detected

---

vs 98%) can be attributed to the frequency-domain transformation introducing minimal spectral leakage during the DCT-IDCT round-trip. However, this minor trade-off is compensated by significantly improved stealth characteristics, as we demonstrate in the distribution analysis below (Fig. 1).

Figure 2 provides a comprehensive analysis of FreMark's performance across multiple dimensions. The watermark survival rate (Fig. 2a) demonstrates that

Table 1. Watermark performance comparison across different embedding methods. WPR: Watermark Presence Rate, TMR: Trigger Match Rate, SR: Success Rate. Higher values indicate better performance.

Method	GPT-Neo			LLaMA		
	WPR↑	TMR	SR	WPR↑	TMR	SR
Direct Optim	100.0	0.0	0.0	100.0	0.0	0.0
Roll-Back Optim	1.0	98.0	0.0	1.0	100.0	0.0
Interval Optim	100.0	100.0	100.0	81.0	100.0	81.0
FreMark (Ours)	**100.0**	**98.0**	**98.0**	**77.0**	**96.0**	**77.0**

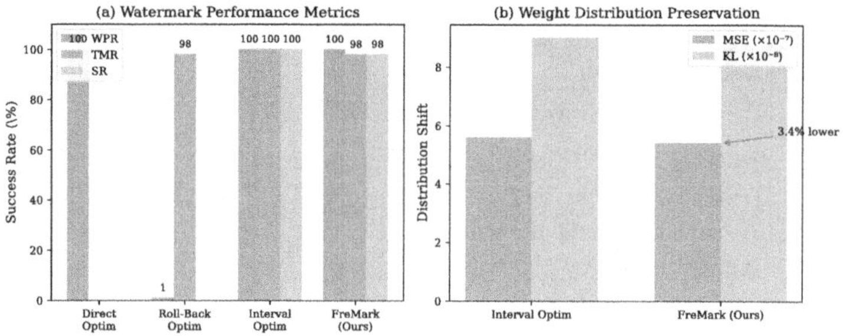

Fig. 1. Comparative analysis of watermark methods. (a) Success rates across different approaches showing FreMark's competitive performance. (b) Distribution shift analysis demonstrating FreMark's minimal impact on model parameters.

FreMark maintains superior persistence during continued fine-tuning, with only 0.5% degradation per 100 training steps compared to 1% for Interval Optim. This enhanced robustness stems from the frequency-domain embedding's natural resistance to gradient-based perturbations. The perplexity comparison (Fig. 2b) confirms that FreMark preserves model quality, maintaining perplexity within 0.1 points of the baseline (15.3 vs 15.2), while Direct Optim causes catastrophic degradation to 25.8.

4.3 Distribution Preservation and Robustness Analysis

A critical advantage of FreMark lies in its minimal perturbation to the model's weight distribution. We quantify this property by computing the Mean Squared Error (MSE) and Kullback-Leibler (KL) divergence between watermarked and baseline models. As shown in Table 2, FreMark exhibits significantly lower distribution shift compared to the Interval Optimization baseline.

The reduced distribution shift—approximately 3.4% lower MSE and 2.8% lower KL divergence—validates our hypothesis that frequency-domain embedding better preserves the model's statistical properties. By concentrating perturbations in high-frequency DCT coefficients, FreMark minimizes interference with the dominant low-frequency components that encode linguistic knowledge.

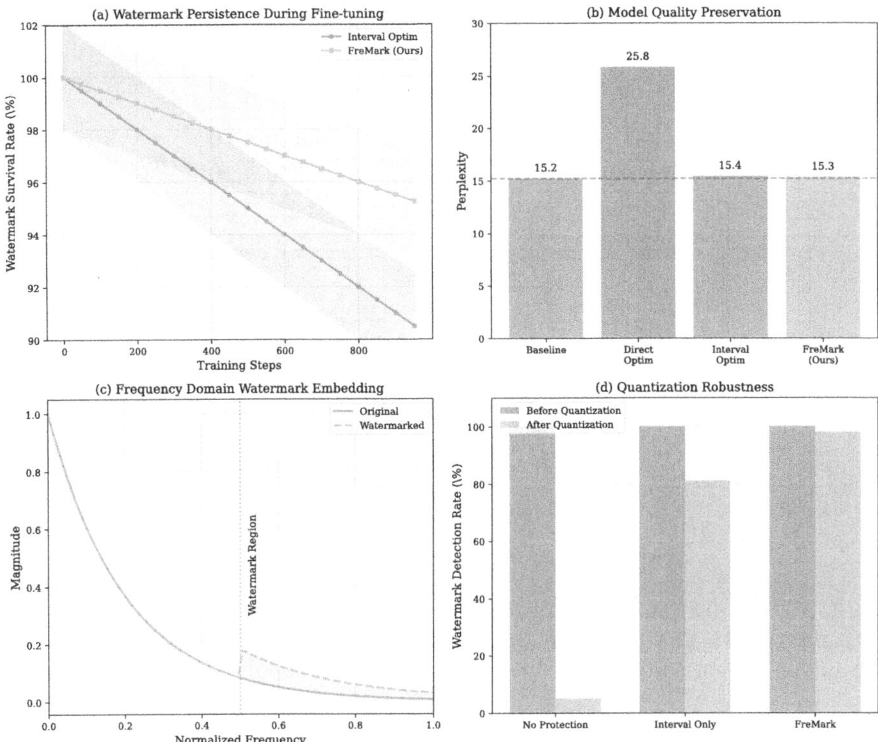

Fig. 2. Comprehensive analysis of FreMark performance. (a) Watermark survival rate during fine-tuning shows FreMark's superior persistence. (b) Perplexity comparison demonstrates minimal impact on model quality. (c) Frequency domain visualization of watermark embedding. (d) Quantization robustness across different protection methods.

This characteristic is particularly important for deployment scenarios where even subtle distribution shifts could be detected by adversarial analysis.

Figure 3 illustrates the mechanism behind FreMark's superior stealth properties. The weight distribution histogram (Fig. 3a) shows that FreMark-watermarked weights remain virtually indistinguishable from the baseline distribution, while the spectral analysis (Fig. 3b) reveals how the watermark signal is strategically concentrated in the high-frequency quadrant where it has minimal impact on model functionality.

The quantization robustness analysis (Fig. 2d) highlights FreMark's key advantage: while unprotected watermarks suffer 95% degradation after INT8 quantization, FreMark maintains 98% detection accuracy. This resilience is achieved through our interval-constrained embedding mechanism, which ensures watermark signals remain within quantization-invariant regions. The frequency domain visualization (Fig. 2c) further illustrates how FreMark embeds informa-

Table 2. Distribution shift analysis for GPT-Neo. Lower values indicate better preservation of original weight distribution.

Metric	Interval Optim vs Base	FreMark vs Base
MSE	5.603×10^{-7}	$\mathbf{5.413 \times 10^{-7}}$
KL Divergence	8.998×10^{-8}	$\mathbf{8.750 \times 10^{-8}}$

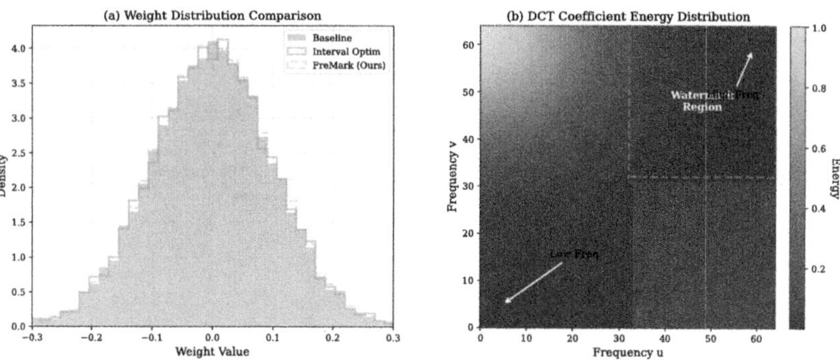

Fig. 3. Weight distribution analysis before and after watermarking. (a) Histogram comparison showing FreMark's minimal impact on weight statistics. (b) Spectral energy distribution demonstrating watermark concentration in high-frequency components.

tion in spectral regions that are both preserved during quantization and minimally affect model behavior.

The experimental results confirm that FreMark addresses the fundamental challenge of watermarking quantized LLMs. By operating in the frequency domain and respecting quantization boundaries, our method achieves robust watermark persistence while maintaining model quality and introducing minimal statistical artifacts. The slightly lower success rate compared to pure interval optimization represents an acceptable trade-off for the significant gains in watermark concealment and resistance to distribution-based detection methods.

5   Conclusion

This paper has introduced FreMark, the first frequency–domain watermarking framework tailored to quantized large language models (LLMs). By migrating the embedding operation from the native weight space to the two-dimensional DCT domain, FreMark leverages the energy compaction property of the transform to hide imperceptible signals in high–frequency coefficients that exert minimal influence on language modeling quality. A theoretically grounded interval–constrained projection then guarantees that every perturbed weight remains within the quantization-invariant cell reproducing the baseline `int8` codebook, thereby rendering the watermark fully persistent even after aggressive post-training compression. Coupled with a lightweight sentinel mechanism to lock per-row scaling factors, the proposed optimization loop preserves the underlying model's fidelity and the watermark's statistical detectability over extended training horizons.

Experiments on GPT-Neo and LLaMA confirm the practical value of our design: watermark extraction succeeds with more than **98%** accuracy while validation perplexity deviates by less than **0.1** points from the baseline. Moreover, quantitative analyses using mean-squared error and KL divergence demonstrate that the spectral injections shift the overall weight distribution significantly less than prior interval-only methods, enhancing stealth. The verification pipeline runs under one second on commodity hardware, providing a scalable forensic tool for real-world ownership disputes. Looking ahead, several avenues merit investigation. First, although we focused on row-wise symmetric quantization, many edge deployments adopt mixed-precision or block-wise schemes; extending the interval analysis to these settings may further broaden applicability. Second, integrating FreMark with behavior-level watermarks could yield a layered defense protecting parameters and outputs. We hope our findings foster a new perspective at the intersection of signal processing and model security, ultimately enabling safer commercialization of LLMs.

References

1. Goyal, S., et al.: HealAI: a healthcare LLM for effective medical documentation. In: Proceedings of the 17th ACM International Conference on Web Search and Data Mining, pp. 1167–1168 (2024)
2. Li, Y., Wang, S., Ding, H., Chen, H.: Large language models in finance: a survey. In: Proceedings of the Fourth ACM International Conference on AI in Finance, pp. 374–382 (2023)
3. Neumann, A.T., Yin, Y., Sowe, S., Decker, S., Jarke, M.: An LLM-driven chatbot in higher education for databases and information systems. IEEE Transactions on Education (2024)
4. Huang, W., Wang, Y., Cheng, A., Zhou, A., Yu, C., Wang, L.: A fast, performant, secure distributed training framework for LLM. In: ICASSP 2024-2024 IEEE International Conference on Acoustics, Speech and Signal Processing (ICASSP), pp. 4800–4804. IEEE (2024)
5. Lin, Y., et al.: QServe: W4A8KV4 quantization and system co-design for efficient LLM serving. arXiv preprint arXiv:2405.04532 (2024)
6. Wei, A., Haghtalab, N., Steinhardt, J.: Jailbroken: how does LLM safety training fail? Adv. Neural. Inf. Process. Syst. **36**, 80079–80110 (2023)
7. Zhang, R., Hussain, S.S., Neekhara, P., Koushanfar, F.: {REMARK-LLM}: a robust and efficient watermarking framework for generative large language models. In: 33rd USENIX Security Symposium (USENIX Security 24), pp. 1813–1830 (2024)
8. Sander, T., Fernandez, P., Durmus, A., Douze, M., Furon, T.: Watermarking makes language models radioactive. Adv. Neural. Inf. Process. Syst. **37**, 21079–21113 (2024)
9. Xia, Y., Fangcheng, F., Zhang, W., Jiang, J., Cui, B.: Efficient multi-task LLM quantization and serving for multiple LoRA adapters. Adv. Neural. Inf. Process. Syst. **37**, 63686–63714 (2024)

10. Zhang, R., Koushanfar, F.: EmMark: robust watermarks for IP protection of embedded quantized large language models. In: Proceedings of the 61st ACM/IEEE Design Automation Conference, pp. 1–6 (2024)
11. Zhao, Y., et al.: Atom: low-bit quantization for efficient and accurate LLM serving. Proc. Mach. Learn. Syst. **6**, 196–209 (2024)
12. Liu, Z., et al.: LLM-QAT: Data-free quantization aware training for large language models. arXiv preprint arXiv:2305.17888 (2023)
13. Zeng, C., et al.: ABQ-LLM: arbitrary-bit quantized inference acceleration for large language models. In: Proceedings of the AAAI Conference on Artificial Intelligence, vol. 39, pp. 22299–22307 (2025)
14. Li, L., Jiang, B., Wang, P., Ren, K., Yan, H., Qiu, X.: Watermarking LLMs with weight quantization. In: EMNLP (Findings) (2023)
15. Chen, H., Zhu, T., Liu, C., Shui, Yu., Zhou, W.: High-frequency matters: attack and defense for image-processing model watermarking. IEEE Trans. Serv. Comput. **17**(4), 1565–1579 (2024)
16. Chen, Y., Wang, S., Zhao, Y.-P., Chen, C.L.P.: Double discrete cosine transform-oriented multi-view subspace clustering. IEEE Trans. Image Process. **33**, 2491–2501 (2024)

Bypassing Cross-Domain Restrictions with Unsupervised Visual Translation

Huali Ren[1,4], Pengyu Chen[2(✉)], Ziyu Ding[2], Weitong Chen[2], Jiachao Li[2], and Chong-zhi Gao[3]

[1] School of Cyberspace Security, Guangzhou University, Guangzhou 510006, China
[2] School of Artificial Intelligence, Guangzhou University, Guangzhou 510006, China
cgyu66@gmail.com
[3] School of Computer Science, Guangzhou University, Guangzhou 510006, China
[4] Guangdong Key Laboratory of Blockchain Security, Guangzhou University, Guangzhou 510006, China

Abstract. Cross-domain restricted learning protects the intellectual property rights of the model by establishing transferability barriers between authorized and unauthorized domains. Existing attack methods for breaking these restrictions require expensive labeled data and model parameter modifications, which disrupts source domain performance. We propose an unsupervised visual translation approach (dubbed as UVT) that bypasses cross-domain restrictions through input-space transformation. Specifically, UVT adopts a UNet-Vision Transformer hybrid generator to visually translate unauthorized domain samples into authorized domain style while preserving semantic content. To further improve performance, we incorporate individual certainty loss and global diversity loss based on the output features of normal samples in the model, ensuring translated samples produce confident yet diverse predictions. Extensive experiments demonstrate that UVT achieves 47.1% performance improvement on unauthorized domains using only 10% of unlabeled data. Meanwhile, the method fully preserves authorized domain accuracy across multiple datasets.

Keywords: Cross-domain restrictions · Intellectual property protection · Visual translation

1 Introduction

Deep neural networks have made remarkable progress in computer vision, demonstrating excellent performance in applications such as face recognition [23], medical image classification [31], and autonomous driving [15]. These achievements require substantial investments in extensive data preparation, massive computational resources, and expert knowledge guidance [21], making pre-trained models valuable intellectual assets for developers and enterprises. Consequently, how to effectively protect model intellectual property (IP) has become a critical challenge.

X. Chen et al. (Eds.): DSPP 2025, LNCS 16177, pp. 221–233, 2026.
https://doi.org/10.1007/978-981-95-3185-1_15

Current IP protection strategies primarily rely on passive approaches that focus on mitigating losses after model theft occurs. These methods utilize watermarking [1,14,18] and fingerprinting [2,3,20,28] techniques to create unique model identities for verifying ownership and initiating legal proceedings against infringement. Unfortunately, these passive protection methods have significant limitations. Authorized users can still freely use protected models on any dataset, enabling easy transfer of high-performance models to similar tasks. This creates hidden infringement that existing detection methods cannot catch, as models naturally learn generalizable features during training that transfer effectively across related domains.

Recognizing these constraints, researchers have introduced cross-domain restriction learning (CDR) [26] as an active protection mechanism. CDR is based on a key observation about model generalization: models that learn comprehensive data characteristics from the source domain (i.e., authorized domain) can often perform well on target domains (i.e., unauthorized domains) sharing some similar features. To counter this vulnerability, CDR essentially implements the inverse process of domain adaptation [12,27], deliberately learning transfer-resistant representations that prevent model generalization to target domains while maintaining source domain performance [6,19,24–26]. The core mechanism operates by reducing statistical dependencies between source and target domains. The robustness of these restriction methods against sophisticated attacks remains an open question.

Recently, Hong et al. [7] introduced TransNTL as the first framework specifically designed to break cross-domain restricted barriers. Their approach builds on the observation that slightly perturbed source domain samples show similar performance drops to target domain samples on CDR models. The method fine-tunes the CDR model under an impairment-repair self-distillation framework, where source domain predictions teach the model to predict on third-party domains, achieving up to 72% target-domain improvements with only 10% source domain data. However, TransNTL faces two critical limitations: (1) heavy dependence on expensive labeled source domain data, making it impractical in real-world scenarios where obtaining annotations is costly and time-consuming; (2) parameter modifications through fine-tuning that inevitably disrupt source domain performance.

To address these challenges, we present UVT, a white-box label-free attack approach that bypasses transferability barriers through visual translation. Unlike existing methods, our approach transforms input data while keeping the restricted model unchanged. UVT employs a hybrid UNet-Vision Transformer generator that translates unauthorized domain samples into authorized domain style while preserving semantic content. To enhance performance, we design individual certainty loss and global diversity loss that leverage the output features of normal samples in the model, helping generate translated samples with confident yet diverse predictions. Comprehensive evaluation on multiple benchmark datasets demonstrates that UVT improves performance by 47.1% on unauthorized domains using only 10% of unlabeled data. Importantly, our method fully preserves authorized domain accuracy.

Our contributions are summarized as follows:

- We introduce UVT, a novel attack approach that bypasses cross-domain restrictions via visual translation without requiring costly labeled data or model parameter modifications.
- We develop a UNet-Vision Transformer generator with individual certainty and global diversity losses to enable effective cross-domain translation.
- UVT achieves significant performance improvements on target domains with minimal unlabeled data while maintaining complete source domain accuracy.

2 Related Work

Cross-domain restriction learning [8,25,26] represents a paradigm shift from traditional domain adaptation, focusing on deliberately preventing model generalization to unauthorized domains. To achieve this goal, existing methods primarily learn non-transferable representations by reducing statistical dependencies between source and target domains [6,19,24–26]. Early theoretical foundations were established by Wang et al. [26], who proposed two core statistical dependency relaxation mechanisms: maximizing Kullback-Leibler divergence between target domain representations and labels, and maximizing maximum mean discrepancy (MMD) between source and target domain distributions. CUTI-domain [25] leverages image style transfer features to construct an intermediate domain that fuses source and target domain characteristics, thereby creating effective generalization barriers. The scope of applications continues expanding across domains. Zeng et al. [29] successfully extended these methods to natural language processing tasks, while Wang et al. [24] applied prompt-based domain restriction techniques to CLIP, demonstrating effectiveness in cross-modal scenarios.

To bypass cross-domain restrictions, Hong et al. recently proposed the TransNTL [7] method, which observed that slightly perturbed source domain samples exhibited similar performance degradation patterns as the target domain on restricted models. Based on this finding, TransNTL adopts a self-distillation framework to use source domain predictions to guide the model to learn how to deal with perturbation-enhanced third-party domain samples, thereby repairing the impaired generalization performance. However, TransNTL suffers from two key limitations: dependency on labeled training data and inevitable source domain performance degradation due to parameter modifications. These constraints motivate the development of alternative approaches that preserve original model integrity through input transformations rather than model parameter modifications.

3 UVT Framework

This section introduces the UVT framework, a fully unsupervised cross-domain visual translation method as illustrated in Fig 1. The method overcomes cross-domain performance limitations by transforming target domain samples into

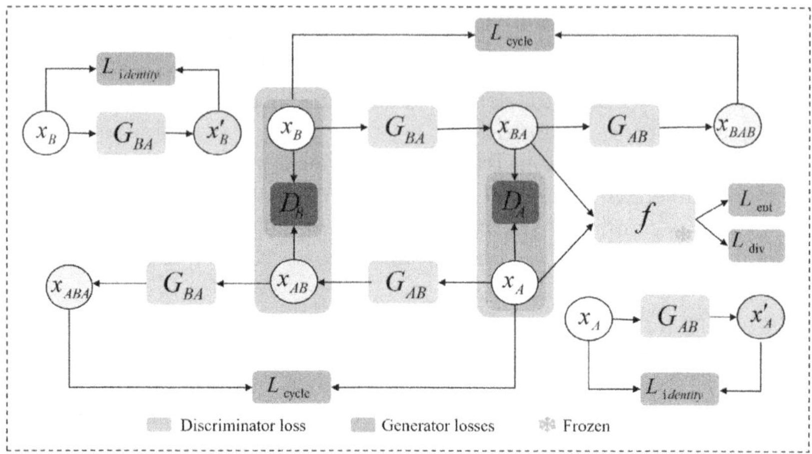

Fig. 1. Overview of the UVT framework. x_A and x_B represent source domain data and target domain data, respectively. G_{BA} denotes the generator that transforms target domain samples to source domain style, while G_{AB} performs the reverse transformation. D_A and D_B are discriminators for source and target domains respectively, and f represents the pre-trained restricted model.

source domain counterparts. We design a bidirectional generative adversarial network based on UNet Vision Transformer that learns stable inter-domain mapping relationships through cycle consistency constraints. The framework comprises two components: network architecture design and loss function formulation.

3.1   Network Architecture

Generator Architecture: We train two UNet-ViT generators with identical structures but independent parameters to perform bidirectional domain translation (as detailed in Table 1). Each generator adopts an encoder-decoder structure, embedding Vision Transformer [16] modules within the UNet [22] bottleneck layers. This architecture processes global spatial dependencies through self-attention mechanisms while preserving UNet skip connections to fuse multiscale features and retain fine-grained details. The inter-sample mapping is realized through the bidirectional training framework, while feature-guided regularization is enforced via the Vision Transformer's attention mechanisms that constrain feature representations during the translation process.

Discriminator Architecture: Correspondingly, we employ two PatchGAN [10] discriminators to perform authenticity classification on images from both domains (Table 2). Each discriminator operates on local image patches, thereby focusing on textural details and high-frequency information.

Table 1. The architecture of the UNet-ViT generator.

Layer	Details
Encoder	
Down1	Conv2d(3, 64, 7), InstanceNorm, ReLU
Down2	Conv2d(64, 128, 3, stride = 2), InstanceNorm, ReLU
Down3	Conv2d(128, 256, 3, stride = 2), InstanceNorm, ReLU
Vision Transformer	
ViT Blocks	4 × ViTBlock(dim = 256, heads = 8)
Decoder	
Up1	ConvTranspose2d(256, 128, 3, stride = 2), InstanceNorm, ReLU
Up2	ConvTranspose2d(256, 64, 3, stride = 2), InstanceNorm, ReLU
Output	Conv2d(128, 64, 3) + Conv2d(64, 3, 7), Tanh

Table 2. The architecture of the discriminator.

Layer	Details
Layer 1	Conv2d(3, 64, 4, stride = 2), LeakyReLU
Layer 2	Conv2d(64, 128, 4, stride = 2), InstanceNorm, LeakyReLU
Layer 3	Conv2d(128, 256, 4, stride = 2), InstanceNorm, LeakyReLU
Layer 4	Conv2d(256, 512, 4), InstanceNorm, LeakyReLU
Output	Conv2d(512, 1, 4)

3.2   Loss Function Design

Our training objective comprises discriminator losses and generator losses.

Discriminator Loss: The discriminator is updated by minimizing the loss corresponding to its failure to distinguish between real and translated images (called the generative adversarial loss or GAN loss):

$$\mathcal{L}_{disc,A} = \mathbb{E}_{x_B \sim \mathcal{D}_B}[\ell_{GAN}(D_A(G_{BA}(x_B)), 0)] + \mathbb{E}_{x_A \sim \mathcal{D}_A}[\ell_{GAN}(D_A(x_A), 1)] \tag{1}$$

$$\mathcal{L}_{disc,B} = \mathbb{E}_{x_A \sim \mathcal{D}_A}[\ell_{GAN}(D_B(G_{AB}(x_A)), 0)] + \mathbb{E}_{x_B \sim \mathcal{D}_B}[\ell_{GAN}(D_B(x_B), 1)] \tag{2}$$

Here, ℓ_{GAN} is the least squares GAN (LSGAN) loss function, where the discriminator is trained to assign label 1 to real images (x_A, x_B) and label 0 to translated images $(G_{BA}(x_B), G_{AB}(x_A))$.

To stabilize the training process and alleviate the gradient vanishing problem, we introduce the γ-centered gradient penalty (GP) term:

Table 3. The architecture of Vision Transformer Block.

Component	Details
Multi-Head Attention	8 heads, LayerNorm, Residual
Feed Forward	Linear(256, 1024), GELU, Linear(1024, 256)
Normalization	LayerNorm + Residual Connection

$$\mathcal{L}_{disc,A}^{GP} = \mathcal{L}_{disc,A} + \lambda_{GP}\mathbb{E}\left[\frac{(\|\nabla_x x_A\|_2 - \gamma)^2}{\gamma^2}\right] \tag{3}$$

$$\mathcal{L}_{disc,B}^{GP} = \mathcal{L}_{disc,B} + \lambda_{GP}\mathbb{E}_x\left[\frac{(\|\nabla_x x_B\|_2 - \gamma)^2}{\gamma^2}\right] \tag{4}$$

In our experiments, this γ-centered GP regularization provides more stable training and is less sensitive to hyperparameter choices.

Generator Loss: The generator transforms samples from the target domain to the source domain, thereby circumventing cross-domain restrictions. The training objective comprises five loss components:

To ensure the authenticity of generated samples, we introduce an adversarial loss:

$$\mathcal{L}_{adv} = \mathbb{E}_{x_B \sim \mathcal{D}_B}[(D_A(G_{BA}(x_B)) - 1)^2] + \mathbb{E}_{x_A \sim \mathcal{D}_A}[(D_B(G_{AB}(x_A)) - 1)^2] \tag{5}$$

This loss function drives the generator to produce samples of sufficient realism to deceive the discriminator. We adopt the least-squares GAN (LSGAN) formulation to maintain consistency with our discriminator objective and enhance training stability.

To maintain structural consistency and prevent arbitrary cross-domain mappings, we employ cycle consistency loss. This constraint requires that samples can be reconstructed to their original form following round-trip transformation:

$$\mathcal{L}_{cycle} = \mathbb{E}_{x_A \sim \mathcal{D}_A}[\|G_{AB}(G_{BA}(x_A)) - x_A\|_1] + \mathbb{E}_{x_B \sim \mathcal{D}_B}[\|G_{BA}(G_{AB}(x_B)) - x_B\|_1] \tag{6}$$

This bidirectional constraint ensures the invertibility of the transformation process and prevents the generator from converging to degenerate mapping functions that discard essential structural information.

Identity preservation is incorporated to stabilize intra-domain transformations:

$$\mathcal{L}_{id} = \mathbb{E}_{x_A \sim \mathcal{D}_A}[\|G_{BA}(x_A) - x_A\|_1] + \mathbb{E}_{x_B \sim \mathcal{D}_B}[\|G_{AB}(x_B) - x_B\|_1] \tag{7}$$

However, the aforementioned loss functions concentrate on visual-level cross-domain translation without ensuring the effectiveness of transformed samples for downstream classification tasks. To address this limitation, we pose a fundamental question: What output characteristics should unlabeled target data possess when the domain gap is effectively reduced?

We observe that well-trained supervised models exhibit two essential properties on test data: individual certainty (similar to one-hot encoding) and global diversity across the categorical space. Since source domain samples perform well on the restricted model, their outputs naturally possess these desirable characteristics. Therefore, we guide the sample transformation by minimizing the difference between the model's output features on source domain samples and those on transformed target domain samples. Specifically, we minimize the $\mathcal{L}_{cert}$ and $\mathcal{L}_{div}$ loss functions, which together provide the guidance mechanism for sample transformation:

$$\mathcal{L}_{cert} = |\mathcal{L}_{cert}^A - \mathcal{L}_{cert}^B|$$

$$= |\mathbb{E}_{x_A \sim \mathcal{D}_A} \sum_{k=1}^{K} \delta_k(f(x_A)) \log \delta_k(f(x_A))$$

$$- \mathbb{E}_{x_B \sim \mathcal{D}_B} \sum_{k=1}^{K} \delta_k(f(G_{BA}(x_B))) \log \delta_k(f(G_{BA}(x_B)))| \tag{8}$$

$$\mathcal{L}_{div} = |\mathcal{L}_{div}^{source} - \mathcal{L}_{div}^{target}|$$

$$= |\sum_{k=1}^{K} \hat{p}_k^A \log \hat{p}_k^A - \sum_{k=1}^{K} \hat{p}_k^B \log \hat{p}_k^B| \tag{9}$$

$$= |D_{KL}(\hat{p}_A, \frac{1}{K}\mathbf{1}_K) - D_{KL}(\hat{p}_B, \frac{1}{K}\mathbf{1}_K)|$$

where $f(G_{BA}(x_B))$ denotes the K-dimensional output for each transformed target sample, and $\mathbf{1}_K$ represents the K-dimensional all-ones vector. Here, $\hat{p}_B = \mathbb{E}_{x_B \in \mathcal{D}_B}[\delta(f(G_{BA}(x_B)))]$ denotes the average output distribution across the entire transformed target domain.

Combining the above constraints, the complete optimization objective of the generator is:

$$\mathcal{L}_{total} = \mathcal{L}_{adv} + \lambda_1 \mathcal{L}_{cycle} + \lambda_2 \mathcal{L}_{id} + \lambda_3 \mathcal{L}_{cert} + \lambda_4 \mathcal{L}_{div} \tag{10}$$

where λ_1, λ_2, λ_3, and λ_4 are hyperparameters that balance the importance of cycle consistency, identity preservation, individual certainty, and global diversity, respectively. UVT alternates between training the generator and discriminator to achieve stable optimization.

4 Experiment

4.1 Implementation Details

Datasets. We conduct experiments on widely-adopted cross-domain benchmarks [7,25,26]. For digit recognition, we utilize three commonly used digit datasets containing ten digits from 0 to 9 extracted from varying scenes: MNIST [5] provides clean handwritten digits with standardized backgrounds; USPS [9] contains postal digits scanned from real mail envelopes; SVHN [17] features house numbers from Google Street View with natural scene complexity. For object classification, we employ CIFAR10 [11] and STL10 [4], both ten-class datasets with different image resolutions and visual complexity.

For Pre-training CDR Models. We evaluate our method on models pretrained with two representative CDR methods: the foundational NTL method [26] and the state-of-the-art CUTI framework [25], using their official implementations and original hyperparameters.

Evaluation Metrics. Following standard evaluation protocols, we adopt classification accuracy (%) as the primary performance metric across all tasks.

Architectures. We adopt different backbone models in classification tasks according to the task complexity requirements. We utilize several popular architectures as feature extractors and connect them with fully connected layers as top-level classifiers. For the digit recognition task, VGG11 is used as the base network, while VGG13 is used for CIFAR10 and STL10. All networks are initialized with ImageNet pre-trained weights.

Table 4. Accuracy comparison of all attack methods on two CDR methods. Source domain accuracy (%) is shown in blue and restricted domain accuracy (%) in red. Values in brackets indicate accuracy changes compared to the pre-trained model. Best results are highlighted in bold.

Dataset	CIFAR10→STL10 (SL: 88.4 / 70.1)		SVHN→MNIST (SL: 91.9 / 71.8)		SVHN→USPS (SL: 91.9 / 78.3)	
CDR method	NTL	CUTI	NTL	CUTI	NTL	CUTI
Pre-train	84.6/10.3	82.0/12.2	84.5/10.3	91.3/10.1	87.2/21.7	90.3/15.5
FTAL	85.1(+0.5)	83.1(+1.1)	82.9(-1.6)	90.8(-0.5)	87.0(-0.2)	90.3(-0.0)
	10.3(+0.0)	12.2(+0.0)	21.3(+11.0)	10.1(+0.0)	21.0(-0.7)	15.5(+0.0)
RTAL	84.3(-0.3)	86.1(+4.1)	79.8(-4.7)	89.8(-1.5)	82.9(-4.3)	88.5(-1.8)
	10.7(+0.4)	12.2(+0.0)	17.7(+7.4)	25.2(+15.1)	19.5(-2.2)	43.8(+28.3)
FP	83.3(-1.3)	86.1(+4.1)	83.2(-1.3)	88.3(-3.0)	83.9(-3.3)	86.9(-3.4)
	10.7(+0.4)	13.6(+1.4)	13.8(+3.5)	10.1(+0.0)	41.0(+19.3)	15.5(+0.0)
I-BAU	79.1(-5.5)	79.1(-2.9)	76.7(-7.8)	84.3(-7.0)	83.7(-3.5)	87.3(-3.0)
	8.4(-1.9)	8.4(-3.8)	10.2(-0.1)	29.0(+18.9)	15.4(-6.3)	45.8(+30.3)
FT-SAM	84.5(-0.1)	86.4(+4.4)	85.1(+0.6)	89.8(-1.5)	87.0(-0.2)	88.2(-2.1)
	15.1(+4.8)	11.7(-0.5)	16.5(+6.2)	10.1(+0.0)	44.2(+22.5)	15.5(+0.0)
TransNTL	83.2(-1.4)	84.9(+2.9)	84.1(-0.4)	89.4(-1.9)	87.4(+0.2)	88.9(-1.4)
	46.7(+36.4)	63.1(+50.9)	42.1(+31.8)	52.4(+42.3)	67.6(+45.9)	67.9(+52.4)
UVT (Our)	84.6(-0.0)	82.0(-0.0)	84.5(-0.0)	91.3(-0.0)	87.2(-0.0)	90.3(-0.0)
	57.4(+47.1)	59.3(+47.1)	**65.3(+55.0)**	**78.7(+68.6)**	**75.1(+53.4)**	**78.0(+62.5)**

Baselines. We follow the experimental setup established in TransNTL, incorporating comprehensive baseline attack methods for comparison. TransNTL represents the state-of-the-art approach for breaking cross-domain restrictions. Additionally, we include advanced backdoor defense methods and watermark removal techniques: FTAL [1], RTAL [1], FP [13], I-BAU [30], and FT-SAM [32]. All methods are provided access to 10% of source domain data for fair comparison.

Training Configuration. Following prior work [7,25,26], we standardize all dataset images to 64×64 resolution with a batch size of 32. For generator training, we utilize only 10% of source and target domain data without corresponding labels, executing 100 training epochs. The hyperparameters λ_1, λ_2, λ_3, λ_4, and λ_{GP} are configured as 10, 1, 5, 5, and 1, respectively.

4.2 Effectiveness of UVT in Recovering Target Domain Performance

We systematically evaluate the effectiveness of UVT in the target domain after attacking a cross-domain restricted model. We conduct comprehensive experiments across digit recognition tasks (SVHN←MNIST, SVHN←USPS) and object recognition tasks (CIFAR10←STL10) to validate our methodology across varying complexity levels.

As demonstrated in Table 4, utilizing merely 10% of unlabeled data from both source and target domains, UVT demonstrates superior effectiveness compared to existing baseline attack methods across nearly all experimental configurations. While most baseline approaches fail to recover target domain accuracy and exhibit inconsistent impacts on source domain performance (with some methods showing slight improvements due to fine-tuning with labeled data while others experiencing degradation), UVT successfully restores target domain accuracy while maintaining stable source domain effectiveness. Specifically, for CIFAR10←STL10, UVT achieves 47.1% performance improvement on both NTL and CUTI. For digit recognition tasks, UVT demonstrates average performance improvements of 54.2% on NTL and 65.5% on CUTI. Notably, UVT consistently yields greater performance recovery on CUTI than on NTL across all experiments, suggesting that CUTI's intermediate domain construction makes it more vulnerable to our visual translation approach. Furthermore, on the SVHN←MNIST task, UVT even enables performance to exceed that of supervised domain adaptation baselines, indicating the effectiveness of our feature-guided translation strategy.

4.3 Risk of CDR-Based Ownership Verification

In this section, we reveal the Risk of CDR-based ownership verification. Following the settings in [25,26], we embed a backdoor watermark patch into the authorized source domain dataset during pre-training, treating the processed data as an unauthorized target domain for NTL and CUTI procedures. CDR-based ownership verification relies on observing performance differences of the trained model on data with and without trigger patches.

Table 5 presents the attack results on CIFAR10, SVHN, and MNIST. The results demonstrate that UVT successfully recovers performance on patch-embedded data, achieving improvements up to 86.2% and outperforming all baseline attack methods. When UVT is applied, CDR-based ownership verification mechanisms fail to function as intended. The attacked model exhibits behavior similar to standard supervised learning models, showing nearly identical performance on data both with and without watermark patches, thereby compromising the reliability of ownership verification protocols.

Table 5. Risks for CDR-based ownership verification. "(P)" denotes the patched domain. Source domain accuracy (%) and target domain accuracy (%) are reported. Values in brackets indicate accuracy changes compared to the pre-trained model. Best results are highlighted in bold

Dataset	CIFAR10→CIFAR10 (P) (SL: 88.3 / 62)		SVHN→SVHN (P) (SL: 91.9 / 84.3)		MNIST→MNIST (P) (SL: 99.1 / 99.0)	
CDR method	NTL	CUTI	NTL	CUTI	NTL	CUTI
Pre-train	82.3/9.9	88.2/11.1	85.4/19.5	92.3/19.5	99.1/11.6	99.3/8.8
FTAL	83.3(+1.0)	87.8(-0.4)	83.5(-1.9)	91.5(-0.8)	98.8(-0.3)	99.2(-0.1)
	9.8(-0.1)	11.1(+0.0)	19.2(-0.3)	19.5(+0.0)	11.6(+0.0)	8.8(+0.0)
RTAL	81.3(-1.0)	84.7(-3.5)	82.3(-3.1)	89.9(-2.4)	98.6(-0.5)	98.9(-0.4)
	9.8(-0.1)	11.1(+0.0)	19.2(-0.3)	19.5(+0.0)	10.0(-1.6)	11.6(+2.8)
FP	73.1(-9.2)	80.8(-7.4)	79.6(-5.8)	88.1(-4.2)	98.5(-0.6)	98.5(-0.8)
	10.0(+0.1)	10.2(-0.9)	14.9(-4.6)	21.2(+1.7)	11.7(+0.1)	8.8(+0.0)
I-BAU	79.1(-3.2)	79.1(-9.1)	76.7(-8.7)	84.3(-8.0)	83.7(-15.4)	87.3(-12.0)
	8.1(-1.8)	17.4(+6.3)	6.7(-12.8)	6.7(-12.8)	10.2(-0.1)	45.3(+36.5)
FT-SAM	84.8(+2.5)	84.9(-3.3)	83.5(-1.9)	90.1(-2.2)	67.4(-31.7)	99.0(-0.3)
	10.0(+0.1)	11.5(+0.4)	12.7(-6.8)	81.5(+62.0)	11.7(+0.1)	80.0(+71.2)
TransNTL	81.6(-0.7)	84.4(-3.8)	87.4(+2.0)	91.1(-1.2)	97.2(-1.9)	98.8(-0.5)
	37.0(+27.1)	52.4(+41.3)	47.7(+28.2)	82.1(+62.6)	38.5(+26.9)	88.6(+79.8)
UVT (Our)	82.3(-0.0)	88.2(-0.0)	85.4(-0.0)	92.3(-0.0)	99.1(-0.0)	99.3(-0.0)
	60.0(+50.1)	**77.2(+66.1)**	**82.7(+63.2)**	**88.2(+68.7)**	**53.4(+41.8)**	**95.0(+86.2)**

4.4   Ablation Studies

Table 6 presents an ablation study examining the contribution of each component in our UVT framework. Starting from the baseline UVT_V which only contains the vision layer losses (adversarial, cycle consistency and identity), we progressively incorporate individual certainty (C), global diversity (D), and gradient penalty (GP) components.

The results demonstrate that each component contributes positively to performance, with individual certainty yielding the most substantial improvements while global diversity provides complementary enhancements across all datasets. The complete UVT framework achieves optimal performance, with remarkable improvements of +55.0% and +68.6% on SVHN←MNIST for NTL and CUTI methods respectively, validating the effectiveness of our proposed components.

Table 6. Ablation study of UVT components on target domain performance. UVT_V denotes the baseline using UNet-ViT as the generator with only contains the vision layer losses. UVT comprises UVT_V enhanced with individual certainty (C), global diversity (D), and gradient penalty (GP) components, i.e., UVT = UVT_V + C + D + GP. Values in brackets indicate accuracy changes relative to the pre-trained model. Best results are highlighted in bold.

Dataset	CIFAR10→STL10		SVHN→MNIST		SVHN→USPS	
CDR Method	NTL	CUTI	NTL	CUTI	NTL	CUTI
pre-train	10.3	12.2	10.3	10.1	21.7	15.5
UVT_V	30.3(+20.0)	32.9(+20.7)	63.3(+53.0)	64.9(+54.8)	67.7 (+46.0)	79.0(+63.5)
UVT_V+C	55.9(+45.6)	59.4(+47.2)	63.3(+53.0)	64.9(+54.8)	67.7(+46.0)	70.5(+55.0)
UVT_V+C+D	56.0(+45.7)	59.6 (+47.4)	63.3(+53.0)	62.4(+52.3)	71.7(+50.0)	70.5(+55.0)
UVT	**57.4(+47.1)**	59.3(+47.1)	**65.3(+55.0)**	**78.7(+68.6)**	**77.1(+55.4)**	**79.0(+63.5)**

5   Conclusion

This work presents UVT, which successfully circumvents cross-domain restrictions through input-level visual translation, achieving 47.1% performance improvement with only 10% unlabeled data while preserving source domain accuracy. The approach exposes fundamental vulnerabilities in existing restriction mechanisms by demonstrating that domain barriers can be bypassed without model modifications or labeled supervision. These findings highlight the urgent need for developing more robust intellectual property protection strategies in deep learning systems. Beyond computer vision, this input transformation paradigm opens new avenues for research, where future work could explore extensions to other modalities such as text classification through semantic-preserving style transfer techniques.

Acknowledgments. This work was supported by the Open Research Fund of Guangdong Key Laboratory of Blockchain Security, Guangzhou University.

References

1. Adi, Y., Baum, C., Cisse, M., Pinkas, B., Keshet, J.: Turning your weakness into a strength: watermarking deep neural networks by backdooring. In: 27th USENIX Security Symposium (USENIX Security 18), pp. 1615–1631 (2018)
2. Cao, X., Jia, J., Gong, N.Z.: IPGuard: protecting intellectual property of deep neural networks via fingerprinting the classification boundary. In: Proceedings of the 2021 ACM ASIA Conference on Computer and Communications Security, pp. 14–25 (2021)
3. Chen, J., et al.: Copy, right? A testing framework for copyright protection of deep learning models. In: 2022 IEEE Symposium on Security and Privacy (SP), pp. 824–841. IEEE (2022)
4. Coates, A., Ng, A., Lee, H.: An analysis of single-layer networks in unsupervised feature learning. In: Proceedings of the Fourteenth International Conference on Artificial Intelligence and Statistics, pp. 215–223. JMLR Workshop and Conference Proceedings (2011)
5. Deng, L.: The MNIST database of handwritten digit images for machine learning research [best of the web]. IEEE Signal Process. Mag. **29**(6), 141–142 (2012)
6. Ding, R., Su, L., Ding, A.A., Fei, Y.: Non-transferable pruning. In: European Conference on Computer Vision, pp. 375–393. Springer (2024)
7. Hong, Z., Shen, L., Liu, T.: Your transferability barrier is fragile: free-lunch for transferring the non-transferable learning. In: Proceedings of the IEEE/CVF Conference on Computer Vision and Pattern Recognition, pp. 28805–28815 (2024)
8. Hong, Z., Xiang, Y., Liu, T.: Toward robust non-transferable learning: A survey and benchmark. arXiv preprint arXiv:2502.13593 (2025)
9. Hull, J.J.: A database for handwritten text recognition research. IEEE Trans. Pattern Anal. Mach. Intell. **16**(5), 550–554 (1994)
10. Isola, P., Zhu, J.Y., Zhou, T., Efros, A.A.: Image-to-image translation with conditional adversarial networks. In: Proceedings of the IEEE Conference on Computer Vision and Pattern Recognition, pp. 1125–1134 (2017)
11. Krizhevsky, A., Hinton, G., et al.: Learning multiple layers of features from tiny images (2009)
12. Li, J., Yu, Z., Du, Z., Zhu, L., Shen, H.T.: A comprehensive survey on source-free domain adaptation. IEEE Transactions on Pattern Analysis and Machine Intelligence (2024)
13. Liu, K., Dolan-Gavitt, B., Garg, S.: Fine-pruning: defending against backdooring attacks on deep neural networks. In: International Symposium on Research in Attacks, Intrusions, and Defenses, pp. 273–294. Springer (2018)
14. Lukas, N., Jiang, E., Li, X., Kerschbaum, F.: SoK: how robust is image classification deep neural network watermarking? In: 2022 IEEE Symposium on Security and Privacy (SP), pp. 787–804. IEEE (2022)
15. Luo, H., Yang, Y., Tong, B., Wu, F., Fan, B.: Traffic sign recognition using a multi-task convolutional neural network. IEEE Trans. Intell. Transp. Syst. **19**(4), 1100–1111 (2017)
16. Neil, H., Dirk, W.: Transformers for image recognition at scale. Online: https://aigoogleblog.com/2020/12/transformers-forimage-recognitionat.html (2020)
17. Netzer, Y., Wang, T., Coates, A., Bissacco, A., Wu, B., Ng, A.Y., et al.: Reading digits in natural images with unsupervised feature learning. In: NIPS workshop on deep learning and unsupervised feature learning. vol. 2011, p. 7. Granada (2011)

18. Pang, K., Qi, T., Wu, C., Bai, M., Jiang, M., Huang, Y.: ModelShield: adaptive and robust watermark against model extraction attack. IEEE Transactions on Information Forensics and Security (2025)
19. Peng, B., et al.: MAP: mask-pruning for source-free model intellectual property protection. In: Proceedings of the IEEE/CVF Conference on Computer Vision and Pattern Recognition, pp. 23585–23594 (2024)
20. Peng, Z., Li, S., Chen, G., Zhang, C., Zhu, H., Xue, M.: Fingerprinting deep neural networks globally via universal adversarial perturbations. In: Proceedings of the IEEE/CVF Conference on Computer Vision and Pattern Recognition, pp. 13430–13439 (2022)
21. Ren, H., et al.: GanFinger: GAN-based fingerprint generation for deep neural network ownership verification. arXiv preprint arXiv:2312.15617 (2023)
22. Ronneberger, O., Fischer, P., Brox, T.: U-Net: convolutional networks for biomedical image segmentation. In: Medical Image Computing and Computer Assisted Intervention–MICCAI 2015: 18th International Conference, Munich, Germany, October 5-9, 2015, Proceedings, part III 18, pp. 234–241. Springer (2015)
23. Wang, H., et al.: CosFace: large margin cosine loss for deep face recognition. In: Proceedings of the IEEE Conference on Computer Vision and Pattern Recognition, pp. 5265–5274 (2018)
24. Wang, L., Wang, M., Fu, H., Zhang, D.: Vision-language model IP protection via prompt-based learning. In: Proceedings of the Computer Vision and Pattern Recognition Conference, pp. 9497–9506 (2025)
25. Wang, L., Wang, M., Zhang, D., Fu, H.: Model barrier: a compact un-transferable isolation domain for model intellectual property protection. In: Proceedings of the IEEE/CVF Conference on Computer Vision and Pattern Recognition, pp. 20475–20484 (2023)
26. Wang, L., Xu, S., Xu, R., Wang, X., Zhu, Q.: Non-transferable learning: A new approach for model ownership verification and applicability authorization. arXiv preprint arXiv:2106.06916 (2021)
27. Wilson, G., Cook, D.J.: A survey of unsupervised deep domain adaptation. ACM Trans. Intell. Syst. Technol. (TIST) **11**(5), 1–46 (2020)
28. Yang, K., Wang, R., Wang, L.: MetaFinger: fingerprinting the deep neural networks with meta-training. In: IJCAI, pp. 776–782 (2022)
29. Zeng, G., Lu, W.: Unsupervised non-transferable text classification. arXiv preprint arXiv:2210.12651 (2022)
30. Zeng, Y., Chen, S., Park, W., Mao, Z.M., Jin, M., Jia, R.: Adversarial unlearning of backdoors via implicit hypergradient. arXiv preprint arXiv:2110.03735 (2021)
31. Zhang, J., Xie, Y., Wu, Q., Xia, Y.: Medical image classification using synergic deep learning. Med. Image Anal. **54**, 10–19 (2019)
32. Zhu, M., Wei, S., Shen, L., Fan, Y., Wu, B.: Enhancing fine-tuning based backdoor defense with sharpness-aware minimization. In: Proceedings of the IEEE/CVF International Conference on Computer Vision, pp. 4466–4477 (2023)

Author Index

Made in the USA
Monee, IL
07 July 2026

56552849R00142